MW00446480

Portrait of America

Portrait of AMERICA

A Cultural History
of the Federal
Writers' Project

Jerrold Hirsch

The University of
North Carolina Press

Chapel Hill & London

© 2003 The University of North Carolina Press
All rights reserved

Designed by April Leidig-Higgins

Set in Monotype Garamond by
Copperline Book Services, Inc.

Manufactured in the United States of America

The paper in this book meets the guidelines for
permanence and durability of the Committee
on Production Guidelines for Book Longevity
of the Council on Library Resources.

Library of Congress Cataloging-in-Publication Data
Hirsch, Jerrold, 1948–
Portrait of America: a cultural history of the Federal
Writers' Project / by Jerrold Hirsch.
p. cm.
Includes bibliographical references (p.) and index.
ISBN 0-8078-2817-3 (cloth: alk. paper)
ISBN 0-8078-5489-1 (pbk.: alk. paper)
1. Federal Writers' Project—History.   2. United
States—Historiography.   3. United States—
Intellectual life—20th century.   4. National
characteristics, American.   5. United States—
Civilization—1918–1945.   I. Title.
E175.4.W9H57   2003
973.917—dc21   2003006858

cloth   07 06 05 04 03   5 4 3 2 1
paper   07 06 05 04 03   5 4 3 2 1

For My Daughters,
Riina and Anna

Contents

Preface

   This study of the Federal Writers' Project (FWP) has lasted long enough to have a history of its own. One beginning might be traced to a day in late August 1971 when an anxious but competitive young man about to begin his graduate studies entered the library of the University of North Carolina at Chapel Hill, walked up to the reserve desk, and asked to see all the books on Professor George Tindall's reserve list. Thus, perhaps the first step on the path that led to this study may have been taken that day in August when I discovered on Tindall's list *These Are Our Lives: As Told by the People and Written by Members of the Federal Writers' Project of the Works Progress Administration in North Carolina, Tennessee, and Georgia* (1939). I include the full title here because that day I reread it several times, and everything in the title intrigued and puzzled me. In that book I discovered what was to me a new kind of history, done by people who called themselves Federal Writers and who had been part of a New Deal relief program.

   In the latter stages of this study, I constantly found myself wondering when I had actually started working on it. I became aware of the ways my life, previous experiences, and the choices I had made prepared me to write this study. Perhaps the beginning was not in August 1971 but in my experience of American diversity, my own provincialism and cosmopolitanism. My grandparents had been Jews who lived in Russia or Poland, not Russians or Poles. In the United States, however, they became people who were both Jews and Americans. I attended an orthodox Jewish day school, though my parents were not orthodox Jews. After elementary school I went to the University of Chicago

High School in Hyde Park, which was then sometimes referred to as the labo-
ratory school, thus evoking memories of its founder John Dewey. For a long
time I did not give any of this a great deal of thought. It seemed simple and
clear cut. I had escaped a parochial world for a cosmopolitan one—progress.
Only later did I begin to feel that the provincial was alive in the cosmopolitan
and that that was good. I was unable to formulate that thought until I had
learned to understand how FWP officials thought about provincialism, cosmopolitanism, and American identity.

The present study could not have been completed without the support of
archivists, librarians, and fellow scholars. Some individuals fit into more than
one category. The friendly folks in the interlibrary loan office at the University
of North Carolina at Chapel Hill library dutifully fulfilled hundreds of requests. During extended periods, I lived in the library's microfilm reading room
and Southern Historical Collection. The staffs in each area were helpful. The
archivists at the National Archives and at the Library of Congress Archive of
Folksong and its Manuscripts Division provided needed assistance and asked
thoughtful questions about my work.

I have been employed by North Carolina State University, Memphis State
University, the University of the South, Harvard University, and Truman State
University during the various stages of transforming what began as a disserta-
tion into a book. I have had the good fortune to be associated with institutions
of higher learning that recognized the importance of supporting scholarly endeavors. The University of the South and Truman State University provided
generous support that enabled me to attend conferences and submit my ideas
to the scrutiny of my fellow historians. An Andrew W. Mellon fellowship at
Harvard University in the curriculum in folklore and mythology gave me the
freedom I needed at a crucial stage in this study. Truman State University's
generous summer research grants and excellent policy of providing stipends
for undergraduates to work with faculty as true research assistants allowed me
to complete this study and for these students—Christine Davids, Matthew
Haggans, David Hurst, Darrin Osborne, Charles Redden, Michael Roth, and
Adam Marchand—to engage in related research projects. I was privileged to
have always the full support of James Lyons, former head of the Division of
Social Science at Truman State, and Seymour Patterson, the current division
head.

Those of us who have had teachers who opened new vistas, who were alive
with passion for their fields and had a desire to share their knowledge, know
how lucky we have been. In Margaret Fallers, formerly at the University of

Chicago High School, and the late Louis Filler, at Antioch College and beyond, I had the good fortune to know teachers who exemplified the exciting intellectual and moral adventure of being an American scholar.

Conversations in person and by letter with people who had firsthand knowledge of the FWP gave a dimension to my research that I could have acquired nowhere else. Leonard Rapport, the late William Terry Couch, and the late Gertrude Botkin took a special interest in this project.

Friends and scholars helped me develop my approach. Doug Swaim introduced me to the idea of vernacular architecture, the meaning of place, and cultural and historical ways of examining landscapes. After reading a conference paper of mine, folklorist Archie Green insisted I had to write more about Botkin. The late Warren Susman enthusiastically encouraged me to follow the approach I had described to him. Michael O'Brien made valuable suggestions during friendly conversations. Folklorists Burt Feintuch, Bruce Jackson, Ellen Stekert, and the late Kenneth Goldstein helped by letting me know they thought I was on to something important. My understanding of the FWP southern life histories benefited from my collaboration with Tom Terrill in editing *Such as Us: Southern Voices of the Thirties* (1978). Ann Banks and I shared ideas gained from our work on different aspects of the FWP life history projects.

The faculty and graduate students in the history department and in the curriculum in folklore in the English department at the University of North Carolina at Chapel Hill provided an environment in which I developed as a scholar. I especially leaned on and learned from Peter Filene, Mary Fredriksen, Joseph Herzenberg, John Kasson, Frank Kessler, and Jack Roper.

Ralph Waldo Emerson said the scholar loses no time in which the man lives. Some special friends—Natalie Alexander, Michael Bell, Nevin Brown, Bob Cummings, Maureen Coulter, Keith Doubt, Debra Foster, Jean Gowen, Tom and Jane Hatley, Joe Herzenberg, Annette Jacobs, Nick Jordan, Coventry Kessler, Frank Kessler, Linda Morely, John and Mary Ramsbottom, Linda Seidel, Pam Sobek, Steve Stern, and Allen Tullos—helped me balance scholarship and living.

Without the initial support my mentor George Tindall gave me in pursuing my own path through the FWP, I would not have been able to complete this study. I am also indebted to Jane DeHart, who supported me in my conviction that the study of the FWP had not been exhausted but had only begun. She took time from her own studies to share her knowledge of the New Deal arts projects. I came to realize that she looked forward to hearing my ideas about the FWP—and that was most encouraging.

My parents have helped me with this study in every way they could and since long before they realized it. My father was the first American historian I ever knew. My mother was the first person I knew who quoted poetry because she liked it. Karen Nygaard Hirsch and I have helped each other learn much about the ways in which we both could grow. More than anyone she has helped me understand something about life as a process of becoming. She took time from her own research and teaching to read and discuss my work. She only helped a very little with the proofreading and not at all with the typing. But she loved to discuss with me the issues at the heart of this work, and she offered penetrating and challenging insights. My daughters, Riina and Anna, grew up with this book. As young children, each appreciated in her own way that I was working on a book. But they did not hesitate to remind me how important it was that we play. I am glad for the times I listened to them. And perhaps that is part of how they got to the point where they wanted to discuss the manuscript with me.

Portrait of America

Introduction

While earlier studies of the Federal Writers' Project (FWP), a New Deal Works Progress Administration (WPA) work relief program established in 1935, focused on the birth, growth, and demise of the project—the administrative details—this study treats it as an episode in American cultural and intellectual history and as part of the cultural component of the New Deal's program of political and economic reform. By focusing on key individuals, developments, and programs, this study provides an analysis of the dreams and accomplishments of the FWP.

Congress voted WPA relief appropriations in response to national adversity, not out of a desire to support a rediscovery of American culture. Nevertheless, national FWP officials seized the opportunity the relief crisis had offered to undertake studies of American culture. In the end, they would direct a project that published encyclopedic guidebooks to every state in the nation and numerous localities and that conducted interviews with former slaves, members of ethnic minorities, ordinary southerners, farmers, and factory workers. National FWP officials, under the leadership of Henry Alsberg, aimed to redefine American national identity and culture by embracing the country's diversity.

The structure of the FWP reflected state and federal interests and intermingled the practical goals of providing work relief with the dreams national FWP officials had of making a lasting contribution to a new understanding of American culture. Thus, in every state of the union a unit of the FWP was established. Each state Writers' Project answered to both state and national WPA administrators as well as national FWP officials. The FWP was a motley crew. The state units were only allowed to hire a small number of writers solely on the basis of ability. The vast majority of state workers first had to qualify for relief before they could join the FWP. Their abilities varied widely. Some were not competent to do the work they had been assigned. Some performed adequately. A few were talented. Almost all of the relief workers came from the areas in which they worked.

In sharp contrast, FWP officials in the national office came from across the nation. Unlike most relief workers, they had traveled within the United States, and some had been abroad. They were not relief workers; rather, they were asked to serve on the project because of their interest in and contributions to American culture. Although they were not the most well-known intellectuals of their day and are not well remembered, they were all individuals who had participated in the debates in the United States in the early twentieth century about national identity and the arts. They had a cosmopolitan view of both the diversity within their own nation and contemporary developments in the social sciences and the arts. Influenced by the new anthropology that had begun to emerge in the 1920s, they were all interested in the relationship between culture as the expressive arts and culture as ways of life. They deliberately blurred the line between these two categories, and this aided them in their effort to explore diverse American traditions. Their role in shaping the vision and work of the FWP still needs to be explored.

Such national FWP officials as director Henry Alsberg, Negro affairs editor Sterling Brown, the first folklore editor, John Lomax, and his successor Benjamin Botkin, and social-ethnic studies editor Morton Royse developed a coherent vision for the FWP. To understand them requires more than familiarity with biographical data. To know them, one has to know something about their work: Alsberg's association with the Provincetown Players (home, for a time, to Eugene O'Neill); Lomax's folklore anthologies and memoirs; Botkin's *Folk-Say* volumes, essays, poems, and book reviews; Brown's poems, essays on the blues, and literary criticism; and Royse's work on minority issues in Europe and his labor studies in Puerto Rico. An examination of the careers and FWP correspondence of these individuals reveals that the anthropological definition of culture, the discussion among writers in the 1920s and 1930s about the possibility of creating literature in an urban-industrial world, and the meaning of modernity were important issues in the work of the FWP. Thus, national FWP officials did not intend to be merely bureaucrats. They saw themselves as part of a larger cultural project.

National FWP officials' emphasis on cultural diversity was part of the larger liberal-reformist politics of the 1930s. The creation in 1935 of a place for New Deal arts projects—theater, art, music, and writing—within the WPA coincided with a renewed popular interest in "rediscovering" America in general and the emergence of a Popular Front cultural milieu in particular. Following a change in Soviet policy, American communists and their supporters no longer opposed and criticized the New Deal. New Dealers and other left-wing groups welcomed an alliance of all liberals and leftists. It would be a mistake, as Michael Denning has demonstrated in *The Cultural Front: The Laboring of American Culture in the Twentieth Century* (1996), to see the Popular Front as simply a response to changes in Soviet foreign policy.[1] Rather, many national FWP officials and other liberal New Dealers supported the political and cultural thrust of the Popular Front because they valued a cultural politics that showed concern for the lives of ordinary Americans, in particular the poor, the industrial workers, and the racial and ethnic minorities—these are overlapping categories—and opposed fascism at home and abroad.

Narrow and exclusive definitions of America had buttressed the status quo in the 1920s, an era of immigration restriction, a reborn Ku Klux Klan that was anti-Catholic and anti-Semitic as well as antiblack, a weak labor movement, and Republican ascendancy. An inclusive community, as national FWP officials envisioned it, was not supposed to strengthen social consensus but to give weight to the claims of scorned groups such as black Americans. The FWP's approach to American culture had both ideological and mythic aspects, and thus the project's publications, especially the American Guide Series, might be thought of as having dynamic qualities that keep them moving back and forth between two poles labeled myth and ideology, leaving much to the determination of the individual reader. To the extent that anything that challenged exclusive definitions of America served the interests of those who had not been allowed to participate fully in the mainstream of American life, FWP programs were ideological and reformist. But in addition, the FWP tried to unite Americans, individuals and groups with conflicting interests, while ignoring issues that divided them, and therefore the project also created a conservative myth that pointed to a harmonious future without indicating how a change from current circumstances to a better future could be achieved.[2]

While the immediate context of the FWP is work relief and the cultural issues of the interwar years, national FWP officials developed a program that spoke to much larger and long-standing debates over the nature of American identity and culture, over the very definition of who was an American, of who the American people were. It was a discussion as old as the nation. FWP programs need to be understood as part of an ongoing dialogue about American culture and nationality. In ways they were not always fully aware of, national FWP officials echoed writers of the American Renaissance, as they addressed persistent questions about the meaning of American culture and nationality. The forms they used to present their answers to the questions at the heart of this dialogue deserve study. Their vision, programs, and accomplishments should be seen in relation to the intellectual traditions they inherited and the recurring nature of these questions in the United States. Their vision can also be clarified through an examination of those who opposed it and by analyzing how it changed in response to such a major challenge as World War II.

The overarching question I seek to answer throughout this study is "What was the approach of the FWP to the study of American culture?" A standard sentence in a history textbook survey dealing with culture in the 1930s and the FWP would talk about the rediscovery of America and the conservative thrust of this uncritical embrace of everything American. If my work led to a revision of this sentence, it would be rewritten to say that there were attempts by New Deal cultural agencies to redefine American nationality in a way FWP officials hoped would create a more egalitarian, democratic, and inclusive community. In doing this, they sought to reconcile cultural diversity, as a fact and (in their view) as a positive value, with cultural nationalism, and to treat a pluralistic culture as a positive aspect of modernity. Both goals were important in all the projects initiated by national FWP officials.

Although they probably did not use such terms to describe themselves, national FWP officials can be described as both romantic nationalists and cultural pluralists. In their search for American materials on which to build a national art and to reunite the artist and his or her society, they were similar to earlier romantic nationalists in Europe as well as in their own country. American romantic nationalists, however, faced an additional problem. They had to prove to skeptics that there were specifically American traditions. In many European countries, romantic nationalists tended to stress the traditions of a predominantly rural ethnic group over other groups within the nation's borders in defining the essence of a national identity and culture. So, too, did some American romantic nationalists. National FWP officials rejected this approach.[3]

Given their interest in defining and asserting the existence of an American folk and lore, it should not be surprising that the discourse of national FWP officials fits within a romantic nationalist framework. What made their work innovative was their effort to reconcile romantic nationalism with cultural pluralism —two isms that seem diametrically opposed—although they did not formulate the task they undertook using these terms. Many of Ralph Waldo Emerson's essays, much of Walt Whitman's poetry, and more immediately, the writings of Randolph Bourne on "Trans-national America," the work of Horace Kallen on cultural pluralism, and most significantly, Franz Boas's anthropological contributions to the idea of pluralism provided an American variation on romantic nationalism on which FWP officials could build. In all of these writings there was an effort to reconcile both universalist ideals and particularist experiences.

Boas's influence on the thinking of liberal intellectuals interested in American culture in the 1920s and 1930s was profound. On one hand, his attack on racist thinking made it possible to consider who was an American in pluralist terms. Keep in mind that racial labels at that time also included many ethnic groups that are today referred to as "white."[4] The universalist strain in Boas's thought was tied to his rejection of race as a way to understand individual difference. He denied that any group was incapable of being American citizens. The particularist romantic nationalist strain in his thought can be seen in his emphasis on a pluralist description of a multiplicity of cultures that had developed in response to specific historical conditions and could not be ranked hierarchically in terms of best and worst.[5] Indeed, as historian Walter Jackson has pointed out, this strain in Boas's thinking can be seen in his interest in the traditions and lore of a plurality of cultures, and thus "part of his mission was . . . collecting texts of myth and folklore."[6] Although Boas focused largely on native American nations, he also addressed the question of alleged racial differences between white Anglo-Saxon Protestant Americans and both African Americans and eastern and southern European immigrants and their children. His students and other intellectuals drew on Boas's work when pondering the nation's numerous ethnic and racial groups.[7]

As Boas's anthropological formulations offered a powerful tool for the many American intellectuals in the 1920s and 1930s who wanted to be both cultural nationalists and pluralists, Van Wyck Brooks's essays in the 1910s and 1920s constituted a challenge to those same intellectuals. Brooks criticized Americans for not having developed and cherished the traditions that make a national culture possible. The FWP and its supporters challenged Brooks's views by offering positive answers to questions that Brooks had helped frame and that he and some other American writers had in the 1920s despairingly answered in the negative. This emphasis on the connection between national traditions and the creation of a national culture illustrates the importance in the 1930s of romantic nationalist assumptions in the discussion of American art.

These romantic nationalist arguments were linked with an implicit pluralism that saw in cultural diversity a vitality that could reinvigorate American life. The idea that knowledge of "communal traditions and achievements," as one contemporary review of FWP publications put it, could produce a new literature reflected not only romantic nationalist values but also a definition of culture that incorporated both the traditional meaning of the term and a newer anthropological understanding.[8]

Although some articles written at the time about the FWP stressed the number of well-known writers on the project, most commentators in the 1930s would have agreed with Bernard DeVoto that the Federal Writers' Project was a misnomer for a relief project that employed relatively few writers. Nevertheless, there was a widespread belief that from this exploration of America might come a renewal of American literature, that FWP guides were contributing both to the rediscovery of American culture and to the reintegration of the American artist into the community. Writers, according to this view, would discover in the FWP description of an indigenous American culture both that "the creative spirit had found a home in America" and the materials from which they could create a widely accessible national art.

Culture and nationalism are linked in virtually every discussion of the FWP. The FWP's emphasis on diversity is almost always noted and is often described as Whitmanesque. Contemporary reviewers pointed to the diversity the FWP guides described as a source of cultural renewal that could counterbalance the forces of modernity that promote homogenization. Labeling the FWP an example of 1930s cultural nationalism, however, is a beginning, not a conclusion. The intellectual context into which the project fits and the conception of American culture reflected in the guidebooks and other FWP projects is still unstudied. Scholars who have focused on the administrative history of the FWP have not treated national FWP officials as individuals with ideas—New Deal intellectuals as much as those who formulated the administration's economic and social programs.

National FWP officials tried to create an inclusive portrait of America. FWP publications were infused with the idea that a discovery, an acknowledgment, and finally a celebration of the nation's cultural pluralism offered a basis for national integration that was inclusive, not exclusive, and democratic, not coercive. FWP officials thought new guides to America were needed and that members of ethnic groups, ordinary southerners, urban workers, and former slaves deserved an opportunity to speak directly to their fellow citizens. In this way, they also dealt with the relationship of minorities to American culture and suggested that cultural understanding could reconcile the fact of pluralism and the need for national integration and unity.

After studying American nationalism, historian Hans Kohn concluded that in sharp contrast to other nations with age-old traditions, America was defined by a set of abstract political principles to which an American was supposed to adhere.[9] Nevertheless, in various periods of American history, some citizens have argued for Protestantism or Anglo-Saxonism or a combination of the two as a definition of American nationality and as a basis for social cohesion. As cultural pluralists national FWP officials rejected religious or ethnic definitions of American nationality. They advocated instead a cosmopolitanism that encouraged Americans to value their own provincial traditions and to show an interest in the traditions of their fellow citizens. They embraced pluralism as the basis for a democratic and egalitarian society and for a cultural definition of American nationality compatible with the traditional ideological definition.[10]

The first section of this study focuses on the effort of the Writers' Project in the American Guide Series to reconcile romantic nationalism and cultural pluralism within the format of state guidebooks. National FWP officials' view of pluralism and modernity is central to the analysis of the FWP's social-ethnic, oral history, and black studies examined in the second section. In this section the South is treated as the region whose racial problems, poverty, and folk traditions provided the FWP national office's democratic and pluralistic cultural nationalism its greatest challenge and its greatest opportunity.

The FWP's pioneering oral history projects were intended to provide not only a social history of ordinary southerners, ex-slaves, ethnic minorities, and industrial workers but also a new view of American life and culture. The existence of regional differences, the presence of blacks, and the history of immigration have always been major considerations in the development of definitions of American nationality. To question traditional views on these topics was to formulate new meanings for the term "American." The FWP's examination of aspects of the southern experience challenged dominant images of the region, and its black history projects offered a different perspective on an ideological definition of American identity that stressed commitment to freedom, equality, and democracy. The FWP's social-ethnic studies were the first government-sponsored program that rejected either a racial or an assimilationist definition of American nationality.

Chapters on the House Un-American Activities Committee (HUAC), chaired by Martin Dies, a Texas Democrat, and on the Writers' Program, as the FWP was rechristened after June 1939, conclude this study. They return the reader to

epic

inherited questions Americans continue to confront today regarding diversity and unity, modernity and tradition. They also point to topics that still need further exploration. The FWP's innovative folklore projects have not yet been adequately studied. Nor has there been any analysis of why the FWP's work had to be rediscovered. These are topics that I will address in a second volume.

In 1938 HUAC, then commonly referred to as the Dies committee, used anti-Communist rhetoric to attack the FWP and its pluralistic vision of American culture. Guidebooks that some historians have described as a conservative endorsement of everything American, HUAC labeled subversive. Martin Dies maintained he objected to the radical attack on American values he saw in the FWP's American Guide Series, but he complained mainly about the treatment of labor, ethnic, and racial groups in the guides' portrait of America. HUAC ignored the pioneering oral history and folklore projects that national FWP director Henry Alsberg thought would constitute a deeper examination of American culture than the guides had.

During World War II tolerance of ethnic diversity became a part of an ideological definition of American nationality as a commitment to democracy and liberty. Much that had been implicit in the work of the FWP became explicit rhetoric in the Writers' Program, while the actual program became more conservative. The Writers' Program discontinued most of the oral history and folklore projects begun by the FWP in order to concentrate on completing the state guidebooks and on war-related activities. While some historians have pointed to the FWP as an example of the conservative cultural nationalism of the 1930s, their analysis better fits the Writers' Program. Analysis of the wartime activities of the Writers' Program can help illustrate how easily cultural pluralism can be transformed from an ideology supporting reform to one that serves mainly as a basis for promoting consensus.

Not until Dies, World War II, and the Cold War consensus were part of history did most of the people who spoke to the FWP interviewers find an audience. That seems less an accident than a reflection of a changing political and cultural landscape. The FWP social-ethnic studies, ex-slave narratives, and living lore projects seem as if they did not exist until they were rediscovered; it is only in recent years that these voices have been heard again.

The Federal Writers often used the word "epic" in describing their work. Like Emerson and Whitman, the Federal Writers found an American epic in the doings of ordinary as well as great men, and in the present as well as the past. FWP officials argued that the familiarity with the American scene that project writers gained from guidebook research and that the information guides provided all American writers would stimulate literary creativity. They saw the possibility of a great American epic emerging from the work of Federal Writers on the oral history projects.

Attempts to create an American epic unite both American romantics and modernists. Rather than endorsing many modernists' claims that they totally rejected romanticism, some scholars emphasize the similarities between the two movements and describe a finely shaded continuum from romanticism to modernism. In recent years, American scholars have been challenging the view that the work of T. S. Eliot and his epigone constitute the story of modernism in American literature. They have argued instead that "modernist" should not be used in the singular, since there were a variety of modernisms. Thus, such FWP officials as regionalist and folklorist B. A. Botkin and poet and literary critic Sterling Brown are now treated by an increasing number of scholars as modernists, although their work on the FWP has received relatively little attention.[11]

The first historians of the FWP have made it possible to shift the focus away from the administrative aspects of the history of the Writers' Project and to deal instead with how FWP officials tried to contribute to American culture as well as to provide relief.[12] In this study the administrative history of the FWP is treated only when it is relevant to understanding the project's programs and goals. Rather than reading the correspondence of FWP officials, memorandums, work manuals, and the work itself primarily to determine what happened next, one must read the documents for what they reveal of project purposes, the questions addressed, and the answers offered. It then becomes clear that the questions and answers are part of both an inherited and a contemporary dialogue. When one follows such an approach, Ralph Waldo Emerson, Walt Whitman, and Carl Sandburg become important in understanding the FWP. So, too, do anthropologists such as Franz Boas and Paul Radin.

Various methods of studying American traditions had sociopolitical as well as cultural implications. Why FWP officials undertook the work they did and what they achieved cannot be comprehended without addressing such matters. Not only their contemporaries but earlier generations of Americans had considered the questions about American culture that concerned FWP officials. Sometimes the dialogue is sharply focused, sometimes not; but in either case, trying to retrieve it contributes to an understanding of the FWP as an episode, not a self-contained unit, in American cultural and intellectual history.[13]

Despite the emphasis on administrative history, scholars have not been able to write about the FWP without giving some assessment of the project's work that went beyond noting what was undertaken and what was completed. The

problem is that these assessments have not fully integrated a historically informed examination of the purposes behind project work and the specific features of that work. Attractive rhetoric sometimes penned by prestigious students of American culture has been repeated endlessly and with only minor
variations: a road map to an indigenous American culture; the finest contribution to American patriotism in our generation; the need born of the depression to chart America and possess it.[14] Recycled, these statements begin to turn
stale. They serve now to close a subject on which too little work has been done.
In the absence of analysis, descriptive phrases, no matter how appealing or
powerful, should not be allowed to pose indefinitely as authoritative judgments.
Quoting the fine things Lewis Mumford and his contemporaries wrote about
the FWP guidebooks proves only that these individuals liked the guides—not a
small point. But it is neither an analysis of why they liked what the FWP was
doing nor an assessment of project work. These critical statements, however,
are a part of the contemporary dialogue about the Writers' Project and thus,
like project correspondence and publications, a part of the cultural history of
the FWP.

All of the interpretations that have been offered of the work of the Writers'
Project were first suggested in the 1930s. Although those who have written
about the FWP have made little attempt to formulate their assessments in relationship to other views of the Writers' Project, it is possible to see the outlines
of a debate, an unacknowledged historiography. Clarifying that historiography
can help sharpen a sense of the issues that have been raised but not examined.

Critics such as Lewis Mumford and Bernard DeVoto welcomed the guides
as patriotic contributions to a rediscovery of an indigenous American culture.[15]
Patriotism, rediscovery, exploration, and culture were key words in reviews that
treated FWP publications as part of a nationalistic celebration of American diversity and vitality. Reviewers made a connection between Whitman's poetic
approach to America and the FWP's work, though they offered no analysis along
these lines. National FWP officials and book reviewers encouraged Americans
to see their own culture as deserving the respect they thought had too often
been reserved for European culture. In varied ways they said, "Explore America through the FWP publications. Discover that Americans, like other peoples,
had traditions, that modernity had not produced a bland homogenized culture
in which all places were alike."

A number of historians of Depression era culture have echoed Alfred Kazin's comments on the FWP guides and other documentary literature of the
1930s in *On Native Grounds* (1942). Kazin regarded FWP publications as part of

a "new nationalism" that resulted in a literature of "unprecedented affirmation" addressing the "question . . . no longer posed from afar—'What is an American?'" We do not need further variations on Kazin's points but an extended analysis along the lines he only briefly sketched.[16]

The need to try to understand the synthesis of romantic nationalist and pluralist ideas that national FWP officials worked out could not be recognized by later cultural critics who rejected this tradition, even if they had once worked in the Washington office of the Writers' Project. Art critic Harold Rosenberg, who had been the FWP art editor and a member of the *Partisan Review* circle, used the occasion of his review of former FWP official Jerre Mangione's *The Dream and the Deal: The Federal Writers' Project, 1935–1943* (1972) to deny that the Writers' Project had made any contribution to American culture. He ridiculed what he saw as "the fantasy promoted by [the FWP's] top echelons, that the project was engaged in creating, against all odds a lasting literary representation of America and its people." "In its fantasy of one America," he contended, the FWP "promoted the belief that the mere assembly of American data could be the equivalent of a great collective creation."[17]

In some cases historical research can sometimes best go forward if historians focus not on the work of their immediate predecessors but on the work of still-earlier historians.[18] This study has benefited from "The Achievement of the Federal Writers' Project," a perceptive article published by Daniel M. Fox in 1961. Fox presented an overview of what the FWP celebrated that should have led to further studies along the lines he sketched. He noted that the organization of the Writers' Project, with its national office and state units, contributed to the guidebooks' emphasis on diversity and unity. The FWP's celebration of diversity, he maintained, was part of a 1930s effort to create a new form of national unity. Fox pointed out that the FWP had a history, that its approach to American culture evolved and "moved steadily beneath the surface of American life" as the guidebooks were followed by ethnic and folk studies. The efforts of the FWP were part of a tradition that ran from Whitman to Mumford. In focusing on regional, ethnic, and racial differences the FWP was dealing with the definition of American nationality. Fox also raised questions about the attitude of Federal Writers—who, he insisted, "were not alienated intellectuals" —toward America.[19]

In recent studies of the FWP, historians have begun to pay more attention to the work of the project; however, these inquiries are limited by the absence of the type of analysis this book seeks to develop. The great strength of *Against Itself: The Federal Theater and Writers' Projects in the Midwest* (1995) lies in Paul Sporn's

framing of the history of these programs in terms of questions that illuminate
the cultural history of the New Deal arts projects. Sporn's approach stands in
sharp contrast to the limited scope of previous state and regional studies of
the FWP. Sporn notes the frequent discrepancies between the ideas of national
officials and the workings of state FWP offices. Still, a history of the FWP at the
state and regional levels needs to pay more attention than Sporn does to the visions of the national office as an important component of the story. While
Christine Bold's *The WPA Guides: Mapping America* (1999) treats the guides as
the product of a discourse within the FWP and offers perceptive insights about
the guides based on Bold's analysis of the role of local Federal Writers and national officials in their production and a close reading of the texts, the author
does not place that discourse within a broad historical perspective. Her view of
the celebration of diversity as an attempt to contain and control the cultural
representations of individuals and groups neither contrasts the New Deal approach to the arts to the cultural politics of the 1920s nor recognizes how con-
temporaneous totalitarian developments abroad influenced these cultural projects. By not treating national FWP officials as intellectuals or as part of American
intellectual history, Bold misses the challenge they faced in trying to reconcile
romantic nationalism and cultural pluralism. Celebrating diversity and unity
was hardly a tension-free and simplistic and reassuring mantra at the time. The
FWP was an attempt to contribute to a renewal of American cultural expression
and to the cultural politics of reform through a more inclusive understanding
of American identity and nationality.[20]

While there has been virtually no direct continuity, no evidence of influence,
between the work of national FWP officials and that of the new social historians, both address similar questions. If the echoes do not indicate influence,
they do reveal persistent issues in American life and cultural studies. Like the
new social historians who came to dominate their profession in the 1970s, national FWP officials wanted to create a history of America that paid attention to
the great majority of people, particularly those on the lowest social rungs: the
workers, the poor, and the ethnic and racial minorities. And they sought alter-
natives to traditional written sources that primarily reflected the viewpoint of
small elites. The end they envisioned, however, was not simply a greater understanding of social change, processes, and structures, but a flowering of American culture growing out of a more inclusive, egalitarian, and democratic community in which all citizens participated. They thought that listening to the
voices of people such as former slaves could not only change the way Americans understood the past but also help create a better future.

The visions of national FWP officials and the work the FWP produced are inherently interesting, and they deserve much closer study than they have yet received. But such a study is also a vehicle for examining aspects of the intellectual history of cultural pluralism in America and of its relationship to the cultural politics of reform and the status quo, to the American variation on romantic nationalism, to conceptions of American identity and nationality, and to the creation of American literature. A cultural history of the FWP offers insight into cultural pluralism as a response to modernity. It tells another part of the story of American liberal intellectuals and provides an important perspective on the development of American anthropology and folklore studies.

In the world in which national FWP officials lived, they thought they saw a choice between pluralism and totalitarianism. That perception reveals much about them and their world. The question of the relevance and the strengths and limitations of that view will provide a subtext for many readers and will constitute the basis for their own dialogue with national FWP officials.

The relationships between art and democracy, provincialism and cosmopolitanism, folklore and modernity, and diversity and unity are permanent issues. They can also be viewed as an American variation on worldwide issues that have accompanied the growth of modern societies. The Federal Writers dealt with these issues, and that is why their visions and work demand study.

Part 1

Romantic Nationalism,
Cultural Pluralism, and the
Federal Writers' Project

Chapter 1

Inherited Questions

American identity and nationality have always been problematic. The classic answer that St. John de Crèvecoeur offered almost two hundred years ago to his famous query "What then is this new man the American?" was based on the assumption that the American was "either a European or the descendant of a European." The passage of time has not made the answer any clearer; it has only shown the inadequacy of previous answers. Thus, historian Robert Wiebe observes that "each generation of Americans has to rediscover America, for its meaning has been a problem that could neither be ignored nor resolved." Time and again Wiebe finds that "try as they might most Americans stopped short of encompassing the nation. . . . Each generation passed to the next an open question of who really belonged to American society." Another student of American life argues that this very problem is our hope: "But the promise of America—the unfinished society—has been that it is a pluralism of groups and individuals who seek grounds for unity." The FWP tried to rediscover America, to encompass the nation, and to provide grounds for unity. National FWP officials insisted on the relevance of American diversity to answering questions such as Crèvecoeur's and rejected answers that excluded any group of citizens. It is essential to understand how the FWP approached questions about American nationality, for approach and answer are intertwined.[1]

National FWP officials developed programs that they thought would make a significant contribution to American culture. Their programs were formulated in the context of national depression, New Deal recovery programs, and the growing crisis in international relations. They also addressed inherited questions about the nature of American identity, nationality, and culture. Their answers reflected their cultural nationalism, cultural pluralism, and cosmopolitanism. In both idealistic and practical terms national FWP officials contemplated the relationships between government and culture and, ultimately, between culture and democracy. The answers they offered to the questions they inherited were shaped by their relationship to the romantic nationalist tradition, the pluralist and cosmopolitan attitudes they had developed out of their personal experience and pre-FWP careers, and the decision that state guidebooks would in the beginning provide a vehicle that would allow the FWP both to fulfill its relief functions and to address key questions about American culture. Like all cultural nationalists they assumed that answers to the question of national identity and the achievement of national unity were intimately tied to the development of the arts. The FWP was a manifestation of cultural nationalism in a period of crisis.[2]

That nationality is an essential part of personal identity is an idea so pervasive in the modern world that the relationship between the two is taken for granted and few are conscious of the history of the efforts in different nation-states to create this link. Cultural nationalism has been a significant component of modern nation building and a widespread response to the growing social-structural differentiation of modern societies, which, in theory, has led to segmentation and a transition from face-to-face to impersonal relations. Examining the history of cultural nationalism in Germany from the Napoleonic wars to the triumph of Nazism, George L. Mosse found that in response to "the atomization of traditional views and the destruction of traditional and personal bonds," myths developed that "were meant to make the world whole again and to restore a sense of community to a fragmented nation." Cultural nationalism in Germany and elsewhere has often been exclusive, reactionary, illiberal, and racist. The pluralist version of cultural nationalism, however, turns diversity into a virtue and celebrates it as a source of national vitality. The creation of an atmosphere in which cultural pluralism could develop was a triumph of New Deal nationalism. The FWP both reflected and contributed to this atmosphere.[3]

Not only were American intellectuals in the 1930s trying to rediscover America, as so many commentators then and since have pointed out; they were also trying to redefine it. The studies published by the Writers' Project tried to broaden the definition of who and what was American. To answer such questions the FWP offered new materials: ex-slave narratives, folklore and folk song, and the life histories of ordinary people. In the American Guide Series, which included guidebooks to every state in the union and to numerous cities, counties, and geographic areas, the FWP tried to provide the nation with a "road map for the cultural rediscovery of America."[4]

FWP officials were hardly the first Americans to address questions about tradition, unity, and the arts in America. Laments about the lack of a unifying national tradition in the United States are as old as the republic. Henry James's oft-cited complaints about American culture are representative. Examining American life, James was struck by "the coldness, the thinness, the blankness," as contrasted to what he thought was "the denser, richer, warmer European spectacle." James focused on the lack of traditional national institutions and classes: "no sovereign, no court, no personal loyalty, no aristocracy, no church, no clergy," and on the lack of a built environment that symbolized a traditional sense of place: "no palaces, no castles, nor manors, nor old country-houses, nor parsonages, nor thatched cottages, nor ivied ruins." Constant uncertainty about whether American life provided a basis for creating an American art has been accompanied by frequent declarations of cultural independence and maturity, such as Emerson's "American Scholar" and Van Wyck Brooks's *America's Coming of Age*. The FWP offered yet another such declaration.[5]

Central aspects of the FWP response to the need for a unifying tradition become clearer when this need is viewed as an enduring American problem. The Depression and the international crisis intensified anxiety about the role of tradition in American life and the search for unity. Democratic results, as totalitarian developments abroad illustrated, were not foreordained. The New Deal drew on and broadened native liberal traditions. FWP officials assumed that knowledge of the experience of ordinary Americans, a celebration of the nation's cultural pluralism, and a cosmopolitan attitude toward the country's diversity would fulfill the functions of a unifying tradition.

"Problems of social cohesion," of "the struggle between rival ways of getting together," have, according to historian John Higham, "been a central theme" in American history. His point "is not the uniqueness of the American experience, but rather the special salience here of disparities every modernizing society seems to confront." Primordial ties, a feeling of unity based on inherited relationships, have played a limited integrative role in the United States. Instead ideological definitions have been offered as a basis for American identity, purpose, and unity. Like ideology, technical unity—bureaucratic, rational, and effi-

cient procedures and modern forms of communication and transportation—
is an integrative force characteristic of modern societies. Reformers during the
Progressive Era had hoped these two ways of achieving unity could prove
complementary and help sustain democratic values. New Dealers had not abandoned this dream. The FWP complemented New Deal experiments in combining various forms of technical unity with an ideology of cultural pluralism.[6]

In any attempt to understand the 1930s, one student of the subject argues,
"no fact is more important than the general and even popular 'discovery' of
the concept of culture": culture not in the traditional view as the achievement
of great thinkers and artists of the past—what Matthew Arnold called "the
best which has been thought and said in the world"—but in the anthropological sense, as a group's shared values and way of life. In most of the FWP publications, however, it was an anthropology closer to early approaches that gave
primary attention to listing and describing the ideas, behaviors, and artifacts
characteristic of a culture, in contrast to the later emphasis on cultural patterns
and processes—the way people learn values and behaviors. Not until the 1930s
did anthropological works focusing on patterns and norms reach a wide audience. Thus, when Governor Clyde R. Hoey of North Carolina wrote in the
preface to his state's FWP guidebook that it offered "a complete inventory," his
comment reflected an approach to culture characteristic of much of the American Guide Series. Still, aspects of the guides and some of the folklore and oral
history projects come closer to less static, more dynamic definitions of culture.[7]

In large part, it was not social science but a romantic cultural nationalism
and a vision of a pluralistic America that underlay the FWP's concern with an
anthropological approach to culture as opposed to an emphasis on the art of
an elite. The issues the FWP addressed related to debates about American art
that had shaped discussion of these topics during the first three decades of the
twentieth century and continued to set the terms of the discussion until after
World War II. Subtle nuances distinguished different views, but it is possible to
distinguish two main groups. On one side were the genteel critics; on the other
were the romantic nationalists.[8]

Both the genteel critics and the romantic nationalists built on aspects of
nineteenth-century European and American thought that emphasized an organic relationship between individual personality, nationality, and the creative
arts. Both groups were also preoccupied with the relationship between American and European culture. The genteel critics, however, were willing to wait
for (what they viewed as) an immature American culture to develop. In the
meantime, they were content to possess and preserve European high culture.

Some thought that perhaps all levels of society could be taught to appreciate the best that had been said and thought in the past. If not, at least it could be preserved. For the foreseeable future, this was the best that could be done. After all, according to this view, the United States lacked a rich indigenous folk culture, and there was as yet no American race or nation—the terms were often used interchangeably.[9]

Such diverse romantic nationalists as Van Wyck Brooks, Randolph Bourne, Constance Rourke, and national FWP officials were as unwilling to wait as Emerson and Whitman had been. They were not content to create institutions whose primary function was cultural preservation—museums, symphonies, and academies. Their impatience echoed Emerson's declaration that "our day of dependence, our long apprenticeship to the learning of other lands, draws to a close. The millions that around us are rushing into life cannot always be fed on the sere remains of foreign harvests." A satisfying national culture had to consist of more than attempts to assimilate the high culture of Europe. Bourne was contemptuous of "our almost pathetic eagerness to learn the culture of other nations, our humility of worship in the presence of art that in no sense represents the expression of any of our ideals and motivating forces." Rourke claimed Americans possessed a rich and abundant cultural tradition that they had failed to recognize, appreciate, and use. She strove to elucidate the cultural achievements of the American folk—their humor, crafts, and mythmaking tendencies. The New Deal found a place for her as an editor of the Federal Art Project's monumental guide to American folk art, *The Index of American Design*.[10]

While Van Wyck Brooks wrote about the need for a usable past in creating a national culture, he could actually find little in the American past to value. Brooks was closer to the genteel tradition than he or his opponents realized. For all of his talk of a usable past, Brooks often sounded like those nineteenth-century Americans and Europeans who thought Americans had no past and thus no way of creating a national culture. Brooks lamented "that, unlike any other great race, we were founded by full-grown, modern, self-conscious men." Without a childhood, Americans had not had the opportunity to develop the myths that would provide the basis for a living culture. This is essentially the same argument sculptor Horatio Greenough offered antebellum Americans: "As Americans we have no childhood, no half-fabulous, legendary wealth, no misty cloud-enveloped background." Disagreeing with arguments like those of Greenough and Brooks meant raising questions about the relationship in America between nationality, race, and culture. It also meant that figures as separated

in time as Emerson and national FWP officials would make the democratic assumption that the source of a society's creative expression is in its ordinary citizens, not in its genteel classes—in the folk culture, not in refinement.[11]

As romantic nationalists FWP officials assumed that the study of the experience of ordinary Americans would contribute to a revitalized national culture; as pluralists they believed all groups had to be taken into account; and as
cosmopolitans they hoped the various diverse groups that constituted America could benefit from learning about fellow citizens who were different from
themselves. National FWP officials were part of an ethnically diverse, liberal
American intelligentsia. Their outlook was national, secular, and cosmopolitan.
One student of the subject argues that these characteristics defined the liberal
intellectual community from roughly 1910 to 1960. During the New Deal, however, significant numbers of individuals from this community entered government service. National FWP officials such as Henry G. Alsberg, John Lomax,
B. A. Botkin, Morton Royse, and Sterling Brown shared much in common with
this community. The general tone and direction they gave to the Writers' Project was not the result of an ever recurring movement between alienation and
acceptance, exile and return, as some intellectuals and their historians have
viewed the relationship between America and its artists. Instead, these FWP officials had a vision of American culture that guided their endeavors.[12]

Like the literary intellectuals in Malcolm Cowley's *Exiles Return: A Literary
Odyssey of the 1920s* (1934), many of these FWP officials had attended prestigious
Ivy League universities. Their careers, however, do not fit his key themes of
alienation and acceptance. Cowley wrote of a generation whose education
"might be regarded as a long process of deracination." Regional dialects had
been transformed into a school-learned "amerenglish." Cowley grew up thinking culture was something to be obtained, to be put on "as a veneer." It was
alien to one's own background, experiences, and language. Cowley ignored those
intellectuals who saw in a romantic nationalist approach to American diversity
a way of countering the forces of deracination and standardization and the
basis for creating a distinctive American form of artistic expression. Eventually Cowley and many of the individuals he wrote about also adopted that
approach.[13]

Alienation, exile, and acceptance described a psychology, not ideas or values.
Paris was more than exile. It was symbolic of a movement from a provincial to
a cosmopolitan orientation—and then one could write about one's province.
The return meant more than simply going back to the provinces. It involved,
Cowley noted, an enthusiastic romantic nationalism: "The exiles were ready to

find that their own nation had every attribute they had been taught to admire in those of Europe. . . . It possessed a folklore, and traditions, and the songs that embodied them. . . . American themes, had exactly the dignity that talent could lend them."[14]

Return, the provinces, and romantic nationalism did not mean the abandonment of cosmopolitanism any more than the trip in the other direction actually meant leaving the provinces behind. Cowley's intellectuals and those in the national office of the FWP were finding ways to integrate cosmopolitan and romantic nationalist perspectives. Perhaps psychologically the "intellectuals were trying to overcome their sense of isolation and loneliness," as Richard Pells argues. Pells and other students of 1930s cultural radicalism, however, do not give enough attention to the tradition of romantic nationalist and cosmopolitan ideas and the emerging pluralist framework that virtually all left-of-center writers actively worked within.[15]

While national FWP officials valued particular cultural differences, they thought that the parochialisms that made it difficult for individuals of different regions, classes, and races to understand, accept, and appreciate one another could be overcome. Thus "their task" was "to introduce America to Americans."[16] They took the cosmopolitan belief that it is necessary to transcend all parochialisms in order to be able to draw on the experience of a multiplicity of groups and to achieve a fuller human experience and translate it into national terms. Cultural differences would remain, but parochial outlooks were to be transcended in order to achieve a richer, more satisfying national experience.

The romantic nationalist, cultural pluralist, and cosmopolitan orientation of the FWP reflects the experiences and attitudes of its directors. The backgrounds, areas of interest, and pre-FWP careers of key national officials reveal that they came to the Writers' Project with definite ideas about American culture. The national office of the FWP was staffed by Americans with diverse backgrounds —Jews, blacks, Italians, westerners, and southerners—representing a diverse nation. To rediscover American culture meant to note and examine the life and creations of different regions, ethnic groups, and social classes. In celebrating the idea of a people's demotic culture, national FWP officials in effect made room for themselves in this culture.

It is striking how similar key national FWP officials were in educational background, which included travel, social work, and in many cases formal education at Harvard and Columbia or both. Henry Alsberg and B. A. Botkin studied at Harvard and Columbia; John Lomax and Sterling A. Brown, at Harvard; and Morton Royse, at Columbia. In some cases specific intellectual influences can be traced. Morton Royse studied with John Dewey. At Harvard, Lomax was encouraged by American literary historian Barrett Wendell and by Shakespeare and ballad scholar George Lyman Kittredge. Botkin also noted Kittredge's role in leading him to study folklore. National FWP officials turned to Columbia anthropologists Franz Boas and Ruth Benedict for advice. Botkin's thinking in particular reflected Boas's influence. The ideas of national FWP officials echoed Wendell and Kittredge's romantic nationalism, William James's open pluralist vision of the universe, Josiah Royce's arguments "in praise of provincialism," and Horace Kallen's arguments for cultural pluralism. Direct influence is not, however, the most important issue. By the 1930s romantic nationalism, cosmopolitanism, and pluralism had become the common intellectual property of members of the liberal intelligentsia. National FWP officials, however, had been educated at institutions where members of the faculty had made important contributions to twentieth-century American thought about romantic nationalism and cultural pluralism.[17]

To understand the outlook that most national FWP officials shared, it helps to begin by looking at the career and ideas of John Lomax, the first FWP folklore editor, who was similar in many ways to his colleagues in the national office and yet quite different from them. The Harvard education, the influence of Kittredge and Wendell, the effort to broaden American folk song scholarship by taking it beyond the search for the survivals of English ballads, and the democratic implications of ballad hunting that found high aesthetic values in the creations of those at the bottom of the social ladder are all aspects of Lomax's career that make him seem to have much in common with other national FWP officials. Lomax contributed to an American romantic nationalist tradition that had its roots in the work of Emerson and Whitman. But Lomax's attitudes toward race and modernity offer a sharp contrast to those of his fellow national FWP officials.

While Lomax thought there was a distinctive American folklore, he also claimed modern life was destroying folk traditions. In his view folklore was associated with the isolated life of rural communities. He regarded the "spread of machine civilization" as a destroyer of folk traditions; it broke down isolation and exposed members of folk cultures to other traditions and to popular culture. He saw folklore surviving only when it was separated from the mainstream of modern American life. Diversity and change were folklore's enemies. It did not disturb him that to preserve folklore, he implicitly consigned those at the bottom of the social scale, such as southern blacks, to permanent poverty and low status. Thus like those who argued that folklore was only survivals from elsewhere, Lomax arrived at the conclusion that such materials were fast disappearing. His goal was to collect American lore before it died out.[18]

Lomax's nostalgia revealed a conservative romantic's rejection of modernity. In his romanticism he looked backward to a lost world, not forward to a new one. His appreciation of cowboy and African American songs was bound up with his feelings about his Texas childhood. This and his acceptance of racial paternalism kept him from questioning the southern social order. Blacks and their songs appealed to his sense of beauty and aroused emotions in him that were deeply felt but evidently impossible for him to analyze. While he admired African American folk songs because they were "so unique, so pliable, that no other folk music in America approaches it," he also thought their major quality was "self-pity." Thus he wrote that he recorded black convicts who "pathetically" sang songs full of "mystery and wistful sadness" but devoid "of self-consciousness or artificiality." To some extent his comments about African Americans reflect an acquired sensibility that had become a habitual way of writing about emotions. The adjectives Lomax used to describe African American folk song distanced him from black people and their songs, placed him in the superior role, and told more about his emotional reactions to the music than about the meaning it had in the culture from which it emerged. For Lomax the African American was still a primitive who did not suffer from the self-consciousness he associated with civilized life.[19]

Lomax shared the romantic nationalist sentiments of his FWP colleagues but not their egalitarian values nor their left-of-center politics. Among this group he was the most provincial. His interest in black folk songs, given his assumptions, demonstrated a parochialism that prevented him from imaginatively entering the life of another culture and that precluded a cosmopolitan outlook. Romantic nationalism was compatible with a hierarchical view of the relative worth of various cultures and with the maintenance of the status quo. As Lomax's case illustrates, romantic nationalist ideas did not automatically lead in the direction in which Alsberg, Botkin, Royse, and Brown took them. They made their own synthesis, a synthesis that Lomax never seems to have made or accepted. By comparing Lomax, a white southerner born in Goodman, Mississippi in 1876, with his colleagues on the FWP, it is possible to begin to trace the difficult path from a conservative romantic nationalism to the liberal and radical variants on that idea that developed in the 1930s.

In the early decades of the twentieth century, travel and social work provided an important educational experience for liberal intellectuals like Alsberg, Botkin, and Royse. Their own experience and contemporary social theory sug-

gested that cultural differences were to be explained in terms of historical experience and were not matters of superior and inferior groups that could be
rated on some absolute scale. Social work in the Jane Addams tradition had
embodied a cultural as well as a social program. The job of a social worker was
as much a form of cultural education as travel, an introduction to aspects of
American diversity, and as much a course in social problems as any offered in
universities. Trying to address the problems of a community, Addams and her
colleagues learned, meant meeting that community's cultural as well as social
and economic needs. For Alsberg, Botkin, and Royse social work experience
had been part of their education, part of their effort to fuse cultural, humani-
tarian, and political concerns and to learn how others different from themselves actually lived.

Alsberg assembled a national FWP staff that shared similar literary, cultural,
and political concerns. Born in 1881 in New York City to a German Jewish
family, he was a cosmopolitan most at home in large cities. Before he became
national FWP director, Alsberg had had a varied career that revealed his Bohemian temperament. He flirted with anarchism, displayed a general sympathy
for left-wing movements, worked at what he called "saving the world from reactionaries," and traveled in the hope that his experiences would help him become a writer. He graduated from Columbia, became a lawyer, gave that up, attended Harvard's graduate English department for a year, and served on the
editorial board of the liberal *New York Post*. From 1919 to 1922 he was a foreign correspondent. He worked for the American Joint Distribution Committee aiding victims of the famine that followed the revolution and civil war in
Russia.[20]

There were obvious connections between Alsberg's social, political, and aesthetic concerns. He brought what he had learned about avant-garde developments in the Russian theater to his work with the Provincetown Players and
combined that knowledge with a creative method that turned to the folk life of
ordinary people, at home and abroad, for inspiration. In Paul Green's *In Abra-
ham's Bosom*, produced by Alsberg, the Provincetown Players presented a serious play performed by African Americans actors. Alsberg's greatest theatrical
achievement was translating, adapting, and producing *The Dybbuk*, by Russian
Jew S. Ansky (Solomon Rappoport). Ansky had drawn his inspiration from the
folk traditions of East European Jews.[21]

For Botkin travel, art, and social work were part of the heady mix out of
which he intended to find himself and create poetry. He wrote of traveling in
search of experience, encounters that would help him define a sense of self

and possibilities: "summers communing with nature in both her Eastern and Western moods." His romantic quest may have also revealed the attitudes of a first-generation American. Botkin knew little of his family history except that his parents were Jewish immigrants from Lithuania and that the family name was Rabotnik, which meant "worker." He was born in East Boston in 1901, but "since we moved every time [my father] moved his shop, I never sank my roots in any one of our four home towns." With the help of scholarships and a variety of summer jobs, he received his B.A. from Harvard in 1920. After he earned an M.A. in English from Columbia in 1921, Botkin became an instructor at the University of Oklahoma. In 1923 he left Oklahoma to return to New York City, where as he later remembered, "I drifted uncertainly and half-heartedly in and out of the Columbia grad school, teaching in an Eastside cramming school, a couple of settlement houses, the Village, Rhytmus, and the homes and shops of foreigners to whom I taught English from Brooklyn to the Bronx." Then, as Botkin put it, "the West recalled me." What he liked to think of as his *wanderjahre* were over.[22]

Through his Sunday reviews in the *Daily Oklahoman*, Botkin had worked to introduce Oklahomans to modern literature and to help them appreciate the folk literature emerging out of the daily life of Oklahomans. He wanted "to make Oklahoma culture-conscious and Oklahoma-conscious (a two fold pioneering)." Botkin was formulating a view of culture in which cosmopolitanism and provincialism were complementary, not hostile, approaches. From 1929 to 1932 he was the editor of the annual *Folk-Say: A Regional Miscellany*, which was an important part of the Southwest renaissance. His essay "The Folk in Literature: An Introduction to the New Regionalism" was both polemical and programmatic. Botkin maintained that cultural diversity was not a danger but a positive aspect of American life. "There is," he argued, "not one folk in [America] but many folk groups—as many as there are regional cultures or racial or occupational groups within a region."[23]

Royse, like Botkin, was interested in American ethnic diversity. His initial interest in ethnic cultures focused on European minorities, a subject that World War I and Woodrow Wilson's talk of self-determination of peoples had made a topic of great import for the future. Royse's career might be seen as the archetypal story of the young man from the provinces. He was born in North Dakota in 1896; went east to attend Columbia, where he came under the influence of Franz Boas and John Dewey; and earned his Ph.D. He also studied in Vienna. Royse, too, engaged in social work activities that united educational, cultural, and political issues. He worked with the Workers' Education Bureau of America and served as head of a teacher training institute in Puerto Rico. One of his colleagues on the education board recalled that "officials in Puerto Rico who were opposing worker's education attacked [Royse] from all sides."[24]

Brown's academic career enabled him to travel and observe black life in various American locales. He drew on this experience in writing his poetry. Born in 1901, Brown had grown up among black intellectuals gathered around Howard University in Washington, D.C., where his father was a professor of theology. Though he did not engage in actual social work, in his poetry and literary criticism Brown did seek to link cultural, social, and political issues. His poetry focused on the history and experience of ordinary black people, and Brown tried to incorporate a black folk voice and point of view. Through his analysis of black stereotypes in American literature Brown intended to reveal the social and political interests that benefited from these distortions of the character of African Americans. The process, he thought, would lead to significant social and political change and to a revitalization of American culture as both blacks and whites were freed of the harmful burdens stereotypes had placed on them. For him as for other national FWP officials, cultural and political issues were inextricably linked.[25]

In the 1930s social work had not yet become merely an institutionalized part of the status quo. It was still close to what one scholar has called its role as the spearhead of reform in the Progressive Era. During the 1920s it provided a base for keeping the reform tradition alive and from which new ideas emerged that came to fruition in the New Deal. Clarke Chambers has suggested that social work in the 1920s was the seedtime of reform, the link between Progressivism and the New Deal. A host of social workers, the most visible of whom was Harry Hopkins, the head of the WPA, held important positions in New Deal agencies. The presence of the arts projects in the WPA program was not merely a logical bureaucratic arrangement. Nor was it simply coincidence that so many arts projects officials had had social work experience. The link between the arts and social work symbolized a reform tradition that had paid attention to both economic and cultural issues—bread and roses. This tradition of reform and social work affected the way these officials thought about the relationships between government, culture, and democracy.[26]

National FWP editors had arrived at a romantic nationalist, pluralistic, and cosmopolitan view of the nation that both influenced and grew out of the way they approached their own field of interest. Their visions affected the making of the guides and led to the creation of other FWP programs in folklore, social-ethnic, and black studies, which were at the heart of the FWP's effort to recon-

cile romantic nationalism, pluralism, and modernity. The FWP's cultural pluralism was not limited to white Americans. Alsberg was aware of black interest
in how African Americans would be treated in the FWP's portrait of America.
John P. Davis, executive secretary of the Joint Committee on National Recovery, an African American organization formed early in the New Deal to protect
black interests in such matters as the National Recovery Act codes and the agricultural programs, wrote Alsberg of the "apprehensions" he had about the Writers' Project. He was concerned about black employment on the FWP and the
treatment of blacks in project publications. He recommended that Alsberg con-
sult African American scholars such as Carter G. Woodson and Alfred Schom-
burg about black materials to be included in the planned national guide. Alsberg
was open to advice from black leaders, who despite their criticisms of New Deal
policies, found there were individuals within the Roosevelt administration interested in their point of view—in marked contrast to previous administrations.[27]

Alsberg saw the work of the FWP as contributing to the rediscovery of a diverse American culture, and from the beginning he thought the Writers' Project should study blacks, ethnic groups, regional cultures, and the nation's diverse folklore. He wanted Brown to work out a program for exploring the black
aspect of the American experience. In the summer of 1938 he hired Botkin as
national FWP folklore editor and Royse as national FWP social-ethnic studies
editor. He planned for Botkin, Royse, and Brown to work closely together on
projects that would examine the participation of diverse groups in creating a
pluralistic American culture. These studies, he thought, would continue to explore in greater depth subjects that the guides had only introduced.[28]

Romantic nationalists in the FWP Washington office gave an affirmative answer to the question of whether the United States had distinct, indigenous
folklore and art traditions that had grown out of the American experience.
Lomax insisted that there were native American folk songs reflecting the experience of the African American, the cowboy, the outcast, and diverse occupational groups. This idea marked a significant break from the traditional position that ballads surviving from the British Isles were the only folk songs in
America, and it had radical cultural implications for intellectuals interested in
rediscovering a diverse American folk tradition and those sympathetic to the
lower classes. From Lomax's point of view, American folklore was more than
the remnant of Old World traditions. Rather, it was the creative response of
diverse American groups to their New World experience. Botkin, who succeeded Lomax as folklore editor, shared a similar view of folklore and American culture. Botkin, however, was interested in urban as well as rural lore, eth-

nic and labor lore, oral history, and the relationship between folklore, anthropology, and modern literature. Unlike Lomax, Botkin did not see modern life and folklore as engaged in mortal competition with the former in danger of winning. In Botkin's view folklore was not a survival from the past that was fast disappearing but something still being created in the city as well as in the country, in the factory as well as in the fields.[29]

Botkin developed a theoretical regionalism that valued both the provincial and the cosmopolitan aspects of American culture, that was compatible with national integration, and that did not uncritically embrace the status quo. Botkin wanted to avoid a nostalgic regionalism. Therefore, he maintained, a line needed "to be clearly drawn between the acculturative and contra-acculturative phases of regionalism," between a regionalism that accepted the process of cultural exchange and change that occurred when different cultures came into contact, and a regionalism that rejected what he viewed as an inevitable development. Contra-acculturative regionalism, he argued, "makes the mistake of identifying culture with a particular trait or complex, a particular way of life . . . of taking a certain background for granted and a certain social order as final." Instead, he saw regionalism as "integrative within differentiation and decentralization," and as capable of contributing to a modern pluralistic American culture.[30]

Botkin hoped the FWP folklore and oral history projects he developed would enable people to speak for themselves and that the published results could create an encounter between reader and narrator in which the reader could see things from the perspective of the speaker. Lomax's confident assumptions that he knew and understood African Americans often prevented this from happening in his work. His vision of a rich folk tradition menaced by modern developments had no place in it for the idea of America as a culture in the process of becoming. Any changes in the social order could only harm the folk tradition. Such a vision distinguished Lomax from Botkin and his FWP colleagues who, like Emerson and Whitman, linked the idea of America as a culture still in the process of realizing itself with their hopes for achieving a more democratic and egalitarian society.

When Royse joined the FWP in 1938, he shifted project work on ethnic groups away from discussion of Americanization, the melting pot, and "contributions." Royse denied that the culture of older American groups constituted the American civilization to which immigrant groups made contributions. In many American communities, he pointed out, the immigrants were a majority of the population. Royse argued "that in such communities these people are the American people. Their culture is contemporary American culture . . . not merely a contribution to American culture." American culture, in Royse's view, was a "composite of cultures."[31]

Brown spent much of his time on the Writers' Project reviewing guidebook material to see if it gave accurate and adequate attention to black Americans. Brown did more than correct the work of others. His strictures became rationales for programs he and others advocated. He viewed the history and culture of black Americans as a significant part of the larger American culture. Brown sought material about the life and history of ordinary blacks as well as about the black elite. His search complemented the research of his FWP colleagues in the national office.

In his FWP plans for "Portrait of the Negro as American," Brown rejected an approach that treated "the Negro as a separate entity, as a problem, not a participant in American life." He found that in the work of black historians who attempted to correct "this neglect . . . the result has been overemphasis, and still separateness." He observed that "where white historians find few or no Negroes and too little participation, Negro historians find too many and too much." Such "race glorification," he held, was a form of parochialism and could, ironically, only create a false sense of separateness, while in reality the African American was "an integral part of American life." Brown's cosmopolitanism had a definite place for a strongly rooted black culture. By not regarding all social and political issues in exclusively racial terms, he was able to emphasize the role ordinary blacks had played in American culture and society and the relationship between the problems blacks and other Americans faced. While never abandoning the idea that there was a distinctive African American culture, his sociologically informed criticism stressed concepts such as class, status, and caste as much as race. For black liberal-left intellectuals in the 1930s a class analysis, as opposed to a chauvinistic approach to race, was a form of cosmopolitanism that enabled them to move outside the parochialism of their own group.[32]

In the careers, publications, and project correspondence of national FWP officials, one finds no evidence that any were as rooted in their particular American subculture as Lomax was, that they viewed the whole primarily from the vantage point of their province, either geographical or ethnic. With the exception of Lomax, they almost all seemed more a part of the liberal intellectual community than any other; thus, unlike Lomax, they approached the study of diverse American cultures as outsiders. It is true that Brown, an African American, focused on the culture, history, and folklore of his own group, but he did so from a national and cosmopolitan perspective. Because of his unquestioned assumptions about the cultural life of his own province and the subcultures within it and their relationship to one another, Lomax the insider became a nostalgic outsider in his analysis of black folk song, although he was one of the nation's great folk song collectors. Assuming they could not speak for others, Lomax's FWP colleagues turned their outsider status to advantage as they went about the task of introducing America to Americans. In the guidebooks national FWP officials strove to introduce Americans to the idea that American diversity was a sign of the nation's vitality and potential, and that celebrating it could provide the basis for a flowering of American culture. Reconciling romantic nationalist theories that had emphasized homogeneity, isolation, and purity with pluralism was a challenge that all New Deal cultural programs faced.

FWP officials and supporters maintained that the work of the Writers' Project would make a major contribution to the development of the arts in America. An FWP official writing to a literary critic asserted that the Writers' Project was "bringing about a sort of rediscovery of America, not only by the people who use our books, but by the many writers who have participated in the preparation of them. Already some novels and short stories and articles have been prepared by workers of the Project or formerly of the Project indicating a new interest in all the nooks and crannies of the country." Alsberg informed a congressional committee that "these FWP books should provide a rich mine of colorful Americana to our writers of this and future generations." This was one of the major arguments FWP officials used to justify the existence of their agency. FWP publicity releases announced, "It is not too much to expect that important literature will result indirectly from the ideas and information which thousands of writers at work for the government are coming into contact with every day."[33]

Romantic nationalist aesthetic theory was more than a rationale offered to win support from writers, congressmen, and the public. It was also a deeply held assumption and a sustaining hope that permeated all levels of the Writers' Project and was shared by numerous publishers, literary critics, and journalists. Two New York City FWP workers thought the legends the project was collecting suggested "possibilities for operas." They reported that when "the subject of an American opera came up" during an interview with noted baritone Lawrence Tibbett, "he was almost delirious with joy over the suggestion that Billy the Kid and Sitting Bull might be put in an opera. He said he would like to sing both roles." In his report on the final disposition of project work, Merle Colby eulogized his agency's accomplishments in acquainting Americans with their country and concluded, "We further hope—that here and there in America some talented boy or girl will stumble on some of this material, take fire from it, and turn it to creative use."[34]

FWP officials compiled lists of writers to whom the project had given "enough to feed, clothe, and house them, while they use their evenings and weekends for creative writing." Such lists helped justify the agency's existence. To their everlasting credit, project officials did aid Richard Wright before he became well known. The dream, however, always involved more than giving writers sustenance, as important as that was. Paul Angle, Lincoln scholar and secretary of the Illinois State Historical Society, told a group of Federal Writers that even the compilation of historical documents was part of an effort to redis-cover the creative potential of American culture: "They constitute rich materi-als for historians and creative writers, which no individual could collect for himself on a similar scale." It was clear, one FWP admirer wrote President Frank-lin Roosevelt, the project merited support "for its significant cultural achieve-ments, for bringing to light an enormous quantity of material that will aid in extending and enriching our native literature." Lewis Mumford saw no reason to criticize the Writers' Project for having "diverted novelists and poets from the free play of their fantasy to tasks that have involved a different discipline." For, he argued, "in the long run, this apprenticeship, this seeing of the Amer-ican scene, this listening to the American voice, may mean more for literature than any sudden forcing of stories and poems." By grounding American art in the details of American life and experience, by studying the "American scene," an optimistic romantic nationalist could conclude, "the Federal Writers Project together with the other creative projects will gradually tend to make literature and art an integral part of the national life." The roots of these arguments lie in the romantic faith that knowledge of the cultural creativity of the "people" would provide the basis for great national achievements in the high arts.[35]

Several national FWP officials held that the creative accomplishments of or-dinary people were in and of themselves significant artistic achievements. While they saw a connection between the rediscovered culture of ordinary Ameri-cans and a revitalized high art, they sometimes discussed cultural achievements in other than hierarchical terms. Roderick Seidenberg, FWP architectural editor, saw that the architectural essays in the state guides gave adequate attention to the cultural, social, and economic forces shaping the built environment, to folk traditions, as well as to individual triumphs of the architect's art. Brown was as concerned with the cultural achievements of ordinary blacks as with the con-tributions of famous individuals. Lomax and Botkin found artistic achieve-ments at all levels of American culture. *American Stuff: An Anthology of Prose and*

Verse by Members of the Federal Writers' Project (1937) included "Phrases of the People," "Six Negro Market Songs of Harlem," and "Square Dance Calls" as well as short stories and poetry.

All the New Deal cultural programs made efforts to democratize the arts, both in the materials they used and in their efforts to create accessible works that could be appreciated by a wide audience. It is easier to see how this worked with arts projects other than the Writers' Project. True, there were occasional FWP publications of creative writing, such as *American Stuff.* These, however, were a small part of the overall FWP program. In part these publications were meant to appease dissatisfied creative writers. Not all project writers were content solely to gather materials that would provide the basis for a great national literature. They wanted the opportunity not simply to gather but to create. Nor was the morale of all project workers adequately buoyed by the FWP's romantic nationalist visions. At some time nearly all writers on the project viewed their research assignments as mundane work, far removed from their creative concerns. Writers who complained that they wanted more time to do creative writing were not easily convinced by their superiors that "the assignments which you call 'routine' . . . very often give considerable opportunity for creative writing."[36]

There were demands from both within and outside the project that the FWP provide writers with a chance to concentrate on their own creative work. In an effort to win support for an FWP creative magazine, Alsberg wrote one of his WPA superiors, "There is great pressure and complaint from all quarters that we are not giving writers a chance in their proper field of creative writing. This is one reason why the support of the Author's League, which is made up of the most important writers of the country has been practically nil." While Alsberg was deeply committed to the FWP program—guidebooks, folklore, slave narratives, and life histories—he also wanted to give creative writers a chance to practice their craft. Despite his best efforts, Alsberg was unable to establish an FWP literary magazine. In 1938 when Botkin established Industrial Lore and Living Lore units in Chicago, New York, and New England composed primarily of creative writers, he encouraged them to draw on their folklore research and ethnic studies in their creative writing. From the beginning, Alsberg was convinced that the work of creative writers on the FWP would show the benefits of their project work, the knowledge gained of American people and places. Creative writers, however, were only a small percentage of the project's employees.[37]

One reason FWP officials had settled on the guidebooks as their principal program was that it was well suited to their function as a relief agency. Project employees had to be selected from the relief rolls, except for a small percentage of supervisors who were exempted from this requirement. FWP officials needed a program that would fit the talents of the people they would find on the relief rolls. The majority of the nation's unemployed writers were in major metropolitan areas. The emphasis on guides, however, meant that the project could employ individuals with varied talents—typists, teachers, journalists, lawyers, mapmakers, and scholars—who would have had no place on a Writers' Project devoted solely to giving sustenance to novelists, poets, essayists, and other "writers." For example, the North Carolina FWP director, after examining the relief rolls of thirteen cities, found 518 teachers and 3 librarians listed, "but not a single name of a writer, journalist, or otherwise professionally qualified person." Alsberg instructed the North Carolina director that there was no need for the project to restrict itself to professional writers. Librarians, lawyers, insurance salesmen, and former executives, he explained, could be employed by the project to "collect and complete the data which can be written by the few real writers later on." By focusing on guidebooks, FWP officials could make their agency national in scope and employ a wide variety of individuals on the relief rolls for whom it was often difficult for WPA officials to find suitable work.[38]

Thus, in a sense, it is true that "Henry Alsberg with his state guides and his heterogeneous assortment of writers, was perhaps least [of the arts project directors] concerned with the need of a creative intelligentsia for a public." Despite the emphasis on the state guides and the varied abilities of FWP employees, Alsberg and other national FWP officials were as concerned as their counterparts on the other arts projects with using the everyday materials of American life in creating an accessible culture. It was not, however, a culture of plays, paintings, concerts, or novels and poems that FWP officials worked to make increasingly available. Rather, in their publications they tried to present to the American people a broad knowledge of their own culture—culture in the anthropological sense—to "introduce" them to its richness and diversity.[39]

Both in conventional terms and from a broadly humanistic point of view, national FWP officials saw the guides as an educational venture. In the pages of the *Journal of the National Education Association* Alsberg explained how the work of the FWP would be of "great value to educators." FWP publications would provide "a new and valuable textbook," which could serve as both a tourist guide and "a social history of the country." But Alsberg's hopes for the FWP and his definition of education transcended the idea of Federal Writers as authors of textbooks. The official report of a regional FWP conference held in Chicago noted that "Mr. Alsberg, in closing the conference suggested the conception of the Federal Writers' Project as constituting in effect a great popular university teaching America in many different ways, and genuinely integrated with contemporary life." Federal Writers performing their task of cultural education would have an organic relationship with the larger culture.[40]

Integration, a key word for national FWP officials, had both a romantic nationalist and a cultural pluralist connotation. Education would help Americans accept and celebrate their diversity and lead to a renewed culture that sustained both its people and its artists. National FWP officials also thought cultural integration could overcome the fragmentation of modern life without demanding that everybody be the same or by excluding those who were different. Education in this vision was helping the nation develop its awareness and understanding of its own culture. Thus for national FWP officials, "the purpose of the guides is to give the nation a detailed portrait of itself." They argued that the FWP was having a "profound influence on the cultural life of the nation" and that outside observers "believe that the effects of these activities will extend far into the future, and be looked back upon as a great forward stride in the cultural development of the American people." Van Wyck Brooks shared with Alsberg his general enthusiasm for the project's work: "The reviewer was certainly right when he said the other day that the American Guide Series will still be going strong when most of our current books are dead and forgotten. For undertaking such a job and carrying it out successfully, every college in the country should give you a Ph.D." Brooks thought of Alsberg and his colleagues as American scholars.[41]

At a special regional conference of FWP officials, John T. Frederick, Midwest regional director, sought to explain the FWP's role in American culture. Frederick, a committed regionalist, had founded an experimental little magazine, *Midland*, in the 1920s. While encouraging regional literature, he also saw regional declarations of cultural independence within the diverse parts of the United States as compatible with a vital sense of American cultural nationalism. He argued that "the job in which we Federal writers are cooperating is one that is an expression of a change in the whole American attitude toward America." Just as Americans were learning to appreciate and conserve material resources, they were also learning to conserve the cultural resources of the nation: "The job that is specifically of the Federal Writers' Project seems to me to fit precisely into a program for the extension of the new appreciation of the American cultural inheritance." He told his fellow Federal Writers that the guidebooks "for the Dakotas and Iowa seemed admirable for this particular purpose." The books would be useful to the tourist, "but their greatest importance is in what they will do for the people of the states themselves, and what they do there it seems is to stimulate and foster a new appreciation of what the state is, what it stands for and what the cultural possibilities are."[42]

Frederick specifically noted how this attitude contrasted with Sinclair Lewis's view in *Main Street* (1921). Lewis's irony, heavy sarcasm, and deep disappointment were apparent on every page: "Main Street is the climax of civilization. That the Ford car might stand in front of the Bon Ton Store, Hannibal invaded Rome and Erasmus wrote in Oxford cloisters." Lewis detested what he saw as the spreading blight of a homogenized and standardized America: "The town is, in our tale, called 'Gopher Prairie, Minnesota.' But its Main Street is the continuation of Main Streets everywhere. The story would be the same in Ohio or Montana, in Kansas or Kentucky or Illinois, and not very differently would it be told Up York State or in the Carolina Hills." FWP officials took a different approach to American culture in general and Lewis's Minnesota in particular. The state director of the Minnesota FWP remembered "being completely baffled by the tendency of all federal editors to regard us as inhabiting a region romantically different from any other in the country." She concluded, however, that "this romanticism of the Washington editorial mind, disconcerting as it often was, is probably responsible for most of the best writing in all the guides."[43]

In Frederick's view the state and local guides could make Americans aware that they possessed a worthy culture, that it was available to them, and that the FWP was providing guides to it:

> It seems to me possible for us to make a real contribution to a new attitude for the home town, on the part of the coming generation. And I think that is a tremendously important thing to do. If we can, in dealing with Galena or Dubuque, or any small city of the middle west, help people who are living there, and growing up there to see that they have something in their own home town that is special and intrinsically worthy, not something to get away from, but something to foster and appreciate, I think that is a pretty good job for us to try to do.[44]

Folklore editor B. A. Botkin wanted Americans to appreciate the nation's diverse folk traditions. He thought that the FWP had a duty to disseminate as well as to collect folklore, for he believed folklore had an important role to play in a democratic culture: "For the task, as we see it, is one not simply of collection, but also of assimilation. In its belief in the public support of art and art for the public, in research not for research's sake but for use and enjoyment by the many, the WPA is attempting to assimilate folklore to the local and national life. . . . The WPA looks upon folklore research not as a private but as a public function, and folklore as public, not private property."[45]

For FWP officials American culture was not a European import; it was something Americans had always possessed but had overlooked. Now they needed to rediscover it. What the FWP helped them rediscover was a pluralistic American culture, not the culture of Anglo-Saxon Americanism or the culture of an emerging American race. "Nationality," "race," and "culture" were terms that were no longer used interchangeably.

Earlier romantic nationalists had attacked the genteel identification of the national culture with Anglo-Saxon Americanism. Rebellious individuals had challenged genteel standards by contrasting them with what they argued were the richer alternative cultures offered by non-Anglo-Saxon groups. They were concerned with defending the rights of minorities to remain different. There had been talk of defining America as a "trans-national culture" or a federation of nations. FWP officials, however, were trying to define a nation in which individuals and groups could participate as Americans while retaining their regional, ethnic, and racial identities. They were influenced by cultural relativism, the emphasis on a plurality of historically conditioned cultures rather than a hierarchical evolutionary scheme of a universal culture in which different groups occupied higher and lower rungs—the idea of culture as an integrative force and the concept of acculturation, which characterized the work of anthropologists such as Franz Boas, Ruth Benedict, and their students.[46]

Looking for an editor to handle materials on the American Indian, Alsberg wrote Boas for advice. Boas recommended Edward Kennard. Kennard spent a large part of his time telling state editors that "use of such terms as 'progress' or 'relative achievement' implies evaluation according to a fixed standard and should be omitted." Plans for a study of the acculturation of Indians were developed by Benedict and Alsberg but were dropped because of a lack of funds. In discussing American culture, FWP officials used such phrases as "composite America" and "the Negro as American."[47]

Cultural pluralism offered a basis for a national integration based on cultural understanding, not merely the technical and administrative ties of a large bureaucracy. It complemented New Deal programs that attempted to address the problems of farmers, industrial workers, blacks, and ethnic groups; it gave them cultural recognition. One historian argues that the New Deal was "a social revolution completing the overthrow of the Protestant Republic." Perhaps.

At the least, it was a significant change in cultural direction. The definition of American culture and nationality was enlarged; it was redefined. It is easy to forget how dominant a narrow vision of America had been. The Republican presidents of the 1920s were not only the representatives of a conservative philosophy but also the physical symbols of an America that defined itself as white, Protestant, middle-class, and rural.[48]

Discussion of Writers' Project publications among FWP officials and in the press proceeded on the assumption that knowledge of the United States, its past, and its diverse peoples and regions would paradoxically create both a cosmopolitan feeling and primordial ties. One's relationship to the nation was more psychological than political or intellectual. As with family relations, whatever the problems and conflicts, the assumption was that a deep knowledge led to understanding, affection, and acceptance. Thus Bernard DeVoto, writing in the *Saturday Review of Literature*, described the FWP guidebooks as "an educational and even a patriotic force, an honorable addition to our awareness of ourselves and our country," and Lewis Mumford hailed them in the pages of the *New Republic* as "the first attempt to make the country worthily known to Americans." The guides, he thought, contributed to the detailed knowledge of American life that would provide the basis for a revived national art and to the regional understanding necessary for a sound future. The guides could put Americans in touch with themselves. They were addressed to every American. Therefore, he concluded, "these guidebooks are the finest contribution that has been made to patriotism in our generation." Mumford's remarks would be quoted by both FWP officials and other reviewers as a description of what the FWP was trying to accomplish. Thus his remarks gave form to widely held sentiments.[49]

The FWP guidebook tours offered a way of rediscovering and celebrating a diverse landscape, a way of creating a consciousness of the United States that could help Americans feel at home in a diverse land—a consciousness that could fulfill the role of a unifying tradition. The guides proposed a way of looking at, approaching, and infusing the landscape with emotional and symbolic content; the guides tried to create a sense of place. They offered knowledge of a variety of American places as a way of making the abstraction "America" into a symbolic place. Identity and place became two sides of the same coin. Travelers were to know who they were by knowing where they were.

The FWP tried not only to complement New Deal efforts at technical unity with an ideology of cultural pluralism but also to foster a sense of primordial unity within a pluralistic and cosmopolitan framework. America's diverse groups and regions were to be rediscovered and celebrated first in a series of state guidebooks and then in a series of projects focusing on regional, ethnic, and folklore topics touched on in the guides. Inherited questions were to be approached in a new way. An approach that sought to reconcile romantic nationalism, cosmopolitanism, and cultural pluralism implied an answer to the problematic nature of American identity and nationality far different from that offered by those who when they dealt with this issue excluded the history and culture of many groups of Americans. The FWP's examination of who and what was American, the relationship between identity and place and between tradition and modernity, and the nature of American national identity began with the guides.

Chapter 2

Visions and Constituencies

Introducing and Writing
the American Guide Series

National FWP officials wrote no theoretical books about American culture. Instead, as government officials in charge of one part of the New Deal's relief effort, they directed the production of books that to a significant degree reflected their assumptions about their culture. The justifications the FWP gave for its program and the intra-agency discussion of methods for producing guidebooks help explain how the guidebooks embodied the visions of FWP officials and the practical realities they faced. The arguments national FWP officials publicly offered in behalf of their agency reflect not only their aspirations but also their reading of what would gain wide approval for their program. Publicity releases and discussions about methods reveal how visions became programs. The guides were put together according to a method national FWP officials continually sought to refine, in a form that helped define and limit their aspirations, and in a style thought suitable to their immediate function and symbolic meaning.

The visions and the dreams of a period can tell as much about aspects of that time as its accomplishments. Discrepancies between vision and accomplishment are a revealing part of the story. The accomplishment may illuminate aspects of the vision that were not openly acknowledged or whose full implications were not understood. To paraphrase the argument cultural an-

thropologist Clifford Geertz made using Chartres as an example, the FWP
guides are words and paper, but they are not just that alone; they are guidebooks, made at a particular time by certain members of a society. To understand what they mean and to perceive them for what they are, we need to know
more than the generic properties of words and paper and more than what is
common to all guidebooks. We must understand the concepts these artifacts
embody. In their time these guidebooks, these artifacts, stored symbolic meaning, fused fact with value. We can begin to understand these meanings only when
the artifacts are seen in as full a cultural context as possible. The guides need to
be understood in terms of the FWP's aspirations, the metaphorical and symbolic weight attached to them, and the way American history and culture were
treated in them.[1]

The American Guide Series was the central vehicle for the efforts of the Writers' Project to rediscover America, to introduce America to Americans, and to
make the culture accessible to the people to whom it belonged. The guidebooks are cultural artifacts of the 1930s, embodying cultural visions and dreams
of their time. The individuals involved left some record of their aspirations for
the FWP and their assessment of its accomplishment. Within a few years these
aspirations and assessments became a standard version of the purposes of the
guides that was acceptable to such official and mainstream institutions of the
culture as agencies of state and local government, universities, chambers of
commerce, major publishing houses, and magazines and newspapers representing a wide spectrum of political views.

A series of multiauthored guides that could provide work for the diverse talents on the relief rolls partly represented a compromise with the exigencies of
an agency whose primary goal was relief. Though FWP officials frequently proclaimed that this was their primary goal, the matter was not as clear-cut for
them as it was for most members of Congress. Though FWP officials knew that
without its relief role there would be no Federal Writers' Project, they also
thought that future generations would "take no account of the circumstances
under which the guides were produced, but only of their accuracy and excel-
lence." The guides were not offered as mere "temporary displays of talent on
relief, but permanent printed records of work done." The *Indianapolis Star* for
example, announced "that the writers' staff was ready to sift state history" and
"compile for future generations all historical facts, major or trivial, that have a
bearing on the state's development." FWP officials thought the American Guide
Series was meant for the ages, to be an enduring contribution of 1930s America to the continuing effort to understand the American experience. On a prac-

tical level, project officials thought that a favorable reception for their publications would help create an appreciative audience, a constituency that they hoped would ensure their agency's future. A favorable reception meant that Henry Alsberg could tell his superiors "that the books we are putting out around the country reflect a definite credit to the administration."[2]

When the FWP was set up in the fall of 1935, project officials found that it was possible to enlist widespread support for the guide program. They also thought there were definite political dangers in that very fact: "It is also inconceivable that the work be undertaken without being completed. Here in Washington, for instance, we have already enlisted the hearty cooperation of powerful organizations that are not otherwise friendly to the administration. At no point have we encountered political opposition. But once having secured nonpolitical support, it would be fatal to disappoint the influential bodies that have granted it." That the argument was also a self-serving way of winning support from New Deal superiors for a newly established agency did not necessarily invalidate it.[3]

While they worried about how long the Writers' Project would last, FWP officials at the same time contended that their agency should be permanent and in many ways behaved as if it were: "There is no escaping the conclusion that this will be a permanent government function similar in certain respects to the census. It will be one of the most important permanent sources of information that the government can offer. Periodic revisions will naturally be expected. It will return dividends for generations to come." In describing to President Franklin Roosevelt the project's achievements and potential, Alsberg proudly noted that "in our files is enough material on the American scene to keep staffs of writers busy for years in editing valuable publications." Testifying at an appropriations hearing, Harry Hopkins made the same point. Arguments that the tasks of the Writers' Project were unlimited and that there were plans and work to fill an indefinite future were offered as good reasons for continuing a temporary agency.[4]

Despite ritualistic assertions to the contrary, FWP officials were more committed to their programs than they were to their relief role, but Congress had committed itself to government-sponsored relief, not government-sponsored art. At a 1941 conference on the arts programs of the WPA, poet and librarian of Congress Archibald MacLeish focused on these issues. MacLeish wanted government support for the arts divorced from relief concerns. Addressing the WPA administrators at the conference, he argued, "What you people did was completely hypocritical. . . . You kept telling yourself [*sic*] you were actually giving people a job, but you were really more interested in your program." No one denied it. But the WPA official who countered, "You must admit it was one of the higher forms of hypocrisy," could have been speaking for them all.[5]

Talk of widespread support, of lasting contributions, and of endless programs cannot disguise the fact that the FWP was on the defensive from the beginning; such talk was partly a response to the pressures and criticism the agency confronted. To critics of relief programs for artists, WPA administrator Harry Hopkins responded, "Hell they got to eat just like other people." But the press wondered at what expense. There were reports emphasizing the seemingly exorbitant per-word costs of the proposed guides. The appointment of Katherine Kellock as tours editor resulted in a barrage of unfavorable headlines when it was reported that her husband, an American journalist, was the Soviet embassy's publicity director.[6]

Many state WPA administrators either cared little about or were openly hostile to their state FWP units. State FWP directors had to depend on state WPA directors in administrative matters involving funding and the placement of relief workers. In their search for state FWP directors, Alsberg and his staff looked for individuals who had both editorial and administrative skills—a rare combination. They sought state directors who could lend the project literary prestige, perform ably as editors, administer the project, and work successfully with the state WPA administrator. Political pressures influenced Alsberg's choices. In Missouri, for example, the FWP became embroiled in political manipulations that made newspaper headlines.[7]

When Henry Alsberg was chosen to head the FWP, it was unclear how long the agency would last. If a hostile Congress chose to, it could always curtail appropriations. At any time Alsberg's superiors might decide that the project was a political liability and not worth defending. Eventually, Congress did curtail the FWP, and New Deal officials made little effort to defend the project.

Tension and uncertainty permeated an agency whose survival was always in doubt. In January 1936 Alsberg informed state directors that they should plan on having "all state copy cleared by Washington not later than May 1, 1936." Necessity was the mother of the unreasonable optimism underlying this request. There was never any certainty that Congress would continue funds at existing levels; any reduction in congressional funding meant retrenchment in all WPA activities. Between appropriations the financial resources of the FWP depended on how the Bureau of the Budget divided limited funds. When President Roosevelt thought the economy was ready to absorb more workers, he favored cutting WPA expenditures. By reducing work relief, the president attempted to dramatize improvements in the economy. After the presidential election in November 1936, Hopkins ordered a 20 percent reduction in WPA personnel. The special 25 percent exemption for nonrelief personnel on the arts projects was reduced to 10 percent. In the spring of 1937 Congress cut relief appropriations for fiscal 1938 by 25 percent. In June, Roosevelt was buoyant about the prosperity that seemed to mark the early part of 1937, but he worried about the danger of inflation. To meet this danger, he ordered a cut in WPA employment. These and other measures helped cause the recession of 1937. Such cuts damaged morale. Many workers spent much of their time worrying about whether they would keep their jobs. Reductions in exemptions for nonrelief personnel often deprived state projects of their best writers.[8]

The Theater, Music, and Art Projects could offer examples of their work almost from the beginning. The FWP could not. Alsberg and his staff tried to explain, both publicly and to their superiors, why it would take longer to write comprehensive state guides than to produce a play, give a concert, or paint a mural. As Alsberg wrote one state director in February 1937, "It is necessary to give rather definite assurance to those who are concerned with the continuation projects that the State guides will reach completion within a reasonable time. . . . Where undue delay is reported in finishing the major product in each state, an attitude of doubt becomes apparent in the minds of those responsible for the Writers' Project."[9]

Project editors in the national office were intensely aware of who ultimately paid the bills and of who their patrons were. They knew that FWP publications would carry the stamp of federal approval, expertise, and authority. The American people, both present and future generations, were a powerful motivating symbol of who ultimately constituted the FWP's patrons and audience. On a day-to-day basis the national FWP staff worked with New Deal administrators, congressmen, state officials, local FWP field-workers, consultants, sponsors, publishers, and journalists—the official representatives of that abstract audience, the American people.[10]

Alsberg and his staff also thought the guides were "the only project the people of the whole country will get behind." From the beginning there was "a consensus of opinion in the national office of the FWP that the Guide could count on the enthusiastic support of all factions and interests irrespective of politics, that the most representative bodies and individuals in every locality and throughout the states would be glad to collaborate once they knew the nature of the project and that local people would consider it the greatest boon of its kind ever offered."[11]

At the end of first year, Alsberg reported that the guidebooks had "aroused enthusiasm everywhere" and that groups such as historical societies, women's clubs, automobile clubs, the Lions, chambers of commerce, and railroads were all eager to help. He thought the guidebook project was "unusual in that these business groups have given support, while at the same time labor groups, and writers' organizations, leftist, centrist, and rightist have given their help just as enthusiastically." Guidebooks, FWP officials insisted, provided a noncontroversial but culturally significant activity for Federal Writers. The government, they recognized, could not involve itself in publishing partisan works, since these publications would "bear the stamp of authenticity placed on them by Federal experts." Striving for authenticity became in part a search for a consensus approach, for a presentation of the American experience that would be widely acceptable—but only in part, for in various ways to be explored in later chapters, national FWP officials tried to offer a new vision of American culture in the guides. In time the limitations of the guidebook format would lead national FWP officials to develop other programs for examining American culture.[12]

Alsberg talked about creating guides to America that could be sold in "teahouses" and "up-to-date" gasoline stations. By playing on the multiple meanings of the word "guide" in determining the purpose of the American Guide Series, FWP officials sought to sound themes that would resonate with the interests of diverse parts of its audience. In search of an audience, FWP officials defined a guidebook whose encyclopedic aspects promised something of interest for virtually everyone, that declared America's cultural maturity and independence of Europe, that would promote economic recovery and growth, and that through both the cultural themes it sounded and the cultural monument it would constitute offered a portrait of a rediscovered land that would interest Americans, not only in terms of their occupations, regional and ethnic backgrounds, and tourist interests, but also as fellow citizens.[13]

FWP officials claimed that the encyclopedic and travel aspects of the guidebooks would appeal to a wide audience. They aimed to make the work "of value to historians, scientists, teachers, and their students." At the same time the traditional tourist function of guidebooks was always kept in mind. But project officials also claimed that the American Guide Series would "be far more than a tourist enterprise; it will represent a survey of America's past and present, such as has never before been undertaken by any organization." They were convinced that in both scope and content the guidebooks were unprecedented: "No previous guidebooks were concerned with the historical, social, and economic backgrounds of the places they described." With so broadly conceived an effort to document an indigenous American culture, FWP officials could claim the guides "will be of value to persons in every position of our society."[14]

Everyone was considered a potential authority on some aspect of American life. The FWP's interest in talking with ordinary people about their local communities and their own lives testified to that. As Orrick Johns, director of the New York City project, explained to a *New York Times* reporter, "Field workers are scouring the town for this information. So if you're stopped by a stranger who wants to know your racial background and how many of your ancestors fell at Ticonderoga don't be ruffled. It will simply mean that you've become a landmark and are to be preserved for posterity in the New York City guide." Thus the FWP encouraged ordinary Americans to participate in the rediscovery of America, to become partners with the Federal Writers in creating the guides: "Will you join with us in this effort to build up the distinctive atmosphere and background of your community?"[15]

Serving as consultants, recognized authorities associated with respected institutions and organizations established links between the FWP and representatives of the nation's official centers of power. Sponsoring institutions who handled arrangements with commercial publishers further extended the ties between the FWP and mainstream political, cultural, and economic institutions. The effort to enlist the aid of consultants was also part of the constant rhetoric about the scope, the magnitude, indeed the grandeur of this unprecedented undertaking. The size of the undertaking and the number of projected and completed volumes became symbols of a task and accomplishment that, it was argued, or hoped, was commensurate with the reality of a vast and diverse America. All of this rhetoric echoed the sentiments of earlier American artists who had assumed that only a large, perhaps panoramic gesture would do. The Federal Writers were fond of the word "panorama." Newspaper and magazine reports and articles helped develop these themes and congratulated their readers for being part of the generation that was undertaking this task. There was also the Whitman theme. From this point of view the FWP, like Walt Whitman, was trying to catalog, embrace, and possess the indigenous materials of a vast nation. Like Whitman, the project, too, used the road as a metaphor for exploration and discovery. The similarities and differences between *Leaves of Grass* and the guides were not examined. Whitman served inspirational, not critical, purposes.[16]

National FWP officials presented the guides as a declaration of American cultural independence from the Old World. Thus they became one more topic in an endless American discussion about the cultural relationship of the United States to Europe and Western civilization. The guides served three purposes in

this discussion. They could be pointed to as a sign that America was a civilization, that there was as much worthy of study at home as in Europe, and that
Europeans ought to acknowledge the accomplishments of American civilization, perhaps by reversing the flow of tourist traffic.[17]

The publication of guidebooks would prove the existence of an American
civilization. "Every other civilized country," Henry Alsberg argued, "possesses
a substantial guidebook." The lack of adequate American guides, in the words
of one critic, was "a serious defect in our culture"—a defect the FWP promised
to remedy. Guidebooks would also assert American civilization's claim to historical immortality. They would constitute a record for the future. And the act
of leaving a record would prove that America was a civilized country: "The nations of old made the first essays in government sponsored history writing.
The inscriptions which they had cut on columns, pyramids, arches, and the
walls and sides of public buildings survive to give us many facts of antiquity
which would have been buried in the rubbish of fallen cities, if their permanent recording had been left to private initiative." Failure to leave a record
would be a sign of America's failure as a civilization.[18]

FWP officials observed that when Americans read about the vandalization of
ancient tombs by the people presently living on these sites, they were wont to
"condemn the vandals as lacking all sense of responsibility as custodians of
their racial heritage," and yet "many American communities are now making
little effort to preserve historic landmarks and literary shrines." Guidebooks,
FWP officials thought, would both develop and embody a new attitude toward
American culture and history, an attitude that would both literally and symbolically "prevent relics of the past from crumbling into dust" by awakening "a
sense of local pride of possession." In the opinion of one reviewer, the FWP
guides gave 1930s America the opportunity to leave the kind of records classical antiquity had left: "Future historians will turn to these guidebooks as one
who would know the classic world must still turn to Pausania's ancient guidebook to Greece."[19]

"Have You Discovered America?" the Federal Writers asked their fellow citizens. FWP officials thought the answer was they had not. The FWP encouraged
Americans to undertake the task of rediscovery. To aid that undertaking they
offered guides. FWP officials thought that the knowledge of local communities
the guidebooks provided would lead to a renewed interest and appreciation of
America, a realization that Americans "have ignored the natural and cultural
advantages of the United States in favor of the carefully exploited features of
a similar nature in foreign countries." After all, as Lewis Mumford argued, "this

exploration of America, which might be no less exciting and fruitful in its special way than the more conventional trip to Europe, has been stupidly ham-
pered" by the absence of thoughtful and detailed guides, the preparation of
which no publisher had the funds or resources to undertake. "Here," he wrote,
"was an ideal opening for a government supported project."[20]

FWP officials knew there were many Americans who felt that "every place
[they] saw on a vacation in the United States was just like every other place. All
the houses were built the same way. All the people wore the same kind of clothes
and drove the same kind of automobiles. When you see one place you see them
all." They had an answer: "This man has seen nothing because he has gone
about with no appreciation of what his country has to interest travelers." The
truth was that "scattered throughout the American states are hundreds of communities which possess distinctive, scenic, historic, cultural, or economic features and which are known to only small groups of people." Without a guidebook "a man may traverse the Oregon Trail and see nothing under his feet but
dirt." FWP officials thought that "no other country in the world has the poten-
tiality that this country possesses to stir our people so deeply and the object of
the American guide will be to stir them—to help them to recall the associations
of places they have known about and forgotten." By awakening "the interest
of people in their own cities and revealing to them the sights which they have
been missing," the guides would show Americans there was as much to see and
discover at home as in Europe.[21]

At the same time the guides helped Americans reassess their own culture,
they would also constitute a declaration that America deserved Europe's attention. Once again foreigners were to be disabused of fancies such as America
being "largely a primeval forest populated by red Indians ready to pounce
upon and scalp them." The truth was that Europeans could benefit from a trip
to America as much as Americans could from a trip to Europe. American communities had "sights to interest and edify" foreigners. FWP officials had heard
the conventional European "complaint that America is 'so new' and 'so lacking in background.'" According to FWP officials, "What America really lacks is
an adequate guide to tell travelers what they should look for and where to look
for it." The guides, FWP officials asserted, "will unquestionably give smaller
communities the best opportunity which they have ever had to gain the attention of foreigners as well as native Americans."[22]

The 1893 Baedeker guide to the United States was to be replaced by an
American-produced FWP series of state guides. Baedeker's guide to America,
written from a European perspective and last revised in 1909, had in the eyes

of FWP officials treated America with traditional Old World condescension. Travel in the United States, it advised, was "as safe as in the most civilized parts of Europe." Despite the cultural nationalism of the FWP, its guides adopted a European form. While the contents of the guides were distinctly American, the format borrowed from Baedeker. Karl Baedeker, a German, had turned guidebook writing into an industry by producing a standard product in a predictable format for a triumphant and traveling nineteenth-century European middle class. "Baedeker" and "guidebook" became synonymous. The form involved essays, points of interest, and tours. The FWP borrowed all of this but nevertheless changed the form into something distinctly American. Part of the process involved the themes of cultural nationalism and pluralism that prefaced, introduced, and permeated the FWP guides; part involved their breadth and depth; and part involved adapting the tour format to the automobile. Still, all the talk about the FWP's accomplishments in adapting the guidebook form to American circumstances and in documenting American history and culture was accompanied by mumbling even among some FWP officials about cultural inadequacy and inferiority. Along with those who said the FWP guides were better than Baedeker, there were those, even on the national FWP staff, who emphasized American youth rather than maturity: "Perhaps when American guidebook making has gone on as long as Baedeker-making has it may approach Baedeker perfection."[23]

Cultural nationalism was also promoted on practical economic grounds. A neglected historic shrine, FWP officials argued, was both a cultural and an economic loss: "It does nothing to create interest because its history has been allowed to fade out of the public mind." Yet, they pointed out, "the Europeans —conscious of the profits to be made from tourists—use historic shrines to build up atmosphere and to popularize foreign travel." They offered to lend their support to a "see America first" campaign. Alsberg argued that by making Americans aware of "what there is to see right here at home," the guides could "bring back part of the six hundred million dollars spent in average years by Americans on travel outside this country." As a New Deal relief program the FWP had little choice but to point out how their agency could contribute to economic recovery. Travel, FWP officials constantly emphasized, had a commercial dimension. In an effort to secure cooperation "in giving your city a first class write-up," Alsberg wrote to the secretary of the Pennsylvania Rotary Club that "the quickening of interest in local sites will cause an improvement of traffic through the development of tours in and about each city. . . . Doubtless your city's restaurants, hotels, boarding houses, and commercial establishments would welcome transient customers from out of town."[24]

The cultural rediscovery of America promised definite economic advantages. The guides, Alsberg explained to the vice-president in charge of traffic of the Association of American Railroads, "will stimulate local pride to a point where all advantages will be exploited and . . . awaken the interest of local people and strangers in the sights to be seen. This will undoubtedly result in an increase in local and national travel." Since production of the American Guide Series was a task no private individual or organization would undertake, in publishing the guides the FWP would aid, but not compete with, private enterprise. The links established with commercial interests provided FWP officials with one more argument in behalf of their agency. The *Boston Globe* headlined a story on the establishment of the state FWP with "W.P.A. Project Expected to Increase Travel" and reported the state WPA administrator's claim that "businessmen throughout Massachusetts are hailing the new project with great enthusiasm." Harry Hopkins, testifying before skeptical congressmen, not only referred to the cultural value of the guides but also to the support the FWP was receiving from such organizations as the Association of American Railroads, the National Association of Motor Bus Operators, and the American Hotel Association.[25]

When Republican presidential candidate Alf Landon disdainfully declared, "This administration has found time to make guide books," the FWP responded, "We say: The transportation associations—railroad, steamship, airline and busline, the hotel associations, automobile clubs, more than 500 chambers of commerce and some 12,000 other individuals and associations, including editors, and other professional people, seem to think it is a pretty good idea to make tourist guide books." In meeting Landon's attack, project officials emphasized the support of commercial, not cultural, institutions and organizations.[26]

American traditions and the guide format ensured that many organizations would welcome the guides for their commercial possibilities. From the writings of America's early explorers through the immigrant handbook and the publications of land and railroad companies, farmers' organizations, and chambers of commerce, exploration and travel have been linked with promotion and development. At every opportunity, FWP officials asserted that the guidebooks would aid local business. Yet they avoided justifying project work on commercial grounds without also referring to the guides as a cultural endeavor. Their vision of the government's cultural role in a democracy, while it acknowledged commercial interests, also transcended them.

Despite their willingness to sound commercial themes, national FWP officials were determined to keep the guidebooks from becoming simply promotional material. FWP editors in the Washington, D.C., office eliminated such superlatives as "largest," "best," "greatest," and "prettiest" from guidebook drafts submitted by state FWP offices. Boosterism, national FWP officials thought, was incompatible with the objective and authoritative tone they were trying to achieve. America, they held, had no shortage of publications that reflected the outlook of local boosters. They, however, intended their guides to be a contribution to the national culture. Boosterism was incompatible with that aspiration. If the rhetoric of the booster appeared in the American Guide Series, national FWP officials were convinced, it would make their guidebooks indistinguishable from other such efforts—and they aimed to transcend the genre.[27]

Only in recent times have fiction and poetry been thought synonymous with literature, for as Paul Fussell has pointed out, "The status of those two kinds [of literature] is largely an unearned and unexamined snob increment from late romantic theories of art." As a result of this attitude, other forms of writing have suffered a loss of status and critical attention. It is worth keeping this in mind when examining the claims of FWP officials and their supporters that the guidebooks were a form of literature and should be distinguished from the usual chamber of commerce promotional material that was "both unreliable and insipid." In addition to awakening writers to the creative materials America offered its artists, Henry Alsberg maintained that writing guidebook copy itself was a literary endeavor. He sought to "dissipate the impression that the guidebooks have no creative side to them." For example, he noted that the national FWP staff "demanded that color and imagination and vividness be used in the descriptions."[28]

Lewis Mumford, writing in the *New Republic,* tried to refute those who held that "such a tract as a guidebook offers no scope for literature." While he conceded that this genre had "no place for free fantasy of fabulous creative invention," he nevertheless insisted that "it offers many a real test of literary capacity: the focusing of the subject, the precise epithet, the acute observation, the novelist's insight into his material and that ultimate purity of literary style which is free from merely individualistic mannerism can all find their place in such writing." These qualities could be found in the FWP guidebooks, he held. In his view the "alert gusto that characterizes" many of the FWP guidebook descriptions distinguished them from "the dull conventional shorthand of a Baedeker." The former were literature; the latter were not.[29]

In a 1940 article Katherine Kellock, the FWP tours editor, offered a preliminary assessment of the guides. She took the position that it was not surprising that the guides had for the most part not been regarded as literature, since "literary criticism is little practiced in the United States." It is not difficult to hear the indictment in those words or to discern the pride she took in the guides and the challenge she posed for future students of American culture in the 1930s.[30]

Freed from chamber of commerce rhetoric, FWP officials intended their publications to be received as a literary contribution to American culture. They aimed for "more than just a conventional guidebook" and another "ephemeral publication." Their guides were to be "permanent . . . records, which will be exposed to critical scrutiny for all time." The guidebook format, FWP officials claimed, gave them the opportunity "to catch the atmosphere of each town and section," to make "a valuable contribution . . . to American culture" and to offer "a directory and guide to the historical and contemporary development of this country"—guides that they also asserted were a social history. Americans would be able to trust guides that bore "the stamp of authenticity placed on them by Federal experts." The guides were to appeal to a varied audience and to introduce that audience to a diverse America. Knowledge of American experience and diversity gained from the guides would contribute to a revitalized American culture and a broadened definition of American identity and community. To achieve such aims required more than statements from national FWP officials of the FWP purpose, though the rhetoric of their aspirations helped create the immediate context in which the guides were written and read. It required the development of a method and a style for writing guidebooks.[31]

The guidebooks were divided into three sections: essays, general descriptions of the state's major cities, and automobile tours. In these sections there was room for material that highlighted regional qualities, ethnic and racial diversity, history, and folklore. The guides reflected the systematic approach inherent in the format and the collective effort involved in creating them. Nevertheless, there were as many ways of using the guides as there were readers. One could open to whatever topic, city, or tour one chose and proceed in any fashion and the book would serve its guide function. The design was responsive to individual need. It allowed the reader to approach travel as a chance for personal growth and discovery. "We are not regimenting travel," declared Alsberg; "we are endeavoring to cover all main routes, indicating the preferable ones, and then permitting tourists to make up their own combination of routes as best suits their purpose."[32]

The FWP was organized somewhat on the model of a large metropolitan newspaper, with its reporters, desk men and women, and editors. Editors issued guidelines and defined assignments. Reports from local field-workers went to district supervisors and then to the state FWP office before being sent to editors in Washington, D.C. Thus the FWP brought together, within a national framework, for the purpose of writing books about the United States, individuals from all points on a local-cosmopolitan continuum.

National FWP editors could send reporters back to gather additional material, they could demand revisions, and they could reject copy. They could not, however, fire and hire at will. They had to work with individuals who came from the relief rolls or were hired under special exemptions for a small percentage of nonreliefers. Before the state guidebooks could be published, they had to be approved by the national office. In this way, Washington officials sought to maintain standards.[33]

Field-workers received guide manuals written by the national office. These manuals were designed to aid workers in understanding their role and tasks. Experience, however, revealed weaknesses in the manuals. Frequent revisions and supplements had to be issued. In the initial stages of setting up state FWP units, members of the national staff, such as architectural editor Roderick Seidenberg, folklore editor John Lomax, and tours editor Katherine Kellock, visited the state projects to help local workers understand what Washington wanted. They also reported to the Washington office on the quality of work being done and on local problems.[34]

National FWP officials took pride in a method that, they asserted, "allows definite local color and feeling to penetrate into the guides." They argued that this was possible because "the material has actually been collected locally, on the spot by Guide workers who are native to the location and catch its real spirit." But this was also the reason national editors had to work hard to keep the guides local and regional in content, but national rather than parochial in outlook. Ordinary field-workers had limited ability to set local material in a broad context. Copy sent to the national office was often so irritatingly inadequate that editors had to be warned about the importance of carefully phrasing their comments, about "not sounding as if we were posing as little tin gods. . . . We must avoid this in order to get the best work out of our state offices."[35] National FWP tours editor Katherine Kellock played a crucial role in developing the guidebook format. Like other key FWP officials, social work experience and travel had been part of her education. She had served as a nurse doing relief work in eastern Europe and with Lillian Wald at the Henry Street Settlement House. At Columbia University she began studying the social sciences but changed to journalism. The Hearst Press, interested primarily in her husband's job as a publicity agent for the Soviet embassy, did not publicize the fact that Harold

Kellock was an old friend of Alsberg's and had worked as a publicist in Progressive Party candidate Robert LaFollette's campaign for the presidency in 1924. Harold Kellock's friends thought him "somewhat anti-communist in his views." Alsberg had asked Katherine Kellock to leave the Resettlement Administration to work for the FWP because of her reputation for research and writing, as evidenced in her contributions to the *Dictionary of American Biography* and other scholarly publications. She had also had a long-standing interest in publishing a major guide for the United States. All of these details are relevant in trying to understand the outlook and approach of national FWP officials, but at the time, it did not seem pragmatic for WPA officials to publicize many facts about Kellock, except that her ancestors had been in America for a long time. As Reed Harris concluded, "Obviously nothing we might say would particularly aid us in the Hearst newspapers."[36]

On her visits to state FWP offices, Katherine Kellock discovered the inadequacies of the original manual. Local workers had a difficult time interpreting the instructions. They had, according to Kellock, engaged in "microscopic analysis of sub-divisions" without any sense of their relation to the whole. In the Birmingham, Alabama, files she found a 1,020-word description of a modern Presbyterian church, 820 words on a Federal Reserve building, and 40 words on local art. Part of the Raleigh, North Carolina, staff, she learned, had been working full time covering every church in town. The 117 project workers in North Carolina had been concentrating in microscopic detail on nine cities, while no work had been done on the rest of the state. The manual had given project workers the impression that for every city they should write 100,000 words, which would eventually be condensed. The manual, Kellock argued, had been made up in haste, and people set to work before they understood the instructions. In her view, the problems with the way the material was being assembled were as much the fault of the manual as of the state directors. The manual, she conceded, might be suitable in states with large urban centers, but in predominantly rural states it had led to comical absurdities.[37]

In reviewing these problems, Kellock outlined a broad conception of a method suitable to organizing material for the guidebook format. She thought reading Charles and Mary Beard's *The Rise of American Civilization* would give "the workers perspective on what is important and what is unimportant." It could "serve as an explanation of the purposes of the guide; the real purpose is, of course to educate Americans to an evaluation of their own civilization." Kellock shared the Beards' great hope—"The history of a civilization, if intelligently conceived, may be an instrument of civilization"—and what she viewed as his relevant statement of method: "Surveying life as a whole, as distinguished from microscopic analysis by departments, the history of civilization ought to come nearer than any partial history to the requirements of illumination."[38]

Henry Alsberg responded cautiously to Kellock's ideas. He agreed with her suggestion that field-workers make use of such reference works as the *Dictionary of American Biography*, the *Encyclopedia Brittanica*, and the *World Almanac*. He doubted, however, that the average field-worker would be able to follow articles in the *Encyclopedia of the Social Sciences*. Regarding *The Rise of American Civilization*, he was sensitive to possible political repercussions: "We might get in trouble with that," he wrote Kellock. Therefore, he advised, "it might be better to give them something less disturbing to their traditional points of view." He was not, however, rejecting the hopes and goals the Beards had articulated. The issue was how to fulfill them.[39]

Alsberg and Kellock differed over the kind of material that was suitable for a guidebook. Both, however, had similar and equally ambitious aims for the guides. In the early stages Alsberg saw the essays as offering the Federal Writers an opportunity to creatively explore American life. The essays, in his view, would make the guides useful to a broad audience. Therefore he was unwilling to view the potential guide user primarily as a tourist. The problems Kellock reported could be corrected by supplements to the manual. Kellock, however, contended that the manual reflected a flawed concept of what a guidebook is. For her, an emphasis on essays on topics such as agriculture, architecture, and history would mean the appearance of materials that belonged in detailed histories, dictionaries of biography, and encyclopedias. Such guides would constitute a bewildering mélange of genres that would confuse everyone and satisfy nobody.[40]

Kellock insisted that the guide reader had to be thought of as a tourist. Her point of view did not totally triumph. The essays occupied more space in the state guides than they would have if the decision had been Kellock's alone. Initially the essays were seen as carrying the burden of the FWP's educational, research, and creative ambitions. As time passed, however, other national FWP officials moved to a position much closer to Kellock's. Though the guides were not put together solely with tourists in mind, the reader as tourist became the controlling symbol that dominated decisions about gathering and organizing material and the style in which it should be presented. The Federal Writers, however, did not condescend to the reader. The format, materials, and style made demands on the tourist-reader they envisioned—too many for the casual tourist. Rather, their tourist-readers had to want to explore and rediscover their country, to broaden their sense of the national community.[41]

National FWP officials had a long list of words they warned field-workers not to use. Style embodied goals and values. Thus Alsberg told Harrison Parkman, a Kansas FWP official, "We question your biggest array of earth moving machinery ever assembled in one locality. We have checked with the U.S. Bureau of Mines and find that equally large machinery exists in Illinois and Montana." The rule of thumb was to avoid as much as possible words ending in "est."[42] Material also had to be presented in a style that would help the tourist see the area he or she was visiting. National editors asked for accurate observation rather than "such florid expression as 'magnificent waterfall,'" for "flowery hyperboles are no substitute for a forceful authentic style." In their view, attaining a style that gave "pertinent details unclouded by local or sectional bias" was no mean task.[43]

National FWP officials worked to create a style of guidebook writing responsive to the needs of the traveler. They sought a style as well as materials that could express their vision of who and what was American. State officials were constantly reminded that "we are writing guidebooks to stimulate the interests of tourists and strangers, and not merely to be read in libraries." Therefore it was essential that "the tourist point of view must not at any time be neglected." The essays, national officials advised, should summarize general tendencies and provide a historical background, "with cross-references to specific manifestations in localities." The manifestations were the concrete examples for the generalization, examples that could be visualized "localized and attached to the spot, tour, or city where they belong." As one set of instructions put it, "Strangers to your State would not be so much interested in the size of the peach crop as where it is grown; what are the things to see; picking processing, etc.—the story of peaches."[44]

It was not that difficult a task, according to national FWP officials. It did, however, require imagination: "Mention any of the great American industries or staple crops and the imagination is at once stimulated to picture places and people at work; lumberjacks in Oregon, Minnesota, Maine . . . beet workers in Colorado, steel workers and coal miners in Pennsylvania, and the like." This went beyond the call for vital and graphic tour copy, the "vivid picture," to encourage local FWP workers and guide readers to see ordinary Americans at work, as the stuff of romance, as heroes.[45]

The tourist, Washington editors held, was an outsider, a stranger who wanted to know what was different, unique, or odd about a place. What appeared on the surface as inconspicuous, ordinary communities, national officials advised, should not be ignored, for they "are likely to interest the outsider who likes the quaint, the unusual, or the picturesque." At the same time they instructed guide

writers to avoid these adjectives—to show, not to assert. By attaching historical facts and anecdotes to visible sights, the Federal Writers tried to create a feeling that time and change had happened here, too, and that Americans, like other
people, had a history. This aspect of the guides did not demand much of the
tourist. A portrait of America as quaint and picturesque provided a charming
and agreeable experience. When the guides used the term "dramatic," it usually
meant only that the sight they were discussing was eye-catching and demanded
one's attention—for the moment. Used in this way, the drama had little to do
with values and ways of life in conflict, with tragedy.[46]

The guides, however, went beyond the usual Baedeker to ask more of tourists than that they simply enjoy a quaint experience. Guide writers used direct
and vivid quotes from letters, diaries, and other personal accounts of past hardships and triumphs to offer perceptions of a different world. Regional and ethnic differences were mentioned. The tourist had to come to terms with the fact
that in these guides the usual distancing factor, the sense of us and them, was
diminished and ultimately did not exist, for both were Americans.

Both American writers of the late nineteenth century and Federal Writers in
the 1930s searched for local color. For the most part, the earlier group wrote
nostalgically and patronizingly about regional and ethnic differences. They welcomed nationalizing and homogenizing tendencies that they thought could not
be resisted. For them these different peculiar groups with their strange ways
were vanishing remnants of the past. National FWP officials, however, encouraged local workers to seek out diversity with the goal of celebrating it as a sign
of American vitality and as a counterweight to the standardizing forces of modern American culture. Thus the guides reassured one reviewer that though the
American countryside and towns had, in his opinion, lost much of their unique
flavor, "ours is still a richer land than we ourselves sometimes suspect."[47]

It is the collective portrait of America found in the American Guide Series
that constitutes one of the FWP's major achievements. True, there are interesting differences between individual volumes, but a shared approach, method,
and set of values makes it possible to treat the series as a whole. The guides illustrate national officials' claims that "the publications of the Writers' Program
constitute a unique example of cooperation between community and nation,
with the aim of preserving the story of our American heritage in such force that
it may become part of the consciousness of the widest possible number of
Americans." Local, state, and national officials worked closely together on state
guides that national officials hoped would be provincial in content and national
in tone.[48]

All the guides open with prefaces and forewords that set the tone and introduce the key themes. Figures of cultural and political authority from outside
the Writers' Project joined local FWP officials to inform the reader about the
guide and its contents, purposes, and uses. They all wanted to make it clear to
the reader that these were "more than conventional guidebook[s]." Harry Hopkins, WPA federal relief administrator, thought that what made these guidebooks special was the opportunity they gave Americans "to understand the
contrasting character of the forty-eight States and to realize how the contribution of each has brought about the unity of the whole." The same theme was
repeated by others. Frank L. McVey, president of the University of Kentucky,
also thought that as "each state studies and describes its history, natural endowments, and special interests, the paradox of diversity and homogeneity will become apparent." He was convinced that while "each [state] has a special personality . . . certain qualities and interests bind them together." McVey did not
mention what these qualities and interests were. Neither he nor Hopkins explained why American unity would emerge from a knowledge of diversity. For
them, as for countless others associated with the FWP or interested in its publications, this was a hopeful faith.[49]

The idea that the guides addressed both strangers and residents paralleled
the emphasis on diversity and unity. Massachusetts Federal Writers explained
that their state guide, though designed for visitors, was "also intended . . . to
present Massachusetts to Massachusetts." Federal Writers in Iowa recounted
that they set out to write a guide for sightseers from other states, only to discover "another purpose unsuspected when the work of making it began—to
acquaint Iowans with Iowa." They learned that Iowans "had yet to know their
own state, to define its history, to appraise their commonwealth's real values."[50]

Self-examination, rediscovery, and a "general awakening of interest," Writers' Project officials claimed, would lead to " a quickening of our national consciousness." This sense that a focus on the local, on differences, could promote
national unity loses its paradoxical quality when one comprehends that the
presentation of the local to the outsider, the stranger, one's fellow American, is
part of an effort to redefine a national community. Thus Pennsylvania Federal
Writers offered their state guide "to their neighbors within and without Pennsylvania."[51] In large part, the essays constituted a record of the state's accomplishments in various areas. In each state guide an introductory essay on the
contemporary scene followed the purposes stated and the claims made in the
prefatory material. These essays served as both introduction and summary, an
invitation to explore and a preview of what the reader would find. Some of the

material in these essays reflected traditional views and images of the various states. Hoosier and Badger, for example, have traditional associations that appear in the Indiana and Wisconsin guides. The emphasis, however, is on diversity and inclusiveness. In stressing these themes the FWP moved away from discussions of state or national character.[52]

Repeatedly, the guides deny that there is a representative state character: "He who would describe a typical Illinoisan may well find, after carefully combing the State, that his only valid generalization is that an Illinoisan is one who lives in Illinois." There is no Missourian character: "The spare Ozark hillman, with his rabbit gun and dog, is a Missourian. So is the weathered open country farmer; the prosperous cotton planter; the subsistence sharecropper . . . the Kansas City business man; the St. Louis industrialist . . . the filling station attendant . . . all are Missourians." To the implied question Is there a typical Arizonan? the state's guide writers responded, "When one speaks of an Arizonan . . . does he mean the Indians, whose ancestors were here first? Does he mean the Mexicans . . . ? Does he mean a grizzled pioneer . . . ? Does he mean one of the 200,000 or so who have come in the last decade from every state and from almost every country on the face of the earth?" Guide readers are informed that in the southern states, differences are more complex than a simple division between black and white. For example, East, Middle, and Western Tennessee are held to be practically three different states, and Mississippi is seen as eight distinct geographic units. Some states, such as Montana, "are too large and diverse for definition or characterization." One's definition of Montana, the reader is told, depends on where in that state one lives.[53]

Underlying the celebration of diversity, of an inclusive community, is a faith in American cultural vitality. These essays declare the wealth of American cultural as well as material resources. The Montana guide writers maintain that scholars at the state university working "for a wider understanding of the value of Indians, cowpunchers, farmers, miners, and lumber-jacks as literary source material" constitute evidence that "Montanans are becoming aware that Montana's cultural possibilities are as vast and as relatively unexplored as her material resources." If, as Alabama Federal Writers asserted, their state "too often vaguely thought of as a 'land of cotton' . . . is in reality a region where sharply contrasted influences have shaped the manners and customs of the people," it was also a state whose "fast changing conditions were drawing Alabamians together into a close-knit group strengthened rather than weakened by their different backgrounds and the different groups that shaped their lives." An increasingly integrated national economy was contributing to new forms of cultural integration. These essays spoke of an American culture that was fluid, not fixed, and capable of integrating diverse elements into something new and worthwhile.[54]

National FWP officials holding to a pluralistic vision of American culture largely succeeded in creating guides that did not contain set, exclusive definitions of what it meant to be an American. While state and local Federal Writers often did not embrace the pluralism of the national office, they did share a revived faith in the nineteenth-century American belief that the New World environment could transform diversity into unity. An affirmation of American diversity as a source of cultural vitality fitted easily with traditional American ideas of progress. American history culturally and economically was still the unfinished story of American growth—the Great Depression was merely an interruption.

Chapter 3

A New Deal View of American History and Art

The Federal Writers' Project Guidebook Essays

Though the New Deal's cultural politics were less tangible and measurable than its economic policy, the two were intertwined, and both were an integral part of New Deal triumphs and defeats. Treating the FWP as part of the New Deal's cultural politics offers a way of understanding both a specific cultural program and a larger cultural policy. Previous chapters have described national FWP officials' views on the relationship between democracy and culture and how those views were reformulated in response to the political realities of their positions as directors of a federal relief agency in the Franklin Roosevelt administration. Out of this process emerged guidebooks that gave form to the dreams and visions national FWP officials had for the ways in which the cultural studies they undertook could contribute to a revitalization of American culture.

All the guidebook essays took a historical approach in treating such topics as education, agriculture, or literature. This approach followed from the romantic nationalist assumptions FWP officials held. It produced what might be called a romantic nationalist social history of American life and art. As romantic nationalists who were also pluralists, FWP officials insisted on a broad, panoramic

display of past endeavors that focused on ordinary Americans in all their ethnic, racial, occupational, and regional diversity. The artist would have a key role
to play in attaining the fulfillment of this vision. In creating an art that was accessible, available, and meaningful to ordinary Americans, an art that reflected
American diversity, the artist would help create an inclusive, democratic community. This could only be accomplished if the artist was familiar with the forms
of expression that had grown out of the past experience of the American people, and if working with that knowledge he or she could express the nature and
meaning of their lives. If artists could substitute for their alienation and isolation an organic relationship to their community—like that Writers' Project officials assumed existed in the past—they could help create a democratic society.
Virtually all the essays in the guidebooks embody a vision of the relationship
between past experience and the development of a culture, between experience and expression. This was a New Deal view of American history and art
that provided little analysis but did develop a hopeful myth that mixed traditional American themes with New Deal pluralism and reform in an effort to
achieve a new basis for national unity.

What kind of social and art history did such an approach produce? What
view of the past did it offer? What vision of the future? What role did the Depression and the New Deal—the present—play in such a vision? A close
reading of the history, literature, art, and architecture essays in the state guides
can provide answers to these questions. The boundless hope permeating these
essays is revealed in the emphasis on progress, the romantic nationalist view of
the ideal relationship between artist and community, and the conviction that
valuing the indigenous and the provincial is easily reconciled with celebrating
diversity and maintaining cosmopolitan standards. The points at which the essays substituted hope for analysis provide an entry into their worldview, its
mythic and ideological aspects, and its strengths and limitations.

An examination of these potentially conflicting hopes takes the subject beyond the debate over whether the guides were critical works. The American
Guide Series did not constitute the "critical portrait" of the nation that some
have seen in them, nor were they merely, as one historian claims, part of an
effort to "cope with the very real terrors of the present by rejoicing in the apparent serenity of the past." Advocates of the critical portrait thesis assemble
examples from the guides of the kinds of facts not usually found in tourist literature. There are a multitude of them; for example, the Tennessee guide provides details about the strikes in the Elizabethton textile mills in 1929. Opponents of this thesis correctly point out that the overall context is celebratory,

but they do not explain what is being celebrated. A treatment of the mythic and ideological aspects of this material can move the argument to new ground and make it possible for historical analysis to serve also as cultural criticism.[1]

The guidebook essays offer a view of American history and art that deals with the past as a source of reassurance about the future, but significantly only to a very limited extent with the present. The present, the Great Depression and its impact on Americans, is hardly dealt with in these essays. Ronald Taber, in a study of the FWP in the Pacific Northwest, was highly critical of the guidebooks for being "in no sense a picture of the 1930s" and therefore "of small value in understanding the 1930s." But the portrait the FWP offered of America is part of the cultural history of the 1930s, part of the history of how in the midst of the Great Depression Americans chose to think about themselves and their country. An account of the past tied to a vision of the future in which present problems are hardly discussed indicates the mythic nature of the guidebook portrait of America, a retelling of an old story in order to give birth to a new pluralistic understanding of American identity.[2]

The FWP's romantic approach to history and art can be understood better as myth rather than as ideology. Myths in a complex society unite different groups and interests by articulating emotionally satisfying utopian hopes and dreams based on a vision of the past that holds promise of a better future. Myths, as Warren Susman argues, offer "a vision of the future without providing in and of itself any essential dynamic elements which might produce the means for bringing about any changes in the present order of things." An ideology, on the other hand, seeks to understand the past in order to find a way to change the future. Rather than promoting unity, it emphasizes conflict, representing the views and interests of some groups and not others. The institutional matrix within which the FWP functioned favored a mythic approach. As government employees working with state and local governments and mainstream cultural and economic institutions, national FWP officials easily gravitated to a mythic rather than an ideological view of America and its future. In this way, difficult problems and conflicting values did not have to be faced.[3]

The distinctive aspects of the FWP's mythic portrayal of the American experience were all evident in the guidebook essays national FWP officials thought of as objective overviews of a specific topic. The idea of a vital pluralist America in which the common person played a central role was linked to an optimistic view of inevitable American growth, of an ever higher standard of living. The history essays have the static, repetitive quality of traditional myth. Times change, but the story is always the same; a wide variety of ordinary people are contributing to American progress. The anguish, uncertainty, and terror that have been seen by many as the central aspects of modern experience and the constant upheavals in economic and social relations disappear when the ordeal of change is treated primarily as the story of American dreams fulfilled through material growth. It is the New Deal of recovery, not reform, that is stressed.[4]

An important part of the myth that national FWP officials were working out focused on expressive culture and was developed in guidebook essays on literature, music, drama, art, and architecture. Important figures in all the New Deal arts projects thought in the romantic nationalist terms of the dialogue about the arts they had inherited. Central issues were the artist's relationship to his or her culture, the possibility of creating an indigenous American art, whether it could be made available and meaningful to ordinary Americans, and the relationships between the fact of American regional and ethnic pluralism and the hope for a national art.[5]

The FWP manuals called for essays that would create a picture of daily life past and present. They asked Federal Writers to provide materials that could help the reader visualize what aspects of life such as education, farming, and transportation had been like in the past. A direct quotation from a diary, letter, or newspaper that created a vicarious experience was to be preferred to statistics, which were to be kept to a minimum. Founding events, because they give meaning and identity to a community, received much attention and were linked to specific people and places whenever possible. One of Montana's first schoolteachers is quoted as a witness to what early conditions were like.[6]

While social aspects of education are mentioned in the state guidebook essays, education in the context of the social relations between classes is ignored. The education essay in the Tennessee guide opens by noting that while "the first settlers in Tennessee had little time or use for book-learning . . . they did have a wide and thorough education in the lore of rifle, plow and broadax— learning which cleared and peopled a wilderness." After the initial concern with portraying the social dimensions of educational history, the focus shifts to a recounting of the development, spread, and growth of institutions. The record is offered as evidence of progress. Problems are mentioned in connection with how much has been done to solve them. Thus the guidebook education essays affirm contemporary American life by endorsing the optimistic faith that as time passes, American life inevitably improves. They did not constitute a critical portrait, since they offer no analytical framework for making critical assessments. In this regard, the education essays are typical of the guidebook treatment of other topics.[7]

National FWP officials' view of the guides as a form of social history proved easily compatible with the guides, if not as boosterism, at least in part as a chronicle of progress. The state history essays in each guidebook offer a good illustration of how these different themes combine. While Washington advised the authors of these essays to "banish the classroom idea" and view themselves "as a chronicler relied upon to set down facts as a bookkeeper would figures," with "no theorizing, no moralizing, no embellishing," they also instructed them "to keep political narrative and description to a minimum." Instead, they were to focus on custom and social and economic life, supposedly along the lines of the "new history" of James Harvey Robinson and Charles Beard.[8]

Stressing origins and growth, the history essays became paeans to progress. The social life of ordinary people was moved to center stage, and descriptions of daily life and progress were easily combined. In Minnesota the sod-house and the dugout gave way in time "to neat frame houses." Towns "usually started with a boxcar station" but were "quickly surrounded by store, church, schoolhouse, and homes." Eventually, grain elevators and water towers dotted the landscape. Similar accounts are given in other state guides. American history was seen largely as the story of the log school being replaced by the red brick schoolhouse. It was the story of American ingenuity, resourcefulness, and inevitable progress—"railroad-branch lines were laid where bridle paths had been."[9]

Often social history was only colorful anecdotes in which origins figured more prominently than developments, events more than the underlying forces they reflected. Thus the Arizona essay offers a description of the life of an early trapper and a miner's account of Tuba, Arizona, in 1858. The reports of earlier inhabitants of a state—the tavern owner, politician, trapper, doctor, lawyer, miner, or riverman—are scattered throughout the state history essays. In this way a sense of the past is evoked even when history is not analyzed.[10]

A few state history essays offered some interpretative comments. The Ohio guide examined both the copying of the New England town pattern in the Western Reserve's first settlements and the advent of the steel mills in those same towns in the 1870s. Cheese manufacturing plants and local industries were displaced. Large numbers of eastern European immigrants moved into an area that "till then had been almost pure Anglo-Saxon stock out of New England." The physical nature of the town changed: "Rows of cheap company houses appeared in the towns along with the mills." All of this had consequences for the social structure of these towns and the relationships among the inhabitants. In short, "there came to be a right side and a wrong side of the tracks."[11]

More often than not, if the historical essay offered an interpretation, it embodied a liberal reformist view in harmony with the New Deal ethos. In recounting farm and labor struggles of the late nineteenth century, the writer of the Illinois history essay made it clear where his sympathies lay: "With this industrial growth came poverty and unemployment, disease and slums. . . . Men and women who had deserted farms and towns for factories and cities were buffeted and beaten. To their aid came the labor organizations."[12]

To some extent the interpretations offered in the history essays depended on chance circumstances, on who was assigned to work on the essay. However, even in conservative states such as Alabama, social legislation and industrial development were seen as twin aspects of progress. The state history essays celebrated both as the signs of growth and progress, of which the New Deal was simply a continuation. New industry and federal aid "kept Louisiana moving forward." New Deal reforms were endorsed because they, like industrialism, promised material progress, not because they promised to ameliorate social injustice and inequality.[13]

Despite the Depression, the New Deal had restored faith that America's material progress would continue. According to the state history essay in the Ohio guide, published in 1940, the hope that the New Deal had breathed into Ohio industrial towns was being fulfilled. There was a revival "of industry of a large and unending diversity." The essay concluded, "In industry these unsettled years have little discouraged the resourcefulness and new directions of manufacture, witnessing the beginning of many potentially great industries." A $3 million effort to improve a large Akron rubber plant was noted as a significant fact symbolic of future trends. History essays in the guides published in the last years of the Writers' Program noted the war effort as a source of economic revival. Given the approach of these essays, the possibility of another world war did nothing to diminish their optimism.[14]

The social history in the guide essays is often rich in detail, and the judicious use of quotation turns information about the past into vicarious experience. Yet little in these essays could divide readers, could make them choose different sides, for issues that had separated Americans in the past were usually only noted. Progress as a central theme was almost as important as the guidebooks' celebration of diversity, for that theme flowed through all the essays and organized a myriad of disparate facts. It created a version of American history that pointed to a past record that offered a basis for expecting a better future.

In the guidebook essays on the arts, romantic nationalist aspirations provided organizing assumptions and central themes but never issues to be examined. By deliberately not drawing a line between folk culture and high culture, the essays on the arts could begin with those forms of art closest to the experience of ordinary Americans in the past and offer them as the basis for a tradition. If present-day artists were to draw on this tradition, they, like its creators, would no longer be isolated from their community; they would succeed in creating an accessible and socially relevant art. At the same time, these essays hailed the growth of artistic institutions that could make all forms of cultural experience accessible to ordinary Americans. Thus, high culture was no longer to be restricted to a privileged elite. Educational institutions would foster a new appreciation for art by encouraging everyone to participate in and learn about the creative experience. These essays cited the New Deal arts projects as both signs of and contributors to these developments. They found in the past and the contemporary scene only evidence that the New Deal's "quest for a cultural democracy" would lead to a future in which the American artist would easily be integrated into the community.[15]

The guidebook essays on the arts make an effort to define their subject broadly. According to the Tennessee guidebook essay, the literature of the state's early settlers is found in the written forms with which they transacted the business of their everyday lives. This material is valuable, "for these trail-clearers, fort-builders, and Indian-fighters" have left the "framework of their collective biography" in these writings. Materials such as this provided the stuff of epics yet to be written. A literature rooted in the experience of ordinary people held the promise of a great literary flowering in the future. Though Illinois has a rich record of literary achievement, there were still "great areas . . . untouched by writers." Varied occupational and ethnic groups, in town and country, were "waiting for novelists, poets, and dramatists whose vision and power are worthy of their material." Illinois literature should be thought of in terms of "opportunity, of praise, and of continued growth."[16]

The underlying assumption in the guide essays on literature was that poring over the documents of daily life, examining indigenous forms of expression, studying local traditions, and contemplating the surrounding landscape constituted not simply a starting point for writers but a procedure from which literary achievement would automatically issue. The artist would find both material and an audience. It was all very simple; in this utopian future, the relationship between artist and society is devoid of any problems and conflicts. The discussion of writers who exist in the interregnum between the early settlers and the future artists who will portray the state scene is not treated as important. The central point is the mythic relationship between the distant past and the creative future.

A WPA publicity release claimed that "in telling the story of art in the United

States, the guide book essays approach painting and sculpture as an activity associated with the changing social life of the locality." All the guide essays on the arts oversimplify this relationship and assume and demand that the arts simply mirror the external social life of the majority. Such an approach shortchanges ideas. Difficult material conditions are the stock explanation for the failure of early settlers to create art in the traditional forms of high culture. Little is said about their attitudes toward art or about the values revealed in the folk arts they did create. The possibility of the artist as a questioner, let alone adversary of his or her culture, is hardly present. The intellectual world of artists and the ideas embodied in their work receive little attention.[17]

The view of the arts presented in the guidebooks was more firmly held by national officials than by members of the state units. National officials had to work to convince Illinois writers that "a single paragraph on folk art is not quite sufficient," that "art has a broad as well as a narrow sense," and therefore that "cabinetmakers and housewives . . . deserve to be called artists." In the folk arts and crafts, national officials contended, was the cultural history of Illinois "as enacted by the mixture of French, English, Scandinavian, Irish, and German pioneers who came to the fertile prairies, seeking new ways of life."[18]

Local art was to be appreciated from a national point of view, to be written about for a national audience, according to national standards as defined by FWP officials in Washington, D.C. They worked to avoid what they saw as the "provincial tendency to evaluate artists on the basis of their birth or loyalty" to the states in which they resided. Utah Federal Writers were taken to task for submitting an essay "conspicuously lacking . . . an evaluation of the Utah region painters according to standards that might apply anywhere." The national office found that the drafts of the state essays often "confused men of prominence with men of historical importance."[19]

National FWP officials insisted that a national perspective and the celebration of the indigenous were compatible. Grant Wood, they thought, deserved considerable attention in the Iowa guide's discussion of the state's painters. The Iowa guide, while praising Wood's work, did not endorse his vision of a rural-pastoral America as an alternative to an industrial way of life. Life in the rural Midwest was but one of many American ways of life. Wood was important not as an ideologue but as evidence of a national artistic revival based on attention to local aspects of life. Regarding Wood, the Iowa essay suggested that "what has been hailed as 'regional art' may well be found, upon examination of the many factors which led to its birth, to be part of a wider and perhaps far more significant movement." The fine arts in Iowa should be viewed in relation to their development in the entire country. Everywhere the guides saw the Federal Art Project bringing "art closer to the daily life of the people," developing native talent and aiding art and artists in gaining "a deeper orientation with respect to the social life of the community." The art, theater, and music projects, as portrayed in the guidebooks, were helping to create an American art based on regional and ethnic traditions and close relations between artists concerned "with the whole life of their times" and relating to the general public.[20]

Overall the guidebook essays on art and architecture were markedly superior in style and content to the other essays on the arts. Roderick Seidenberg, national FWP architectural and art editor, deserves much of the credit. Seidenberg was a Columbia-educated architect who had designed the New Yorker hotel and occasionally wrote for the *Freeman*, the *New Republic*, and the *Nation*. His friendship with Henry Alsberg went back to their days together at the Provincetown Players. He also shared friendship and interests with Waldo Frank and Lewis Mumford, romantic nationalists who in their various cultural studies were contributing to the rediscovery of America.[21]

Seidenberg was markedly reticent about his past, but he was part of a left-of-center, cosmopolitan intelligentsia sharing a romantic nationalist and pluralist vision of America. At the outbreak of World War I, Seidenberg registered as an absolute conscientious objector. He was drafted in May 1918 but refused service. On November 13, 1918, two days after the armistice, he was court-martialed. The formal charge was refusing to help clean the parade grounds. For this crime he spent a year and a half in prison.[22] One positive result of this experience, he later wrote, was that "I began to lose something of my New York provincialism and to learn of this America. Here were men from all quarters and from all walks of life: religious farmers from the Middle West who alone seemed capable of community living; I.W.W.s from the Far West; Socialists from the East Side of New York; men from Chicago, from the South; men who had been sailors, carpenters, college students, tailors . . . each with his own story."[23]

The occasional pieces Seidenberg wrote about the arts in the 1920s focused mainly on avant-garde artistic experiments; however, they gave evidence that he saw culture and politics as interrelated. Like other national FWP officials, Seidenberg had a secular, left-of-center, cosmopolitan, and pluralist view of the world. Writing on the Zionist movement, he expressed a pessimistic view of a "Palestinian enterprise . . . cradled in the lap of British imperialism" and further feared that a Zionist state "once established in Palestine . . . may swing

backward into an obscurantist orthodoxy. Always it will be necessary to overcome the tendency towards an intensified ritualistic life, drawing inspiration
from the sanctified soil." He looked more favorably on "the left-wing expo-
nents of Zionism who wish to fuse the conception of a cultural nationalistic
autonomy with advanced theories of economic internationalism." In 1929 the
Soviet Union could still be regarded by many on the left as a radical cultural
and political experiment. Seidenberg spent four months that year working on
a project with Soviet housing authorities.[24]

During his FWP years Seidenberg seemed to share his colleagues' faith that
an inclusive democratic community that welcomed regional and ethnic diversity could create a revitalized American culture, an alternative to the dehuman-
ization of a bland, standardized mass culture. Later Seidenberg publicly rejected that faith. In two critically well-received philosophic essays, *Posthistoric Man*
(1950) and *Anatomy of the Future* (1961), Seidenberg despairingly argued that the
future would inevitably see the growth of an increasingly bureaucratized society in which individuality no longer existed. His friend Lewis Mumford appreciated the books as warnings but denied that the future Seidenberg painted was
inevitable.[25]

In the 1930s Seidenberg's and Mumford's views on architecture were similar. Writers' Project files contain letters from Mumford on architectural and
other cultural matters. So close were Mumford's outlook and those of national
FWP officials that they would cite his *New Republic* review of the first guides as
a definitive critical gloss on their goals and achievements. Mumford thought
the guides "were indispensable to creating a new sense of the regional setting
and history." Only then, he contended, will there be "citizens who will understand the problems that grow out of their intercourse with the earth and with
other groups: citizens who will eventually learn the art of socialized living and
regional planning and will make the earth their collective home."[26]

For Mumford, an architecture relating to and expressing the life of a region
had a key role to play in achieving such a world. This had been a major theme
in his seminal studies of American architecture, *Sticks and Stones* (1924) and *The
Brown Decades* (1931). It was also a major theme in guidebook architectural essays that celebrated regional vernaculars as functional responses to available
materials, local climate, and human needs and as a precursor of a modern architecture seeking functional solutions to contemporary problems. Thus Louisiana Federal Writers described how early buildings "evolved out of the material
on hand, the exigencies of the climate, and the needs of the colonists." Though
Minnesotans had ignored them, European visitors had discovered "the stark

unornamented functional clusters of concrete—the Minnesota grain elevator." The grain elevators, the Minnesota guide held, were an unconscious expression of "all the principles of modernism." Ironically, while seeking "for
artistic expression in other directions," Minnesotans had already achieved it in
their "grain elevators, a signal triumph of functional design."[27]

The architectural manual instructed Federal Writers in the basic tenets of a
modern, functional approach. Architectural history was not to be thought of
as simply a succession of styles, for "style is a matter of conception; not a means
of treatment." Only an analysis of form, structure, and purpose made it possible to "'place' a building stylistically." Federal Writers had to be careful "to
avoid the pitfall of relying solely upon the externals of a style—the ornamen-
tal earmarks of a period." Rather, since buildings had to meet the needs of the
people, knowledge of the building plan was essential. It was unfortunate, according to the manual, that "this basic consideration which is vital to a proper
understanding of architecture, is all too often neglected in favor of comment-
ing upon the exterior alone." Instead, Federal Writers had to note "the main elements of the structure and their relation to each other and the building as a
whole." These elements were to "be clarified in terms of . . . purpose and function." Reviewing a draft of the Vermont architectural essay, one of Seidenberg's assistants commented, "Architecture cannot be arbitrarily divided into
aesthetic qualities and functional realities." In a critique of an inadequate architectural description, Seidenberg concluded, "It is essential that the picture of
the whole problem be indicated in order that we may appreciate the solution"
—a variation on Louis Sullivan's famous dictum, "The very essence of every
problem is that it contains and suggests its own solution."[28]

These guidebook essays were to describe the "history of the diverse social
and racial influences that have molded the architecture of the region." From
the tourist's point of view, Seidenberg thought adequate treatment of architecture necessary to any guidebook venture; but beyond that, he contended, the
guides offered an opportunity to instruct American taste and to help ordinary
Americans know and appreciate the built environment. Here was an opportunity "to clarify . . . a broader conception of architecture as an expression of
historic (and social) forces—as a resolution, in visible form, of the trends and
tendencies of our civilization." This theme was sounded in the guidebook essays, although sometimes it was only repeated rather than developed. It gave
the New Mexico essay a thesis, method, and outline: "Architecture more than
almost any other art reflects the history and culture of the people and region
to which it is related. The architecture of New Mexico based on forms and

materials indigenous to the State is particularly representative, modifications having occurred with successive invasions and subsequent changes in social conditions."[29]

Anyone who thinks of himself as a "well-informed traveler," the Connecticut essay declared, "is as much interested in the architecture of a country as he is in the manners and customs of its people. For in essence one is a reflection of the other." Regarding architecture, the Federal Writers were in love with the term "essence." By claiming to deal with essences, they could also claim the universality of their approach: "Whether in Bali, Gizeh, Nurnberg, or our own Connecticut, the structures reared by a people are the most public and often the most permanent expression of its social life—the translation of habits and modes of thought into wood and stone." Maine Federal Writers were convinced that their state architecture "reflected the conservative, substantial, and practical characteristics of Maine people from the time the first roof was raised in the state to the present day."[30]

Local Federal Writers and the architectural historians they consulted often rejected or simply failed to comprehend the approach of Seidenberg and his staff. In a critique of the Washington State architectural essay, a national editor pointed out assumptions that he contended he and his colleagues had to fight. In his view, the problem with the Washington State essay was that it reflected the outlook of a local consultant, "who represents the typically unimaginative bourgeois urban architect, uninformed on architectural history, with no respect for traditions and no sensibility to local influences."[31]

National FWP editors found equally objectionable the sensibility that could not call a building architecture unless it could identify a traditional historical style. From that perspective, neither the vernacular southern dog-trot, a Sullivan skyscraper, nor a public construction such as a Tennessee Valley Authority dam or a housing project were architecture. Vermont Federal Writers, for example, had to be told that "it does not appear necessary to apologize for the 'lack of architecture' in Vermont, if one's definition of architecture and point of view toward it is sufficiently comprehensive."[32]

Seidenberg and his assistants had to explain to local Federal Writers that "the distinction between the builder's and the architect's art is a dangerous one." By breaking down the distinction, national FWP editors sought to emphasize the continuing relevance of the traditional vernacular as embodying a method that took regional realities into account. The essayists acknowledged that the early architecture of the ordinary people of their state was rarely a totally indigenous creation. Yet they did not, as some architectural historians do, see this as merely an inferior copying of a higher culture. Instead, the FWP approach was closer to a more recent definition of architectural vernacular "as a local hue or coloration given to something that exists, or has existed, elsewhere as well." The vernacular, in this definition, is an intermediary level playing back and forth between folk and high architecture: "It has both its conservative aspect —as when a folk survival contributes to a sense of place—and its progressive aspect—as when adaptation of a folk tradition produces a locally idiosyncratic building vocabulary."[33]

Along these lines, the FWP guidebooks argued that the adaptation of both the folk and high culture English housing tradition to a New World environment should not be seen simply as a cultural survival but as the creation of something new. The same process occurred within the rest of the nation. The general principle is clear in such guidebook declarations as "Oklahoma architecture has achieved interesting and often-distinctive qualities through the adaptation of borrowed designs to local traditions." For national FWP officials a multiplicity of regional and ethnic styles was the expression of an American style in architecture. Pluralism was not a problem to be dealt with but an opportunity to be exploited.[34]

The American version of the functionalist aesthetic that shaped the FWP's view of architecture was strongly influenced by Walt Whitman, as Louis H. Sullivan testified in *The Autobiography of an Idea* (1924). Sullivan's metaphors for his famous "form follows function" principle were organic rather than mechanistic: "For instances," he declared, "the form oak-tree resembles and expresses the purpose of function oak." The American vernacular, as national FWP officials saw it, had a close organic relationship to the local landscape and native building materials. In addition, the FWP emphasis on the creations of ordinary people also reflected an idea officials shared with Whitman—a belief, as the poet put it, that the "genius of the United States" is most manifest in the culture of the "common people." The guides expressed a romantic nationalist faith like Whitman's and Sullivan's that art growing organically from local needs would express the democratic ethos of the American people. The guides implicitly echoed Sullivan's rejection of the idea that a national style could be obtained by "contemplating the matured beauty of Old World art" and then bringing it to America by "a grafting or transplanting process."[35]

It was a basic principle among Seidenberg's staff that "the builders' vernacular style preceding the eclectic periods and the modern style of the last ten years—neither of which fall into traditional categories of styles"—could be viewed as intimately related. Frank Lloyd Wright's buildings were regarded as symbolizing this relationship. Washington architectural editors contended that the main "thing about folk architecture is its use of local materials and the adjustment of the design to the landscape." The same considerations, they argued, were central to Wright's work. In their view the vernacular was a model of a functional response to specific needs. In Wright's architecture they saw a response to modern developments that adapted the lessons of the machine to the region without abandoning the qualities that gave an area its identity. This was in sharp contrast to the developing European architectural functionalism and the international style, with its new formalism and its promise of universally applicable solutions to architectural problems.[36]

Seidenberg and his staff, after much effort, obtained architectural essays from the state FWPs that discussed the vernacular, the sod-houses and silos, their functional qualities, and modern architecture in its private and public manifestations. Like the other guidebook essays on the arts, they rejected a genteel criticism that had come to stand for a separation between art and experience.

What made the architectural essays distinctly superior to the other essays on the arts was their concern with form. Although all these essays had a hortatory quality, a shared utopianism, only the architectural essays, by using the functionalist idea, had a view of how experience could be expressed in artistic form. However, as intellectual history, the architectural essays were only slightly more successful than the other essays. They aimed to link the "salient characteristics of the architecture of the region, with its stylistic development, its history in terms of the industrial, economic, geographic, and cultural factors that have affected its development," but they achieved only partial success, even in such strong efforts as the Mississippi architectural essay.[37]

John Lyons, the Wisconsin FWP director, questioned the Washington office's basic approach to writing the history of art in a state. Alsberg had advised him that "the major social stages of Wisconsin's development should be shown as background for its artistic growth; i.e., pioneering linked to folk art, agricultural community life with landscape and portraiture, industrialization with European influences and modern-age styles." Lyons responded that Wisconsin Federal Writers could find no such "point by point correspondences." Even trying to show such correspondences, he thought, would require extensive research beyond the state project's abilities. Alsberg claimed Lyons had misunderstood him: "We did not intend to imply that a causal connection or point by point correspondence exists" in these matters. Rather, the goal was to indicate that various "types of painting have flourished . . . concurrently with specific historical periods." This much the essays accomplished; however, in the limited scope the essays allowed, the implied causal relationship was unrevealingly formulaic. The external environment was viewed as a primary cause but hardly ever as material on which Americans had tried to impose their view of the world; there was little sense of a dialectical relationship between the two.[38]

Given the deflated ambitions and ironic tone of postmodernist architecture, the utopianism of the guidebook's architectural essays has a peculiar flavor, not simply in its pluralistic cultural nationalism, but in the belief that modern architecture could be the harbinger of a new social order. Behind the public statements of the guide essays there were private doubts. After visiting Techwood and University Homes, public housing projects in Atlanta, Georgia, Stella Hannau wrote Seidenberg that she did "not think they are interesting enough architecturally to be included in the essay. (In fact, to my layman's eye, they are quite ugly and unimaginatively designed.)" In the Georgia guide such private doubt was translated into the ambiguously neutral, they "are severely plain structures, showing the influence of modern utilitarian design." For private doubt could not compete with the public hope that, as the Illinois guide stated, "the problem of architecture for those left behind" could be solved. Therefore, "from a sociological point of view these projects may be more significant in the history of architecture than the towers of the loop."[39]

The functionalist approach brought the architecture essays closer than any other guidebook essays to a statement advocating and explaining how to bring about change. All of the guide essays praised the vitality and creativity of ordinary people and in good romantic nationalist fashion sought an American vernacular, which, it was assumed, would revitalize American culture. Only the architectural essays with their functionalist point of view hinted at how an American vernacular might be translated into vital contemporary forms. But in the final analysis, the FWP's functionalism also appears more successful in contributing to the formulation of myth than to the study of an aspect of cultural history. Functionalism often becomes a formulaic refrain in a myth where, as in the other guide essays, an expression of hope about the future substitutes for a programmatic statement. Understanding the ways in which the architectural essays are more mythic than ideological statements illuminates the approach to American culture embodied in the guides, the aspirations expressed, and the issues that could not be confronted.

The guide essays on the arts were one of many efforts in the 1930s to awaken Americans to the culture they had created, a contribution to the popular triumph of liberal romantic nationalist views over the genteel tradition. Yet in at least one way these essays shared the narrowness of that tradition. Neither outlook saw popular culture as worthy of much consideration as art. While the guide essays lauded the vernacular arts, they implicitly rejected the popular arts. Except for industrial architecture, the guidebook essays largely ignored the aesthetics of modern industrial-capitalist culture. The essays on art and architecture and the correspondence of the Washington editors who read these essays reveal an ambivalent attitude toward industrialism that reflects a variation on European romantic nationalist hostility to modernity as the destroyer of traditional culture. Without ever taking an explicit position, sometimes the essayists and editors blamed industrialism per se, and at other times they blamed industrial capitalism. The FWP directly attacked neither industrialism nor capitalism, but the guides, and certainly national FWP officials, were more skeptical about the latter than the former—a position compatible with the agency's place in the New Deal reform program.

In the essays on art and architecture, nineteenth-century industrial developments are cited as the destroyer of the handicraft tradition and the cause of an architectural eclecticism FWP editors held in low esteem: "The soft whir of spinning wheels and the rhythmic clack of looms could be heard throughout Arkansas during the first three quarters of the nineteenth century. Then the railroads came." Industrialization or industrial capitalism also explained the development of an unsatisfying relationship between artist and community. In a sweeping generalization, one of Seidenberg's assistants contended that in the nineteenth century there had been a "downward swoop in the progress of creative expression." He attributed this to "the force of materialism, with its resultant compromise or surrender by the artist to gentility and privateering, or his efforts to preserve his integrity through isolation or expatriation." Fortunately there were "evidences of native skill struggling for orientation among the bewilderments of the times." Terms such as "force of materialism," "privateering," and "bewilderments" encapsulate a vague analysis of the sources of change.[40]

The guidebook essays constitute a mythic view of the arts in the United States that promises a resolution of the problems in the relationship between artist and people. Once art and artists had been organically bound to the community. That situation could exist again in the future, but not, however, by going backward. The changes in economic and social relationships brought about in the development of a modern society, or progress as the guidebooks preferred to call it, were not to be repudiated. Beyond advocating that contemporary artists study the folk arts, the FWP offered no program. Programs were potentially divisive. The unstated and unexamined question was whether a revitalized

American culture could be created without fundamental political and social change.

The relationship between artist and community, while a significant concern in the guidebook essays, was dealt with not in terms of the economic situation of the artist in various periods or in terms of ideas and approaches that led to acceptance or alienation from the dominant culture but, rather, as part of an effort to redefine American culture. Matthew Arnold had argued that a fundamental weakness of English and American culture was the absence of a center of intellectual and aesthetic opinion that organized creative life. National FWP officials, however, placed themselves in opposition to the very idea of a center. For them, the reality of a center was the dominance of either the culture of white Anglo-Saxon Protestant America, especially in its genteel expression most manifest in the Northeast, or of mass standardization. To open up the question of American identity meant rejecting the idea of a center and instead advocating pluralism. Americans and their artists, they held, should reconsider the country in terms of its diversity.[41]

The guidebooks tried to demonstrate that American experience and materials were richer and broader than the various efforts to create a center had been willing or able to acknowledge. Instead of analysis, the guidebook essays offered a vast display of the creative response of all kinds of Americans to their world as the foundation for building a democratic community in which art would not be an ornament but an integral part of the common experience. Thus national FWP officials had high hopes that cultural programs would help achieve democratic goals. They accepted essays that indicated a relationship between culture and social change but that did not explore the connection between culture, society, and politics. Perhaps this reflected not only that FWP officials were limited by the political restraints of being a New Deal agency but also the strengths and limitations inherent in New Deal liberalism.

In working against the idea of a center, national FWP officials found themselves face-to-face with the question of whether local attitudes should be allowed to serve as cultural authority. They did not, however, altogether disagree with Matthew Arnold's criticism that "the provincial spirit . . . exaggerates the value of its ideas for want of a high standard by which to try them." They clearly imposed their values in encouraging (and sometimes insisting) that, for example, local Federal Writers include material on ethnic minorities, on handicrafts, and on vernacular and modern buildings. Such an approach added the notion of cultural relativism to the problem of defining cultural authority.[42]

Although the evidence from the essays lends itself to an interpretation that the FWP advocated a mythic approach to American history and art, the issue is not so easily resolved. To some extent national and regional FWP officials themselves were not fully satisfied with the ways the guidebook essays allowed them to deal with these issues. In many guidebooks separate essays on folklore, blacks, and ethnic minorities were added to the general pattern and contributed to the effort at inclusiveness and redefinition. These essays pointed to the areas national FWP officials wanted to explore beyond the guidebook format. FWP folklore and oral history projects in the South and among blacks and ethnic and working-class Americans would address questions about regional and minority experiences in America that raised profound questions about the nature of the national experience and the possibilities of creating a democratic and egalitarian form of national integration. Folklore and oral history projects would also address significant questions about American identity, the nature of the American vernacular, and its relationship to modernity.

Americans in the 1930s, however, knew the work of the FWP almost entirely through its state guides. It is more than passing strange that their political representatives would reject the FWP's redefinition of American culture as embodying an unpatriotic and alien definition of America. They saw what now appears to many historians to be a conservative myth as a radical ideology. Neither conservative Americans nor national FWP officials were content with the guidebooks' portrait of America. But before we can turn to conservative critics of the guides or to the programs FWP officials thought would lead to a deeper understanding of American culture, we need to look at how the guidebooks dealt with the vernacular through the exploration of the American landscape in the automobile tours.

The guidebook tours also confronted the issues of romantic nationalism and cultural diversity, the meaning of American history, and questions about American identity and nationality. But to the issues that emerged in the essay part of the guides the tours added questions about the meaning of the American landscape, about place and time in modern America, and they gave the reader an active role as an explorer rediscovering and redefining America.

Chapter 4

Picturesque Pluralism
The Guidebook Tours

The heart of the guides, Federal Writers and their critics have always insisted, was the city and automobile tours. Bernard DeVoto, writing in the *Saturday Review of Literature*, went so far as to argue that the guides would have been better without the essays, their "conspicuous weakness." The tours, on the other hand, were, in his opinion, the great triumph of the guides. In them he saw "a rich, various, and rewarding spectacle . . . a heartening reminder of how complex the current scene is and on what a variegated and fascinating base it rests."[1]

While few commentators were as critical of the essays as DeVoto, all praised the tours. Vermont Federal Writers proudly asserted that the FWP guides were "a new kind of book," and "the newness of the book consists primarily of its tours." They contended that the tours constituted a major "effort to interweave the background of a state—the scenery, the history, the society and the culture of Vermont—so that the visitor may become conscious of our landscape in a genuine, a three dimensional fashion." The Wisconsin guide provided additional insights into what the Federal Writers hoped to achieve in the guidebook tours. Places, the Wisconsin state director explained, were interesting to Federal Writers not for the natural scene but "chiefly for the people who inhabit them." Essays and tours dealt with time and space as they guided "the reader to Wisconsin's people, down through the years as well as across the miles." In addition to the practical purpose of getting the tourist from one place to another, the tours aimed "to present the State once again, not in the large outlines of the first section, but, as it were, in mosaic; isolated bits—chips of description, of history or legend, of geographic or economic situation—are pieced together to make a variegated but single picture of Wisconsin."[2]

From Walt Whitman's songs of the road to Charles Kuralt's televised reports, the road has always had a powerful cultural and historical resonance for Americans. It has served as a metaphor for discovery and as a symbol of unity. In the foreword to the Nebraska state guide, Addison E. Sheldon, the superintendent of the Nebraska State Historical Society, noted that "some of us in Nebraska know what it is to have made the first wagon track across an unbroken sea of grass into a new land, with no guide but the sun, the hilltops and our own resolution." He also remembered creating roads: "We had to find our own way, discover our own fords, devise our own gully crossings, and leave a trail which others could follow and improve." There was, in his view, continuity between the experiences of pioneers and the efforts of the Nebraska Federal Writers. The Nebraska guide, he declared, "is another road starter."[3]

The form and content of the guidebook tours raise large issues about the cultural politics behind the landscape images the Federal Writers created in the tours. The aspirations of national FWP officials regarding the contributions the tours could make to American culture reflected their assumptions about the relationship between place and identity, tradition and modernity. They contemplated such questions, however, within the framework of producing tourist guides. Thus large issues could become reduced to a concern for the picturesque. The results were tour guides that had picturesque, mythic, and historic qualities that contributed to their strengths and limitations. The picturesque pluralism of the tours offered a portrait of America that rejected the divisive cultural politics that after World War I had destroyed the progressive reform movements that had flourished before the war. Thus while the guides sought to make a significant statement about American culture, they also reflected the effort of New Deal cultural programs to create an atmosphere that supported political and social reform.

Actual landscapes, cultural geographers have demonstrated, are often idealized and made into symbols. Donald Meining has shown that Main Street America is one such symbol. In the idealized version of the community represented by this symbol, the people are predominantly white Anglo-Saxon Protestants. This is the case despite the fact that, as Meining points out, "a panorama of the landscape of most towns in the Middle West . . . would reveal several other groups," such as Irish-Catholic workers, poor whites, blacks, and "new industries full of foreigners." In this case, he concludes, "the symbol did not encompass the actual diversity of its landscape reference." The gap between symbol and fact was eventually seen as a gross distortion of reality. As Meining observes, a large body of American literature reflects the revolt against Main Street as an inadequate symbol of American community. Though Main Street still has evocative power, Meining's evidence indicates that its greatest appeal was roughly in the period from 1890 to 1930. In their own way the FWP guidebooks were part of the American literature that sought to discredit the Main Street symbol, for the FWP embraced all American landscapes as aspects of the nation. Rather than focus on an idealized Main Street that excluded many non-WASP Americans, national FWP officials worked to create guidebooks reflecting an ethnically and regionally diverse America. Country and city, farm and factory—all are part of the landscape Federal Writers wished travelers to identify with, to possess, and to claim as American. While Main Street embodied the view that basic American virtues were found only in the dominant WASP groups, the FWP guides did not equate American virtues or American identity with any one group.[4]

The connection between ethnic groups and various towns and occupations receives much attention in the state guides. Chicago's Federal Writers bragged that by 1900 their city had the largest Scandinavian, Dutch, Polish, Lithuanian, Bohemian, Croatian, and Greek communities in the nation. Not only were ethnic groups in the major metropolitan centers included in the FWP guides, but those in small towns and in rural areas were also part of the American landscape covered in the FWP tours: the Cornish miners of Globe; the Czechs of Cedar Rapids, who "first came to Linn County in 1852 to work in the T. M. Sinclair packing plants"; the German dairy farmers in Wisconsin; and the French Canadians who helped operate New England factories. The examples are endless.[5]

Attitudes toward the future of ethnicity in the United States vary in the state guides. Nowhere, however, is there a nativist rejection of the ethnic composition of America. What can be seen is given sharp visual expression and is included in the traveler's itinerary: "Flagstaff, [Arizona,] with its Indian, Mexican, and Negro population, is a town of traditional, ethnic, and occupational contrasts —exemplified by the cowboy's spurred boots, the lumberjack's hobnailed shoes, and the Indian's moccasins, worn on the streets." There are Mexican neighborhoods and customs as well as a "section of small unpainted, smoke blackened frame houses, occupied by Negroes brought from Louisiana to work in the lumber industry." These are not the usual tourist sights of great historical events, magnificent architecture, scenic beauty, or recreational opportunity. They are, however, the guides repeatedly assert, part of the traveler's America and have a place in any effort to introduce America to Americans.[6]

National FWP officials and 1930s critics saw the tours as a helpful response to the problematic nature of American nationality and to the complex question of the place of tradition in the modern world. Both concerns were voiced in a newspaper reporter's description of what she thought the Federal Writers were learning about America. Mary Hornaday conceded that "the history of American settlements is brief compared with those in other parts of the world." Nevertheless, she was convinced that the FWP's initial plans for a single national guide would produce a work that "will prove to its readers that it is not too soon for them to have customs, personages and landmarks distinguishing them from their neighbors." She also saw it as providing a counterweight to ubiquitous modern developments: "Chain stores and gasoline filling stations may give tourists the impression that all American towns are alike, but writers of the American Guide have discovered that, down underneath, every settlement has an individuality all its own."[7]

In these guides American identity was closely tied to creating a feeling of definition and possession about the diverse places that constituted the nation. The tours were often appreciated for the way they juxtaposed diverse facts. One critic saw in the tours "the profuse disorder of nature and life, the dadaist jumble of the daily newspaper." Again one discovers a paradox that highlights the tension between modernity and tradition and the effort of FWP officials to cope with the conflict. On one hand, the guidebook tours did parallel the arbitrary juxtaposition of materials that the Dadaists offered as art. Dadaism conveyed the idea that context and place had been destroyed by modern life. Yet using a method that resembled Dadaism, Federal Writers tried to create a sense of distinguishable places. Perhaps only in recent times would a juxtaposition of facts linked only with regard to place but by no theme or thesis seem a way of asserting the importance of place and tradition in a changing world.[8]

The function of the guidebook tours was to create a sense of distinguishable places that could be toured by automobile. Yet as the Federal Writers knew, the automobile was seen by many Americans as a modern force contributing to the destruction of all sense of place. Automobile touring had become a part of American popular culture, and oil companies, automobile makers, and auto clubs promoted this form of tourism. But not everyone was impressed by this form of travel. Cultural critics of the 1920s such as Charles Merz wrote scathingly of Americans and their automobiles. Merz wondered, "Where are they going? Why are they speeding? What do they hope to find?" As to whether it all made any lasting impression, he answered: "Impression? Yes impression of a never-ending road, a thousand farms, grade crossing signs, back axles, towns passed through at twenty miles an hour." Like many of these critics of American life who were satisfied with the well-phrased attack on the philistines, Merz worked hard at making his point, almost compulsively, but offered little in the way of an alternative. Modern in concept, the FWP guides recognized, as had Merz, the triumph of the automobile, the reality of America "on wheels." In the tours, however, they tried to help drivers see more in the landscape than grade crossings and back axles. An American Baedeker, FWP officials realized, had to acknowledge the automobile as the emerging dominant mode of travel if it was to have any impact on American life. In both practical and cultural terms, the FWP approached the automobile as a challenge to and an opportunity for meaningful travel.[9]

The mobility the automobile provided, the Federal Writers understood, "has opened up fresh new field of interest to the tourist." Yet while "high speed automobiles and hard surface roads have enabled millions of Americans to go places and see things that would have been out of the question a few years ago," these "same factors have made it impossible for travelers to get the full pleasure and benefit of the historic and picturesque points through which they pass." FWP officials thought that because of the guides, "this condition is in the process of being remedied." In the tours, the Federal Writers tried to create numerous distinct but nevertheless American places located in a meaningful landscape in which the tourist could use the automobile as a vehicle for the discovery and exploration of American diversity. No longer, as one critic commented, "will the traveling motorist have any excuse for regarding the road as merely the shortest distance between two points." Rather than rushing by, tourists would find that the tours could acquaint them with a place, and "it will be a dull spirit indeed which is not quickened by that acquaintance to a lively interest."[10]

It was interest that Matthew Arnold had coolly declared American civilization lacked. From the perspective of the Federal Writers, he was simply unacquainted with the country. State FWP units that submitted manuscripts to the national office labeling some places dull or uninteresting had the material returned with specific suggestions for further research. National FWP editors proceeded on the assumption that "hardly any place in America is wholly uninteresting if we are thinking in terms of background as well as present conditions." Local writers were advised that if they would simply read back issues of the area's newspapers, they would find "a wealth of amusing, quaint, or revealing items."[11]

The goal was to find material that could be "localized and attached to the spot." Katherine Kellock contended that "it was the need to find something to say about every community and the country around it that forced the close scrutiny of hill and dale, the search for what makes each community different from the others that eventually created the first full-length portrait of the United States." Reviewers generally agreed with Kellock, though they usually offered only vague, if any, explanations of how tours constituted a portrait of America or told the American story. They dwelled more on the list of interesting facts they welcomed as a sign of American vitality. These disconnected items gleaned from the guides today, however, suggest the fascination people often uninterested in either history or culture display in trivia, a peculiar sense of authority derived from the equally peculiar idea that in memorizing facts, they have mastered a body of knowledge. What distinguished these guidebook facts from trivia was the symbolic meaning persons interested in the guides saw in them. "This 'X marks the spot philosophy,'" Frederick Gutheim maintained, "is the hall-mark of every guidebook" and is central to the 1930s interest in them.[12]

Roads themselves embodied aspects of American history, for as the Federal Writers knew, "roads have not developed by accident." This fact could constitute a method for constructing a tour. "Thus," national officials advised local writers, "the tour route is often a thread on which a narrative can be built with history, from the days of Indian occupation to the present told in geographical rather than topical or chronological sequence." It could be a broad history in which all aspects of life would be touched on, for "the social, economic, cultural, and political histories of towns along routes are related to the history of the route itself and most points of interest are closely related to the main theme."[13]

If Americans "really" wanted to know their country, they would, according to FWP officials, have to become "familiar with the nation's great resources of scenery, recreation, its history, its industry, its cities, and infinitely varied landscape." The Tennessee guide acknowledges that "the Tennessee that the tourist knows, with its standard highway and hotdog stands, its industrial areas, cities, and hustling chambers of commerce—all smoothly integrated in surface America—is much like the tourist's Maine or Ohio," but insists that is only the surface, an appearance. FWP officials acknowledged that modern life made it possible "to jump from New York to San Francisco in about sixteen hours," but they nevertheless did not think that the speed with which Americans could

cover space had to destroy a traditional sense of place and meaning if the traveler remembered that such phenomena as transcontinental flight did "not
mean there is nothing to see in the thousands of miles you have skipped." If
Americans stopped and looked, they would see that "we are a nation of infinite
variety, of various races, historic developments, religious observances, and even
of language and dialect." Europeans could say whatever they chose, but it was
time for Americans to realize that their own culture was interesting. It was "time
that Americans who travel in their own land should have a book," declared national FWP officials, "which will tell them where and how to find the countless
things of interest that lie at their own doors."[14]

National FWP officials rejected the "generally accepted opinion that there is
little variety in the towns and cities of America." Just on the visual level alone,
they contended, "a wide divergence exists." In their view, every major city has
"a street like none other in America." Not only are there the "colorful story-
book avenues" such as Beale Street in Memphis but also the row houses of
Baltimore and Philadelphia and the cottage-lined streets on the outskirts of
Chicago. These guides, they thought, were "designed to meet the desire of the
man or woman who really wants to see and get acquainted with this country."[15]

The guides were never completely devoid of parochial values, regardless of
the efforts of the national FWP staff to eliminate or modify such material. At
the same time, the guides would be poorer without the local perspective. A national FWP editor could know that the history of Globe, Arizona, was closely
tied to that of the Old Dominion Mine, but most likely it was an Arizona Federal Writer who knew that "for every old-timer who looks at the Old Dominion and strokes his whiskers and says, 'There's as good copper in her as has
ever been mined. She'll come back,' there is somebody younger who smiles and
says, 'Well, even if she doesn't, we'll get along.'" For both the visitor and the
resident the mine identified Globe: "On a green and rose-colored hillside at
the northern limits the remains of a great copper mine stand as the landmark
of a famous old mining camp." The visitor would be able to see that "tailings
leached to colors as fine as those of the surrounding mountains occupy the
creek valley like mellow sand dunes."[16] While this made a "pleasing picture" to
the visitor, it had a different meaning for those who could not only identify the
place but who also had become part of it, who possessed it: "To the old-timers
of Globe the Old Dominion Mine is not part of the scenery. It is a gravestone,
harsh-looking and sad, commemorating Globe's career as a great Arizona copper
camp—one that flourished with the Old West, and, so they say, died with it."[17]

An emphasis on the old-fashioned, the uncommon, and the unfamiliar as

tourist sights characterized part of the guide's tone, part of the effort to capture the atmosphere of other ways of living, different environments, and past
times. Still, the travel guide format was not wholly compatible with the FWP's
larger ambitions. In writing guidebooks, FWP officials did not escape inherited
modes of perception associated with tourism. The tours embodied aspects of
the picturesque emphasis on the exotic, quaint, and outlandish. Superficial de-
light in such material makes it possible for tourists to observe persons different
from themselves in a patronizing manner and to see even poverty as picturesque. The celebration of diversity in the guides shades into a collection of
picturesque sights. Without trying to define the art historical meaning of the
term "picturesque" and the period in which it flourished, one can still describe
aspects of the view of the world it refers to and that have remained closely associated with tourism and can be found in the FWP tours. It involves regarding
the world as a picture, a pleasing arrangement of reality that calls forth no
strong intellectual or moral responses. The viewer's interest comes from the
variety of rugged textures and irregular surfaces, light and lines that could be
found either in nature or, for example, in an old house or a painting emphasizing aspects of such scenes. The aesthetic and emotional response of the viewer
is disengaged; the scenes are interesting. It is a point of view that, from the
nineteenth century to the present, has been closely associated with tourism.[18]

There are both emotional and moral dangers in seeing the world as a collection of picturesque sights. Much that does not fit such expectations, such de-
light in surface, cannot be felt or seen by those in search of the picturesque. In
this way poverty can be regarded as picturesque. The picturesque was a class
privilege. Charles Dickens much earlier offered an insight into the moral dangers of celebrating the picturesque. While traveling in Italy, he wrote to a friend,
"I am afraid the conventional idea of the picturesque is associated with such
misery and degradation that a new picturesque will have to be established as
the world goes onward."[19]

The FWP guidebooks strove for a new picturesque while not completely
shedding the old. They encouraged educated middle-class Americans to travel
or contemplate travel, both because America was colorful and because they
needed to broaden their vision of the country, of who they as Americans were.
In the first instance the guides visualized the world in the old picturesque way.
In the latter, they were creating a new picturesque pluralism. Through an emphasis on the local and the particular, the idiosyncratic and the anecdotal, the
FWP guides incorporated material that reflected local folkways, regional diversity, and ethnic pluralism.

Often the tours were preceded by a note on the characteristics of the route as a whole, the type of countryside traversed, the history and economy of the area, and the way of life of the inhabitants. The Arizona guidebook, for example, informs the traveler that though a tour runs through "long arid stretches," it "is never monotonous," for there is a "brilliance of color" in the natural landscape and in the variety of Arizonians who inhabit it: "The people along the route are as varied as the country, which ranges from plateau more than a mile above sea-level and snow patched even in summer to the subtropical Salt River Valley; along the northern end are lumberjacks living in camps, near the center are Arizona metropolitans in houses of extremely modern design, and along the lower end are the Mexicans—whose adobe houses can always be identified from afar in the fall by the strings of scarlet chili peppers."[20]

A Connecticut tour from Norwich to the Massachusetts line passes through a rural area where "one-room schoolhouses at the crossroads, mill platforms beside the road, rural mail boxes that sometimes lean at crazy angles" are to be viewed "as typical of this countryside as are the textile mills and foreign-born operatives of the cities and towns through which this route passes." With the color provided by the strings of scarlet peppers and mailboxes at crazy angles, and with the impression of diversity imparted by the rural and urban settings, occupations, and ethnic backgrounds, these two descriptions are examples of the guidebooks' pluralistic picturesque.[21] Examples of economic and social change are occasionally presented in a picturesque manner that fails to acknowledge the poverty in the scene. An Alabama tour covers a land that was "once cotton country" but where dairying and cattle raising are becoming widespread. It is nevertheless also an area with "many old unpainted cabins, some of them log with wooden shutters, reminders of ante-bellum plantation days. Many of them house descendants of slaves who were field hands on the same plantations."[22]

Yet the tourist is often brought face-to-face with evidence of economic and social upheaval, although conflict is presented as something that has led or will lead to progress for everyone. Given such assumptions, there is no need to examine deeply conflicting interests. Traveling from New London, Connecticut, to Massachusetts, the tourist passes through "textile towns and villages . . . where frequent mill failures have altered at least temporarily the socio-economic pattern. The land utilization section of the Resettlement Administration is now making limited purchases of submarginal lands and adding to the State park and forest preserves in this region." The consequences for different groups of such change need not be discussed if they can be labeled temporary and evidence that there are signs of progress can be introduced.[23]

There is no mistaking the visible poverty on Wisconsin roads that once linked the first settlers.

Between Phillips and Prentice, State Route 13 clears a swath through jumbled miles of cutover in which wagon and foot trails begin nowhere and end nowhere, cutting across the road at right angles and disappearing in green and black mazes of trees. Some are as old as the first white settlements back in the brush, so well-worn by pioneer horses, wagons, and boots that nothing has grown on them since. Many houses appear germ-ridden and badly insulated; some lack floors and beds. What little income the farmers here earn comes from primitive roadside stands, small milk checks, or scraggly potato crops.[24]

The guidebooks were of two minds about poverty. Guidebook readers, Federal Writers thought, needed to know that "in the northern section U.S. 141 cuts an almost straight path through a country of markets and upland, desolate timber-stripped cut-over. . . . Little villages, once busy lumbering centers, now serve as trading posts for farmers living in crude cabins and tar-paper shacks." But readers were also tourists, to whom the Federal Writers also thought it necessary to say, "If this land is the farmers' despair it is the vacationist's paradise with its wild natural beauty, camp sites and resorts, and deep streams stocked with fish." Still, they believed "the grim business of making a living from the fluctuating tourist trade" was a step down from the role a town like Crivitz had played "in the changing history of the river from fur-trading and lumbering days."[25] In the final analysis, the guidebooks were for tourists, but they stretched the usual tourist modes of perception as far as possible in an effort to create a portrait of the relationship between the physical artifact and human events, past and present, that would constitute a new democratic picturesque. The ability to perceive this picturesque would not be so much a sign of class privilege as an indication of a revitalized and broadened vision of American community.

In the automobile tours, Federal Writers tried to stimulate a desire to rediscover American places and landscapes. They dealt with places in terms of identity and possession, orientation and wholeness. Within the constraints of the tour form they thought they would capture the American experience. "The tour form," Henry Alsberg repeatedly claimed, "can contain as excellent material and skillful writing as any sonnet or ballad." Whatever conclusions one might draw as to content, there was little doubt that the rules of tour writing were as strict as those for composing a sonnet. Mileage and directions had to be precise. The various tours had to be intermeshed. National FWP officials were confident that the tour form and art were compatible. They boldly asserted that "mileages and other practical information could be inserted in Thoreau's *A Week on the Concord and Merrimack Rivers* without making it any less a work of art." Initially, North Carolina FWP officials doubted the tours could be made "readable, because of the machinery, the route numbers, mileages, directions, interruptions for side tours, etc." Yet by the time the North Carolina guide was ready to be published, they agreed that if any cuts needed to be made to reduce the size of the manuscript, they should come from the essays, not the tours.[26]

"Every effort," Alsberg insisted, "should be made to make the traveler feel when he is traveling this or that highway that he is covering historic ground."[27] It was a historic ground both travelers and inhabitants could share. As state FWP officials and local sponsors acknowledged, residents as well as outsiders needed to become better informed and better acquainted with their place and the landscape in which it was located. The piling up of details was intended to help travelers identify the places they were seeing and to help the inhabitants strengthen their sense of possession. For the Federal Writers everything in the environment could potentially be included in automobile tours to serve as symbols recalling past experiences and creating shared information for both traveler and resident, a sense of familiarity with a place. The sheer volume of facts in a tour conveyed the idea that Americans knew neither the places they lived in nor those they had heard about. The Federal Writers tried to create in the automobile tours a portrait of places and landscapes that invited public exploration. Identification was a stage in rediscovery that could lead to a sense of possession, a sense that the part of America being explored through a tour was a part of oneself.

The attention the guidebook tours paid to the vernacular landscape placed them in a tradition of American writing that proceeds from the assumption that material reality is the starting point for contemplating nonmaterial matters. As one American art critic argues, "The need to grasp reality, to ascertain the physical thereness of things, seems to be a necessary component of the American experience." If Moby Dick is to have symbolic meaning, Melville feels he must give the whale corporeal reality. The chapters on different types of whales must be accurate if we are not to get lost. Similarly, tour mileages and physical descriptions of local sites must be accurate if we are to be able to contemplate the things that happened at a particular place—events that can only be imagined, not seen.[28]

Rather than erecting memorials to locate the past in the present, the FWP tried to make the existing American landscape into a monument, to infuse it with emotion and symbolic content. The guides hardly analyze what Americans had done to the landscape as an index to their historical experience and cultural values. What was important to the Federal Writers were the facts they could, for example, attach to buildings, thus turning them into monuments and linking them to the stories that were now to be associated with them in the traveler's mind.[29]

The guidebook tours tell of the ordinary doings of the famous and the extraordinary doings of the ordinary. Follow, for example, tour 12 in the Tennessee guide and learn that the Dandrige County Courthouse has the marriage bond of Davy Crockett and Polly Finley and the record of an earlier license, "returned unused," issued to Crockett and Miss Margaret Elder, and that in the Huntingdon Courthouse a record book "saved" from two courthouse fires "shows that Crockett was paid a bounty here for wolf skins." Looking at Durham, North Carolina, that state guide noted, the tourist will find that "the universal demand for tobacco, coupled with the business genius of the Duke family, is exemplified in long rows of red-faced factories where thousands toil daily, filling whole trains with their products." The guide pointed out that "here was created the fortune that endowed Duke University." Without those who toiled, the trains would have remained empty and there would be no Duke University. The guide attempts to portray the army of workers, "men and women, white and colored," entering and leaving these factories, for this, the guide contends, is when the reality of Durham as an industrial center is clearest—this is the "bustle"; the rest is "relative calm." In the guidebooks the vitality of America is linked to hard-working, ordinary people. They are the key to the FWP's picturesque: mid-nineteenth-century lumbermen and rivermen who "thronged into Bangor[, Maine], fresh from the log-drives with a winter's wages and the accumulation of a winter's thirsts and hungers"; Columbia, Tennessee, on "First-Monday market day"; Gary, Indiana, steelworkers.[30]

One does not have to be famous to have one's extraordinary doings commemorated in the guidebook accounts of American history and life. In the Tennessee guide, the old Mabry place, 12.6 miles west of Knoxville on US 70, provides an occasion for a vignette of antebellum life and this detail of Civil War–related passions: "A quarrel between two union soldiers ended in the murder of one in spite of Mrs. Mabry's attempt to save the man's life by locking him in the lower front room." The Fur Craft Shop of J. W. Hickey and several roadside stands he operates are located near Mammy's Creek, Tennessee. Hickey's skills as a trapper and curer of hides are described and related to local traditions.[31]

The FWP guides focused on the daily and seasonal round of communal life in their portrait of America. Turn to the Tennessee guide's description of the slaves who made the bricks for the Thomas J. Page House, the sorghum making along the roadsides around Camden, the foot washing and communion service at Hollow Rock Primitive Baptist Church near Bruceton, and the Brunswick stew suppers, the shopping crowds downtown on Saturday, and the Taylor Tabernacle Revival in the area of Brownsville and Haywood County. Confronting a myriad of facts about American places with a sense of wonder, national FWP officials thought, the tourist following the automobile tours would find no American places and landscapes uninteresting.[32]

The guidebooks tried to make buildings and other objects part of the landscape in which they were located. They linked significant facts to objects. The object—house, inn, jail, cemetery, church, or factory—offered the occasion to introduce the traveler to the social, cultural, and economic history of the place, as in this example from the North Carolina guide:

THE LILESVILLE BAPTIST CHURCH, organized in 1777, is one of the oldest Baptist congregations in the State. Here preachers Tirant (Methodist) and Durant (Baptist) debated from sunrise until dark on the question of infant baptism. The first log church was succeeded in the 1840's by a frame building with a slave shed in which the Negroes, required to accompany their masters to church, were separated from the white congregation by a low wall that permitted them to see the preacher and hear the services without being seen. The present white frame building, with a square belfry over the small vestry, was erected in 1871.[33]

If the information was interesting enough, it could be offered even though the object with which it was associated was no longer present. The odd fact, the legend, or the career of a local figure or of a national figure in his or her local aspect is not trivia in the context of these tours. Take tour 16 in the Tennessee guide, cross the Wolf River, go through Byrdstown, pass Starpoint, and take a right at State Route 53, and you come to the birthplace of Cordell Hull, who long before he became secretary of state in the Franklin Roosevelt administration was a shy youth noted locally "for two accomplishments—his ability to pilot log rafts safely down the river, and his skill in debate."[34]

Material reality transports travelers into another world and makes them ponder the juxtaposition of past and present. Following the tours, the traveler can view the built environment not only as evidence of the present but, like an archaeologist, as the revelation of successive phases of a civilization:

Roper, [North Carolina,] 42m. (13 alt., 660 pop.), a farm village, was formerly a busy settlement called Lees Mill, which served the needs of the wealthy planters of Tyrell County in Colonial days. At the close of the 17th century, Capt. Thomas Blount of Chowan, a blacksmith and ship's carpenter, settled on the eastern bank of Kendricks Creek. Later he bought the Cabin Ridge plantation where the town of Roper stands, and in 1702 built the first mill in this section. He died in 1706, and his widow married Thomas Lee. In time both the mill and the settlement were called Lees Mill. The mill was used continuously until 1920. Only the water wheel and a small part of the building are left to mark one of the earliest developments of water power in North Carolina.[35]

The tours tried to create a sense that the places the tourist passed through were part of a distinctive landscape. An alert traveler following, for example, the first tour in the North Carolina guide, from the Great Dismal Swamp to Shallotte, would know that more than a geographical designation, eastern North Carolina was a particular place. Other people had been there before the traveler and had left evidence that they had preceded him or her, and their descendants continued to live there in their way and manner.[36]

Not only could tourists visit the Great Dismal Swamp, but the guide also let them compare their observations with a selection from Colonel William Byrd's *Description of the Dismal with a proposal to drain it* (ca. 1730). This reminded travelers that Colonel Byrd had preceded them, and so also had runaway slaves and other fugitives. The same tour also takes the traveler through Winton, North Carolina, a town named for the DeWinton family of England. Here, too, past and present occupied common ground:

> During the War between the States the town was burned except for one log cabin. The first courthouse was set on fire in 1830 by Wright Allen, who sought thus to destroy a forged note. He was exposed, tried, and publicly hanged on the courthouse grounds. Winton levies no local taxes; its revenue is derived from municipally owned and operated farm lands. Citizens protested so vigorously against the noise, smoke, and dust of trains that the railroad tracks were laid 30 miles away. Winton was the birthplace of Richard J. Gatling (1818–1903), inventor of the Gatling gun.[37]

Which of these events were most important? The guide did not say; the tours contained no thesis. Travelers would have to draw their own conclusions.

The guides describe history from a local perspective; they emphasize origins rather than developments, and events rather than trends. History revolves around a particular site. The guides give no indication that some historical events are more significant than others. For the traveler at Fort Fisher Beach the guide offers no comment on the significance of the Civil War in terms of national destiny or human freedom: "The Site of Fort Fisher, Confederate stronghold during the War between the States. The only remains of the emplacement are stretches of grass-grown breastworks, marked by a monument to northern and southern soldiers who fought in the battle (Dec. 20, 1864–Jan. 13, 1865). The Federal fleet alone, in two attacks, fired more than 2,000,000 pounds of projectiles. Cannon balls and skeletons of men have been found on the beach where the ocean is washing away the earthworks."[38]

Mileages indicating distances from one point to the next gave a firm orientation as the road inevitably led from place to place. It was not enough for readers to identify a place and to feel a sense of possession. The guides further asked travelers to link the place to the larger tour, the tour to the state, and ultimately the state to the nation. The guide took travelers through the evidence of the past as it directed them through space. By offering travelers and inhabitants references to past experiences associated with a specific place that, although it had changed over time, continued to exist, these tours made readers conscious that they occupied a point in time as well as space.

Both Federal Writers and project supporters claimed that the guidebooks also constituted a history of America, its story and portrait. In a letter to Bernard DeVoto, national tours editor Kellock conceded that Iowa "has relatively few real points of interest." By "real points of interest" she seems to have meant sites connected with well-known public events and grand national scenes. Given this situation, she explained, the Iowa editors had chosen to use "the tours to describe the life and customs of rural areas." The entire guide series was rich in such material. Church suppers, coon hunts, county fairs, tenant farmer moving days, and band concert nights had a place in any broadly and democratically conceived history of the American people. And Kellock insisted that the tours were history. By "weeding out the lush panegyrics on the glories of the old culture," she thought, the national office had helped Mississippi Federal Writers prepare tours that told the history of their state. All that was necessary, according to Kellock, to write history using tours was that you "have very interesting material," for "the descriptions of the various towns and plantations when united in the tour, tell the history of the whole western side of the State without a single editorial generalization." This absence of generalization did not mean that the editors "shied away from erosion, reconstruction and tenant problems, though they let the facts speak for themselves."[39]

It was a curious historical method that could avoid generalization either in organizing materials or in drawing conclusions. In effect, the Federal Writers claimed to be writing history while refusing to assume the traditional responsibilities of the historian. It was, as historian Daniel M. Fox much later complained, not a historical method at all. In his view, the Federal Writers displayed either "impatience with the past, or antiquarian-like fascination with certain aspects of it." They had failed to display any comprehension of "the relative importance of historical events." Still, he acknowledged that they did capture "in panorama fashion, the unity and diversity of the American landscape." He did not, however, recognize that they dealt with tradition and history in an effort to create identifiable American places that citizens could feel they possessed and that were somehow connected, one to another, in that larger whole called America —an abstraction the Federal Writers tried to turn into a symbolic place. What is remarkable is that for Kellock, her FWP colleagues, and other Americans interested in the guidebooks, this was seen as the same thing as writing history.[40]

The guidebook tours abandon the historian's traditional task of constructing a meaningful explanation of past events. From a historian's point of view, the tours' vast array of facts constitutes a failure to distinguish the significant from the trivial and the central from the marginal, or to seek to establish the relationship between the facts. Only the place and landscape connects these facts as the tour jumps from an item associated with one period to an incident associated with another era without indicating any relationship. Few causal relationships are noted, let alone explored.

By jumping from one period to another and juxtaposing events separated by decades, often centuries, the tours give the impression that nothing happened in a place between the items noted. Such an approach makes it impossible to analyze the conflicts that underlay the social and economic transformations that the guides view as progress. Even when the tours pass through areas in economic decline, there is no clear sense of how different groups or classes were affected by this. No effort is made to distinguish whether some residents gained or lost more than others. The traveler could not discover from the tours that change had ever been an ordeal. Economic and social revolutions took little toll; they simply produced progress.

To the extent that national FWP officials used a romantic nationalist and pluralist approach to try to unite Americans while ignoring conflicts that divided them, they created a mythical view of the nation. An ideological view of America would have stressed history and conflict and would have sought to understand the interests of a particular social group and to change its circumstances. The guidebook essays and tours worked to create an inclusive American community by portraying it. There was an inherently paradoxical attempt to both preserve and celebrate differences while seeking to transcend them in a sense of shared nationality. In modern societies one of the functions of social myths is to unite individuals and groups with different interests. Such myths embody visions of the society's past and hopes for a utopian future. They do not indicate how a change from present circumstances to a better future can be achieved. That would be divisive. Thus, to a large degree the guidebook series is mythic. In part, it was this mythic quality that made the guidebooks acceptable to the official private and public cultural and political institutions that lent their authority as sponsors and consultants.

As historian Daniel Fox recognized, the FWP attitude toward history was unique neither to that agency nor to the 1930s. Ironically, he saw it as part of an American tradition manifested in "the bulk of poetry of *Leaves of Grass*, the early books of Van Wyck Brooks and the essays of H. L. Mencken." More than the absence of a sense of history relates the FWP to American transcendentalism, to Emerson and Whitman. National FWP officials, however, did not self-consciously cultivate the idea that they were working in such a tradition. Fox sees them as typical American intellectuals less interested than their European counterparts in integrating and understanding their own traditions. Yet a vague sense, vaguely articulated, that like Whitman the FWP was dealing with "a nation of nations," that it was dealing with issues with which he had dealt, can be gleaned from project correspondence, publications, and book reviews. Neither Fox nor anyone else has analyzed how Whitman and the FWP were addressing similar problems—issues that have never been resolved but that both Whitman and the FWP testify are a persistent and unresolvable part of American life as well as an opportunity constantly to revitalize and redefine an American sense of identity and community.[41]

Like Ralph Waldo Emerson and Walt Whitman, the Federal Writers found an American epic in the doings of ordinary as well as great individuals, and in the present as well as the past. Emerson declared in "The American Scholar," "I ask not for the great, the remote, the romantic; what is doing in Italy or Arabia; what is Greek art, or Provencal minstrelsy; I embrace the common. . . . What would we really know the meaning of? The meal in the firkin; the milk in the pan; the ballad in the street; news of the boat." This list has more than a little in common with Kellock's idea that the ordinary social life of a particular place is a real point of interest.[42]

Many an FWP statement of purpose echoes Emerson's conviction that "our logrolling, our stumps and their politics, our fisheries, our Negroes and Indians, our boats and our repudiations, the wrath of rogues and the pusillanimity of honest men, the northern trade, the southern planting, the western clearing; Oregon and Texas, are yet unsung." But Emerson asked for more than a collection of "our incomparable materials." He wanted an American poet who could "show me the sublime presence of the highest spiritual cause lurking, as always it does lurk in those suburbs and extremities of nature"—the sublime in the commonplace. If Whitman was the poet Emerson had called for, he was also, as some of his admirers occasionally conceded, guilty of offering interminable lists, formless catalogs presented as poems. The argument has always been about whether he was more than this. F. O. Matthiessen, who found much to praise in Whitman's poetry, thought he "failed on those occasions when he tried to express a loose America simply by writing loosely." Much of what the FWP offered in the guidebook tours was a cataloging of America without any transforming point of view. That was left to the travelers. From the incomparable materials offered in the tours they would, so to speak, have to make their own poems.[43]

The Federal Writers talked about the guides as an American epic, not as catalogs. Their notions are similar to those discussed in earlier American attempts to make the epic, an Old World literary form, suitable to American circumstances —an epic for a diverse and democratic people allegedly with little sense of history. The present looked at imaginatively, Emerson contended, was as inspiring as any glorious past: "Banks and tariffs, the newspaper and the caucus, Methodism and Unitarianism, are flat and dull to dull people, but rest on the same foundations of wonder as the town of Troy and the Temple of Delphi, and are as swiftly passing away."[44]

By placing himself at the center of his poem, Whitman treated both himself and America as engaged in a process of self-realization. It was not an epic that celebrated past heroic deeds and that accepted and justified present social arrangements but, instead, a new epic of becoming. Out of his experience Whitman sought to create a new personality for a democratic age—"tallying, the momentous spirit and facts of its immediate day"—and thus guide others in discovering their possibilities. Unlike Whitman's *Leaves of Grass*, there is no self at the center of the FWP tour expressing and fusing private lyric and public epic. Still, the guides do invite an exploration of the open road; they do invite Americans to place themselves in the center of the automobile tours and to realize and celebrate a pluralistic culture still in the process of becoming, and thus to know themselves in a new way.[45]

All citizens are heroes in both Whitman's and the FWP's American epics. Whitman largely refused to discriminate between the ugly and the beautiful, for all material facts revealed spiritual realities. In Whitman's view, Susan Sontag observes, "nobody would fret about beauty and ugliness . . . who was accepting a sufficiently large embrace of the real, of the inclusiveness and vitality of actual American experience." The FWP tours documented America in a similarly inclusive manner. They dignified the commonplace. This was one of the qualities that William Stott contends make the documentary form "a radically democratic genre."[46]

In the guidebook automobile tours, the FWP tried to help tourists confront previously unimagined aspects of American life. The emphasis, however, was not on social documentary trying to remedy problems by so moving readers that hardships other people faced would become of such concern to them that they would feel compelled to address those problems. Rather, the focus was on culture, on American ways of life. Cultural differences were celebrated on the assumption that no one group had a superior way of life that could be defined as the American way. In fact, every American's sense of identity and nationality would be enriched if, like Whitman, all Americans could see and incorporate as part of themselves the life of their fellow Americans. In this way, inequalities in American life are implicitly attacked. In retrospect, novelist and Missouri Federal Writer Jack Conroy saw himself as "a witness to the time rather than a novelist. Mine was an effort to obey Whitman's injunction to 'vivify the contemporary fact.'"[47]

The guidebook tours constitute neither a conventional history nor a historic epic nor a traditional myth, although they had characteristics of all these genres. And that is not simply coincidence. Rather, it illustrates the efforts of national FWP officials to use the guidebook format to address inherited questions in ways compatible with their commitment to romantic nationalism, cultural pluralism, and New Deal reform. In stressing pluralism, integration, and inclusiveness, they sought to overcome the cultural divisiveness of the immediate past.

Critics Lewis Mumford and Bernard DeVoto and WPA administrator Ellen Woodward talked about the guides as a form of patriotism, as books that would help Americans love their country and value it more dearly. They all spoke in terms of psychology and of emotion. Neither the guides nor FWP officials nor critics talked much about traditional American political ideas and institutions that had in the past been seen as unifying Americans. Instead, the focus was on cultural diversity as a vital and positive aspect of American life.[48]

The emphasis on emotions such as patriotism and love and on ways of life rather than abstract ideas reflects, in part, the extent to which the New Deal responded to the emotional and cultural divisions inherited from the 1920s. The 1920s had been a decade of fundamental cleavage between rural and urban Americans, between fundamentalists and nonfundamentalists, and between nativists and minorities. In national politics, reform programs were equated with foreign ideologies, and the status quo was endorsed. In the most extreme manifestations of these divisions, there was an attempt to seek cultural unity by crusading for "one hundred per cent Americanism," by regarding all minorities and nonconformists as the source of American problems. This type of program provides the individual with the definition of nation that satisfies one's need for security. As social psychologist Gordon W. Allport observed in *The Nature of Prejudice* (1955), the nation becomes for such an American an "in group." He sees "no contradiction in ruling out of its beneficent orbit those whom he regards as threatening intruders and enemies (namely, American minorities)." In such a formulation, Allport finds, "the nation stands for the status-quo. . . . Nationalism is a form of conservatism." In contrast, the FWP's epic of American nationalism aimed to revitalize American culture through an inclusive celebration of American diversity, of an America in the process of becoming and of realizing itself. This version of cultural pluralism was compatible with reform as manifested in New Deal political and social programs.[49]

The limitations of the FWP's guidebook tour approach to American life and history as a contribution to cultural liberalism and the dilemmas of modernity are more apparent now than they could have been at a time when archconservatives rejected the portrayal of the United States offered in the guides as un-American. Pluralism in the interest of democratic equality deferred addressing the problem of cultural authority. The question of who deserved a citizen's allegiance in conflict situations was not addressed and, in the circumstances surrounding the FWP, could not be faced. The Writers' Project guidebooks interpreted the nation's landscape so as to create a monument to America's cultural pluralism. They provided no definite answers to who and what was American, but they did insist that any answer would have to be broadly inclusive. At the same time they sacrificed any attempt to assess critically where the nation had been and where it was going. FWP officials never tried to determine what would hold this pluralistic nation together. They assumed that an acknowledgment that the United States was a diverse nation was a necessary starting point. What were the underlying values that could bind Americans together? Project officials envisioned a diverse and inclusive national community, but they never confronted the question of whether all the parts were compatible. Were all aspects of various regional and ethnic cultures valuable? Which were not?

Can tourism serve as a culturally viable way of dealing with modernity, or has it become a pathological symptom of a general cultural malaise? Does the modern museum or tourlike appreciation of cultures make it possible to understand the quality of other people's experience? Or is cultural critic Susan

Sontag's more pessimistic conclusion correct? "In a world that is well on its way to becoming one vast quarry, the collector becomes someone engaged in a pious work of salvage. The course of modern history having already sapped the traditions and shattered the living wholes in which precious objects once found their place, the collector may now in good conscience go about excavating the choicer, more emblematic fragments."[50]

In *The Tourist: A New Theory of the Leisure Class* (1976), sociologist Dean Mac-Cannell describes tourism as an attempt to cope with the structural differentiation that gives the modern world both its sense of freedom and its fragmentation, discontinuity, and alienation. "Sightseeing," he argues, "is a ritual performed to the differentiations of society," an attempt to make out of fragments, out of bits and chips of information, "a unified experience." MacCannell, however, is convinced that tourism "is doomed to eventual failure: even as it tries to construct totalities, it celebrates differentiation." Yet MacCannell sees tours as having the possibility of constructing a unified representation of reality that has a "moral claim on the tourist," because in combining "natural, social, historical and cultural domains," the tour takes on a universal quality. For MacCannell that universality also comes in large part from the fact that tours deal with modern structural differentiation and fragmentation.[51]

In the tourism MacCannell analyzes, he sees no hope, as the Federal Writers did, that travel could lead to a rediscovery and broadening of identity and help produce a more integrated society while fostering an appreciation of differences. Rather, MacCannell contends that "consciousness and integration of the individual into the modern world require only that one attraction be linked to another: a district to a community, or an establishment to a district, or a role to an establishment." Ultimately, tourism represents the triumph of modernity: "Restored remnants of dead traditions . . . are reminders of our break with the past and with tradition, even our own tradition." National FWP officials expected tourism to accomplish more than that. The FWP guides are richer in material than any of the travel "literature" MacCannell quotes and more demanding in their expectations of the traveler. Yet the guidebook tours do not discuss traditions to find out how to solve problems, how to behave in particular situations, how to view the world, or what to value.[52]

Can an FWP tour take the traveler beyond a superficial view of other people's experiences? National FWP officials had their doubts and undertook a number of folklore and oral history projects designed to supplement the guides and to give greater depth to the FWP portrait of America. In a 1938 letter to Lewis Mumford, Alsberg explained his desire to undertake studies that would examine American life in greater depth than the guides had. Alsberg saw the FWP as fol-

lowing in the steps of Mumford's pioneering studies of American culture. The
FWP was linked to a democratic romantic nationalism whose main concerns
first received creative literary expression during the American Renaissance.[53]

Ironically, during the Great Depression the FWP invited Americans to travel.
Everyone was invited. This was not an aristocratic grand tour, a finishing school
for an elite. The invitation was democratic in theory though phrased in middle-
class terms. The FWP asked Americans, either literally or imaginatively, to step
outside their daily routine, to leave their places in the spatial, social, and class
structure of their nation—to travel. They could share the excitement of the
explorer's sense of new discoveries with the tourist's certainty of knowing exactly where they were.

Anthropologists studying tourism have described the individual leaving the
ordinary workaday world to vacation as engaging in the modern world's equivalent of the more traditional alternation of profane and sacred days. Some of
the FWP rhetoric about travel places the proposed tours in the tradition of religious pilgrimage. But while traditional pilgrimages drew individuals out of
their diverse places in the social world into a community focusing on symbols
of unity, the guidebook tours emphasized social differentiation. What appears
to be worshiped (or in more secular terms, explored, studied, and honored) is
society itself, not anything transcendent. From this perspective Federal Writers
hardly differed from totem makers, who without being fully aware of it, were
constructing ways for their society to worship itself.[54]

Still, the FWP journey through America involved more than self-worship.
The guides invited Americans to travel not only for the opportunity to live temporarily outside their ordinary world but also for the chance to develop a sense
of community with people different from themselves, people who might appear foreign and strange but who were fellow Americans.

What constitutes historical consciousness is open to discussion. It is not
necessarily the same as cultural and historical analysis. The FWP tried to give a
mythic meaning to American places and landscapes. In the geographical presentation of history provided by the tours, elements of past and present are
presented in a way that makes them seem simultaneously available to the traveler. Time is largely undifferentiated and unified only by place and landscape.
But neither the Federal Writers nor the audience they wrote for were any longer
capable of viewing the world in completely mythic terms. Their sense of past,
present, and future slides between myth and history.

The guidebooks tried to make buildings and other physical objects indigenous to the place and landscape in which they were located. They linked anec-

dotal facts of local significance to objects in an effort to make them part of an indigenous mythic history. In the guidebooks, as in painting, the goal of an anecdotal method is not analysis of the object being treated. Rather, the object is used to tell a story that transcends it—a story many of whose significant details cannot be seen in the object itself. Thus in the automobile tours project workers were not deeply concerned with whether in architectural terms a building reflected an indigenous style or an outside influence. More significantly, they did not see buildings as an expression of a cultural process and towns and regions as cultural patterns on the land. They did not see buildings as an image of a people's view of the world—a house as a universe in microcosm. A different approach would let buildings speak to travelers about questions concerning process and pattern. In the tours the Federal Writers did not ask why a past builder used a particular form for a building designed to perform specific functions. They did not ask what those choices revealed about that builder, his world, and his view of his place in that world. In dealing with both man-made and natural objects the tours provided only brief descriptions and then quickly moved on to make some connection between the site and an event they thought worth noting. A more analytical approach would have involved spending more time reading the object itself.[55]

Nevertheless, associations are important elements in creating and conserving a sense of place. A place associated with past events can become part of a mythic or a historic consciousness. Looking back at his youth, F. O. Matthiessen, one of the founders of the American studies movement, thought "it is appalling how much can get left out of an American education." It was only much later in his life that he learned "that Starved Rock and the Illinois river where I had gone canoeing near my grandfather's house was the scene of some of the most vivid pages in Francis Parkman's *La Salle and the Discovery of the Great West*. La Salle had been simply the name of my grandfather's town. That it was the name also of a French explorer was lodged somewhere abstractly in my memory, but I had not had the irreplaceable experience of sharing, as a boy, in a rich consciousness of history."[56] In their guides to Illinois and the other states, the Federal Writers put together tours designed to help Americans make such associations.

At the very moment Henry Alsberg was planning to take the FWP beyond writing guidebooks, both domestic politics and international conflict were developing in ways that would have a major impact on the Writers' Project.

Part 2

Modernity, Cultural Pluralism,
and the Federal Writers' Project

Chapter 5

Long Live Participation!

Ethnicity, Race, and the Federal Writers' Project

Few topics have been as central to discussions of American national identity as race and immigration. One important indication of the way many old-stock white Americans have defined freedom and equality and their sense of national identity has been their attitudes toward African Americans and immigrants. New Deal cultural programs concerned with race and ethnicity offered new definitions of national identity. National FWP officials saw a history of slavery and emancipation as central to both African American history and the struggle to define freedom in a multiethnic society. They thought the story of the role of immigrants and their children in America needed to be viewed in the same way. For the most part, the interest of the FWP in the history of immigration focused on the so-called new immigration from southern and eastern Europe that began to rise in the 1880s and did not significantly decline until World War I and the passage of immigration restriction laws in the 1920s.

Regarding both African Americans and the new immigrants and their children, FWP folklore editor B. A. Botkin, Negro affairs editor Sterling Brown, and social-ethnic studies editor Morton Royse concentrated on experiences that not only had unique aspects but that, they argued, were also universal and representative of key themes in American history. Epic migrations, a transition from an agrarian to an industrial world, a quest for freedom and a better life, and a struggle to adapt tradition to dramatic changes in circumstances were central to the historical experience not only of African Americans and various groups of new immigrants but of all Americans. Momentous and continuous change was emblematic of America in particular and the modern world in general. The failure of Reconstruction to secure the civil rights of African Americans, the industrialization of America, the migration of blacks, and the immigration of eastern and southern Europeans had raised issues about the nature of American identity and culture and the very definition of the term "American." To a large degree the FWP was dealing with these issues, which the New Deal was reopening in their economic, political, and cultural dimensions.

By addressing these matters from a pluralistic perspective, FWP officials had virtually guaranteed that someone like Texas Democrat Representative Martin Dies would label the Writers' Project a subversive, communist conspiracy. Although the FWP was certainly not engaged in subversion, Dies was right to sense that the Writers' Project challenged his vision of America and that it sought a revision of America. Who constituted the nation? Whose experience was part of the national history? How did the arrival of newcomers affect who Americans were? What role did assimilation or acculturation play in answering these questions?

To help create a more inclusive American history, national FWP officials understood that they needed to search for new sources of information. They rejected the pervasive assumption that the culture of the dominant educated group —the group most likely to leave written records that were preserved—represented the culture of the whole. To move beyond these materials, they used life histories and folklore as sources. The language of oral tradition and oral biographies became central to their task. By having FWP field-workers record oral accounts, they intended to help the inarticulate write themselves into history. Language, oral or written, could be both poetry and history. Asking Americans to listen to the diverse voices that constituted their nation intertwined the cultural politics surrounding language, art, historical understanding, and national identity.

In the 1920s Botkin and Brown had contended that each of the many diverse groups in the United States had created an oral literature. On the FWP, Royse joined Botkin and Brown in arguing that oral tradition and individual firsthand and life history narratives were not only historical sources but also a form of historical narrative. As Brown later put it, "I became interested in folklore because of my desire to write poetry and prose fiction. . . . Then later I came to something more important—I wanted to get an understanding of people, to acquire an accuracy in the portrayal of their lives." Brown called this the "socio-historical approach" to what (borrowing from Botkin) he termed "living-people-lore." Botkin noted the resistance among folklorists and historians to the study of what he referred to as folklore in the making and living lore. Scholars, Botkin argued, preferred to study "the folklore of the past [that] has acquired prestige value because it has the immunity of the old and the safe," while "folklore in the making on the other hand, has a more direct relation to contemporary or recent social structure and is the expression of social change and conflict." He concluded that "social taboos and scholarly inhibitions" blocked study of this material. Botkin and his colleagues in the Washington office intended to break taboos.[1]

Botkin, Brown, and Royse valued anthropological theory that focused on the functional and integrative role of culture. Botkin was deeply interested in anthropologist Paul Radin's argument for a cultural history in which individual life histories played a central role. The anthropological concept of culture gave FWP officials a way to construct the type of history that interested them and that was then found in the work of few historians. The American historical profession, in the name of objectivity and empiricism, relied heavily on documents likely to be found in existing archives. As historian Caroline Ware argued in the introduction to *The Cultural Approach to History* (1940), "Although the literate parts of the population were always in the minority, these were necessarily regarded as the 'people,' since it was they concerning whom the historians had direct evidence."[2] (Botkin and Royse contributed to this volume and had participated in the American Historical Association meeting on which the volume was based). The result, Ware argued, had only begun to greatly concern some historians in the years between the wars. Questions about the social and cultural history of ordinary people would not become a central concern of historians until the 1960s. At that point the FWP's slave narratives began to be regarded as a major source that would allow historians to address some of these questions, but the unwillingness and/or inability to use folklore as a historical source has persisted longer than the resistance to using oral history materials.

In the period when Botkin, Brown, and Royse served on the FWP, African American history was considered a marginal subject of doubtful legitimacy. How to examine immigrant and ethnic history was only occasionally discussed, and few studies were published. Black historians were segregated from the mainstream of the profession, and Jews had difficulty receiving appointments in history and English departments. Botkin himself had experienced anti-Semitism in his search for a position at the University of Oklahoma. Brown spent his academic career in African American institutions. The prevalent view was that African Americans and the new immigrants had not been active participants in American history and that neither blacks nor "foreign groups"—immigrants and their children—could be entrusted with the task of writing the nation's history. Conservative romantic nationalists made a parallel argument regarding the history of American literature, since in their view language and art were central to national identity. They made no effort to reconcile romantic nationalism and diversity. They privileged an allegedly homogeneous Anglo-Saxon American culture as the source of legitimate American culture. They narrowly defined American culture, who had helped create it, and consequently, who was American.[3]

The approach Botkin, Brown, and Royse brought to the study of race and ethnicity placed them on the side of the emerging urban-industrial, working-class American culture and the diverse groups creating it. The studies they initiated were an implicit endorsement of this new America as much as the refusal to study it and/or denial of its existence or worth was a rejection of the new in the name of an older rural Protestant America that still controlled the historical establishment. Shots in these battles were still being heard in the 1960s. In his 1963 address as president of the American Historical Association, Carl Bridenbaugh worried that the new generation of historians lacked the shared sense of a common culture and a rural upbringing once prevalent among historians. Too many historians were now "products of the lower middle-class or foreign origins." The address was widely interpreted as anti-Semitic. By 1963 this was a rearguard action. But that was not the case in the 1930s.[4]

The approaches of Botkin, Brown, and Royse to black and ethnic studies were shaped in response to an inherited American dialogue about these topics and especially by the impact of World War I and developments in the 1920s. World War I had triggered great outpourings of emotion about who was to be included in the nation—Who was a real American?—and a resurgence of exclusive definitions that emphasized race and ethnicity. Both the New Negro Renaissance and the development of the theory of cultural pluralism addressed the nationalistic issue of how to define America. They provide the immediate backdrop for the development of FWP programs.

Botkin, Brown, and Royse initiated black and ethnic studies that were among the FWP's most thought-provoking and innovative cultural studies. The projects they directed are also an inherently interesting part of American thought

on race and ethnicity (especially regarding the relationship between these topics and American literature and history) that has received little attention. An
examination of the historical context in which these three FWP officials developed their outlooks regarding the significance of race and ethnicity, their own
evolving ideas, and the FWP programs they instituted illuminates the history of
the Writers' Project and aspects of how Americans have thought about national identity.

The programs Botkin, Brown, and Royse sought to develop depended on
the cooperation of the local Federal Writers in the state units. Often local Federal Writers holding the parochial views of the dominant groups in their area
rejected the vision of Washington officials. Furthermore, the need to give the
state guidebooks priority, the Dies committee hearings, and the deteriorating
international situation meant that innovative FWP programs had little time to
develop. Nor can analysis that focuses entirely on the programs that the national office initiated give a full sense of the work the FWP did in African American and ethnic studies. All of the state guidebooks dealt with aspects of these
issues and not always in ways compatible with the outlook of national officials.
Brown in particular spent a great deal of time either encouraging more treatment of blacks in the state guides or disputing the treatment he saw in drafts
for the guidebooks. State FWP units also initiated projects and publications
dealing with blacks or ethnic groups.

The FWP's black and ethnic studies need to be examined not only in terms of
an inherited intellectual dialogue about these topics but also as a contemporary
dialogue in which local Federal Writers were key participants who implicitly
and sometimes explicitly rejected points of view held by the national office.
The contrast between the views of the national office and members of the
state units indicates that the ideas of national FWP officials, while reflecting the
New Deal ethos, did not represent the variety of views regarding race, ethnicity, and the definition of American nationality that could be found among the
general population and that were present among Federal Writers. Within the
living memory of many Americans in the 1930s (and part of the continuity of
memory of other Americans), emancipation, Reconstruction, and World War
I had raised fundamental questions about who was included in the national
community—questions about the meaning of terms, like "freedom" and "democracy," that are so closely associated with American self-definition. Each of
these events had held out the promise of a renewal of democracy. The end of
Reconstruction represented a crushing of that hope, but it did not mark an
end to the struggle of blacks and their white allies to give meaning to emanci-

pation. The increasing northward movement of blacks after 1910 became a torrent during World War I. More than a response to the economic opportunity created by a labor shortage, the black migration was a protest movement, a folk movement voting with its feet. Black soldiers served during World War I with distinction. Volunteering to make the world safe for democracy and thereby hoping to secure democracy at home, black soldiers returned to an America torn by race riots in 1919—riots in which whites attacked blacks and blacks fought back.

World War I and its aftermath also marked a crisis for white ethnic groups as a call for unity became a demand for conformity and an attack on anyone who maintained traditional "old-country customs." They suffered repression, physical violence, and the passage of immigration restriction laws that not only limited immigration but also sought to define white ethnics as less American than white Anglo-Saxon Protestants. Robert Sklar argues that "no cultural crisis engendered by the First World War was more severe—or more fundamental to the nature of American social life—than the ordeal of coercion and rejection suffered by immigrant ethnic and nationality groups."[5] After World War I, nativists felt that attempts to Americanize the immigrant had failed. This convinced them that immigrants from southern and eastern Europe were members of unassimilable races and must be kept out of the country. A reborn Ku Klux Klan (which had first appeared during Reconstruction) spread across the nation in the 1920s with a program that in the name of traditional Americanism was antiurban and rejected both blacks and white ethnics (mostly Catholic and Jewish groups, who were an increasingly important part of the nation's major cities) and maintained that an American was a white Anglo-Saxon Protestant.

World War I and its aftermath not only generated hostility toward African Americans and white ethnic groups but also played a role in their growing public assertion of pride in group identity. Philosopher Alain Locke and other black Americans talked about a New Negro and asserted the importance of the African American contribution to America. During the "tribal twenties," philosopher Horace Kallen, an American Jew, argued for the value of cultural differences, for the benefits of ethnic pluralism to a democratic society.[6]

For Alain Locke, editor of the pathbreaking anthology *The New Negro* (1925), Woodrow Wilson's ideal of the "self-determination" of peoples took on meanings the wartime president could not have foreseen. Locke offered an interpretation of the meaning of the self-determination of peoples for a new emerging black urban population in places such as Harlem: "Europe seething in a dozen centers with emergent nationalities, Palestine full of a renascent

Judaism—*these are no more alive with the progressive forces of our era than the quickened centers of the lives of black folks*" (emphasis added). However, it is important to note, as Robert Hayden has pointed out, that "the main thrust of *The New Negro* is clearly integrationist, not separatist. . . . Race consciousness and race pride [were] positive forces making the Negro aware of the true worth of his contributions to American society and helping him to achieve his rightful place in it." In Locke's view, "Negro-American culture" would contribute to an "America seeking a new spiritual expansion and artistic maturity."[7] Sentiments such as these were also commonplace in the 1920s in works about the relationship between American writing and the canon of European literature and between regionalist (Botkin's *Folk-Say* volumes were one example) or white ethnic writing and the canon of American literature.

Horace Kallen's ideas about cultural pluralism developed partly in response to the intolerance of ethnic diversity he saw growing out of World War I. He rejected a definition of American nationality that included only white Anglo-Saxon Protestants or that would include other groups only if they totally assimilated to the ways of the dominant group. Kallen's premise that the survival of ethnic identities was essential to democracy led him and others to celebrate diversity and to attack inequalities in American life: "Democracy involves, not the elimination of differences, but the perfection and conservation of differences." Concretely he talked of a federal republic consisting of "a democracy of nationalities, co-operating voluntarily and autonomously in the enterprise of self-realization through the perfection of men according to their kind." His image of different instruments in an orchestra playing in harmony captured his underlying faith that diversity and concord were compatible. Kallen's argument was defensive. He stressed the right of ethnic minorities to remain different and assumed a static group identity. While national FWP officials accepted Kallen's basic arguments, they gave a different emphasis to pluralism. They stressed the right of minorities to participate without discrimination in American society and the impact of the dynamic effects of the reality of participation on the identity of both minority groups and the larger American society.[8]

In the 1920s the claims of blacks and white ethnic groups to recognition as Americans were often stated in the aesthetic terms common to romantic nationalist discussions of cultural contributions. Locke argued that the African American's "immediate hope rests in the revaluation by white and black alike of the Negro in terms of his artistic endowments and cultural contributions, past and prospective." Thus he restated an approach that had stressed that there were distinguished blacks who had made important contributions to

America exclusively in terms of culture, here defined as the arts. In Locke's vision, the African American "now becomes a conscious *contributor* and lays aside
the status of a beneficiary and a ward for that of a *collaborator and participant* in
American civilization" (emphasis added). In this way, artists/redeemers would
achieve the political and social benefits of equality for African Americans:
"The especially cultural recognition they win should in turn prove the key to
that revaluation of the Negro which must precede or accompany any considerable further betterment of race relationships."[9] National FWP officials would
use words like "collaborator" and "participant," but they would move away
from an emphasis on the arts toward cultural and social history, which they
hoped would have important social and political benefits for creating a more
egalitarian society and a redefined sense of American identity—and also help
revitalize literature in America.

Botkin initially hailed the work of the Harlem Renaissance as evidence that
blacks were contributing to civilization and thus deserved a higher status than
they had been previously accorded. For him the implication of such cultural
facts supported egalitarianism. Thus, in a 1926 review of Countee Cullen's
poems, Botkin found it significant that the *New Masses* had three black contributing editors who were, he maintained, "taking equal part in the new en-
lightenment alongside their white brothers." To Botkin the "cultural flowering
of the Negro" was a sign of the "bursting of the barriers of repression" and "a
force to be reckoned with in our civilization." He listed the names of African
American artists past and present to prove "that the Negro has established his
place in the brotherhood of the arts." In Cullen's poetry he found not only
"sweetness and light" (an allusion to Matthew Arnold and his view of culture)
but also "the sign of the new dawn of an old race, bowed under the sins of the
world." Botkin was not counseling resignation. For self-expression was taking
place in this "age of 'self-determination of peoples.'"[10]

Even in 1926 Botkin was an Arnoldian with a difference. The collection and
publication of black folk songs was, in his mind, as important as the publication of individual black authors.[11] A decade later he rejected the notion that it
was individual contributions that earned African Americans the right to respect.
The study of contemporary anthropology had led him away from Matthew
Arnold's definition of culture and civilization as the history of great individual
triumphs of thought and art—the canon of high culture. In the 1920s Botkin
and Brown had seen a new art as the way to social reform. In the 1930s they
stressed instead the importance of cultural and social history as a necessary
complement to political, social, and economic reform and as a basis for a new

revitalized American art that would contribute to a new conception of America that would promote cultural understanding and aid reform.

Botkin's social concerns and his approach that centered on folklore and oral history meshed easily with Brown's and Royse's outlook. In the oral history projects FWP officials conducted, they played on the theme that interviewing ordinary people had democratic significance and that the reader needed to acknowledge both the importance of undistinguished individuals and that these individuals were fellow citizens. During the 1930s the link between democratic values, a reformist outlook, and the life history method was firmly established. In a democracy, FWP officials maintained, everyone had a right to be heard. Understanding America required listening to new voices. FWP studies gave voice to points of view that had been undocumented. In the life histories, the FWP tried to create a sense of community between the person being interviewed and the reader and to suggest that the situation the interviewee was in was largely not of his or her own making and demanded social and economic reform.

In trying to redefine national identity, FWP officials focused on groups that had been considered lower on either some genetic scale or scheme of cultural evolution—groups whom some politicians and poets, like Martin Dies and T. S. Eliot, thought of as a foreign invasion, a source of contamination. Botkin and Brown knew that accounts of blacks in America suffered not only from racist assumptions but also from static accounts that ignored the dynamics of the African American's relationship to American life. Thirty years later when historian George Tindall reviewed historical writings on African Americans, he made the same criticism.[12]

Brown's career as a poet, literary critic, and FWP official illuminates some of the challenges to be faced in creating a multiethnic account of American life. His work also reflects change and continuity between the literary concerns of writers in the 1920s and their social concerns in the 1930s. The work Brown did as FWP Negro affairs editor was a logical outgrowth of the poetry and literary criticism he had begun publishing in the 1920s. Implicitly, Brown's poetry denied the validity of a contributions approach to art. His poetry did not assume the burden of trying to prove that African Americans could make a great contribution to literature—an approach that in the 1920s rejected the use of dialect. In writing powerful poetry that reflected common patterns of black speech, Brown was helping to demolish walls that had been preventing black poets from providing a full portrayal of black participation in American life. As critics have recognized, Brown's poetry made "no concessions to white prejudice or to Negro pretense" in its effort to capture "the frankness and honesty of black people talking among themselves. . . . black folk whose labors, loves, and hardships reflect in very real terms the texture of the black character."[13] Brown's literary criticism developed in tandem with his poetry and complemented his poetic achievements. His major themes were the social functions of the literary stereotypes found in the writings of white authors and a call for black writers to strive to portray African American life in all its dimensions without fearing the possible reactions of either white or black audiences. Brown's work on the FWP represented an extension and broadening of his earlier themes. He emphasized the participation of blacks in American life, rather than the contributions of distinguished individuals. He tried to see that stereotypes did not substitute for knowledge, and he attempted to ensure that black voices would have an opportunity to participate in the larger American public's discourse about its history and contemporary life.

The positions Brown developed toward the issues he thought black poets had to wrestle with influenced the work he did on the FWP. Brown was intensely interested in the relationship between language and history, oral tradition and the individual artist, and the individual and the group. Although Brown's earliest poems appeared in *Opportunity*, a journal of the Urban League that published many of the writers of the Harlem Renaissance, he denied that he was a part of that movement. By doing so he has forced students of his poetry and of African American literature to ponder the nature of his relationship to the Harlem Renaissance. Literary critic Henry Louis Gates Jr. claims that "Brown's [*Southern Roads* (1932)] even more profoundly than the market crash of 1929, truly ended the Harlem Renaissance, primarily because it contained a new and distinctly black poetic diction and not merely the vapid and pathetic claim for one."[14]

The Harlem Renaissance and the FWP have not been examined in terms of change and continuity, and yet here, too, the FWP can be better understood by comparing its efforts to rediscover and redefine national identity and culture with similar efforts in the 1920s. Brown's career and developing outlook highlight some of the differences and similarities. In both periods, key issues centered around the notion of cultural contributions, the nature and significance of the black vernacular, and its place in poetry and history. Brown's answers to these questions led James Weldon Johnson and Alain Locke to reconsider the influential aesthetic positions they had taken in helping to promote the Harlem Renaissance. Brown's poetry and literary criticism helped him arrive at the participation approach to black studies that he and his fellow poet/ historian B. A. Botkin had been formulating before they began to work together on the FWP.

After Brown graduated from Williams College in 1922 and received his M.A. from Harvard in 1923, he enrolled in what he called "The Academy of Black Folk." Teaching appointments at Virginia Seminary in Lynchburg (1923–26); Lincoln University in Jefferson City, Missouri (1926–28); and Fiske University in Nashville, Tennessee (1928–29) gave him the opportunity to seek out folk professors he had had little contact with in his formal education. Big Boy Davis of Lynchburg, he later recalled, was an outstanding educator: "He was a treasure trove of stories, songs. He was a wandering guitar player. I wrote about him in *Southern Roads*. He knew blues, ballads, spirituals."[15]

Brown's view that there was an academy of black folk worth enrolling in was often regarded as a dubious proposition by both faculty and students at the black universities where he taught. One of his students at Lincoln University recalled, "There were those who considered 'Prof' Brown a bit 'teched' to be spending so much time with 'those weird characters,' who frequented 'The Foot,' an area that bordered the campus. But then they didn't place folklore high on the learning priority list—most of them were busy getting far away from it." He helped change the view of this student and others: "After a while we learned that dialect can be beautiful as well as philosophical." As Brown moved such "weird characters" to the center of his poetry, he would later on the FWP try to move them to the center of the study of African American history.[16]

Brown's use of black dialect in his poetry addressed aesthetic and philosophical issues. The way he resolved these issues led to the creation of a significant body of poetry, indicated his relationship to the Harlem Renaissance, and foreshadowed the way he would approach his work on the FWP. Like Botkin, he was influenced by William Wordsworth's search among ordinary people for a revitalized language, for the emotional intensity of lyric poetry combined with the objectivity of the ballad. Like Botkin, Brown was moved by the work of Carl Sandburg, a modern American poet who found inspiration in the language of both rural and urban Americans. Both Botkin and Brown found the Irish Renaissance, especially the work of John Synge, inspirational. Brown also admired A. E. Houseman, Edward Arlington Robinson, and Robert Frost for their sense of stoicism, critical realism, psychological portraits, and concern for the dramas of ordinary daily life. Like them, Brown searched for new subject matter and a language that was not sentimental, stilted, and divorced from contemporary life. He was convinced that in poetry about the lives of ordinary black people he could express the full dimensions of the human experience. He tried to incorporate a black folk voice and point of view in his poetry. His biographer Joanne V. Gabbin maintains that Brown's poetry is a testimony that "the very elements that make Black expressions uniquely expressive of Black life make them at the same time 'deeply representative' of American life."[17]

To create a portrait of black life in its varied dimensions, Brown strove to re-discover and recover varieties of living black speech that were part of an oral tradition that embodied the creativity and history of African Americans. The stereotypes embodied in the white minstrel show and the plantation tradition versions of black dialect had stood between black poets and the actual speech of ordinary black folk. During the 1920s many black writers argued that this barrier could not be overcome. In *The Book of American Negro Poetry* (1922), James Weldon Johnson distinguished between "the mold of convention in which Negro dialect in the United States has been set," what he recognized as "the mere mutilation of English spelling and pronunciation," and actual black speech. He urged the New Negro poet to "break away from, not Negro dialect itself, but the limitations on Negro dialect imposed by the stifling effects of long con-vention." It is possible to read Johnson as calling for a way of retrieving a black language in poetry that would be "capable of voicing the deepest and highest emotions and aspirations, and allow of the widest range of subjects and the widest scope of treatment." But along with most black writers of this period he stressed mainly the extent to which the existing dialect tradition was a trap for the black poet.[18]

In his critical analysis of the poetry of the Harlem Renaissance, Henry Louis Gates turns the tables on Johnson's view of dialect: "The overriding requisite of black art [in the view of critics such as Locke and Johnson] was that it en-noble the races' image-qua-culture bearers in the pantheon of Western peo-ple's art. This was the first and foremost function; it was a trap." Perhaps this is why it did not occur to Johnson to encourage black poets to walk among black folk and listen. To his credit, Johnson did recognize that Sterling Brown had done exactly that when he published *Southern Roads*, for which Johnson wrote the introduction.[19]

For Johnson, dialect was associated with a phase of black life that would soon be completed: "a log cabin amid fields of cotton or along the levees. Ne-gro dialect is naturally and by long association the exact instrument for voicing this phase of Negro life; and by that very exactness it is an instrument with but two full stops, humor and pathos." Johnson seemed eager to move beyond the rural southern "phase" of the black experience and the dialect associated with it. The very notion of phases seems to deny a connection between the African American southern past and the new urban present. In the preface to the second edition of *The Book of American Negro Poetry* (1931), Johnson maintained that black writers were abandoning dialect: "If he addressed himself to the task, the Aframerican poet might in time break the old conventional mold; but I don't think he will do it, because I don't think he considers it now worth the effort." A year later, in the preface to Sterling Brown's *Southern Roads*, Johnson announced that he was wrong. Brown, he declared, had "made more than mere transcriptions of folk poetry. . . . He has deepened its meanings and multiplied its implications."[20]

Alain Locke argued in his review of *Southern Roads* that Brown was "the New Negro: Folk Poet." It was poetry, he recognized, that built on the black folk tradition. Brown had found a way of using African American folklife without being caught in the white minstrel tradition and other parodies of black folk speech and tradition. Thus Locke announced that Brown "has reached a sort of common denominator between the old and the New Negro." Locke recognized that the term "New Negro" reflected defensiveness and rejection as well as pride and self-assertion: "Too many of the articulate intellects of the Negro group—including sadly enough the younger poets—themselves children of opportunity have been unaware of these deep resources of the past." Brown's poetry, in Locke's view, demonstrated continuity and adaptability in a black folk tradition devoid of phases that had allegedly been left behind: "Underneath the particularities of one generation are hidden universalities which only deeply penetrating genius can fathom and bring to the surface." Taken together, Johnson's and Locke's praise of Brown repudiated many of the basic premises of Harlem Renaissance poetry—premises they had played a central role in formulating.[21]

Brown's response to Locke's idea of the New Negro's cultural maturity was different from that of most of his contemporaries, with the noteworthy exceptions of Langston Hughes and Zora Neale Hurston. Brown was not interested in the African American as an exotic, a primitive, or a model solution to the problems of modern man. Nor was he especially interested in Africa. Brown was interested not in the myth of the old Negro, but in the old Negro as he actually was—the old Negro as Brown himself had seen him and knew him, the old Negro as he lived even during a period of constant talk of the New Negro. Locke was impressed by Brown's sense of a black ethos, his grasp of the subtle variations in folklife from place to place, and his mining of "the communal wisdom of the folk." Thus Locke concluded, "I believe *Southern Roads* ushers in a new era in Negro folk-expression and brings a new dimension in Negro folk-portraiture." Literary criticism and cultural and social history along with poetry became essential components in Brown's exploration of African American life. Significantly, portraiture was a key concept for national FWP officials.[22]

Botkin and Brown had been in contact before they began to work on the FWP, and their views on American poetry and history and on the significance of race and ethnicity in America had been converging. In a review in *Opportunity* of Brown's *The Negro in American Fiction* (1937) and *Negro Poetry and Drama* (1937), Botkin argued, "These books convince us of the importance of the comparative method and the wisdom of placing emphasis on the Negro's participation in America's cultural diversity and social action instead of his contribution to a dominant pattern—one of the stereotypes of criticism in this field." Botkin hailed Brown for having "inaugurated a new era in Negro literary criticism," an era Botkin greeted with enthusiasm: "The 'contribution' stereotype is dead! Long live participation!"[23]

Both Botkin and Brown rejected what they termed the "contributions approach" to the study of African American culture and history. That approach, they argued, treated African Americans as a group set apart from the life of white America, thus reinforcing the idea of separateness. A focus on social problems in the African American community had led to an almost exclusive preoccupation with a depiction of black culture as undergoing disorganization and decay as it tried to cope with modern life. The contributions approach reinforced the idea that distinguished individuals in the group being examined were contributing to a group with a superior culture. Those who emphasized social problems tended to assume that a folk culture could not adapt to American life. This approach was similar to the methodology anthropologist Paul Radin claimed led his fellow scholars invariably to assume that "primitive" cultures were in a state of decay and could not adapt to new circumstances. In arguing for a view that stressed black participation in American life, Botkin and Brown were denying the validity of these assumptions. They focused on the African American as a participant in American society and as an integral part of American life. Whether as slaves or as a segregated group, blacks had participated in creating American culture, and their experience was part of the American experience.[24]

Looking back at the FWP, Brown described the project's treatment of African Americans in these terms: "Many Negro historians believe that what is called Negro history should be approached as the history of the Negro in America, not as a separate entity. They insist that the Negro has been an integral part of

American life, however grudgingly received, a participant quite as much as a contributor."[25]

Brown's criticism, like his poetry, sought, in the words of Alain Locke, "a common denominator." The New Negro would emerge when the old Negro was truly known. For the most part Brown argued that American literature had hidden the old Negro behind stereotypes that "evolved at the dictates of social policy." His literary criticism, like much of the sociological writing of the 1930s, examined the social consequences of racial stereotypes with their omissions and exaggerations. Brown's argument was clear-cut: "Like other oppressed and exploited minorities, the Negro has been interpreted in a way to justify his exploiters." His work was part of a 1930s counterattack on literary traditions in which white authors who claimed "to know the Negro better than Negroes themselves" had portrayed contented slaves, wretched freemen, comic Negroes, brute Negroes, tragic mulattos, local color Negroes, and exotic primitives.[26]

Both Brown's and Botkin's work in folklore and literature had grown into an interest in folk history. To each of them it was a new kind of history in which individual voices revealed the nature of the folk group's experience and history. It was a small shift from the kind of poetry Brown had been writing to the kind of history he wanted to do on the FWP.

Brown spent much of his time on the Writers' Project reviewing state guidebook material to see if it gave accurate and adequate attention to blacks. He did more than correct the work of others. His strictures became rationales for programs he and others advocated. Brown sought material about the life and history of ordinary blacks as well as about the black elite. His search complemented the searches of his FWP colleagues in the national office.[27]

In the 1930s, romantic nationalist, pluralist, and radical assumptions among liberal-left intellectuals cut across racial lines. Brown was not alone. Lawrence Reddick, a black historian writing in 1938, argued, "The historian may become more penetrating if he turns away a little more from the articulate professional classes to the welfare, feelings and thoughts of the common folk—the domestic servants, the tenant farmers, the dark men on the city streets." Brown's FWP colleague Botkin envisioned a new American history: a "history produced by a collaboration of the folklorist and the historian with each other and with the folk; a history of the whole people . . . in which the people are the historians as well as the history, telling their own story in their own words—Everyman's history, for Everyman to read." Contrary to earlier white scholars who had seen black folklore as African, not American, a white contributor to *America Now: An Inquiry into Civilization in the United States* (1938) argued that African

American lore was "as indigenous to our soil as the legendary cowboy or gold-seeking frontiersman." To a significant degree, FWP guidebooks, ex-slave narratives, life history collections, and ethnic studies reflect this outlook, although other points of view held by local Federal Writers can also be found in them.[28]

Brown tried to ensure that material that reflected the premises of evolutionary anthropology and contained racist statements, such as "while the Australians do not have . . . kinky hair . . . they are still lower" and "[blacks] dominate most other groups in their love for pageantry and fancy dress," were removed from the drafts of guidebook essays. Using direct but understated language, he and his assistants were fairly successful. They told Ohio Federal Writers that the above quotation about African American dress "is a general statement lacking proof." They informed Louisiana Federal Writers that the idea that whites had "a natural repugnance for an inferior race was difficult to prove."[29]

Brown emphasized accuracy and fairness. He told Wisconsin Federal Writers that it was more correct to say African American soldiers were massacred at Fort Pillow "than that they died heroically," and that if they were going to give so much attention to George Washington Carver, then they should certainly mention H. E. Just, whose scientific accomplishments were greater. Why, Brown wanted to know, was there no material on the antebellum free Negro? A comment such as "threats of cruel punishment," he insisted, was a "whitewash," since slaves were not merely threatened with punishment. Brown argued that humorist Octavius Roy Cohen, despite his great popularity, should not be treated as the final authority on black life in Birmingham. The Alabama guidebook later gave Cohen a paragraph but noted, "There is, however, much minstrel exaggeration in [Cohen's] presentation of characters, and the dialect does not always conform to the Negro's speech."[30]

By carefully monitoring guidebook copy from northern as well as southern states, Brown made sure that African Americans were not totally ignored or always portrayed in unfavorable terms. But Brown wanted to achieve more than that. He instructed Florida Federal Writers that city descriptions in the guidebook copy needed material on the black population. Such material, he pointed out, could appeal to readers who saw American diversity in terms of picturesque local color. While Brown noted that mention of the African American community could add "color" to the city description, he also insisted that this was necessary to make the guides representative of what he saw as American reality.[31]

What constituted representative treatment was often a subject of debate when national FWP officials dealt with state Federal Writers, who often did not

share their liberal, secular, and egalitarian values. The most clear-cut examples
came from the South, but the conflict occurred elsewhere as well. Responding
to Brown's editorial comments on the Florence, Alabama, copy, state director
Myrtle Miles complained to assistant national FWP director George Cronyn
that "a striking similarity in all cities will result if we give the same data on the
Negro in each of the cities where he simply comprises a part of the laboring
class and has *contributed nothing to the city's culture or beauty*" (emphasis added). She
concluded with what she saw as a reasonable editorial concern: "We do not
wish attention to the Negro to overbalance that of your foreign population in
other states, for example, or to seem fantastic and perhaps offensive to Alabamians." In her view, Alabama blacks could be thought of as comparable to
a foreign population. Her major concern was not offending her primary audience, Alabamians, who for her were only the whites, and who had the culture
to which blacks had not contributed.[32]

Brown spent a good deal of time criticizing the ethnography of local Federal Writers, who most often were implicitly cultural evolutionists (although
few would have been familiar with the expression) and either measured everything in terms of contributions or saw only disorganization and decay. North
Carolina Federal Writers, for example, thought the African American contributed to the state's folkways and lore only by "perpetuating Anglo-Saxon folkways." Washington officials looked at the same phenomenon in a different light.
They saw "the part played by the Negro in adapting Anglo-Saxon lore to his
own genius and purpose," and this "remodeling and adapting," they insisted,
constituted a distinctive contribution, a new lore reflecting a folk culture in
transition. Furthermore, they insisted, some of this lore had African roots.[33]

Brown's requests for more material dealing with African Americans were
often rebuffed by southern state FWP directors, who thought that Brown "wants
us to tell things about the colored population that we would never dream of
telling about the white." Myrtle Miles, Alabama FWP director, argued that Brown
was biased and that his idea of the facts "could not possibly be received by our
fellow citizens of good judgment with approval." She concluded that "Alabamians understand the Alabama Negro and the general Negro situation in
Alabama better than a critic whose life has been spent in another section of the
country, however studious, however learned, he may be."[34]

While Edwin Bjorkman, North Carolina FWP director, claimed to be fully in
sympathy with the policy of doing justice to the African American community,
he also feared an adverse reaction from North Carolina whites if the guide
covered activities of blacks that were overlooked in the case of whites. In his

opinion, Brown was "harp[ing] on the status of the negro."[35] The fact that Bjorkman's fears were not groundless quickly became clear when the North Carolina guide was published. However, Brown, unlike Bjorkman and other southern state FWP directors, rejected the view that the sensitivities of white southerners toward any discussion of blacks should determine guidebook treatment of African Americans. After the publication of the North Carolina guide, Isaac London, editor of the *Rockingham Post-Dispatch*, made it clear that he thought the guide had given "a grossly unfair and false description of Rockingham. If this sort of reading matter depicts others as inaccurately as it does Rockingham, then the book should be consigned to the furnace. It certainly should not be circulated in this or any other state."[36]

What so upset London was the guide's description of Saturday, "Negro day" in Rockingham: "Since [the Negroes] live mostly on the cotton plantations, where the land is level, the rows long, and the summer sun scorching, Rockingham grants them one day to call their own. The carnival spirit prevails as whole families stroll about in their best clothes." *The State* magazine advised the Rockingham editor, "Take It Easy Ike!" and noted that the guide had not dismissed Rockingham as a "nigger town." The first paragraph of the guide's description, commented *The State*, mentioned interesting facts about the city's history and resources, and as for the paragraph that so offended London, "it applies to most every other town in the state."[37]

The draft of the local guide to Beaufort, South Carolina, described African Americans as "a picturesque group," "a happy people, primitive, unmoral," who "for all their seventy odd years of freedom . . . have never really learned to stand alone." Brown objected. Mabel Montgomery, South Carolina FWP director, pointed out that the sponsoring group, the Beaufort County Clover Club, whose members, with one exception, were the descendants of Federal army officers and northern missionaries, liked the guide. Since the president of the club was a Smith College graduate, Montgomery maintained, she could be expected to take a broad view of Beaufort and its black inhabitants. Montgomery argued that Chlotilde R. Martin, who had written the draft, also had a broad perspective. According to Montgomery, Martin had been all over South Carolina, "therefore her viewpoint is not altogether local." As intake secretary for the Beaufort ERA (Emergency Relief Administration), Martin, Montgomery noted, had "dealt with Negroes daily" and thus had "secured an accurate knowledge of the mores of these people." In a southern context, social work was often modeled on the traditional patronizing charity whites extended to blacks. What Beaufort needed, Montgomery wrote Washington, was "understanding treatment. Beaufort residents are tired of being portrayed from a Northern viewpoint."[38]

Montgomery thought the choice was between a "picturesque and interesting account or a sociological discourse carrying a Northern slant," between a genuine and popular account or a controversial one. Brown responded that he saw no necessary connection between a genuine account and one that would be popular with a white South Carolina audience. He felt that "half truth is not enough, however picturesque," and that what was offered as picturesque addressed sociological issues in a simplistic and misleading way. Brown did not dismiss claims that Martin was well informed, but he found the idea that "an Intake Secretary of the ERA is necessarily a better authority on mores than some of America's best known sociologists (southern in birth and upbringing) is hardly warranted."[39]

Here was a test of national FWP officials' desire to reconcile provincialism and cosmopolitanism. For them cosmopolitanism meant a recognition that no one tradition had a complete knowledge of the value and meaning of life, and therefore knowledge of other traditions would broaden one's own perspective. Being provincial was not, in their opinion, incompatible with trying to learn about other traditions. They found support for the idea that provincialism and cosmopolitanism were compatible in the work of anthropologist Franz Boas and his students. Boasian anthropology had strengthened cosmopolitan ideas among intellectuals. National officials objected to parochialism, the inability or unwillingness to look beyond one's own tradition. The southern FWP writers, for the most part, lacked any belief in cultural relativity: "When I am asked to tell what the negro has contributed to the culture in such different cities as Winston-Salem and Elizabeth City," Edwin Bjorkman declared, "I feel something like despair. In one of these cities you hardly see him. . . . In the other you see him only too frequently, but that is all that can be said about him." Bjorkman thought of culture in artistic, not anthropological terms, and of art as high culture. This was a point of view national FWP officials rejected, since they thought of culture as a way of life, not only as artistic creations. They saw cultures in relative terms and found much to admire in art outside the Western tradition of high culture.[40]

The difference between the vision of America held by national FWP officials and that of project workers in the South was clear, but only occasionally directly stated. The Georgia FWP writers who worked on *Drums and Shadows: Survival Studies among the Georgia Coastal Negroes* (1940) did not see their search for African survivals as simply part of the argument about whether African cul-

ture had survived and black Americans had a cultural heritage and identity with visible African roots. Rather, they placed the issue of survivals in the context of an evolutionary theory of culture. They thought of culture as a series of stages in a progressive human development. Cultural materials from an earlier and inferior stage might survive, but with progress they would disappear. They linked these ideas to a view that individual psychology had a biologically and racially determined character. Thus, "he responds under excitement to the fundamental racial traits of his heritage. . . . It is these natural reactions that link the educated African-American citizen to his African forbearer and to the humbler types of Negroes, still primitive in his outlook." It was to the latter, "the survival type," that Georgia FWP writers claimed one had to turn to as a source of folklore. The evolutionary view precluded any recognition of cultural relativity; any sense that acculturation, change, exchange, and adaptation was a two-way avenue; and any acknowledgment that folklore was in part a product of the creative and functional response of a culture to a new situation. In short, Georgia FWP writers were in total disagreement with national FWP officials. *Drums and Shadows* was published, but with almost no narrative or analysis.[41]

The attitude of the Georgia FWP toward African survivals is only one example of the treatment in the southern guides of the African American community from a distance, from the outside. The southern guides almost always discuss the black community in the third person. The use of "they" for African Americans always implies that the writer and other white residents of the region are the southerners. Thus there are Alabamians and the Alabama Negro, Beaufort residents and Beaufort Negroes, Tar Heels and North Carolina Negroes. Brown had plans for an FWP study to be titled "The Negro as American." The logical southern corollary would have been "The Negro as Southerner." Such a study was never proposed and for an obvious reason. It would have required white southern FWP workers to broaden the term "southerner" to include all the residents of the region, just as national FWP officials wanted to broaden the term "American." *The Negro in Virginia* (1940), significantly not "the Negro as Virginian," was the most that could be done. W. T. Couch, FWP Southeast regional director, warned that it would be a good idea not to release it until after the Virginia state guide was published.[42]

Reading the landscape for the meaning behind appearances is not a simple empirical task. The readings Brown suggested and those southern white FWP workers offered represented contrasting values. Brown could convince them to mention that there were black middle-class professionals as well as laborers in their cities. He could not, however, change their assumptions about the social and cultural meaning of the visible landscape. In the Mississippi guidebook the white author of the essay on the Negro found the Mississippi Negro, "a genial mass of remarkable qualities . . . carefree and shrewd. . . . As for the so-called Negro question—that, too, is just another problem he has left for the white man to cope with."[43]

Brown was deeply upset that he had not been able to prevent the publication of that essay. In the end, the southern guides take their place in a discussion among white southerners about tradition and change in the region. True, the discussion was affected by the New Deal experience, but it was still a dialogue in which significant parts of the southern population did not participate. The guidebook format did not lend itself to the examination of the daily life of any group. There was room to mention details about African American life, but not to study it. The inherent limitations of the guides were further compounded by the racial assumptions of Federal Writers, who were overwhelmingly white.

Brown knew that good ethnographic description required an insider's as well as an outsider's perspective. Even accurate and sympathetic material on African Americans in most state guides reflected an outsider's view of contributions and social problems. In Virginia an all-black unit directed by Roscoe Lewis of Hampton Institute wrote the essay on the African American and captured a perspective on black culture found nowhere else in the guides. Stereotyped local color scenes assume a different meaning when seen from a black perspective. What is taken for reality by whites is described by blacks as merely the outer appearance that shelters the inner reality. Many guides noted African American neighborhoods and business districts but did not mention the function of the business street or the race pride of blacks as the Virginia guide did: "The lure of the crowd is strong among Virginia Negroes. Every city and town has a 'street' that serves as the social and business center of Negro life. Here Negroes from every walk of life congregate to purchase from Negro merchants, to ply their trades, to discuss the latest developments in Negro America, or simply to see who else is abroad. Here race pride is triumphant; drug stores, cafes, barber shops, pool rooms, grocery stores, theaters, beauty parlors, and garages are operated by and for Negroes."[44]

Virginia's black Federal Writers knew how black street scenes looked to outsiders who did not understand their meaning. They sought to explain that such scenes were a sign of a healthy, functioning culture, not an emblem of disorganization: "To the uninitiated, the crowd is a group of idlers wasting time in meaningless banter. That banter, however, is the Negro's escape from a day of labor in the white man's world. No matter how carefree the outward appearance of Negroes may be, behind their happy dispositions is the imprint of poverty, disease, and suffering—birthmarks of a people living precariously, but of a people wholly Virginian."[45] They knew they were not a foreign population, but Americans who were also both blacks and Virginians.

The FWP black studies Brown and his colleagues in the Washington office encouraged focused on the individual and his or her relationship to a culture in a state of transition. The underlying assumptions were that black participation in American life resulted in a constant reworking of traditional African American lore, incorporation of white lore into black patterns, and the creation of new materials that could take root in old traditions. The FWP ex-slave narratives deal with the last generation of slaves and thus with both slavery and freedom, a transition point in African American history. Brown initiated a study on the antislavery struggle that treated black participation in the movement. Appropriately, it was titled "Go Down, Moses." Brown also envisioned an FWP "Portrait of the Negro as American," a "composite portrait . . . set squarely against the background of America," an "essay in social history and biography." Individual blacks would be examined in a cultural context, and the standard of measurement would be as much that of the black folk as of the dominant white culture. In the contemporary period Joe Louis, Father Divine, and Bojangles Robinson would receive ample space, but they were to be examined in their relation to less well known African Americans, "the sharecroppers, factory workers, students, businessmen—all those who make up the mosaic of Negro life in America."[46]

"Portrait of the Negro as American" was never completed. There are, however, several FWP-published books on African Americans that illustrate the approach Brown was following. The emphasis, Brown wrote, was on social history and biography, the folk culture, and the individuals who embodied its traditions and values. In a WPA press release Brown hailed *The Negro in Virginia*, a product of the Negro unit of the Virginia FWP, as "the first book of its kind to treat adequately the part played by the Negroes in the state's history." In his opinion, it examined "facts little known to the American public and often neglected by students of history." This had been accomplished, he maintained, by using testimony from ex-slaves. Employing the slaves' "colorful folk-speech" helped give a fuller "social picture." Such a method constituted "a departure from the usual historical reporting." Today *The Negro in Virginia* stands as a precursor of historical writings that use oral history and that focus on cultural and social history. It also reflects the romantic nationalism and pluralism of the

FWP and a larger concern in American anthropology and literature about the relationship between the individual and his or her culture and between tradition and modernity, especially as these issues manifested themselves in the lives of American minorities, cultures on the cutting edge of the transition from agrarian to industrial life.[47]

The Negro unit of the Virginia FWP presented a black perspective on events that had too often only been observed from the point of view of white Virginians. Thus, Robert E. Lee's surrender at Appomattox was described not as a defeat but as a victory that assured black slaves their freedom. The role of African Americans as a people "who have helped build America" was a major theme. Black culture as it was created and transmitted from generation to generation by those who lived in the Great House and those who lived on slave row and by those who were artisans and those who were called free Negroes was captured in the words of those who made and lived the African American tradition.[48]

By allowing the reader to listen to the voices of former slaves, *The Negro in Virginia* taught about the religion and family life of the slaves, about what they thought about the life they had lived, and about how they had reacted to such momentous events as the Civil War and Reconstruction. This method was also used to describe black life from Reconstruction through the Great Depression. The churches and schools as well as country and urban life received treatment that would have been impossible using the contributions approach. A broad-gauged history of African Americans—what would today be called social and cultural history—national FWP officials called a folk history. As in *The Negro in Virginia*, they intended to achieve that kind of history by recording the accounts of individual members of the folk group, whose collective voices would author an African American folk history. Such a history combined with similar studies of other groups in the United States would relate the history of American folk groups, not as isolated or peripheral cultures, "but rather as integral parts, associated and active in the cosmopolitan life of the nation."[49]

The approach followed in *The Negro in Virginia* was not confined to the South. Similar studies were undertaken in several northern cities, although only *The Negro in New York* (1967) has ever been published. That study depicted a viable, dynamic, and creative African American folk culture surviving in northern cities as well as in the rural South. Both *The Negro in Virginia* and *The Negro in New York* portrayed the creative strength of black Americans living through great changes in American and black life.

Not all the FWP black studies followed an approach that stressed folk tradition and black participation in American life. *Cavalcade of the American Negro* (1940), a publication of the Illinois Writers' Program was organized around the contributions approach and had exactly the weaknesses Botkin and Brown had found in that way of writing about the black experience in America. It sought to win higher regard for African Americans by stressing individual accomplishments in a manner that separated individuals from the group, ignored black cultural life, and implied that the standards of the dominant group were the only measurements of achievement. On the other hand, the Arkansas Writers' Program's *Survey of Negroes in Little Rock and North Little Rock* (1941) followed the social problems approach. Sponsored by the Urban League, the book tried to present a sympathetic portrait of problems in black life. The discussion and statistics, however, were so unremittingly bleak that the reader could only conclude that African American life was in a state of utter disorganization and decay. Sympathetic or not, the study portrayed a black culture totally inadequate for the demands of modern life. Perhaps *The Negro in Virginia* and *The Negro in New York* erred in the other direction by stressing the strength of black culture over the damage done to it by white oppression. Reconciling both perspectives has remained a major challenge in African American historiography. In the 1930s, however, the FWP focus on black culture was not a matter of choosing one of several existing approaches, but of working out a new way of looking at African American history that professional historians would not develop until the late 1960s.[50]

In *They Seek a City* (1945), Arna Bontemps and Jack Conroy rewrote and expanded material they had first begun collecting while on the Illinois Federal Writers' Project. *They Seek a City* followed the participation rather than the contributions approach. Black migration was the central focus of the book. Bontemps and Conroy dealt with both southern and northern and rural and urban African American folk traditions. They focused on a southern black folk tradition as it grew and adapted to the northern city. Although there were many capsule biographies blended in with generalized descriptions of the group, the creative reciprocity between the individual and the folk group was not analyzed. Nor had it been in *The Negro in Virginia* or *The Negro in New York*. All three works sought to be evocative and stressed narrative rather than analysis. But the voices of real individuals were much less prominent in *They Seek a City*. That work instead contained composite individuals, or typical representative group portraits—the "they" of the title. In a work that sought as much to evoke a folk experience as to explain it in historical and sociological terms, this was not a serious weakness. It was a limitation that *The Negro in Virginia* and *The*

Negro in New York shared to a lesser degree. In none of these works does the reader learn to understand or feel the relationship, the tension, between individuality and folk pattern. As history they richly portray aspects of black life. As literature they constitute a wonderful source of fragments, but the historical chronology alone does not provide a structure that highlights the universal dimensions inherent in the subject matter.[51]

The differences between traditional ways of discussing recent immigrants and ethnic groups and the way the FWP tried to study them paralleled the differences between traditional ways of looking at the lives of African Americans and the FWP's approach to writing about that group. Questions about American nationality, identity, and culture were also questions about whether Old World traditions could survive and adapt to modern American life and whether such traditions were barriers to succeeding in the modern world. Was there more than one way of being American and of participating in modern society, or did the white middle-class Protestant culture offer the only viable model?

FWP officials thought that European ethnic groups were a significant part of American culture. In writing about ethnic groups, essayists found it impossible not to address questions about who and what constituted American culture and the future of that culture. Terms such as "Americanization," "assimilation," "melting pot," "contributions," and "cultural pluralism" reflected views of American culture and nationality. The FWP inherited the vocabulary that had dominated discussion of immigration in the first third of the twentieth century. Project works dealing with ethnic groups can be divided into three categories: state and local guides, ethnic studies that were undertaken through local or state initiative, and the nationally directed studies.

Only after World War II was immigration apotheosized as a quintessential part of the American experience. Historian Oscar Handlin argued, "Once I thought to write a history of the immigrants in America. Then I discovered the immigrants *were* American History." John F. Kennedy honored that history with *A Nation of Immigrants* (1964). Old-stock Americans, however, have not always celebrated immigration as a positive factor in American life, as a history of recurring nativist movements testifies. But confidence in the power of the New World environment to transform human nature was also an important idea in American thinking. The land would automatically bring unity out of diversity. Nineteenth-century Americans, historian John Higham writes, had "fashioned an image of themselves as an inclusive nationality, at once diverse and homogeneous, ever improving as it assimilated many types of men into a unified, superior people." But the shift in immigration from northern to southern and eastern Europe aroused grave anxieties. The "new" immigrants were viewed as a social problem, not as a "dynamic factor in American development." So dominant was this approach that as late as the 1930s historian Marcus L. Hansen remarked that "by long established custom whoever speaks of immigration refers to it as a problem." Under stress many Americans would lose confidence in the nation's ability to assimilate immigrants. In special circumstances immigrants were viewed as an internal minority posing a threat to the nation's cultural integrity, unity, and survival.[52]

The idea of Americanization was a twentieth-century phenomenon. Anxiety about national, cultural, and social cohesion stimulated a movement to Americanize the immigrants. No longer did old-stock Americans assume that assimilation would be automatic. It seemed to many that the assimilative process would have to be consciously directed. Americanization reflected not only nativistic but also democratic and cosmopolitan traditions. One aspect of Americanization emphasized the transformation of the immigrants. They abandon their native language and culture and give their undivided loyalties to the new nation. There were more liberal and tolerant approaches. Liberals argued that each immigrant group should preserve the best in its heritage and that each group had something to "contribute" to America. The mingling of old and new, they believed, could create a finer American culture. However, the idea of immigrant gifts or contributions could, and often did, become an easily parroted phrase devoid of any significant content.[53]

In time, the power of the pluralist ideas would make terms such as "Americanization" and "melting pot" seem offensive. This occurred partly because the ambiguity of these terms has been forgotten. The melting pot image was used to symbolize either a process that required the stripping away of inherited culture and conformity to Anglo-Saxon customs or a process in which American society as well as the immigrant was changed. One reviewer criticized Israel Zangwill's famous play *The Melting Pot* (1908) because of its vision of an unfinished American culture. He was concerned about the "indiscriminate commingling of alien races on our soil" and could not see how "the scum and dregs of Europe" could improve America. In the 1930s terms like "Americanization" and "melting pot" were still widely used, but in varying, sometimes contradictory ways.[54]

These terms can be found in the FWP guidebook treatment of ethnic groups. It was these terms, not pluralism, that still dominated the discussion. The immigration restriction law passed in 1924 had, in effect, defined the national character in terms of existing ethnic components. One unexpected result of the end of unrestricted immigration was a visible increase in ethnic assimilation. Ethnic pluralism was, in part, a product of and a protest against assimilation. The FWP guides, however, for the most part talked of ethnic groups in the context of Americanization, assimilation, and the melting pot.[55]

Many state guidebooks had essays focusing on "racial elements." State FWP directors were advised by the national office that "racial and foreign groups are also a part of the state's historical picture, the various strains of immigrants, where they settled, what they brought to the culture of the State, how they lived at first, and what survivals of earlier folk ways still persist." Although essayists were instructed not to "write up foreign or racial groups as independent bits" and that "the essays should be closely integrated," the various guidebook essays rarely had themes that tied the material in them together. Not every state guide had an essay on "foreign groups." Sometimes the different groups were treated as independent "bits," as one group after another was mentioned with a short comment but with no effort to relate the groups to one another or to a common whole. A few essays simply gave statistics and dates and no other comments or analysis. But even this represented a significant departure from linking foreign groups to a discussion of social problems.[56]

The state guides provide evidence of varying attitudes toward the future of American culture. In some instances the use of the term "Americanization" reflected a vision of a future in which ethnic groups had disappeared. The Minnesota guide noted that "with the Americanization and the cessation of immigration, the practice of holding services in a foreign language has steadily declined." In Portland, Maine, there were "small Americanized groups of Irish, Jewish, Italian, and Scandinavian people." The evidence that these groups were Americanized was that the "foreign quarters" were disappearing. The New Jersey guide observed that "the Europeans wear American clothes, talk 'American' and in many cases have exchanged their own traditions for those of their adopted country." In this case, however, the fact of Americanization elicited a sense of loss: "The process has cost New Jersey many colorful ceremonies formerly common among immigrants." Nor was Americanization always presented as a one-way process: "In the inescapable process of Americanization, the city's races and nationalities are slowly losing their individuality. A strong reciprocal influence between them and the older American population shows itself in many spheres." The contributions of members of ethnic groups was offered as additional evidence of Americanization: "An interesting feature of all these groups is the extent to which their representatives have achieved distinction in the arts and professions."[57]

The guides demonstrated a renewed confidence in the nation's ability to absorb new groups. Americanization was again seen as inevitable; it did not have to be directed. Paradoxically, this renewed confidence could be attributed to the Depression. In New Jersey's "large cities economic necessity has called forth considerable cooperation among the once isolated groups. The depression itself proved in most cases a uniting force."[58]

Differing definitions of Americanization appeared in the guides. Sometimes it seemed to mean only that ethnic groups would learn to conform to the culture that existed before their arrival. At other times there was an indication that perhaps a new culture was being created out of the mix of peoples. Occasionally there was a pluralistic vision of American culture and nationality.

Some of the New England guides reflected a special anxiety about what impact ethnic groups would have on what the essayists identified as traditional New England culture. In the introductory essay to the New Hampshire guide the writer asserted that "New Hampshire folks are the merriest of the Puritans." He realized that "there are those, of course, who say they are no longer Puritans at all, so large is the infusion of French-Canadian blood and of that very recently from Europe." But he was confident that "the old influences that made New England New England, and America America still prevail. These influences have the power to make over the new stocks into consonance with the old."[59] Massachusetts, however, celebrated its new cosmopolitanism: "Many new strands have been added to Anglo-Saxon culture. Slavic, Semitic, and Celtic influences have permeated Massachusetts thought, enriching folkways, enlivening speech, and giving a new perspective to graphic art, music and literature."[60]

New York and Pennsylvania emphasized their long-standing cosmopolitan traditions. Thus the New York guide argued that "the restriction of immigration during the past few years has given the potpourri of peoples in the State a chance to boil down to an even consistency." And "out of this welter of peoples, faiths, customs, and influences, Pennsylvania had somehow wrought the miracle of a homogeneous, and in a large sense, truly indigenous culture." In both these visions of the melting pot, American culture as well as the immigrant is transformed into something new.[61]

The common element in all the guides is that ethnic groups are viewed as a dynamic factor in American culture, not as a social problem. The Iowa guide offered a vision of American culture that combined a melting pot and a pluralist vision, ideals usually incompatible: "In general, racial lines are tending to grow less distinct as the population merges into a unified whole. Enriching the culture of Iowa, many groups have retained the identity and customs they brought with them from the Old World."[62] In neighboring Minnesota, however, the melting pot image symbolized a process in which the immigrant is stripped of his or her culture and learns to adapt to Anglo-Saxon culture. In part these varied responses were a product of different state traditions and different contributors to the guides.[63]

As the guides neared completion, state officials considered other work that could be undertaken. Numerous projects were started but never finished. However, some ethnic studies were published. They were the product not of a coherent nationwide program but of the interests of local project workers and state FWP officials and the presence of an interested sponsor. These studies suffer from poor editing and writing and are largely compiled from secondary sources. Nevertheless, they do address basic questions about the role of immigrant groups in American culture.

For the most part these studies argued that ethnic groups would disappear from American life. In the preface to *The Armenians in Massachusetts* (1937), Ray Billington, Massachusetts FWP director, wrote that the "colorful, changing pattern of old-world design is still perceptible, but it is fading and disappearing. . . . The slow process of assimilation is inexorable."[64] *The Italians of New York* makes the same point: "The Italians will disappear in that countless mass of native Americans whose origin it is as difficult to establish as it is to trace the streams whose waters have flowed into the ocean."[65] The *Bohemian Flats* guidebook is about a section of Minneapolis where recent immigrants had found they could live cheaply. The emphasis of this brief pamphlet is always on the "quaint and charming." The perspective is that of the outsider, the tourist. The social dynamics of the community are almost totally ignored. The purpose of the pamphlet is to "preserve for posterity a story that will soon be lost."[66]

The main themes of *The Italians of Omaha* are more complex. A chapter titled "The Americanization Process" argues that "a desirable exchange in this social adjustment is giving to the immigrant the best the community has to offer and permitting him to retain the best he has brought from his homeland." "Little Italy" is a part of "a melting pot city." If "Little Italy with its old world picturesqueness will disappear under the press of Americanizing influences," this does not necessarily mean that Italian identity will disappear. Thus one member of the community argues, "Though America must be first does not mean that we cannot cherish a love for our mother country. A man does not need to hate his mother because he loves his wife."[67]

These locally initiated ethnic studies were often sponsored by immigrant associations and thus represent an authorized view; this is how group leaders chose to present the group to the outside world. These studies have a defensive tone. The study of the Armenians sees assimilation into a preexisting and superior American culture as evidence of Armenian accomplishment: "The American-born Armenians in Massachusetts, as well as in other States, can hardly be distinguished from other Americans. With the possible exception of their food, which is prepared for them by their parents, there is nothing foreign in their customs and habits. . . . The Armenians as a group, always sensitive to an environment superior to that of their origin, are rapidly merging into the American pattern."[68]

Winning acceptance by indicating a willingness to conform, by endorsing a conservative version of the melting pot, and by emphasizing contributions by individuals in the group being studied appeared to be the major goal of these studies. One stated purpose of *The Italians of Omaha* was to "enable readers to think of the Italian not as an outlandish individual, but as one who is striving to preserve the rights and blessings he helped establish on our shores." *The Italians of New York* ingeniously argued that the great Roman civilization was a product of a melting pot of races, and thus "great civilizations are the product, not of one, but of many peoples." Italian contributions to every aspect of New York life are mentioned, and various criticisms of Italians are either refuted or examined in the light of mitigating circumstances.[69]

The sections on culture in these locally initiated studies are merely descriptive lists of Old World customs. There is no discussion of what function, if any, these customs play in the life of the ethnic group. It was these and other weaknesses that national FWP officials wanted to eliminate from future ethnic studies. Botkin and Royse cooperated in setting up a variety of social-ethnic studies throughout the country. These studies dealt with individuals in relationship to their ethnic group and used oral sources and folklore to understand the ethnic experience.

The emphasis in the social-ethnic studies was on participation and acculturation rather than on individual leaders and contributions. Henry Alsberg had a grand, liberal, and pluralistic vision of the story the social-ethnic studies would tell: "The building up of our country knows no parallel in historical times—in the influx of peoples from all ends of the earth, and in the freedom and opportunities which beckoned to the impoverished and oppressed of all lands. How a social and cultural unity was achieved by these people, without stamping cultural differences into one mold, producing the unique American civilization, and how the fabric was enlarged is the crux of our story."[70]

The topics to be covered were extensive: Old World backgrounds, migration and settlements, geographical distributions, living standards, adjustment and adaptation, organized life, the foreign language press, and folk culture and expression. The emphasis was on "ways of living and making a living." Three types of ethnic studies were planned: intensive studies of a single group, cross-sectional studies of whole communities, and extensive regional studies. Royse constantly emphasized that ethnic groups "should always be studied in relation to the rest of the community—to avoid the overstressing of exotic things and also to avoid distortions."[71] Instead of emphasizing the separateness and peculiarities of a group, "the aim should be to show how the group functions in the life of the community, through contact; to what extent it varies from the general pattern through survival of Old World traits; and how it contributes to cultural diversity, through its effect on the community . . . changing the pattern as well as being changed."[72]

The goal was to create "human documents." Otherwise, FWP officials thought, these studies would "become dry academic pamphlets which nobody will read." In a proposed examination of Detroit auto workers, the idea was to let a typical member of each group tell his or her story between descriptive accounts of the group as a whole. "The significance of any worthwhile study," Royse explained to a state FWP director, "is always in terms of human interest: as living, earning a living, cultural aspects (always tied up with earning a living)." Oral history and folklore were the key human documents in these investigations. The folklore studies under Botkin's direction were closely coordinated with the social-ethnic inquiries.[73]

Royse was keenly aware that how scholars examined ethnic groups reflected their view of America. He rejected an approach that emphasized the outstanding individuals in a group. For one thing, many had gotten ahead by "sloughing off their traditional culture. . . . Moreover the majority of every group is made up of workers, farmers, and others of lower social and economic status whose culture is very imperfectly revealed in that of the rare 'outstanding' individual." He was convinced that the participation approach held much greater validity than the contributions approach. Royse denied the usefulness of a model that "implies that the culture of old-American groups constitutes 'American civilization' and that bits of immigrant culture are added to it." He labeled the idea that "American culture is the culture of the old-American, Anglo-Saxon group" a historical myth comparable to the Nazi myth about German nationality. To those who argued that ethnicity was a transitional phase, Royse responded that hyphenated Americans were a product of American circumstances, not a passing stage: "The culture of the American people at any time is a composite of the culture of these groups." For him metaphoric language that posited "a constant pattern" absorbing waves of immigrants or "a separate stream with a cultural momentum of its own" was misleading. He maintained that the Polish, Irish, Greek, or French population in traditionally white Anglo-Saxon Protestant New England or elsewhere "is American culture, not merely a contributor to American culture." Put another way, "their culture is contemporary American culture as truly as is the culture of Iowa-American farmers or Appalachian-American hill-billies."[74]

B. A. Botkin, Morton Royse, and Sterling Brown saw a greater potential for cultural resiliency in the subcultures of racial and ethnic minorities than did the majority of their contemporaries as well as an earlier generation of scholars, or even many later scholars. Like recent social historians they viewed these groups as participants in American life who helped shape the larger American society and culture and who in participating in American life created subcultures of their own. Nowhere did they see a closed system. Rather, they thought that American diversity meant that America was always in the process of becoming. Acknowledging the participation and the adaptability of such groups, national FWP officials thought, would help redefine American identity in more inclusive terms. They also thought that an acknowledgment of what they saw as American reality would guarantee that America would remain an open society following an open road, fluid not fixed, like the personality and culture Walt Whitman had celebrated. Ideologically, they saw portraying these cultures as creative adaptations to American life, rather than as either inferior or decaying, as a step toward a new definition of American community that would contribute to reform.

The gap between vision and accomplishment was large. In the end, the only social-ethnic study ever published was *The Albanian Struggle in the Old World and New* (1939). While it was superior to the local or state-initiated ethnic studies, it did not fulfill the goals Royse envisioned, and he acknowledged that.[75] Little of the folklore material gathered under Botkin's direction has been published, except the materials he later included in his folklore treasuries. Brown's proposed studies of African Americans were never completed. One reason the vision was so much greater than the actual accomplishment was lack of trained personnel on a relief program. But this was not the crux of the problem. The crucial factor was that Congress withdrew its support for the FWP experiment. Another problem is how long it has taken students of American life since the

FWP to show a curiosity about the vision of Botkin, Brown, and Royse and to express an interest in the unpublished work that was done under their direction.

Botkin thought that the FWP had "the tremendous responsibility of studying folklore as a living culture."[76] More than a half-century later, it is our responsibility to show an interest in the material that Botkin and his FWP colleagues gathered. A proper use of these materials, however, will require an informed understanding of the intellectual and cultural assumptions underlying these studies. The way the FWP approached black and ethnic studies is part of American intellectual and cultural history.

A dialogue with Botkin, Brown, and Royse about American culture might sound strikingly contemporary. Royse rejected the idea that ethnicity was merely a transitional stage, but neither he nor Botkin nor Brown thought American culture was a static entity. Modernity and the multiethnic composition of the American population had created a situation in which all Americans lived in a state of transition and had to self-consciously deal with the relevance of the past to the future. National identity in this view was not fixed and static but, like anthropological views of culture, a product of the dynamic interaction between past and present. Then and now, arguments about an American cultural canon are arguments about national identity, as are discussions of the cultural politics of language in art and history, about change and continuity between an older, agrarian and a newer, industrial America (and now, an allegedly still newer postindustrial America), and as are the search for metaphors for cultural processes and nationality.

At the beginning of a new millennium, Americans must wrestle with these cultural questions in truly multiracial and multiethnic terms and not focus primarily on African Americans and white ethnic groups from southern and eastern Europe, as the FWP did. It is an open and debated question whether a firm line should be drawn between what are culturally constructed as racial groups —people of color—and white ethnic groups (who in the 1930s were still often viewed as distinct races), the way the FWP tended to do, or whether it would be more useful to think of color as a dimension of ethnicity. Issues of cultural politics and scholarly methods are at stake now as they were in the 1930s. The voices Botkin, Brown, and Royse wanted to allow to enter the discussion about American life and history still need to be heard. It would benefit us not to privilege our own voices over those voices or over those of B. A. Botkin, Sterling Brown, and Morton Royse.

Chapter 6

Before Columbia

The Federal Writers' Project and American Oral History Research

Allan Nevins's plea in *The Gateway to History* (1938) for "an organization which [would make] a systematic attempt to obtain from the lips and papers of Americans who had lived significant lives, a fuller record of their accomplishments" appeared the same year officials of the FWP were dramatically expanding their efforts at collecting the life histories of ordinary Americans. The meaning of the terms "significant lives" and "accomplishments" have been contested for a long time.[1]

Today it is possible to look at the work of the FWP, call it oral history, ask about its antecedents, and question the common view that oral history began with Nevins and his Columbia University program. Such easy revisionism, however, simplistically assumes that by arranging in chronological order evidence about earlier efforts—at what today might be called oral history—one will have discovered origins and traced influences. That approach, however, would create a false sense of continuity regarding the development of oral history research in the United States, an endeavor in which disjuncture and discontinuity are more prominent than continuity.

The FWP and the beginnings of the Columbia University oral history program are pivotal episodes in the history of oral history research in America. It is possible to locate each of these developments in relationship to the sense of ancestors—claimed and rejected—that those involved in these projects developed. It is more problematic to make assertions about which later developments have been influenced by either of these two programs. Similarities do not prove influence. They may testify, however, to persistent issues with which the very structure of modern American society confronts students of the history of the United States, both as scholars and as citizens. That the FWP had virtually no impact on oral history research in the 1950s and early 1960s is startling. The rediscovery of the FWP's pioneering efforts at oral history in the late 1960s also begs for some explanation. But perhaps the most potentially illuminating question that can be asked is why the FWP's efforts at oral history failed to affect scholarly historical discourse for so long. The more recent interest in these materials has not, for the most part, been accompanied by an interest in retrieving and understanding that discourse. Nor has it led to paying adequate attention to the efforts of FWP officials at interpreting their own work. Historians Roy Rosensweig and Barbara Melosh have lamented the lack of a history of the New Deal oral history projects, "one of the most massive oral history projects ever undertaken."[2]

In a field in which so much discontinuity exists, the best strategy for placing the oral history efforts of Nevins and the FWP in an informative historical context might paradoxically be to start with the present before returning to the past. Who do oral historians today want for ancestors? And why? Few scholars calling themselves oral historians in the period from 1948 to the late 1960s wanted the FWP as an ancestor. The celebratory and triumphalist mood of the Cold War had encouraged little interest in either the types of people the FWP interviewed or in the FWP, which by the 1950s was associated with what had become unpleasant memories of the Depression and with the somewhat suspect New Deal. Today those questions might engender a debate. Why is it possible now to make a case for the FWP as an ancestor—mistaken as that strategy might be? By trying to address that question at the beginning, it may be possible to answer it at the end in a way that not only illuminates what happened in the past but also highlights underlying currents affecting recent trends in oral history research in the United States. These are trends that affect the very structure of oral history research and that reflect both the impact of a changing American social structure and an effort to affect that structure.

Regarding the FWP as an ancestor of current work in oral history is an appealing strategy. More than Nevins's efforts at Columbia, the FWP seems to connect to current research trends. Clearly, oral history research is no longer as exclusively focused on the prominent and influential as it was for almost two decades after the founding of the Columbia oral history program. Works in social history using oral history research routinely win praise and prizes. What raised eyebrows in the case of *Like a Family: The Making of a Southern Cotton Mill World* was that the book had multiple authors, not that it used oral history.[3]

It is now hard to read the historically significant but intellectually dreary symposiums that members of the oral history movement participated in during the 1950s and 1960s.[4] It cannot be denied that in an inhospitable environment, they defended oral history, worked to institutionalize it, and maintained their morale by aggressively insisting that they were engaged in a worthwhile endeavor. Nevertheless, after a few pages of this dreary material, there is almost something refreshingly engaging in agricultural historian Fred Shannon's dismissive, reactionary, and sexist remark that he was not interested in the "reminiscences of garrulous old men, not to say anything of old women," people who *merely* liked to talk about "Horseshoe chawin' terbaccer." The vast majority of oral historians today would reject Shannon's point of view; nevertheless, Shannon, unlike many of the oral historians of his time, at least focused on a key issue. Perhaps it comes as no surprise that in the course of grappling with the question "Is Oral History Really Worth While?" none of the earnest advocates of oral history in a symposium published in 1958 defended the value of recording the voices of ordinary folk.[5]

There was only the most limited dialogue between folklorists and oral historians in the 1950s and 1960s. On various occasions folklorist Richard Dorson recycled his vague and fundamentally innocuous thoughts on the relationship between folklore and oral history. Folklorist Roger Welsch offered his perceptive insights about folklore and oral history in a most deferential style at the National Colloquium on Oral History in 1968. Dorson and Welsch seem to have perceived that for the most part those who so earnestly promoted oral history were defensive and largely interested in interviewing the prominent to acquire more empirical data along the same lines as conventional historical studies that did not use oral history.[6]

Not only has there been a sea change regarding oral history "from the bottom up," but there is also a developing interest in questions about the social construction of memory, the relationship between what the interviewee says and the implicit ideology in the narrative structure of the interview. "Memory and American History," a 1989 special issue of the *Journal of American History*, focused on the relationship between memory and history, and John Bodnar's contribution, a study of automobile workers, used oral history in addressing that relationship. In 1992, folklorist Barbara Allen contributed an article to the *Journal* on the value of identifying and studying stories in oral history interviews as evidence of individual variations on shared community attitudes. Perhaps conscious of the history profession's past attitudes, Allen avoided using the word "folklore."[7]

The defensive discussions about the validity of oral testimony and assertions about the various ways that interviews could be useful that were so central to conferences about oral history in the 1950s and 1960s have begun to recede. It is difficult to imagine their playing such a large role in any future colloquiums on oral history. How validity is determined is now treated as a more complex question and highly contested issue than it was when validity was linked to an allegedly impartial historian's noble quest for objectivity. No longer do as many researchers engaged in oral history projects feel compelled to assert that oral history is a valid source solely because it can help us secure objective information if obtained by an impartial interviewer with an appropriate background in history—guild certification. The issues surrounding subjectivity and the construction of narrative have again become the major concerns that they were to some FWP officials.[8]

Work on the cutting edge of oral history has moved on to new questions that are part of a larger discourse among contemporary historians, scholars in other fields, and occasionally the people who have been interviewed. Many of these questions make it seem extremely unlikely that those engaged in oral history research will advocate, as they routinely did in the not-so-distant past, that once tapes are transcribed, it would be cost effective to reuse them. The voice of the past is now heard as constituted in a spoken language that is inherently different from what can be obtained in any written transcription. Ironically, directors of FWP oral history programs—who did not have tape recorders— better understood this point than did Nevins and the archivally based oral historians who with tape recorders in hand followed in his footsteps.[9]

The institutional base for oral history research within the historical profession is more solid today (although still probably more subject to drastic cuts in hard economic times than other aspects of a history department's mission) than it was during the period of the FWP or for more than two decades following the creation of the Columbia program. Major oral history programs are now based within the history departments of universities. Americans engaged in oral history research have their own scholarly *Oral History Review*. Since 1987 the *Journal of American History* once a year provides articles reviewing new developments in oral history and various established fields of research. In addition, the *Public Historian* treats oral history as a central concern for large parts of its readership.

Initially, the FWP's location within the federal government might seem impressive to those who do not know what a weak base that proved to be. By contrast, the location of the Columbia and other early oral history programs under the aegis of libraries and archival institutions was relatively more secure. The respective institutional bases of the FWP and the Columbia oral history program provided one way of paying the special bills that oral history engenders. Nevins has left a vivid account of the need for most oral history programs to solicit donors. The FWP and the Columbia program's institutional locations placed the work of these two groups on the outside, or at best, on the periphery of the discourse about the past that professional historians thought mattered, although a basis in the world of libraries and archives gave oral historians access to the *Wilson Library Bulletin* and the *American Archivist*. However, unlike the later archivally based oral historians, FWP officials did not see themselves as primarily collecting records for professional historians to use. They viewed publication for a nonscholarly audience as the ultimate aim of their oral history projects.[10]

The directors of the FWP neither sought the support of the American historical profession nor expected much help from historians in the kind of oral history research they were pursuing. While the New Deal and the Depression lasted, national FWP officials had a base in the unemployment programs the Roosevelt administration sponsored. They found no way to permanently institutionalize their projects. The FWP gradually faded away as the unemployment crisis declined and the administration, the Congress, and the nation focused on the war effort.

As a professional historian himself, Nevins provided early efforts in oral history research with a link—albeit tenuous—to scholarly circles. Not only Nevins's advocacy of oral history but also his efforts to encourage historians to aim for a more popular audience than they usually addressed were greeted with skepticism by many professional historians. His endeavors on behalf of the Society of American Historians and in establishing *American Heritage Magazine* were not universally supported by his colleagues. His criticism of dry-as-dust academics alienated some of them. The beachhead for oral history programs in the Columbia mode was the university library, occasionally the private corporation or foundation, in time governmental bureaus, but only much later the history departments of research universities. One can still easily rattle off the names of prestigious history departments that do not offer a course in oral history.[11]

What would today be called public history was at the heart of both Nevins's and the FWP's efforts. In *The Gateway to History*, Nevins talked about the need for historians to address a general audience, and after World War II he sought through *American Heritage* to achieve that goal. For both Nevins and the FWP, oral history was linked to concerns over the development of national identity. Memory was a central issue. For Nevins collective memory in its role in helping to constitute bonds of shared nationality was implicitly treated as unproblematic. The validity of individual memory, however, had to be determined in relationship to canons of scientific history defined as the search for the objective truth. For FWP officials, however, American identity was problematic. For them, oral history was central to what they treated as contests over whose experience was considered valuable in constructing America and which individuals and groups should play a role in helping to build a sense of the American past.

Historians interested in oral and public history tend to be familiar with Nevins's call in the preface to his *Gateway to History* for a popular historical magazine and for oral history projects. The underlying assumptions about history that frame *The Gateway to History* receive less attention. Nevins himself listed "frames of reference" along with "patterns of culture" as incomprehensible "pseudo-philosophic jargon" that was distancing professional historians from the ordinary reader. Nevertheless, Nevins's own frame of reference and self-expressed lack of interest in patterns of culture reveal a great deal about his view of history in general and oral history in particular.[12]

The idea that history was "a branch of literature" and that "it is first a creator of nations, and after that, their inspirer" were central and intimately related themes in *The Gateway to History*. Nevins portrayed history as literature that actively helped constitute a nation: "By giving peoples a sense of continuity in all their efforts, and by chronicling immortal worth, it confers upon them both a consciousness of their unity, and a feeling of the importance of human achievement." He maintained that "the strongest element in the creation of any human organization of complex character and enduring strength is the establishment of common tradition by the narration of its history."[13]

For Nevins national tradition and identity are not simply inherited but are constructed by the act of narrating the past. He may have seen "Americans who led significant lives" as potential narrators about the period from roughly the end of Reconstruction to the appearance of *The Gateway to History*. He certainly saw them as providing data for an account of "a period in which America has been built into the richest and most powerful nation the world has ever seen, and socially and economically has not only been transformed but re-transformed." The plot for such a history is the rise and triumph of America. This suggests an epic along the lines of the nineteenth-century American and European romantic histories Nevins so greatly admired—an epic that celebrated past heroic deeds and that accepted and justified present social arrangements. For Nevins this conservative romantic view of the American experience as triumphalist historic epic is reconcilable with respect for "proper [historical] standards."[14]

Although Nevins clearly stresses the value of history as literature, he is not so much challenging the ideal of a scientific, objective, and impartial history as he is trying to reconcile a popular romantic nationalist version of history with scientific history, the "proper standards," as he terms it. For him, oral history is useful because it creates for the recent past the types of documents that he— and countless others since—argued will increasingly be lacking in the modern age. Two decades after the beginning of the Columbia oral history program, Charles T. Morrisey aptly summarized Nevins's position: "Nevins had long felt that much knowledge of historical value was being lost to future historians because no one was recording it. Telephone conversations and air travel were two obvious reasons why men of power and decision in this century tended to carry their files in their heads." Neither Nevins nor the majority of the individuals active in the early archivally based oral history movement viewed oral history interviews as contributing to a new approach to the past. Rather, for them such interviews were a means to continue writing traditional history, with the traditional historical actors, while claiming in the face of the skeptical Fred Shannons of their world that they were not challenging the tenets of scientific history.[15]

Like Nevins, key national FWP officials were romantic nationalists. They, too, saw the key role of tradition, history, and language in constituting national identity. They differed, however, in their emphasis on the experiences of daily life, in a concern with social problems, in a fascination with folklore, and in attempts to reconcile romantic nationalism with pluralism. FWP officials were more interested in the new social classes modernity created than they were in how technology was destroying the records left by individuals traditionally regarded as prominent and influential.

After a long delay, the FWP oral history materials that existed before the Columbia oral history program began are finding their way into scholarly and popular discourse. No common pattern distinguishes the way these materials have emerged. Anthologies of unpublished southern life histories, like *Such as Us: Southern Voices of the Thirties* (1978) and *Up before Daybreak* (1982), have used these sources in scholarly monographs. At the same time, it is clear that work in the new social history has led to efforts to review and publish previously unpublished FWP work. Enough of the material has now appeared and the new social history has become so much a part of historical writing that both these developments encourage new efforts to publish and analyze FWP oral history projects that had for many years been neglected. Given increasing interest in the history of the lives of ordinary Americans and the variety of unpublished FWP materials, there is little chance that the scholarly or popular interest in these materials will abate in the near future.

The anthologies that have appeared share most of the assumptions that led Writers' Project officials to initiate these programs. They emphasize that people not usually heard are gaining the chance to speak. They dignify the ordinary. They attach importance to the common person's view. In the best of these anthologies of FWP materials, the editors provide a historical context for the interviews. They also reflect on what new perspectives these interviews offer on aspects of the American past. In *America, the Dream of My Life: Selections from the Federal Writers' Project's New Jersey Ethnic Survey* (1990), David Cohen insists that the social-ethnic studies "represent for immigration history what the more famous Federal Writers' Project collection of slave narratives has meant for African-American history." In selecting interviews from unpublished FWP social-ethnic studies for his anthology, *The First Franco-Americans: New England Life Histories from the Federal Writers' Project, 1938–1939* (1985), C. Stewart Doty contends that he provides readers with an account of people that does not treat them as an "anonymous mass or . . . filter Franco-American experience through the perceptions of Francophone elites." He maintains that the publication of these interviews "accelerates the development of a new kind of Franco-American history." By having made it possible for voices from the past to reach later generations, the FWP has helped enrich and democratize the dialogue Americans can have about their past.[16]

In *First Person America* (1980), Ann Banks concentrates not on a particular group or place but instead introduces Americans to a wider variety of FWP social-ethnic and living lore interviews than any anthology previously published. In her book one can find interviews with Congress of Industrial Organizations (CIO) supporters who worked in Chicago's back-of-the-yards packinghouses; North Carolinians who made their living from tobacco; monumental stone cutters in Barre, Vermont; and jazz musicians. Banks wanted new generations of readers to benefit from the way "the Federal Writers' Project pioneered the collection of first-person narratives by people who would not otherwise have left a record."[17]

All the editors of these anthologies point out that a key part of the appeal of the FWP materials is the narrative power of these interviews. Tom Terrill and Jerrold Hirsch argue that "through these stories [in *Such as Us*] the impact of facts, trends, and forces can be felt as well as understood, felt as they were felt by those whose lives they helped to shape." Ann Banks made the "story" aspect of FWP social-ethnic and folklore studies a central part of her introduction to *First Person America*. In trying to explain B. A. Botkin's outlook, Banks could not help but discuss the relationship among memory, history, and folklore as embodied in the first-person stories in her anthology. She referred to Botkin as "the man most responsible for the stories in this book." In the 1990 edition of *First Person America*, Banks concluded that "American historians have become more sophisticated in their approach to the workings of memory during the decade since the book first appeared." Recent psychological research, she noted, looked at "remembering [as] a process of creative construction, not merely of replication. . . . A storyteller is not the sole author of his tale, he collaborates with his audience in shaping the story. Every story, in other words, is a conversation, even when only one person does the talking." Banks pointed out that "none of these findings would seem new or startling to . . . Benjamin Botkin." This growing interest in memory promises to balance the initial tendency to discuss the validity of these FWP interviews largely in terms of whether the nuggets of data historians might extract from the material were trustworthy. As David Thelen, a former editor of the *Journal of American History*, has observed, for some purposes "the social dimensions of memory are more important than the need to verify accuracy."[18]

Nancy J. Martin-Perdue and Charles L. Perdue Jr. have spent more than two decades making a treasure trove of materials from the Virginia FWP available to both scholars and the general public. *Talk about Trouble: A New Deal Portrait of Virginians in the Great Depression* (1996) is especially rewarding because of the editors' attention to the ethnographic and folkloric value of these FWP oral history interviews. Rather than simply itemizing customs, the Perdues are concerned with what they refer to as "collective narratives of memory" and how experience is narrated. Drawing on their knowledge of history, folklore, and anthropology, they set their FWP materials in a rich context that presents a full picture of folklife in the region. Among the many valuable anthologies of FWP materials, the Perdues' work may come closest to achieving the goals of FWP officials.[19]

As long as it took for historians to turn to the FWP slave narratives, it took them even longer to give attention to the social-ethnic studies, the living lore materials, and the southern life histories. The appearance of studies of slave

culture in the 1970s using the FWP slave narratives and in the 1980s and 1990s
of anthologies drawing on the FWP social-ethnic studies materials followed, in
part, the development of black power in the late 1960s and the ethnic revival
of the 1970s. Such a conclusion would fit historian I. A. Newby's analysis of
recent historiographical trends. In *Plain Folk in the New South: Social Change and
Cultural Persistence, 1880–1915* (1989), Newby maintained that historians' "recast-
ing of the history of slaves, ethnic minorities, and other groups, including
women, is a recent example of the way they respond to current events." He
held "that example suggests that sea changes in historical treatment of social
groups occur only when basic improvements take place in the status of the
groups themselves." Historians, Newby insisted, have given southern plain folk
relatively less attention than these other groups because there has been so little
improvement in the status and treatment of people often dismissed as "red-
necks." "Even today," Newby laments, "[plain folk] are one of the few recog-
nizable social groups that the media can and do present in negative, stereotyp-
ical fashion, and that academics and liberals can and do disparage by name."
Nevertheless, Newby does see a change occurring among scholars and in the
media.[20]

In *Plain Folk in the New South*, Newby used the FWP southern life histories to
give people who have been "alternately disparaged, patronized, and ignored
. . . what every group is entitled to—a sympathetic look into their history that
seeks to understand them in their own terms." Newby's views about the historical and cultural treatment of southern plain folk differ little from the justification W. T. Couch offered for initiating the FWP's southern life history program.
It was the desire to change the treatment and status of disparaged and ignored
groups of Americans that led FWP officials to initiate interview projects.[21]

The public history and scholarly uses of these emerging FWP materials have
hardly been exhausted. They will continue to enlarge our experience and understanding of the American past as both scholars and laypeople listen to the
interviewees with new questions in mind. Newby demonstrated in *Plain Folk in
the New South* the value of the southern life history collection to a study of the
southern plain folk who experienced the transition from an agrarian world to
the textile mills. In *Rural Worlds Lost: The American South, 1920–1960* (1987), Jack
Kirby employed the FWP southern life histories to examine the experiences of
a wider variety of southerners. These FWP materials speak to questions that
FWP employees had not actually considered. Jacquelyn Jones demonstrated in
"'Tore Up and a-Movin': Perspectives on the Work of Black and Poor White
Women in the Rural South" that the southern life histories offered insights into

the differences and similarities in the situations of southern white and black women and the significance of gender, race, and class in their lives.[22]

If Newby is right about the relationship between social change and the work of historians, the belated rediscovery of the FWP's interview materials is an ironic vindication of a program that was first disparaged in its own time and then ignored by later Americans. It had been the hope of national FWP officials that the interview projects could create a new sense of shared nationality that would help diminish the stereotypes about and low status of African Americans, industrial workers, ethnic minorities, and ordinary southerners. They could not have envisioned that it would take between thirty and fifty years before an ever increasing number of Americans would express interest in these interviews. Nor could they have envisioned that before the publication of this material would take place, significant improvements in the treatment and status of these groups would have had to occur. As optimistic New Dealers, they had hoped to make a difference in their own time. Their assumption that the work they were engaged in focused on vital American realities has been retrospectively endorsed by subsequent social and scholarly developments that make the FWP interview projects increasingly important. Now that these materials are no longer ignored, historians are determining how to assess and use them.

Less has been written about the strengths and weaknesses of the FWP southern life histories than about the ex-slave narratives. Much of the analysis of the slave narratives, however, has concentrated on how to mine these sources for data about slavery. More work needs to be done regarding how to read and analyze all of the FWP interview materials. In a discussion of the slave narrative genre, literary scholars Charles T. Davis and Henry Louis Gates Jr. note the "alarmingly irresponsible naiveté" of historians in dealing with these texts. They warn that "historians can no longer remain unaware of the marvels of close textual analysis, if they seek to employ texts as documents in their own 'fictions' of 'history.'" At the same time, they draw too sharp a distinction between analyzing "these texts as narrative discourses . . . important to criticism for their form and structure" and their importance "to historiography for the 'truths' they reveal about . . . 'the slave community.'" Part of the historical "truths," as Botkin understood them, of these and other FWP interviews was embodied in their narrative structure.[23]

An examination of the challenge of reading the ex-slave narratives and southern life histories is relevant to the problems of analyzing materials from any of the FWP oral history projects. Botkin suggested that the ex-slave narratives could collectively be read as the African American interpretation of slavery. Relatively little consideration has been given to analyzing the accounts of these narrators the way scholars analyze the accounts of other historians. Perhaps understandably, the first efforts have been to determine whether the FWP ex-slave interviews provide accurate information about slavery, and therefore a subsidiary question has been "Were the accounts colored by the passage of time?" Gradually these documents have been used to examine later periods, such as Reconstruction. They have not, however, received much analysis as a source about the last generation of slaves and the first generation of freedpeople. The question has more often been "Do these interviews reflect what these elderly blacks thought when they were slaves, or do they reflect later attitudes?" The assumption has been that "later attitudes" are a distortion for which the historian has to allow. If one also asks "How did ex-slaves interpret their experience?" then what for some purposes are limitations in the FWP narratives become strengths.

Historians have wondered about what experiences can be counted in the FWP ex-slave narratives in order to define the typical and the representative. Yet the analytical issues involved in reading the ex-slave narratives and those connected with counting behavior cannot be separated. Most of what historians would like to quantify in the accounts of ex-slaves is embedded in a historical narrative in the form of answers given to an interviewer's questions. Attempts to read and quantify these materials illuminate much about their value as historical evidence. Useful tables can indicate the percentage of FWP interviews with field hands, house servants, and artisans; types of punishments that slaves received; the kinds of occupations that they followed after freedom; and patterns of migration during Reconstruction. All of this constitutes helpful information. More problematic are tables that try to identify the impact of particular variables, such as "Did the responses of ex-slaves who owned land differ from those who did not?" or "Were some forms of resistance more characteristic of house slaves than of field hands?" Such an approach assumes that all narratives deserve to be given equal weight. But thoughtful reading indicates some narratives speak with more authority than others.[24]

Both an interviewer and an interviewee appear in these narratives. The methods, assumptions, compulsions, and goals of the interviewers shaped and became part of the interview. Questions about these documents are similar to questions that scholars ask about memoirs, diaries, and the work of other historians. A key difference is that these documents were the result of a collaboration between interviewers and interviewees, who were putting together a historical account in the format of a "conversational narrative." The linguistic, grammatical, and literary structure of the interview offers the best evidence on the relationship, the interaction between interviewer and interviewee, and how the interviewee presents his or her life and history to the interviewer, to him- or herself, and to the larger community. These structures give form to reality. John Blassingame has suggested that students of the ex-slave narratives "should begin by mastering the skills of the linguist and then systematically examine the internal structures of the interviews, the recurrence of symbols and stereotypes, the sequence of episodes, and the functions they serve." It is not true, as Paul Escott argued, that "prose portraits of sharecroppers' cabins or flowery description of trees and surroundings" yield "little useful information." These narratives need to be read not only to obtain answers to questions posed by scholars but also for the assumptions that those involved brought to the creation of these histories—information often revealed in the sections of the narratives Escott discounted. Only then can sophisticated questions be formulated.[25]

The naive hope that the filters through which the past is viewed can be eliminated and that an unmediated picture of reality can be obtained needs to be abandoned. The filters are not merely a necessary evil that must be taken into account but, rather, a significant part of the story. In the search for data, the historian cannot afford to disregard the nature of these collaborative historical narratives. A careful reading of the interviews with former slaves reveals the frequent confrontation between white and black views of the past. If scholars try too hard to make elusive materials give hard and certain answers, they run the risk of losing sight of the subtleties inherent in this type of document —the very reason they were interested in this material in the first place.[26]

Examples drawn from the FWP southern life history project Couch directed can further illustrate ways of reading that are relevant to all the FWP interviews. Like traditional narrative historians, the interviewers were neither especially self-conscious nor revealing about their assumptions and methods. Perhaps like traditional narrative historians, they thought that the form, the art, demanded that they hide the scaffolding on which they built. I do not mean to argue that they saw themselves as historians. It is an analogy only meant to heighten our awareness of what they were doing. Whether they intended to or not, they became coauthors of narrative histories. Thus, these materials need to be read with the same attention to detail as textual critics give to literature.[27]

The southern life histories reveal that, like North Carolina Federal Writer Bernice Kelly Harris, most of the interviewers either chose people they had known for years or, like Ida Moore, chose "the people to be interviewed more or less by instinct . . . saying I'd like very much to stop by for a few minutes and talk with them." The pattern was the same in all the FWP oral history projects. One black interviewee in Georgia said he was willing to talk to Grace McCune because he had regarded her father, the sheriff, as a white man who treated African Americans fairly. The selection of subjects was not random in the scientific sense. Sometimes the attempt to record dialect reveals as much about the interviewer's perception of the subject as it does about how the interviewee actually spoke.[28]

The interviewers had little knowledge of the science or art of interviewing, and they did not have tape recorders. Since the interviewers did not preserve their questions, the queries can only be inferred by changes in direction and transitions in the narratives. Often important points are not pursued. The interviewers had been told not to intrude or to judge. Often they did both, and in the process they revealed much about themselves we would not otherwise know. The interviews were intended to be open-ended.[29]

There is little evidence that the interviewers were aware of their effect on the interviewees, of any bars to spontaneity, or of the desire to please. Though the interviewer may not have been conscious of these factors, a close reading of the text makes them apparent in many cases. The structure of the interview offers the best evidence on the relationship, the interaction between interviewer and interviewee, and how the interviewee presented his or her life and history to the interviewer, to him- or herself, and to the larger community. These accounts also need to be read with attention to the way they may have been influenced by literary genres: local color writings, fictional treatments of poor whites from William Byrd to John Steinbeck, and true confessions. The interviewee as well as the interviewer often shaped personal experience in terms of these genres. One woman told an interviewer, "I use to tell Morrison our lives would make a good true story—like you read in the magazines and hear on the radio—Ma Perkins and the others." A major value of these life histories is that they reveal the shape people gave to their experience, and thus the meaning they found in their lives.[30]

Unlike such 1930s sociologists as John Dollard and Hortense Powdermaker, the FWP interviewers in the South did not offer explicit analyses of their biases and other problems inherent in their work. Powdermaker noted, "While I had to be respected and accepted by whites, I could not afford to be too intimate with them otherwise Negroes would not have trusted me." They and other researchers were aware that a "conversation would generally be influenced by its excuse for being in the first place." One writer suggested never asking direct questions because people will only tell you what they think you want to hear. He advised just trying to start a conversation. Though the FWP interviewers on the southern life history project did not comment on these issues, the narratives nevertheless frequently reveal how they dealt with these aspects of the interview process. They indicate how they approached a subject, the greetings they exchanged, how they were received, and where the interview took place: on the porch, in the kitchen, or in the fields. The writers were, for the most part, seen as agents of a sympathetic, friendly, and interested government. No doubt they were also seen as men or women, whites or blacks, strangers or acquaintances. Yet the southern life histories reveal that their role as representatives of the New Deal often overshadowed their other roles. For example, a black interviewee often welcomed a white interviewer as a member of the community and as a representative of the New Deal. Because of the latter capacity, the interviewee revealed things he or she might not have said to other local whites. In recent anthologies of FWP interviews, the editors have demonstrated how useful it can be to examine how the background of the FWP interviewers, their relationship to the interviewees, and their role as representatives of the government affected other FWP oral history programs.[31]

Friendly subjects did try to give interviewers what they thought they wanted. In many cases they interpreted that as telling their government how they viewed their lives. In the attempt to explain and relate past experience and present circumstances, the interviewers and interviewees found themselves writing history. Much of that history is told in terms of the family, its past and present, and its expectations of the future. Race relations were not an explicit concern of the southern life history program interviewers. They rarely seem to have asked direct questions about race. Yet racial matters received much comment in these southern life histories.[32]

Using these southern life histories as a source offers historians an opportunity and a challenge. The problems they present to researchers need to be taken into account. It would be unfortunate, however, if we lost the opportunity because we shied away from the challenge. These are difficult materials for scholars to work with, and their particular limitations can be frustrating. Still, all documents have their limitations, and there is little value in dwelling on the fact that the FWP interviewers were "untrained researchers." That fact obscures an equally evident but, for historians, much more significant point: The people who did this work approached the interview task differently from the way trained oral historians would. The FWP interviewers are not us. That, rather than simply constituting a weakness, is part of their interest.[33]

Both the interviewers and the interviewed were aware that their efforts might allow them to reach a larger audience. Perhaps some of them sensed that here they had an opportunity to reach across time and speak to later generations. They spoke in a time and in a voice different from ours. Their words must not only be read, but heard. The experience, the memories, and the history are in the words, in the way things are put. Anthropologist Dennis Tedlock argues that spoken language is closer to poetry than to prose.[34] In this sense, these life histories can be compared to poetry. As Francis Berry, the English literary critic, maintains, "A poem is composed of active language, but the language in the constitution of a poem is the experience: the poet in writing creates his experience in the act of making the poem."[35] Had Lettice Boyer worked hard? "Hard work? Lord, honey, I's done some hard work! Don't ask me what I has done, but what I ain't." What is building oil rigs like? "In work, outa work and in again—but mostly out. That's rig-building."[36]

All of the FWP interviews are most valuable as a source of qualitative evidence about hopes, fears, and aspirations—as the historical account of people not normally heard from. The authenticity of the voice of the person allegedly speaking is therefore a persistent question for scholars certain the materials need to be used, but uncertain how to allow for the possibility that some interviews or parts of them are inauthentic. No easy answers are available, but it is possible to suggest ways of addressing the matter and putting it in perspective. This requires attention also to factors that lie outside the text.

The existence of more than one version of a slave narrative or a southern life history as well as the editorial rewriting indicated in the original typescripts reveals that someone—the interviewer or an editor—either deleted or added material, rewrote passages, and sometimes changed the wording of the quotations attributed to the interviewee. In part, this was done because the interviewing task was too difficult for many FWP field-workers. The state director of the North Carolina FWP initially thought that the instructions for collecting life histories were "too detailed and complicated for use by our workers." He thought it would be difficult to make the instructions "clear enough to be grasped by the people who do not even know what research work is." Therefore, the original interviews were often edited by the more competent writers on the state FWP units.[37]

The goals of the editors of the FWP oral histories involved more than standardizing spelling or correcting grammatical errors. Both the correspondence of FWP slave narrative and southern life history editors and the nature of the comments on the typescript interviews show editors working to achieve "literary" aims. Sometimes they sought only to illuminate the interviewers' comments. On other occasions they suggested that the material be rearranged for greater clarity or placed in a conventional chronological order, regardless of whether that violated the actual order of the interviewee's testimony. On occasion an editor, with the approval of the original interviewer, altered the quoted remarks of a subject. Thus sometimes the editing went beyond any standards that oral historians today would find acceptable. The local FWP editors' primary aims were journalistic, and their criteria for a good interview reflected their knowledge of the expectations of a conventional middle-class newspaper reader.

Though the editing constitutes evidence that some interviews are inauthentic in detail, it would be a mistake to assume that FWP officials were indifferent to this issue. Some went to great lengths to ensure that the texts accurately reflected what was said in the interview. A Mississippi district supervisor informed the state FWP director that "the order in which details are related has been copied exactly as the field worker submitted. If a Negro told about the Civil War, reminisced about his childhood days before the War, and returned to stories of the Civil War, the narrative shows it." She insisted that she would not alter "the sequence of a narrative" even if that would make "a more interesting or readable story." However, like most Federal Writers, she thought a narrative arranged in chronological order more readable. Outside the national office, few, if any, of the Federal Writers entertained the idea that temporal sequence was but one way of giving order to a narrative, as both folk materials and modernist novels illustrate. Thus John Lomax, while advising that interviews "should, as nearly as possible, quote the exact words of ex-slaves," also approved reordering material to give it greater coherence, which meant a conventional temporal sequence.[38]

Sterling Brown was also concerned about the limitations of the interviewers. He recommended "that the words 'darky' and 'nigger' and such expressions as 'a comical little old black woman' be omitted from the editorial writing. Where the ex-slave himself uses these, they should be retained." Reading the ex-slave narratives requires sensitivity to the failure of most editors and interviewers to make the distinction Brown made.[39]

Project directors and editors in the various states made judgments about the trustworthiness and ability of an interviewer and the quality of his or her work. Most of the FWP oral histories fall short of a verbatim account. The danger of posing the question of authenticity in either/or terms is that it creates a false dichotomy that can only lead to a simplistic acceptance or rejection and an equally simplistic use of the materials.

Focusing on the interviewer can be helpful in assessing the credibility of an

FWP oral history. Since FWP interviewers usually lived in the areas in which they worked, it is possible, even at this late date, to secure biographical information on former project workers. A few are still alive. Project correspondence contains information, often biographical, about the interviewers, including their race—an especially significant factor. Many FWP interviews give the name and address of both the interviewee and the interviewer. By reading all the narratives collected by the same interviewer, it is possible to discern individual characteristics of that interviewer. When Botkin and his assistants on the Writers' Unit of the Library of Congress Project—created after the demise of the FWP —inventoried the ex-slave narratives, they tried to do this as part of their effort at evaluating and indexing the material.

The project ended before the evaluations were completed or the index started. While these assessments are hardly definitive, they suggest the outline of an approach others can follow. For example, one of Botkin's assistants praised the ability of Ruby Pickens Tartt of Alabama to secure information about folklore and folkways from her informants. The assistant also concluded that Travis Jordan of North Carolina "misjudges the subject of the enterprise, and gives himself to the compilation of incredible blood-and-thunder yarns that have a strong resemblance between one another and are told in a glaringly fake dialect." Both Tartt and Jordan also collected southern life histories. Tartt established a national reputation as a local folklorist, and there is a biographical study of her life and work that contains material pertinent to understanding her FWP interviews. John Lomax's *Adventures of a Ballad Hunter* (1947) mentions Tartt and provides evidence that both of them were white paternalists. Another evaluator noted that one interviewer "quotes his informants but uses the same language for illiterates as for college graduates."[40]

Any attempt to analyze the various FWP interviews, for either qualitative or quantitative purposes, should take into account the dynamics of the interview process and the reliability of the interviewer and the interviewee. A large part of the process involves careful attention to internal evidence. C. H. Wetmore, a member of the Writers' Unit of the Library of Congress, thought a close reading showed that "several Indiana interviews bear evidence of having been faked: That is, the interviewer visited an ex-slave, then used imagination to complete a story." Botkin was forced to conclude that regarding the ex-slave narratives, "all judgments of reliability must be based on purely internal evidence." He pointed out that "valid tests of reliability are the tests of evidence, such as competence of the witness, internal consistency, and consistency with historical facts and with common sense." Botkin acknowledged that additional information about the informants and interviewers would have been helpful, but that it was not available to him. He knew that "the interviewer is as important as the informant," but he had "no way of checking on either." Working together, scholars can locate external evidence about the participants in the interview—evidence that Botkin would have liked to have had.[41]

For some purposes it is not crucial whether or not the interviews are verbatim accounts. For example, historians have been exploring boarding as a social institution, the reasons some households took in boarders, and what kind of people became boarders. There is much valuable information on this topic in the southern life histories. Widespread generalizations about American family history can be challenged on the basis of the southern life histories. These interviews do not support the common tendency to make a sharp contrast between nineteenth- and twentieth-century family history. Much that is held to be typical of the nineteenth-century family fits equally well as a description of the twentieth-century southern families described in the FWP interviews. Specifically, the idea that transitions became more age-graded and uniform in the twentieth century does not seem to apply to the rural South. Yet relatively little work has been done on the southern family. Such work would illuminate southern history, provide a basis for regional comparisons, and offer a chance to develop and refine theories.[42]

Rather than taking a frozen moment in the history of the family as the basis for describing a family structure, the southern life histories illustrate phases in the family cycle. If read carefully, they can provide the kind of information about changing family structure that Lutz Berkner and other scholars have shown is essential to understanding family history. These southern life histories also offer abundant evidence that household is not synonymous with family. The recounting of relations with kin shows that the family extends beyond the household. There is much information about the nature and significance of kinship ties in these southern life histories.[43] The alleged weaknesses of the FWP interview materials are not an insurmountable barrier. Historians finally are working at separating the wheat from the chaff.

FWP officials had a vision of a democratic culture in which scholarship was a contributing component, not an end in itself. Part of that vision involved bringing to a wide public the accounts of diverse groups of individuals that would otherwise have remained private and asking that in the academic world and the dominant popular culture those voices be treated as commentary on the American experience. In the 1980s, historians, folklorists, and students of American literature contributed to making possible the radio dramatizations of *First Person America: Voices from the Thirties* and *America, the Dream of My Life.* The Library of Congress's American Memory Project has made all the FWP life history materials in its possession accessible through the internet. This has made it easier for researchers to use the collection regarding a host of topics, and some of these topics are still unimagined. The American Memory Project has made it possible for anyone, not just scholars, to do research in the FWP life history collections. Computer search functions allow interested individuals to construct their own dialogues with the memories captured in this collection.[44]

All of the major tendencies present in oral history today can be found in the various programs of the FWP. The FWP's heuristic value as an ancestor, however, lies in the way national officials attempted to reconcile romantic nationalism and cultural pluralism and built on, modified, and sometimes repudiated earlier investigations and formulations of sociological and folkloristic theories. The specific concerns and formulations of FWP officials are now somewhat foreign to the working assumptions of contemporary oral historians—and therein may lie their historical value—despite their common concern with pluralism, ethnicity, and modernity.

The liberating potential of the past can only be fully realized when we confront not the ancestors we have invented but past students of American life who had their own agendas. An openness to both similarities and differences, to continuity and discontinuity, can make for a creative dialogue with a past that can be a partner in constructing the future of oral history research in America.

National and regional FWP officials were self-conscious about the purpose of the oral history projects they conducted. Unlike many of the scholars who first assessed and used these materials, key FWP officials such as Botkin knew they were dealing with the significance of memory and its relation to history and culture. They also knew that folklore was one of the forms memory took and, therefore, that in recording memory they would also record folklore. FWP officials believed that they were making it possible for new voices to be heard, and that voices are more than sources to be mined by historians in traditional ways, even if we have only the printed page with all its limitations in trying to capture that voice. The FWP interviewees are not simply informants. They are also narrators and historians, preservers and creators of memory.

Chapter 7

The People Must Be Heard

W. T. Couch and the Southern
Life History Program

"With all our talk about democracy it seems not inappropriate to let the people speak for themselves," W. T. Couch wrote in the introduction to *These Are Our Lives* (1939), a collection of thirty-five life histories of ordinary southerners that he saw as the first in a series of volumes of southern life histories. *These Are Our Lives* has been widely hailed as an example of a new approach to the study of American culture and history.[1]

As Southeast regional FWP director, Couch supervised a southern life history program that shared some of the goals of the projects B. A. Botkin, Sterling Brown, and Morton Royse developed in the national office. National FWP director Henry Alsberg encouraged the work of all of these individuals. Nevertheless, the intellectual and administrative history of Couch's project distinguishes it from the programs that Botkin, Brown, and Royse undertook.

Couch initiated the southern life history program, formulated the approach the program would take, and administered it without any significant input from the Washington office. He was not part of the dialogue that took place among Botkin, Brown, and Royse as they thought about how to study American culture. Nor did he respond to the same inherited discourse about American identity that influenced how they approached the subject. As this and the next chapter will make clear, Couch's ideas were formed in response to an inherited discourse about southern society and identity. The FWP made it possible for Couch to administer a life history program that allowed ordinary southerners, white and black, to speak to their fellow southerners, to Americans in other regions of the nation, and to future generations of Americans. However, House congressional hearings led by two of Couch's fellow southerners, Texas Democrat Martin Dies and Virginia Republican Clifford Woodrum, contributed to changes in the Writers' Project that prevented Couch from continuing the southern life history program.[2]

In the New Deal's program for economic recovery and reform the South loomed large. The New Deal cultural projects complemented the thrust of its social and economic programs, and here, too, the South was a significant concern. Although Couch supported the New Deal, his concerns differed from those of national FWP officials. His ideas reflected his involvement with longstanding debates about southern character. *These Are Our Lives* and the southern life history program were not only a response to an inherited southern discourse but also a contribution to an enduring history of images of the South that influenced the way Americans both within and outside the region thought about the South.

Couch wanted to give ordinary southerners an opportunity to tell their own stories in their own words, to let them participate in long-standing discussions about the nature of southern poverty and the southern poor. Images of poor whites have been with us from William Byrd's colonial description of "Lubberland Land" to Erskine Caldwell's *Tobacco Road* (1932) and beyond.[3] So, too, have depictions of the plain folk and yeoman farmers. This ongoing discourse is as much a battle of counter-images involving the psychological and ideological needs of the participants as it is an attempt to describe reality. The debate is over the character of the subject, and the terms are only vaguely sociological. The same is true for the discussion of black southerners. Character is ascribed to these southerners either on the basis of a hasty and condescending impressionism or simply on what has been gleaned from other books. Southern mill workers, one scholar had insisted, behaved docilely because they came from an agrarian background. Another had claimed they were fiercely independent for the same reason. A northern reformer had contended that diversified farming would make for a less boring lifestyle than cotton culture and thus eliminate behaviors he found repugnant. Much of this speculation Couch hoped to push aside.[4]

Couch had been appointed associate state director of the North Carolina

Writers' Project in the spring of 1936; not until the spring of 1938 did he become the Southeast regional director. Alsberg's immediate goal in appointing Couch was to obtain his editorial and administrative skills in helping the North Carolina project make greater progress on the state guidebook. But even before the North Carolina guide was completed, Couch had been contemplating other projects the FWP could undertake to provide more penetrating examinations of southern life.[5] As director of the University of North Carolina Press, he had gained a wide knowledge of conditions in the South and was full of ideas regarding the type of studies that were needed. Unlike other university presses, Couch claimed that the University of North Carolina Press conceived of itself as having a duty to the region in which it was located: "Never before has any publishing firm set out to study the whole environment and life of a particular region and then shaped its program according to the needs of that region. We have done this. We believe the intellectual atmosphere of the South has improved as a result of the work we have done during the last ten years."[6] The press, however, always walked a financial tightrope. Its "realistic treatment of Southern situations," University of North Carolina president Dr. Frank Porter Graham explained to a northern foundation, "had not won for it an endowment by the vested interests of the region." Although Couch had successfully obtained some foundation support for the press, it was never enough for the programs he envisioned.[7]

Couch's vision of the work the FWP should pursue in the South reflected his reaction to contemporary currents of thought in the region and the nation. The sudden end of a period of seemingly endless prosperity had brought new attitudes and programs to the forefront of national affairs. The dominant criticism of American life in the 1920s had focused on the shallowness of middle-class life, the excesses of prosperity, and what was considered the cultural backwardness of large segments of the population. The South, along with Main Street and Winesburg, Ohio, provided critics with symbols of much that was wrong in American life. In the 1930s the South continued to be a symbol of the nation's problems. But as one historian later recalled, "The Bible Belt seemed less absurd as a haven of fundamentalism, more challenging as a plague spot of race prejudice, poor schools and hospitals, sharecropping and wasted resources." Couch responded to these new currents in southern and national affairs. He served with the liberal Southern Conference for Human Welfare, backed Graham in his liberal crusades, and worked for change in the southern tenant system.[8]

Much of the writing that made the South in the 1930s a symbol of the Depression focused on the plight of the southern tenant farmer. More than any other book, Erskine Caldwell's *Tobacco Road* inaugurated the new interest in southern tenant farmers. The world Caldwell created in *Tobacco Road* was inhabited by degenerate, stunted, and starving people. The comedy in the novel came from the behavior of individuals "so stripped of economic and social hope that they became grotesques and parodies of human beings, twisted by the simplest hungers and lacking in dignity and integrity." Caldwell's main character, Jeeter Lester, had lost his chance to play a useful role in society. Jeeter should have become a symbol of the clogged social and economic system that could find no use for a growing number of people. This was not, however, what he came to represent to most Americans. The adaptation of Caldwell's novel to the New York stage resolved all the difficulties the book had created for its readers into a clear portrayal of the story as a form of low comedy.[9]

Couch found little to admire in Caldwell's *Tobacco Road* or in his volume of impassioned reporting, *You Have Seen Their Faces* (1937). Caldwell's plea in the latter work for collective action on the part of the tenant farmers and for governmental control of cotton farming failed to impress Couch, who remarked, "If tenant farmers are at all like the Jeeter Lesters and Ty Ty Waldens with whom Mr. Caldwell has peopled his South I cannot help wondering what good could come of their collective action. Nor can much be expected from government control if the persons controlled are of the type that Mr. Caldwell has led us to believe now populate the South."[10]

Federal Writers, Couch maintained, could be used to obtain a more accurate picture of southern life than novelists such as Caldwell or defenders of the southern agrarian way of life had provided. His original plans, submitted in 1937, for studies of cotton mill villages, slum sections in southern towns and cities, and rural slum tenant problems had the endorsement of numerous students of the South and the sympathetic interest of Alsberg. Nevertheless, the bureaucratic structure of the FWP initially made it impossible to implement Couch's program.[11] May E. Campbell, North Carolina WPA director of women's and professional projects, explained to Alsberg that although she was "intensely interested" in the proposals Couch had made, she did not see how they could be approved by the North Carolina office when they involved work in all the southern states. Nor, in her opinion, was work far enough advanced on the state guide to allow competent writers to be spared for other projects. She suggested, however, that the work could be undertaken if an office for this project was established in Washington and the work administered from there, or it could be administered from North Carolina if the national office authorized it and provided funds. Edwin Bjorkman, the North Carolina FWP director, was no more encouraging when Couch discussed his plans with him in the spring of 1938. While acknowledging that the projects proposed by Couch were "most interesting and worthwhile," Bjorkman argued that they would require more qualified workers and travel money than was available. In his opinion, "Work on . . . local guides together with what remains to be done on the State Guide, represents all that the project can hope to undertake in this state during the remainder of its existence."[12]

The limited vision of state officials delayed the life history project for a year, but Alsberg eventually found a way to fulfill his promise to Couch to "put [his proposal] through if . . . at all possible." When in the spring of 1938 national FWP officials developed the idea of regional directors, offices, and programs, Couch was able to pursue work along the lines he had proposed earlier. National officials turned to the idea of regional directors because they wanted to relieve the Washington office of some of the mounting editorial work on the state guides. They still held out the hope of eventually publishing regional guides and of encouraging regional programs, such as Couch's. In May 1938 Alsberg and his staff began discussing with Couch the nature of his new duties as regional director, but the appointment did not become official for several months.[13]

Couch elaborated in formal proposals the kinds of studies he thought could and ought to be made by the FWP in the South. He believed the FWP could help meet a pressing need "in the South for more books on local subjects, especially books on social and economic subjects, on nature study and on conservation, written on elementary and high school levels." On an even more ambitious scale he proposed twenty projects that, if completed, would have examined numerous important aspects of southern life and culture.[14]

The methodology he suggested for obtaining material on various aspects of southern life differed sharply from conventional approaches. The case histories Rupert Vance used in his study *Human Factors in Cotton Culture* (1929), "to go behind the statistics and show the cotton system as it works," provided Couch with an initial model. He argued that writers could collect life histories of tenant families, farm families, mill village families, and other important occupational groups. In addition, he proposed to collect material on black artists and their work; landlord-tenant relations; laws, customs, and habits governing relations between the races; eating and drinking habits; southern health and disease; poor whites in the South; blacks who had achieved distinction; river bottom cultures; the early history of state universities; criminals condemned to death; rural and urban slums; consumers' and producers' cooperatives; and the quantity and quality of recreational facilities in the South. In each of these areas he described work that had been previously done in the field and what remained to be done.[15]

Couch also defined the advantages of using life histories as opposed to more conventional methods. He thought that if southerners were given a chance to speak for themselves, they would demonstrate that southern life was more complex than easy generalizations had led numerous people to believe. He argued against "the possible objection that only sociologists can get case histories that are worth getting. The fact is that when sociologists get such material, they generally treat their subjects as abstractions." Couch was providing a rationale for using writers unfamiliar with the study of sociology. The life histories would reflect the social situation without becoming statistical abstractions; they would have that elusive quality of human interest, unlike the material gathered by sociologists. Fiction, he thought, was equally inadequate in capturing people's lives, "because of its composite or imaginary character." Since sociologists generally treat people as abstractions, and novelists create composite characters, it would be better to use individuals who lacked background in both fields, such as the majority of project workers. Though sociology and fiction offered the models from which Couch drew in formulating his ideas, the life history program was nevertheless a pioneering effort in social history.[16]

The emphasis was on the present, but the format of the life history led to a discussion of change over time—a discussion of history. Unlike the FWP ex-slave narratives, the life history program was not conceived of in relation to an existing historiography on the topic. The ex-slave narratives, FWP officials thought, would allow an alternative to the standard written histories of slavery; slavery would be examined from the slave's point of view.[17] Until recently, however, the history of ordinary southerners, both black and white, had been written by sociologists and novelists. Couch set out to disprove the traditional notion that the southern poor, white and black, were innately inferior. His work fitted with the underlying themes of reformist social documentary so popular in the 1930: social problems were a product of a system that could be reformed.

The life history outline given to project workers instructed them to ask questions about topics such as family, income, politics, occupation, medical needs, diet, and education. The outline was oriented to the present, and the approach was that of the social worker. However, the outline also reflected concerns about the past and the future. For example, interviewees were asked not only how many years they had attended school but about the causes for limited education and their educational expectations for their children. The life histories are more than an inventory of fact and belief or an opinion poll in narrative form. The emphasis on the words and the voice of the narrator conveys the sense of reflections on personal experience directly communicated so that factual information becomes felt knowledge. Nevertheless, sociological and fictional writings shaped Couch's approach to the collection of life histories. Participant observation and the use of case histories were prominent in 1930s sociological and journalistic writing, and Couch was influenced by them.[18]

The first life histories were collected by Ida Moore, a destitute young woman from South Carolina. Her mother had died when she was a child. She had been a principal in a South Carolina high school when her father died. Saddled with the responsibility of taking care of her younger sister and brother and dependent for a livelihood on a South Carolina school system that was no longer able to pay its employees, she jumped at the offer of a friend to live in her cottage at Skyland, North Carolina.[19] Moore found employment with a federally sponsored adult education program in the area. An article she wrote in an Asheville paper about her experiences working with illiterate adults landed her a job with the North Carolina Writers' Project. Under Couch's direction, she wrote not only the first life histories but the outline used by other workers in collecting life histories. Ida Moore's life histories of textile mill workers dispelled possible objections to work along these lines. It had been "thought that the effort to get stories from people living in textile mill villages would arouse suspicion and that any person attempting to get material would very likely be rejected. It was also said that the people would not talk." Despite these objections, Ida Moore "took the first chances, and proved the job could be done."[20]

With a carefully planned program, the approval of the University of North Carolina to locate a regional FWP office on its campus, and the promise of co-operation (which did not materialize) from the prestigious Institute for Research in the Social Sciences, Couch thought he was ready to begin work and that he could complete four to six volumes of life histories within a year. Therefore, he was dismayed when his official appointment as regional director was delayed. He concluded that WPA officials who did not understand the significance of the program he had proposed were holding up the appointment. The only solution, he explained to Alsberg, was to try "to go over their heads" even though it might "eliminate all chance to do the job."[21] He preferred to take this risk rather "than go into the work under the present circumstances, with responsibility to superior officials who have no understanding of what it is all about, with the danger that some ignoramus may stop the job for frivolous reasons when it is half done."[22]

Frank Porter Graham promised Couch his total support in obtaining approval for the project. Graham had recently been appointed chairman of the committee, created by President Roosevelt, to examine economic conditions in the South and had friendly access to the offices of high government officials. He was willing to talk with Harry Hopkins or any other high official Alsberg suggested in order to secure approval for Couch's program, and Graham assured Alsberg that with Couch directing the program, he "need not worry about the quality of the final product." Paul Green, the prominent North Carolina dramatist, also urged Alsberg, whom he knew well from the days when Alsberg was associated with the Provincetown Players, "to do all you can to get Mr. Couch's appointment approved." In his opinion, Couch was "the best man in the south for the job, there's no question about it. The results will prove it." To gain additional support, Couch sent samples of the life histories that had already been collected to such prominent New Deal officials as Clark Foreman, a liberal southerner who had served Secretary of the Interior Harold Ickes as an adviser on Negro affairs and then as a high official of the Public Works Administration, and Arthur Goldschmidt, a WPA official who had been instrumental in establishing the arts projects. The samples were "quite effective propaganda" and provided the "final push" in obtaining official approval for Couch's appointment as regional director.[23]

In August 1938 Couch became regional director for the southeastern states: Virginia, North Carolina, Tennessee, Georgia, South Carolina, Florida, and Alabama. The appointment gave him the opportunity to draw on personnel from outside the ranks of the North Carolina project and thus secure life histories from other southern states. He took advantage of the exemption state FWP units were given to employ a small number of nonrelief workers. He hired several talented writers who were in financial need but who did not qualify for relief.[24]

Relying on the contacts he had made as director of the University of North Carolina Press, Couch was able to recruit additional writers and secure a small regional staff. Walter Cutter, who had much experience in social work and had served with such New Deal agencies in North Carolina as the Emergency Relief Administration and the National Youth Administration, became assistant regional director. Muriel Wolff, Leonard Rapport, and Bernice Kelly Harris went to work for the project in nonrelief positions. Wolff had been a member of the Carolina Playmakers and had worked for the press from 1931 to 1937; Rapport had also come to Couch's attention as an employee of the press. Harris had, like Wolff, been a member of the Carolina Playmakers. Couch was considering publishing her first novel. He was convinced she had the talent and ability to write life histories and thought work in this area would provide her with an opportunity to get in contact with different types of people. Thus he hoped to help her as a writer while also benefiting the Writers' Project.[25]

At the end of January 1939, Couch sought the response of friends in Chapel Hill to a sample of life histories that the project had collected. Sociologist Rupert Vance responded that "the sketches are unique . . . among all the things that have been done in the social field." Perhaps most encouraging was his opinion that "without further editing it seems to me that they can be integrated into a volume which will give us something of real biography of the common man of the South." Playwright Paul Green was equally impressed and thought the life histories would "be a storehouse for the creative writer as well as those of a scientific bent."[26]

In some areas project workers did not conduct as many life history interviews as Couch desired. Despite repeated encouragement, project workers found it difficult to obtain life histories of middle-class individuals; thus a life history of a doctor appears in *These Are Our Lives* but not one of either a minister or a lawyer. In trying to secure life histories of blacks, Couch discovered that project workers not only found the assignment difficult but were reluctant to attempt it. They had to be reminded that "we must have life histories that reveal the way people in the South live, and Negroes and members of other racial groups are people just as well as whites." That there was only a small number of African Americans on the state projects in the Southeast handicapped the work. Only one of the black life histories, "Didn't Keep a Penny," in *These Are Our Lives* was written by an African American.[27]

Couch also looked for stories that were well written. The rejection of fiction did not mean the rejection of literary devices. There was room in the life histories for descriptions of surroundings and individuals. Though an outline guided the project workers, the life histories were not written in a dry question-and-answer format, but more like short stories. This meant that material gathered by the field-workers often had to be revised by the few nonrelief workers on the project. Project editors thought that "field workers were able to get the material, but they had no sense of literary form." All changes in the arrangement of the material were approved by the original interviewer. Still, many of the project workers used the life histories to try to demonstrate their literary skills. This added an element of distortion. On one hand, Couch and his assistants talked about authenticity, but on the other hand, they wanted to reach a large audience. Thus they often edited and changed material to make it better organized and easier to read.[28]

Unless the first volume of life histories was successful, Couch assumed there was no hope that the work would be allowed to continue. This may have been why he excluded "a number of extremely sordid stories," arguing that though they were important, other material merited first attention. William McDaniel, the Tennessee state director, argued for the inclusion of "Burn All I Can," a life history of a prostitute, Bessie Mai Boatwright. "Bessie Mai," he pointed out, "represents a general class of people in the South and that they have a definite influence on social and economic conditions cannot be denied." Nevertheless, Couch rejected the story, which had "caused some consternation" in Bjorkman's office, where "all our typists are young married women." Couch eventually accumulated enough material for a volume "that would make Caldwell's degenerates look like fine upstanding citizens." But he had "scruples about publishing such stuff," and though he was convinced it ought to be published, he was unsure "how it can be handled and not make a bad situation worse." He had long combated the idea that most poor white and black southerners were hopeless degenerates, and he had no desire to contribute to "the merriment over psychopaths," to which he attributed Erskine Caldwell's success.[29]

Couch selected the life histories to be included in *These Are Our Lives* with the aim of capturing the life of a community composed of individuals "who are of different status, perform different functions, and in general have widely different experiences and attitudes—so different indeed as to be almost unimaginable." Sociologists, he thought, had previously used case histories only to illuminate "narrow segments of experience" and to buttress a particular point they wished to make. In contrast Couch claimed that his selection revealed that "I did not start on this job to get anything on anybody or any class of people, to condemn anyone or to excuse anyone; I started on it to get the real stuff, the real feelings of people of all kinds and classes."[30]

One project worker felt it necessary to apologize for the life histories she had submitted, because "the people I have covered do not seem to be in such dire straits as those Mrs. Moore described." Couch explained to her that she was wrong to feel that she had not "picked good ones." He insisted, "I definitely do not want you to pick people who are in dire straits and write only about them. I want you to write about all the most important kinds of people that live in the villages, giving most attention to those that seem to you most important by virtue of their numbers, interest, or some other good reason. I believe I told you *we are not trying to prove anything, but on the contrary are trying to get as honest and accurate a picture of mill life as possible*" (emphasis added).[31]

Only by permitting individuals to tell their own stories from their own point of view, Couch thought, could the statistical and sociological evidence that already had been gathered be given meaning and context. What can we learn, he wondered, from knowing that the average sharecropper moved several times a year unless we understand what it meant to him in the context of his own life? Underlying Couch's emphasis on the worth of material "written from *the standpoint of the individual himself*" was a strong commitment to democratic values.[32]

There had been, he argued, numerous "books about the South . . . written from other books, from census reports, from conferences with influential people." When the people have been consulted, Couch argued, "they have been approached with questionnaires in hand and with reference to particular problems of one kind or another."[33] This he thought was unsatisfactory. In his opinion, "the people, all the people, must be known, they must be heard. Somehow they must be given representation, somehow they must be given voice and allowed to speak, in their essential character."[34]

The democratic impetus of the book was reflected not only in the voices of the people who had never been heard from before, but also in the way the material had been gathered. The men and women who recorded these life histories were not professionally trained sociologists, nor were they in most cases accomplished writers. Mary A. Hicks had been a nurse, and her only experience in writing consisted of completing a course offered by the Newspaper Institute of America and the editing of a small local National Youth Administration magazine. T. Pat Matthews had been a public school principal, a physical culture instructor, and a factory worker. Claude Vivian Dunnagan, Willis Speight Harrison, and Edwin Massengill, after leaving the University of North Carolina in 1938, turned to the Writers' Project when no other employment was available. Dunnagan's and Harrison's experience consisted of a Bachelor of Arts in journalism; Massengill had majored in business. These individuals and others like them made valuable contributions to *These Are Our Lives*.[35]

In *These Are Our Lives* victims of the Depression recorded the stories of their fellow southerners. They were not far removed from the people they wrote about. Most of them had been born and raised in the South, and often they wrote the life histories of people they had known all their lives. Bernice Kelly Harris traveled with her husband, a cotton ginner, throughout the area around her home in Seaboard, North Carolina, interviewing people they had known for years. Only when she ventured into the "Portuguese Colony," an isolated mulatto community that valued its privacy, was she unwelcome. Willis Harrison recalls that the subject of "Marsh Taylor Landlord" thought the story Harrison wrote about him was "a stab in the back from the house of a friend." Field-workers approached those they did not know in a casual and random manner. Ida Moore remembered choosing "the people to be interviewed more or less by instinct . . . saying that I'd like very much to stop by for a few minutes and talk with them." This friendliness, this sharing "of a few minutes," often between neighbors, perhaps explains why, unlike much similar material, these life histories do not seem to have been cajoled from beleaguered and defenseless individuals unsure of how to cope with people who wished to study them. James Aswell thought that project workers succeeded in collecting life histories because "Southern people are born talkers. Interest in themselves and in others takes the place of interest in books and causes."[36]

The life histories submitted by the field-workers often had to be edited by more competent writers on the project. The field-workers, however, possessed qualities that compensated for their lack of writing skill. William McDaniel, the director of the Tennessee Writers' Project, remarked of one relief worker, "Her greatest attribute is that she is one of the people. She shares their views, religion, and mode of living, and through that gets into her stories the essence of their community life."[37]

Perhaps this closeness, this sense of community, between interviewer and interviewed accounts for the sympathetic tone that permeated the book. The point of view is always clear; these are people like people everywhere: they hope, they struggle, and they persevere. A poor farm laborer still hoped, someday, to satisfy his wife's desire for lace curtains. Gracie Turner, a black sharecropper watching a neighbor moving, exclaimed, "Dat's de way we'll be soon— tore up and a-movin'. I wish I could have me one acre o' land dat I could call mine. I'd be willin' to eat dry bread de rest o' my life if I had a place I could settle down on and nobody could tell me I had to move no more. I hates movin'."[38] A woman living with her aged mother in a shantytown along a river bottom showed perceptiveness and pride in her analysis of "city folks who come trotting up there gitting under our feets. . . . Half of them wouldn't no more set foot in your house low water time than nothing at all." But she thought she

> ought not to say a word against them. . . . I 'preciate what they does. But it's mighty hard for them that's had it easy all they lives to know what 'tis to be poor. They's always one saying to another, "Do you suppose them people got little enough sense to go back to them shacks when the river goes down?" And that's jest the little sense we've got—to come back to where we've got a little spot for a garden and a house we've built to live in without putting out rent money when you ain't got money for eats, much less rent. Yes Lord, we'll always go back to Shanty Town till the river rise someday and forgets to go down.[39]

Not all of the stories in *These Are Our Lives* emphasize hardship. The life history of a country doctor, a small-town merchant, and a justice of the peace portray not only individual lives but also social change in a rural society. But true to the census reports, it is hardship that predominates. What the census reports could not show, and what Couch wanted to point out in *These Are Our Lives*, was that along with hardship there was also a struggle to endure, to achieve dignity and self-respect, and not to lose hope.

Critical response to *These Are Our Lives* was overwhelmingly favorable. It was a distinctly minority opinion that argued that the "book points out what every one knows, and does it without skill or beauty," and that "its characters are approached as 'human types' rather than as human beings, and as members of a class, rather than as individuals." Instead, the work was widely viewed as having literary merit and was praised for its emphasis on the individual. *Time* claimed "it gave the South its most pungent picture of common life and the Writers' Project its strongest claim to literary distinction." The reviewer in the *New York Times* thought it was "as important as any book that has been written since the cultural renaissance dawned below the Potomac" and that the life histories were told with "the simplicity of a Chekhov." Historian Charles Beard maintained that "some of these pages are as literature more powerful than anything I have ever read in fiction, not excluding Zola's most vehement passages."[40]

Praise came from local southern papers as well. They recognized in the pages of *These Are Our Lives* "our neighbors and the folk who crowd the streets. . . . Some we recognize as old acquaintances, and some we see for the first time." Equally they lauded the book as an illustration of the complexity of southern life that defied stereotypes: "We in the South have been called an economic problem. That is not true. We are millions of problems! We are millions of individuals."[41]

In a review titled "Realities on Tobacco Road," Virginius Dabney wrote, "One thing which appeals to me in the volume before us is the absence of . . . degenerates. After all, degenerates are the exception, rather than the rule both North and South." No doubt much of the favorable response to the book in the southern press stemmed from a feeling that it provided an answer to *Tobacco Road*. Yet as Dabney also noted, *These Are Our Lives* "presents a vivid picture of the poverty and ignorance, the destitution and degradation of many Southern toilers. Yet a number of the poorest and most unsuccessful of those interviewed are seen to be persons of innate dignity, frustrated in their strivings for better things by the system under which they have been forced to live and work."[42]

Part of the strength of the book was that it offered no easy answers. The question of how to regard the lives and conditions recorded in *These Are Our Lives* remained open to debate.[43] Donald Davidson could argue that "this book suggests to me that the possibilities of the self-reliant spirit among our people have been quite overlooked by our plan-makers. . . . It shows there's probably as much of the older American spirit in the so-called backward 'feudal' South as anywhere else, and probably even more of it."[44] In contrast Erskine Caldwell called it a "revolutionary book . . . a biographical dictionary of the hamstrung and thwarted people of America."[45]

After the manuscript for *These Are Our Lives* had gone to the printer, the collection of life histories continued because Couch was "more convinced than ever that the work we are doing is important and that ways will be found to use the life histories that are written." A week later the University of North Carolina agreed to sponsor four more volumes of life histories. Couch was convinced the project could "have ready in three or four months an important book on tenant farming in the South." Instead of just another book on the deplorable conditions in this area, Couch thought it would be helpful to have a volume that focused on "the habits and mode of living of those tenants and landlords . . . who have been successful" and thus "reveal the reasons for their more healthy condition." He described to Henry Alsberg a future volume of life histories that would deal with workers in such occupations as "coal and iron works in the Birmingham area, transient laborers in early fruits and vegetables in Florida and on the gulf coast, workers in rice and sugar in fields and processing plants in Louisiana and workers in oil in the Southwest and other vital, but little acknowledged areas of Southern life and labor." In addition, Ida Moore and Leonard Rapport were gathering life histories for books on people in mill villages and in the tobacco industry. With Alsberg's aid, Couch tried to build the foundation for future work.[46]

Couch had begun a program in August 1938 that had proved so successful that he was ready in the spring of 1939 to expand it to include the entire South. But from the beginning, the possibility that Couch would be allowed to continue this work had been becoming less and less likely with each passing month. In retrospect it is possible to see that Couch's work on life histories was in jeopardy from its start. From the almost simultaneous commencement of his work with the hearings of the House Un-American Activities Committee (HUAC) in August 1938 emerged a pattern of events that ended Couch's association with the FWP.

When the new relief act was first proposed in April 1939, Couch saw that it threatened the work he was trying to do. To North Carolina senator Josiah Bailey he expressed his fear that if the new relief bill required that local and state governments provide part of the funds for the arts projects, project units in urban areas might continue while those in rural areas would be discontinued. Cleverly parodying the rhetoric southern politicians had used in assailing the administration for allegedly discriminating against the South in economic matters, Couch argued that the new rules would "perpetuate and exaggerate . . . harmful differentials between southern states and the Northeast." Couch also asked Frank Graham to write the Woodrum Committee indicating his support for the arts projects. Clifford Woodrum of Virginia, chair of a special subcommittee of the House Appropriations Committee, was holding hearings to determine what recommendations to make on the proposed relief bill. Because Couch viewed the congressional threat to the FWP as "part of the effort of reactionaries to curtail work relief and establish the dole," he thought it important that a volume of life histories about people on relief should be collected and published. A volume of this kind, Couch suggested to Alsberg, would inform people of "the real problems involved in relief."[47]

Alsberg thought it would be helpful if Couch sent reviews of *These Are Our Lives* to members of the Senate Appropriations Committee. Along with the reviews he asked Couch to include statements from publishers "that books like *TAOL* [*These Are Our Lives*] could not be produced under any other set-up except Federal control of the Writers' Project." Couch wrote the members of the committee that he thought curtailment of the authority of the national director and the switch to local control and sponsorship would have the following negative results: (1) it would mean a lowering of standards governing the work; (2) the project would be more susceptible to local political influence; (3) because of inadequate personnel many states would not produce good work without outside direction; (4) important projects that required interstate cooperation would become impossible; and (5) state officials without the support of a national director would be "unable to get the attention of publishers."[48]

On all these points Couch spoke from experience. Despite his misgivings about how the bureaucracy of the WPA and the FWP operated, Couch knew that his numerous plans for volumes of life histories could not proceed without the authority to establish interstate programs, and he also realized that he could have accomplished little without Alsberg's support. But the efforts of Couch and other supporters of the arts projects did not prevent a Congress bent on emasculating these and other relief programs from working its will. The congressional forces pushing for changes in the administration of relief abetted by an increasingly cautious New Deal were not to be denied. The Emergency Relief Act passed on June 30, 1939, made changes in the FWP that soon led Couch to conclude that under the new rules the life history program could not proceed. But before he reached that conclusion, he continued to make plans for future work on the life history program that are interesting as reflections of the cultural and intellectual history of the 1930s and as programmatic statements about the study of southern cultural and social history. That the work did not continue is part of the story of what happened to the FWP after June 1939.[49]

The dismissal of Alsberg in August further demoralized project officials. Couch found it distressing that at this, "the most confused moment we have had," Alsberg was fired. He expressed his gratitude to Alsberg for giving him the "chance to do TAOL" and explained that he would continue with the FWP "if I see any chance to get any more work done of any value," but he admitted that "the outlook is anything but hopeful."[50]

Despite the dismal outlook, Couch continued to advocate work on life histories. Eager to obtain the aid of sociologists in carrying out this work, he corresponded with a number of the nation's outstanding scholars in that field. Notwithstanding the general acclaim for *These Are Our Lives*, Couch was disappointed that sociologists did not give it careful attention. Paul Underwood Kellogg, editor of *Survey* magazine, a journal whose history and interests were intimately tied to its origins as a forum for the social work and social welfare issues that emerged during the Progressive Era, was enthusiastic about Couch's work. Kellogg, more interested in social work than social theory and in reform than in research, thought that sociologists who lacked interest in *These Are Our Lives* "were all wet. We've put in a lot of licks for this very type of case history." On the other hand, Ellsworth Faris, a professional sociologist at the University of Chicago, thought that while the success of the book "must be a source of satisfaction and encouragement" to Couch, it was "natural and proper" that sociologists did not concern themselves with it. In his opinion the work did not "come under the most liberal definition of sociological concern." *These Are Our Lives*, he argued, was a "type of propaganda" comparable to *Tobacco Road*, *Gone with the Wind*, and *The Grapes of Wrath*. He maintained that a distinction had to be made "between objective, scientific research and the warm hearted efforts to promote a cause." He failed to specify what cause he thought *These Are Our Lives* advocated.[51]

Couch denied that there was any propagandistic purpose behind the life histories. What he had hoped to do, he insisted, "was to find and use a method which would reveal the real experiences of persons in different levels and in different occupational groups." Sociologists, Couch thought, could help him gather statistical information "to test the typicalness of much of the experience in the life histories." Only by presenting the life histories of individuals, he believed, could the statistical facts be given a meaningful context: "Surely sociologists are aware of the danger of using isolated facts without context— the more real the context, the more nearly it comes to representing the whole living complex in which fact functions, the more 'truthful,' or if you prefer, the more 'scientific.'"[52]

Other social scientists expressed a more positive interest in Couch's work. Hadley Cantril, a distinguished student of public opinion, wrote Couch of his interest in the work on life histories. Plans were made for Hope Tisdale, a member of the Institute for Research in the Social Sciences at the University of North Carolina, to supervise the collection of life histories for the proposed volume "Victims of the Depression." For the first time, Couch would have the aid of trained sociologists. The possibility of Paul Green bringing his literary talents and knowledge of the southern folk to aid in the work on life histories was discussed. Couch was so impressed by poet Allen Tate's review of *These Are Our Lives* that he wished Tate could help him edit future volumes. These plans were so far removed from a concern with mere propaganda that Couch sought the aid of sociologists committed to a "regionalist" approach to southern problems, a liberal playwright, and an Agrarian poet.[53]

Although Couch now had the support of interested scholars and the promise of their help in the collection of life histories, he was not optimistic about the possibilities of continuing the work under the FWP. He explored the possibility of obtaining foundation support either as a supplement to FWP funds or, if necessary, as an alternative. Only after several months of fruitless negotiation with government officials did he abandon the hope of continuing the work through the Writers' Program.[54]

In November 1939 Couch finally concluded that there was no longer any purpose in continuing with the Writers' Program. In his letter of resignation Couch offered a detailed critique of the program's weaknesses. Foremost among his reasons for resigning was that he "had not been able to get any work done since May 1939." What made matters worse was that "much that was previously done had been undone." From the project in Oklahoma Couch had secured nearly enough material to publish a volume of life histories on people in the oil industry, but "for some reasons never yet made clear, the Oklahoma staff was dropped." More than a month earlier, Washington officials had promised to inform Couch when he "could go ahead" on other volumes. That approval never arrived "in spite of repeated inquiries." He pointed out that three or four additional volumes of life histories could have been published by this time and work begun on others if only Washington officials had extended their support.[55]

Although only a part of Couch's plans for the southern life history program were completed, the more than one thousand life histories collected offer ample materials to scholars that they have only recently begun to exploit. *These Are Our Lives* provides only a limited introduction to the life histories collected by the FWP. Couch's editing of this volume reflected his reformist and instrumental view of the life history project. His sample is biased. All of the life histories in *These Are Our Lives* deal with hard-working, virtuous people coping with their problems. A more recently published selection from the life histories, *Such as Us: Southern Voices of the Thirties*, edited by Tom E. Terrill and Jerrold Hirsch, focuses on many of the same areas as *These Are Our Lives*; however, there are people in *Such as Us* who had become their own worst enemies. They are wasteful, they drink to excess, or they beat their wives. Even when read together, the two volumes give a limited view of the richness of the collection. Many life histories of such diverse occupational and ethnic groups as miners, turpentiners, fishermen, Chinese laundrymen, and Cuban and Italian cigar makers remain unpublished and virtually unknown.

While the idea behind the life history program was Couch's, his authority in implementing it was limited. He determined what was published, but he could not control what was recorded. The life history collection represents not a single vision but a collective one—a vision that reflects the efforts of ordinary project workers and the people they talked with. Relying on their personal and, occasionally, eccentric understanding of what was required, southern FWP fieldworkers had gone about their task, each one picking his or her own subjects for his or her own reasons and often taking great liberties in following the suggested interview outline. The nature of that collective vision and the historical uses of the southern life history collection are explored in the context of larger issues dealt with in the next two chapters.

The unpublished southern life histories are one of the enduring legacies of the FWP. They are a product of Couch's ideas and energy, the intellectual currents of the 1930s, and the contribution of southern Federal Writers. They are evidence that despite the makeshift air surrounding the Writers' Project and its conflicting roles as a relief agency and an art project, significant work was completed. In retrospect it can be seen that the publication of *These Are Our Lives* in 1939 represented what writer Harvey Swados has called "not only the high-water mark but the last wave of an unprecedented tide of government-sponsored creative work by writers, artists, and theatre people during the depression years."[56]

Chapter 8

Toward a Marriage of True Minds
The Federal Writers' Project and the Writing of Southern Folk History

"If we admitted no impediments to a marriage of true minds between folklore and history, the product of their union would be folk history," B. A. Botkin declared before a 1939 meeting of the American Historical Association. In his role as director of FWP folklore programs and as chairman of the joint WPA committee that linked all the WPA agencies that had any connection with folk arts, Botkin encouraged studies that sought to achieve that union. In his approach to the study of folklore and his view of the relationship between folklore and historical studies, he was years ahead of scholars in either field. Only recently have some southern historians begun to employ the concepts of cultural anthropology and the methods of the ethnographer in their work and to treat oral traditions and folkways as significant historical sources. The FWP's guidebooks to the southern states in the American Guide Series, the life histories of southern tenant farmers and mill workers, and the interviews with former slaves are important sources for the study of southern folk history.[1]

The FWP southern studies did not develop in a simple linear fashion from state guidebooks to life histories and interviews with former slaves culminating in a marriage between folklore and history. Indeed, it is important to understand that most of the Federal Writers in the South directly or indirectly rejected Botkin's approach to the study of southern culture. The tensions within the FWP over the best way to study the South illuminate change and continuity in how white southerners have viewed their culture and adapted traditional patterns of thought to new circumstances. Then and now the meanings that those who study the South assign to the terms "folk" and "folklore" involve not only methodological issues but also those students' cultural politics—their hopes and fears. Although they have begun to use the FWP southern life histories, interviews with former slaves, folklore studies, and guidebooks as historical sources, historians have largely ignored the intellectual and cultural climate in which the Federal Writers produced these works. It is necessary to place the FWP's southern studies in a broad intellectual context, for these programs developed in response to an inherited and contemporary dialogue about both southern history and folk culture.

The federal structure of the FWP led to a unique dialogue between national FWP officials—who for the most part were members of a nationally oriented, left-of-center, cosmopolitan, and ethnically diverse intellectual community (there were few southerners among them)—and locally oriented, mostly conservative, middle-class, southern white Federal Writers. The number of blacks on each southern state unit could be counted on one hand. The exceptions were Virginia, Louisiana, and Florida, which had separate black units. In any case, there were not enough blacks on the southern FWP projects to affect the dominant approach of the southern FWP units and the assumptions underlying most of the published work.[2]

National FWP officials embraced cultural pluralism and egalitarian values as central to an understanding of American history and identity. The vast majority of southern Federal Writers rejected both pluralism and egalitarianism. On one level the discussion between these conflicting groups was about how to interpret southern folklore and history and how to explain change and continuity; on another level it revealed how national, regional, state, and local officials themselves responded to change or the possibility of change. In the broadest terms the issue was the relationship between tradition and modernity; in a southern context, that meant the dominant issues were the relationship between traditional agrarian folkways and industrialization, and the place of African Americans in the southern social order.

At the national level, cultural pluralism complemented New Deal programs that sought to address the problems of industrial workers, farmers, and blacks and other ethnic minorities. There was an implicit liberal-reformist alliance between New Deal officials directing political and cultural programs at the na-

tional level. In contrast, conservative approaches to culture and politics went
hand-in-hand in the South. Conservative white southern Democrats feared
that the New Deal might reopen political questions about class and caste relations in the South—questions that they preferred to regard as settled.[3]

Local southern Federal Writers shared the dominant views of history and
culture that prevailed in their region—views that helped legitimize the social
and political structure of their society. Within the FWP these regional differences
often resulted in work pursued on the basis of different assumptions and values.

The various approaches that national, regional, state, and local Federal Writers advocated toward the study of the South reveal differing definitions of folklore and conflicting assumptions about southern folk culture. Similarly, the attitudes toward change exhibited by southern Federal Writers versus those held
by national FWP officials reflect contrasting definitions of folk culture: the southern writers stressed a static, eternal southern culture; the national officials emphasized the dynamic, adaptive, acculturative processes that characterize subcultures in a pluralist society. These attitudes were clearly linked to larger values
concerning race relations within the South, southern economic development,
and the South's relation to the rest of the nation.

Whatever their orientation, southern Federal Writers and national FWP officials all addressed such questions as Who should be included in talking about
the southern folk? Could southern culture change and adapt to new developments and still remain distinctive? When was it better to resist new developments, and when was it preferable to adapt to them? These questions link the
work of the FWP to debates that have been at the heart of the way white southerners have thought about the South since the defeat of the Confederacy, for
questions about defining southern folklore and the central themes of southern
history have always been implicitly (and sometimes explicitly) about whether
the South has a future as a distinctive culture.

For many twentieth-century students of southern culture, the very existence
of a distinctive southern culture has been a major topic of debate, and positions
taken on the issue often have reflected political agendas. Conservative white
southerners have feared change would destroy southern culture and identity;
their references to "tradition" often have commingled with talk about maintaining racial and cultural purity. Liberals, on the other hand, both southern
and nonsouthern, have taken more ambivalent positions on these issues, although some liberals have equated the disappearance of a distinctive southern
culture with progress. Key FWP officials, such as Botkin and Couch, arrived at
their own positions on these issues partly in response to the discussion of the

nature of southern identity that took place between the Nashville Agrarians and the Chapel Hill Regionalists. The Agrarians rejected industrialism and social change in favor of their version of the folkways of the agrarian past. The Regionalists, although favoring industrialism and social change, also sought to describe and maintain a distinctive southern folk culture—goals the Agrarians argued were irreconcilable.[4]

Botkin's appointment as national FWP folklore editor in 1938 was a turning point in the history of the Writers' Project. Folklore studies were an obvious and indispensable part of a romantic-nationalist program like the FWP. Until Botkin joined the project, however, it was unclear how folklore fit into the FWP's effort both to reconcile romantic nationalism and cultural pluralism and to study contemporary American life.[5]

Like romantic nationalists elsewhere, national FWP officials undertook folklore studies as part of their effort to record and celebrate an indigenous culture that would provide the basis for a national identity and a national literature. Some romantic folklorists, including John Lomax, considered modernity and pluralism as mortal threats to folklore, and they regarded isolated and homogeneous communities as the only places in which a pure and uncontaminated folklore could survive.[6]

Many of the traditional assumptions underlying romantic-nationalist and evolutionary approaches to folklore studies were compatible with neither the pluralistic and egalitarian values of national FWP officials nor their ideal of America as an inclusive national community that recognized and encouraged differences. Lomax's approach to folklore did not help FWP officials reconcile romantic nationalism with cultural pluralism. Although Lomax was a famous collector of songs of southern blacks, there was little in his approach that threatened the values of local white southern FWP field-workers. His emphasis on purity, homogeneity, and uncontaminated traditions was easily reconciled with a commitment to a segregated social order, as his own published writings indicated.[7]

 Botkin's background, experiences, perspective, and cultural and political commitments complemented those of his colleagues in the Washington FWP office, but they were very different from those of most white FWP southern field-workers, and they also differed in significant ways from those of either Lomax or Couch. His interest in the South was cultural and political; although this interest was intense, it was also detached and theoretical in a way rare among native southerners.[8]

The relationship of the South to the rest of the nation and the relationship between whites and blacks in the region posed challenges to Botkin's view of a democratic, egalitarian, and pluralistic society. By stressing change, process, adaptation, and acculturation, Botkin was urging historians and folklorists to move beyond static definitions of the folk and folk culture, beyond abstract juxtapositions such as agrarianism and industrialism, and beyond the search for reified eternal qualities that define southerners, whether black or white. Botkin understood that the democratic and egalitarian thrust of his view of a diverse American folklore as a cultural asset had political implications, perhaps more for black Americans than for anyone else.[9]

Botkin's functionalism allowed him to see that folklore could be created in industrial and urban environments, and that folklore could be found among the literate and educated as well as among the illiterate and uneducated. He thought that technological media did not destroy folklore but in complex new ways became part of the process of transmitting it; he was convinced that industrialism and the end of geographic isolation would not destroy folk traditions. Given his assumptions, Botkin did not share the fears that many southern intellectuals held regarding the future of tradition in an industrializing and urbanizing world.[10]

Southern folklore, black and white, was central to Botkin's working out his views of both folklore and American diversity as cultural assets. In struggling to arrive at an understanding of the dynamics of folklore in a pluralistic society, he gave the South and its folk traditions considerable attention. On the theoretical level the issue was whether folk traditions had a future in an industrializing society in which geographical isolation was breaking down. On the social and political level the issues were racial and economic inequality. Botkin concluded that neither industrialization nor the end of segregation would threaten the existence of southern folklore.[11]

The Agrarians viewed tradition as a static inheritance that could be maintained only in a homogeneous rural society. Botkin saw tradition as dynamic and changing, adapting to new circumstances and thriving among factories and cities as well as in the fields. The pluralistic and relativistic anthropology that informed Botkin's view of the folk and their lore worked against the evolutionary anthropology that was part of the Victorian intellectual inheritance that informed the thinking of the Agrarians. The Agrarians, the Chapel Hill Regionalists, and Botkin all inherited romantic-nationalist cultural notions and tried to use them to resolve identity, to impose wholeness on a fragmented reality, and to overcome alienation. Both the Agrarians and the Regionalists found that their ideas about the South unified a fragmented modern society. Similarly, Botkin set himself the task of reconciling romantic nationalist notions based on the assumption of the necessity of cultural homogeneity with his desire to embrace and celebrate America's cultural pluralism. For him, the idea of a pluralist America played the same role in translating the romantic tradition to fit modernity that the South played for the Regionalists and the Agrarians.[12]

Botkin was drawn to Agrarian poet Allen Tate's idea that tradition was a set of manners and ways of feeling that one took for granted and did not have to learn. Tate thought such traditionalism would prevent "atrophy" of one's "power of contemplation." Botkin, however, finally rejected Tate's outlook because he was convinced that it was bound to lead to atrophy of one's power of social perception, that indeed Tate's view meant taking "a certain social order as final" —in this case, the southern caste system.[13]

In arguing that the southern Agrarians made the "mistake of identifying culture with a particular trait or complex, a particular way of life . . . [and] of taking a certain background for granted, and a certain social order as final," Botkin was using anthropological positions to make both theoretical and normative judgments. Few FWP southern field-workers would have understood or agreed with Botkin's argument that "cultural minorities and other nondominant groups . . . were not static but dynamic and transitional, on their way up." These field-workers' underlying assumptions about folklore and their view of southern society were fundamentally opposed to Botkin's. They regarded the southern caste system as a fixed and final solution to race relations in the South, as can be seen in the work they turned in and in many of the southern FWP publications.[14]

Couch successfully resisted attempts to combine his southern life history program with the efforts of the national office to coordinate folklore studies with black and social-ethnic studies. Both Botkin and Couch advocated collecting life histories, but there were substantive differences in the way each man conceived of the life history interview. Botkin saw the life history as part of the folklore interview. In his view, the field-worker merely began with the personal history of the informant; but if the interview went well, the field-worker would soon be recording "folk knowledge and folk fantasy." At that point the interviewer would be tapping the folk experience and history of a group. Such interviews, Botkin argued, helped capture a sense of the tremendous historical changes many groups of Americans had experienced in only a few generations —the migration (often immigration) from a rural to an urban world, and the transition from rural to urban patterns of work and play. The interviews documented the creative reciprocity between the individual and his or her folk group and illuminated the dynamics of the acculturative process. Taken together, Botkin thought, a collection of such accounts constituted a folk history.[15]

Couch, on the other hand, thought of life histories as primarily representing different social types and classes. His view of the life history was rooted in journalistic and sociological approaches to the social problems that modernity had exacerbated. He aimed to obtain material that had literary qualities sociological writing lacked yet did not present "the composite or imaginary character" of the fiction writer. In part, the differences between Botkin and Couch reflected the differences between anthropology and sociology in the 1930s. Botkin emphasized the strength and adaptability of folk traditions in a modernizing society, the norms and patterns that gave coherence to group life; Couch focused on the problems created by the growth of a market-oriented agriculture and an industrial workforce in a traditionally hierarchical and biracial society—the problems, in short, of the tenant farmer and the textile worker.[16]

Like national FWP officials, Couch was a supporter of the New Deal, and as such, he advocated examining and possibly reforming much that many white southern Federal Writers did not question. But there remained ways in which Couch was closer to the local southern Federal Writers than to the national officials, for many of his views were responses to inherited and contemporary southern folk, popular, and intellectual attitudes and ideas that were a part of his cultural background. His way of studying a changing South was itself an example of how southern intellectuals adapted to change.

Couch, the son of a Baptist country preacher, was born in 1901 in Pamplin, Virginia. During his undergraduate years at the University of North Carolina, he became widely known for his articles in the *Carolina Magazine* attacking southern conservatism. In 1925, while still a student, he became assistant director of the University of North Carolina Press. In 1932 he was appointed director. He worked to publish books that he thought would help southerners develop a critical attitude toward the social problems they confronted, that would provoke debate, and that would explore the ways various groups of southerners lived. Couch was also deeply concerned that knowledge and discussion of these problems not be confined to experts. Knowledge, he thought, was power. It could promote reform.[17]

Couch saw in the FWP a means of examining southern life in a way that upholders of the status quo in the region would not support. In turning to the FWP to gain leverage against those who approved of things as they were, Couch was willing to break with southern tradition and—in a sense—seek federal interference. He was one of a growing number of southern liberals who in the 1930s found a supportive network in government programs developed under the New Deal.

Couch thought that by interviewing tenant farmers and textile workers and members of other occupational groups, Federal Writers could help move the discussion of southern reality beyond stereotypes and abstractions, beyond the conventional wisdom that helped rationalize the status quo. To argue, as so many southerners did, that "we are held down by the Negro" or that "the masses of white people are not particularly helpful material," Couch insisted, was to "help keep things as they are." Despite novelist Erskine Caldwell's appeals for the reform of sharecropping, Couch regarded Caldwell's portrayal of Jeeter Lester and his family in *Tobacco Road* as reinforcing stereotypes about the southern poor. On the other hand, he rejected what he also saw as the abstract and unrealistic position of the Agrarians. In his view their rejection of industrialization and their idealization of a simpler agrarian society constituted a misreading of southern culture and history and offered no realistic hope for those at the bottom of southern society. The Agrarians, Couch contended, "assert that virtue is derived from the soil, but see no virtue in the Negro and poor white who are closest to the soil." Couch insisted that "the South must recognize that the kind of evils Mr. Caldwell describes actually exist in this region, and must do what it can to correct them."[18]

If southerners were given a chance to speak for themselves, Couch thought, their accounts would move the discussion of southern social problems away from the vast body of oral and written tradition that attributed the plight of poor southerners, black and white, to their inferior character and heredity. In place of the sentimental antimodernism of the Agrarians and the bloodless statistical abstractions of the sociologists, readers of the southern life histories, Couch argued, would encounter the voices of specific individuals recounting from their own perspective the impact of the tenant farm system, industrialization, and the Great Depression on their lives.[19]

Nevertheless, the very sources of the strengths of the southern life history project are the reasons it did not result in a marriage between folklore and history, a folk history. Couch, for all his interest in the daily lives and problems of ordinary southerners, was not particularly interested in their folk culture, and this was revealed in the life history outline and in the stories themselves. Some folk material inevitably turns up in the southern life histories; but it was not sought out, and the interviewers were not especially interested in learning about it. For example, how southern textile workers adapted old folkways to a new means of making a living as they creatively responded to new circumstances remained unexplored. The interviewers failed on numerous occasions to ask additional questions when interviewees referred to their folk culture. To a significant degree the explanation lies in the southern context within which Couch formulated his outlook.

Couch not only made analyses that blamed the social and economic system rather than individuals for their plight, but he also worked within the context of an inherited set of regional attitudes about the character of the poor. The life histories in *These Are Our Lives* demonstrate Couch's desire both to blame the system and to show the strength of character of ordinary southerners. On the whole, the inherited southern discourse (which, ironically, had a significant folklore component) about the poor had more influence on how the southern life history project was conducted than did anthropological approaches; therefore, the southern life histories did not pursue southern folk history and culture to the extent they could have. Traditional southern attitudes about character could be reconciled with a sociological approach, but it prevented a deeper anthropological examination of culture.

In a review of *These Are Our Lives*, Allen Tate insisted that, given the absence of an underlying formal structure to lend them enduring significance, these interviews conveyed only information, not knowledge. Tate, however, found most satisfying two stories that he thought reflected the imaginative qualities of fiction. "'Tore Up and a-Movin'" and "On the Road to Sheriff," he argued, exhibited "the qualities of two very old types of literature, the medieval exemplum and another form of medieval expression best known in 'Piers Ploughman,' a late development of the early mystical vision into an allegory of social protest." Tate found underlying allegory, myth, and vision in the life histories only by comparing them to earlier forms of literature from the culture of another time and place. It does not seem to have occurred to him that the interviewees, drawing on their folk culture, might have given narrative pattern to their stories and filled them with visual imagery and metaphoric language. It did not occur to Couch either.[20]

Couch's problem-oriented view of southern social needs remained within the bounds of a very old southern discourse about the character of the poor; at the same time, it caused him to miss the opportunity to explore more fully change and continuity in the culture of ordinary southerners, white and black. Botkin's focus on what were widely regarded as erroneous and irrational folklore materials, mere survivals of a vanishing way of life, could have provided a view of the impact of change on the traditions of ordinary southerners that Couch's rational, problem-oriented approach could not offer. Like Couch, however, Botkin was limited in what he could do by the perspective brought to the FWP projects by the middle-class white southerners employed on them.

Local southern Federal Writers, for the most part, shared a view of southern culture and folklore that differed from either Couch's or Botkin's. They accepted many of the traditional beliefs about poor whites and blacks that Couch
thought stood in the way of the South's addressing its economic and social
problems. Given their assumptions, southern Federal Writers easily echoed the
views of traditional folklorists who regarded industrialism and pluralism (in a
southern context, racial equality) as enemies of folk culture—a view of folklore Botkin had rejected. The traditional assumptions underlying conservative
romantic-nationalist and evolutionary approaches to folklore studies proved
compatible with these writers' commitment to a racial caste system and a nostalgic view of agrarian folkways. Romantic-nationalist definitions of folklore
had stressed the importance of homogeneity, isolation, and an agricultural way
of life. Folklorists working within an evolutionary framework regarded folklore as being composed of survivals from an earlier stage in the progress of
human beings. It was easy for white southerners to develop variations on these
themes, adapting them to their determination to maintain a segregated society
and to their anxiety about industrialism.[21]

The determination of most southern Federal Writers to make the former
slaves' narratives confirm the white South's traditional view of blacks and slavery is one of the limitations of these interviews as a source on African American slavery. Yet what in one context is a limitation in the sources is a strength
in another. The reaction of white southerners to the assignment to interview
former slaves reveals much about their outlook, about what can be called their
white folk view of black folklore. Chalmers S. Murray, a South Carolina Federal Writer, confided to his state director that he "thought from the first it was
rather a mistake to write these ex-slave stories. . . . The general run of negro is
only too glad of opportunity to record his grievances"—grievances Murray
dismissed as either unfounded or exaggerated. In many of their interviews
with former slaves, white southern field-workers strove to confirm the image
of plantation slavery familiar to them from white southern folklore, popular
culture, and the novels of writers such as Thomas Nelson Page.[22]

The FWP guidebooks to the southern states reveal that local Federal Writers
—and most of the other southerners asked to contribute to the guides as spe-
cialists—worked within a conservative, antimodern, hierarchical, romantic
southern plantation tradition that viewed the past with nostalgia, rationalized
the status quo, and looked at folklore as material endangered by change. In
many ways this view constituted a mirror image of Botkin's liberal/radical romanticism, which looked forward to change; envisioned a more inclusive, dem-

ocratic, and egalitarian community than what had existed; sought to document the ways in which folklore demonstrated how people adapted their traditions to a changing world; and regarded folklore as an important source of social history. Although national FWP officials wanted to produce encyclopedic guides that would "introduce" Americans to the diverse traditions that existed in their country, the guides never completely transcended the tourist mode.[23] The southern guides presented folklore and life within the limits of a plantation tradition genre that patronized black folkways and many white folkways as merely exotic and quaint.

The guidebooks to the southern states represented not only an outgrowth of the plantation tradition but also, in part, a contribution to it. For white southerners the plantation tradition was an important discourse about their relationship to the past, to the former slaves and their descendants, and to the new nation that emerged from the crucible of war. Its mythic description of a lost idyllic world of friendship and affection between master and slave, and of devoted, contented, and comic "darkies," helped rationalize a caste system in the New South. Through repetition and variation, white southerners molded the plantation tradition to reflect and fulfill the purposes of the white community. The portrayal of blacks in the plantation tradition tells more about white southern folklore about blacks than about the folklore of southern blacks themselves; it reveals more about how whites wanted blacks to function in white society than about the functions of folklore and oral tradition in black culture.[24]

The plantation tradition glorifying the Old South had developed in tandem with a New South creed that advocated industrialization and urbanization under the guidance of a conservative southern elite determined to maintain a traditional social and racial hierarchy. In the guidebooks to their states, southern Federal Writers linked discussions of the New South that they saw developing around them with references to the Old South and the blacks. According to the Alabama guide, "the ante bellum mansion and the towering steel mill still symbolize Alabama's dual personality." But the "clash of the once conflicting interests of agriculture and industry has lost some of its former bitterness as activities in both fields show the value of co-operation." Mississippians, that state's guide asserts, are "earth-rooted individuals . . . who collectively face an industrial revolution with hoes grasped tightly in their clay-stained hands." Change, however, could be more dramatic than some white Southerners could accept. Young people in Georgia, guidebook readers are told, having traveled more than their parents, "have lost some of their sectional individuality" and closely resemble young people throughout the nation. Therefore, "their attitude toward the educated Negro, for instance, may be different from that of their parents who still prefer the old-fashioned unlettered kind." Throughout the southern guides, traditional images of African Americans are offered as reassuring signs of stability amidst change. The writers welcome industrialization, but with mixed feelings. For example, the Louisiana guide writers insisted that "while Monroe is [an] essentially modern and semi-urban [city] in aspect, its people cherish many old southern traditions, especially as regards relations between whites and Negroes, hospitality, and a chivalrous attitude toward the ladies."[25]

The southern guides are full of traditional pictures of black folklife that draw on the plantation tradition and portray African Americans as an unchanging folk element linking white southerners of the New South to their Old South ancestors. The Texas guide tells readers about African Americans spending their days "chopping and picking cotton," noting that "their faded jeans and bright sunbonnets are part of the southern tradition," that "old customs of the golden age of cotton survive," and that while the tenant houses of these African Americans constitute a "squalid scene," their "usually smiling faces . . . lend cheer."[26]

Throughout the southern guides, Federal Writers offer traditional images of blacks as reassuring signs of stability amidst change. As muckraking journalist Ray Stannard Baker had pointed out earlier in his *Following the Color Line: An Account of Negro Citizenship in the American Democracy* (1908), "Many southerners look back wistfully to the faithful, simple, ignorant, obedient, cheerful, old plantation Negro and deplore his disappearance. They want the New South, but the old Negro." Baker focused on how a segregated society worked, reported on lynchings, and described white-initiated riots that resulted in attacks on blacks and their property. In the FWP southern guides there are only passing references to these matters.[27]

The guides also contrast the Old and New South by using adjectives such as "slow" and "swift," which reflect what southern Federal Writers perceived as traditional versus modern concepts of time and space and as acknowledging change in their world. The Mississippi guide writers noted that Laurel presented a sharp contrast to "many Mississippi towns richly flavored with the essence of the ante-bellum South." Rather, Laurel exhibited "in a few fast-moving chapters a swift transition from forest through lumber camp to a stable industrial city in the course of fifty years." Life in Florence, Alabama, "continues to move easily despite industrial activity initiated by the Tennessee Valley Authority." While it is true that "khaki-clad Government engineers move briskly," the local "citizens pause on the courthouse lawn to escape the hot summer sun and to discuss politics, and the well-filled knife-marked benches under the trees may be thought of as symbols of this leisurely city." In Selma, Alabama, and throughout the South, "Negro and white citizens have lived in an atmosphere of sympathetic understanding, tinged by a friendly paternalism on the part of whites." The repeated use of the same picturesque scenes replaces direct observation; indeed, it substitutes for any knowledge of the black perspective, of black folklore and ways.[28]

The guidebooks portray white and black southerners as separate groups, each with its distinctive folklore. They explain any similarities within an evolutionary framework and not as the product of acculturation. Southern Federal Writers portray the interaction between these two folk groups as unidirectional, from white to black, from higher to lower levels on the scale of cultural evolution. Georgia Federal Writers working on the study that became *Drums and Shadows* argued that the African American had "innate instincts stronger than the new civilization," which even in the educated members of the race constituted only a "thin veneer." Reconstructing folk history along evolutionary lines, which was still common in American folklore scholarship in the 1930s, white southerners could recount the "history" of African American folklore without relating it to a southern historical experience shared by blacks and whites, and without acknowledging the active role of blacks in helping shape a distinctive southern folklore.[29]

In the essay "Negro Folkways" in the Mississippi guide, the writer makes clear his distance from his subject (always referred to as "him," so that the subject turns into an object). That space makes possible a patronizing tone characteristic of the southern guides: "Those who know him well enough to understand something of his psychology, his character, and his needs, and like him well enough to accept his deficiencies, find him to be wise but credulous —a superstitious paradox." The writer found both amusement and reassurance in the Mississippi black, "a genial mass of remarkable qualities . . . carefree and shrewd. . . . As for the so-called Negro question—that, too, is just another problem he has left for the white man to cope with." The third-person description effectively silences the black subject; its use in this context links the guides to the southern plantation tradition. As Francis Pendelton Gaines pointed out in his study of the southern plantation tradition, "A popular literary device, repeated again and again, was to hand down the legend of splendor and joy through the mouths of the slaves themselves." By casting blacks in the role of clown, court jester, guardian of the tradition, and "sable curator of folk-lore," the plantation tradition tried to make a racist worldview appear benign. It employed the stereotyped portrait of the black as humorous primitive to make the ideal of the blissful race relations of the plantation believable; it used the

African American's own folklore, as interpreted by whites, to justify slavery in the past and the creation of a caste system to replace it.[30]

In part the plantation tradition was a deeply conservative form of antimodernism that profoundly influenced the way southern black folklore and life were presented to a national audience. In a clear but subdued form, the FWP southern state guides embody variations on the genre. According to Gaines, the "genuine darkey" of the plantation tradition, "the folk figure of a simple, somewhat rustic, character, instinctively humorous, irrationally credulous, gifted in song and dance, interesting in spontaneous frolic, endowed with artless philosophy," represents the romantic longings of the "public." Implicitly, the public is white America. These qualities of the "folk figure" draw on a long-standing conservative European romantic nationalist tradition as well as on indigenous racist traditions. In the South, however, the folk/nonfolk dichotomy is also a white/black dichotomy, and the allegedly positive qualities of the "folk" Negro win black Americans no status; rather, they rationalize inequality. These "folk" qualities appear frequently in the work southern Federal Writers submitted to their superiors.[31]

Southern Federal Writers, like other white southerners, used the plantation tradition to dichotomize past and present, to offer a view of a lost world deemed superior in many ways to modern circumstances. Their approach was a variant on a conservative European romantic interest in folklore that saw in the folk and their lore survivals from a past world free of the ills of modern life. The working out of the question of race relations within a tradition that could capitalize on nostalgic reactions to the stresses of modernity helped gain the plantation tradition a national audience. The plantation tradition also gained popularity "as a kind of American embodiment of the golden age," allegedly fulfilling the need of a youthful nation for "a misty, heroic long ago."[32]

As a conservative romantic nationalist myth, the plantation tradition worked against every goal that national FWP officials hoped to achieve. While these officials were seeking to reconcile romantic nationalism and pluralism and to redefine American identity and nationality along more inclusive, egalitarian, and democratic lines, the southern Federal Writers' use of the plantation tradition conveyed the message that a racially diverse society could only work when one group dominated. This message's implicit criticism of the present offered no program or hope for change; it was an accommodation to a form of modernization that exacerbated inequality. It wrote blacks out of the national culture except as subordinates confined to white-defined roles. It celebrated a slave society and helped justify a system that denied black Americans their rights as citizens. In this national myth about the southern past the black point of view was excluded.

The FWP studies of the South embody the conflicting visions of national FWP officials and local southern Federal Writers. That conflict makes the materials a difficult, but nevertheless valuable, source for southern folk history and an especially rich source for studying how white middle-class southerners adapted their folk traditions to change even while trying to limit and deny the impact of change.

Southern Federal Writers either ignored or rejected Botkin's approach to the study of folklore as a neglected source of social history. Questions of methodology were only the tip of the iceberg; the cultural and political implications of different approaches led national FWP officials and local southern Federal Writers each to object to the approach of the other. Southern Federal Writers, unlike national FWP officials, had no desire to reconcile romantic nationalism with cultural pluralism. Couch's reformist approach to the study of ordinary southerners was no more helpful than that of local southern FWP field-workers in illuminating how southern tradition adapted to change, especially as seen in the relationship between changing ways of living and ways of making a living. Working within the plantation tradition, southern Federal Writers sought to celebrate a static southern folklore in an unchanging social structure; in doing so, they were contributing to that same nostalgic tradition—a version that helped accommodate economic development even while serving as a barrier against political and social change. The writers' assumptions made it impossible for them to study and understand how white and black southerners adapted their folklore to a continually changing world—to an emerging industrial order and an increasingly market-oriented agriculture—within a paternalistic and hierarchical society. The southern field-workers treated both black and white folk cultures as homogeneous wholes. They largely ignored the impact of class divisions on folkways. They denied and left unexplored the evidence that a dynamic acculturative process affected the lore of both blacks and whites, although they often recorded the evidence of this very process.

Nevertheless, despite the aims of southern Federal Writers and the resulting limitations in the material they collected, their work can make a contribution both to scholarship and toward realizing the vision that guided national FWP officials. Two works that Botkin later edited, both drawing on FWP southern studies, offer powerful examples of his vision of the role of folklore in studying social history; both meet what he called "the tremendous responsibility of studying folklore as a living culture and of understanding its meaning and function not only in its immediate setting but in progressive and democratic society as a whole." Using excerpts from the FWP interviews with former slaves, Botkin edited *Lay My Burden Down: A Folk History of Slavery* (1945), which sought to bring the black oral tradition into a public forum and allowed the generation of blacks who had experienced slavery and freedom, Civil War and Reconstruction, to present a history that questioned every assumption of the plantation tradition. In *A Treasury of Southern Folklore* (1949) Botkin did not simply stick to traditional and safe topics—agrarian lifestyles and the beliefs of isolated mountaineers—but instead emphasized the folklore that emerged from the interaction between cultures. Labor conflicts, such as those between mill owners and textile workers, he maintained, "created a new folklore-in-the-making."[33]

Botkin's emphasis on folklore as a process kept him from searching for fixed southern qualities, such as personalism, the love of the concrete, hierarchy, and biracialism. In his view, external and concrete measurements did not adequately define the region. He was interested in consciousness. He insisted that folklore as a living tradition, which together the individual and the folk group molded and *remolded,* offered insights into areas of culture to which traditional historical sources provided only limited access. Botkin's methodology embodied values he wished to promote, and he found a happy congruence between his scholarly positions and his values as a citizen.

Ironically, the attitude of local southern Federal Writers toward folklore was also an example of one of the dynamic ways southerners adapted their traditions to change. While the approach of local Federal Writers is less helpful to historians today trying to understand southern social history than Botkin's, his methods can be employed to understand their folklore. Botkin attacked the theoretical approaches to folklore that denied that tradition was a part of the process of adapting the past to the present; he also rejected the views of white southerners who held such theories much more for political and social rather than scholarly reasons. In effect, Botkin argued that the demise of the caste system, the growth of a more democratic social order, and the spread of industrialism would not mean the demise of southern identity if southerners worked to adapt what was valuable in their traditions to the world he and other New Deal liberals envisioned. The history of the FWP, however, indicates that the demise of a particular theoretical perspective among folklorists and historians is no guarantee that conservative southerners will not find new ways to confront, and sometimes to promote, change within a conservative framework.

Part 3

Denouement

Chapter 9

Conflicting Definitions of America

The Dies Committee and the Writers' Project

"In every one of those books [the Minnesota, Montana, and New Jersey FWP guides]," declared a witness in 1938 before HUAC, "I have noticed throughout the tours, descriptions of buildings, descriptions of monuments, there is inserted, absolute propaganda for the labor movement against capital and toward stirring up hatred between the two classes." In sharp contrast, national FWP officials saw their work as contributing to national unity. As the guide series progressed, they contemplated programs the FWP could undertake that would let the Federal Writers explore aspects of American life more deeply than the guide format allowed. To a degree, Henry Alsberg conceded, tourist guides could not help but be superficial. He worked to make them inclusive, representative of American regional, ethnic, and racial diversity, while trying to avoid criticism. He hardly saw them as controversial. Rather, he was concerned that they had only skimmed the surface of American life. Such different views make it seem as if HUAC chairman Martin Dies, his witnesses, and FWP officials lived in different worlds. They did not, but they did have different views of the America in which they lived and different ways of talking about their vision of the nation.[1]

Later students of Depression era America, such as Alfred Kazin, Henry Steele Commager, and Charles Alexander, saw the guides as an example of the literature of rediscovery and cultural nationalism that reached its full development in the late 1930s. In their view, it was a literature that tried to meet a "need born of the depression and the international crisis, to chart America and to possess it," that offered a "reconsideration of the significance of America" and a "renewed interest in national values and traditions and a yearning for a uniquely American statement." None of them noted anything radical in the guides. Instead, they all held that the Depression and the international crisis had a psychological dimension and that the guides were part of the literature that tried to help Americans renew their faith in themselves and their country. Emotional needs, historian Richard Pells argued, explained why "many men yearned not for revolt but recovery, not for change but stability, not for conflict but community." Pells saw the guidebooks as characteristic of the late 1930s celebration of the American heritage as a history of "the average American's ability to endure and triumph over any calamity" and as "an affectionate reassessment of the nation's history."[2]

Dies's assessment of the Writers' Project stands in sharp contrast to that of virtually every historian who has written about either him or the FWP. There have been several attempts to evaluate the accuracy of the charges the Dies committee and its star witnesses hurled against the FWP. Analysts have found HUAC irresponsible and politically motivated, and the evidence for this is convincing. The easy response would be to dismiss Dies and his committee as simply engaged in a right-wing effort to weaken the New Deal by whatever means possible. Following that interpretation, one would indeed grasp part of what happened. Beyond that, however, Dies and his cohorts on the committee, and the national constituency to which they appealed, opposed the FWP's view of America. Rhetoric about Communism was a mode of discourse for voicing a rejection of the political and cultural values of the New Deal.

The committee majority and its supporters rejected the FWP's effort to incorporate excluded groups in a redefined national community. It was this redefinition of the American community to which the committee and its star witnesses objected. Communism was a good catchword for all they rejected. By treating Dies and his committee as an indicator of cultural conflicts with serious political implications, it is possible to further define the FWP's approach to American life and history and to understand why some Americans found the project's approach threatening. It is necessary to look at both national FWP officials and Dies as participants in an inherited and ongoing debate about the meaning of America.[3]

Dies's handling of the hearings on the FWP demonstrates the degree to which his outlook reflected a nativist response to the history of the new immigration, a strand of populism and progressivism that celebrated the independent farmer and small businessman, and white fears, especially those of white southerners, of any change in what they thought of as the traditional racial status quo. Responding to change, Dies warned of conspiracy. He claimed to see the strength of American identity, traditions, and institutions being weakened by subversive groups. Dies saw the New Deal as a product of subversive forces infiltrating the government rather than as emerging from a democratic political system. His frequent use of the Trojan horse metaphor places him in a long line of Americans who, from the Revolution to the present, have feared conspiracies allegedly designed to subvert the republic. A persistent factor in American history, historian David Brion Davis observes, "the image of a vast subversive force subtly appropriating and transforming American institutions might well reflect anxiety over the problem of preserving a consistent sense of national identity in the face of rapid social change." Because, as Davis notes, "American identity has usually been defined as a state of mind rather than as a familial heritage," change is often perceived as a conspiratorial attack on American traditions and institutions. Depression conditions seemed unparalleled in American history. The severity and length of the economic decline threatened everyone. Unprecedented New Deal programs were seen by conservatives as an attack on the American system. While the cultural conflicts of the 1920s had not played a major role in the first half of the 1930s, they had by no means disappeared.[4]

For Dies, American identity was already established. It was not unfinished—in the process of becoming—but under attack. Looking back at the birth of the republic, Dies thought he saw a country that "was practically homogeneous, with similar political, constitutional and cultural traditions." The men who established American political institutions, he held, were products of a "homogeneous race." In a 1935 article in the *Saturday Evening Post*, Dies explained his views on "the immigrant crisis." It was a curious crisis, for the number of immigrants entering the United States had dropped dramatically in the 1930s. The 23,068 immigrants who entered the United States in 1933 represented the smallest number since 1831.[5]

Until the end of the Civil War, Dies argued, "the racial unity of the United States was intact." Then in Dies's dramatic version of the nation's history, "the great alien invasion of the United States took place": the immigration from southern and eastern Europe. It was Dies's thesis that the "greedy industrialists" and "stupid legislators" who permitted this "invasion" betrayed the heritage of freedom won by the founding fathers. Without this invasion, Dies contended, America would have escaped the class and industrial conflicts of the Old World. Instead, Dies charged, "we invited the evils of the Old World's social, political and economic disorders by offering our fertile lands and priceless resources, which our fathers designed as a heritage for their children's children, as a refuge for the jobless and the malcontents of Europe." Dies used nationality and race as interchangeable categories. He was like those white southerners who W. J. Cash thought "felt they represented a uniquely pure and superior race, not only as against the Negro, but as against all other communities of white men." National FWP officials, by contrast, took for granted that African Americans and the new immigrants and their children were a part of the national community. In presenting what Sterling Brown called a "Portrait of the Negro as American," the Writers' Project posed as great a threat to Dies's vision of the nation as had the alien invasion of the United States.[6]

Dies, casting himself as a firm opponent of big business and a defender of small farmers and businessmen, initially supported New Deal programs. "Laborers," as Dies used the term, referred to small farmers and shopkeepers, not industrial workers. As the New Deal moved from a program of recovery to one of reform, Dies became increasingly critical. The *New York Times* noted the change in Dies, who "thus far has been a thoroughgoing New Deal advocate." The 1937 sit-down strikes in the automobile industry marked a turning point in Dies's relationship to the New Deal, though that same year he supported the president's plan to add more justices to the Supreme Court. In the latter part of the decade the alien issue took a backseat to Dies's attack on the CIO, although it played a not insignificant role in the fear of that alleged conspiracy as well.[7]

There were, as Dies never tired of repeating, Communists in the CIO. In addition, the CIO's industrial unionism and its tactics were radical innovations. Though the New Deal had not launched the CIO and President Franklin Roosevelt had initially had serious reservations about the Wagner Act, the administration was nevertheless supporting unprecedented changes in the relationship between business, government, and labor. All of this posed a genuine threat to conservative interests and points of view and provided a basis for fearing a conspiracy. Furthermore, in its effort to organize by industry rather than by craft, the CIO was more successful in the South than the American Federation of Labor had been and constituted a threat to the southern caste system as well as to traditional relations between classes. In the South, one contemporary journalist observed, "the C.I.O. has now become synonymous with

'Yankees, Communists, and Jews' and its representatives must explain over and over that they are not working to establish the Soviet System in America." Dies, assuming the role of defending America from aliens and Communists, became a firm opponent of the New Deal.[8]

New Deal supporters speculated that the Dies committee was a right-wing conspiracy to weaken the New Deal and the labor movement. The committee did indeed attack both while riding a wave of congressional revolt against the administration. Yet, as one historian has shown, "rather than a plot organized by a shadowy group of anti–New Deal 'conspirators,' the committee's actions followed the preconceptions of the committee members themselves"—pre-conceptions that meshed with those of large numbers of other Americans—and thus the committee generated countless headlines during the hearings. Dies, Parnell Thomas, Noah Mason, and Joe Starnes dominated the commit-tee. New Jersey Republican Thomas held that John L. Lewis and the CIO were the "greatest single radical menace this democracy has ever known," and he warned that "if Lewis isn't checked we will see the Red flag flying over the White House." Mason, an Illinois Republican, had attacked virtually every New Deal measure and vehemently opposed the CIO. Starnes, an Alabama Demo-crat, had supported the New Deal and had had little to say about the CIO or Communism. He did, however, voice his dislike of radical aliens and of the growing federal bureaucracy. During the hearings, Starnes joined Dies, Thomas, and Mason in their attacks on the administration and the CIO.[9]

The severe criticisms that have been made of the committee's methods are well founded. The hearings proceeded with little attention to due process and much flag waving. Allegations were treated as evidence. Leading questions elicited the answers Dies and his cohorts wanted to hear. Only witnesses who challenged the committee's preconceptions were cross-examined. The com-mittee's preparations seem to have been minimal. No committee member fo-cused on FWP programs to interview and study such working-class Americans as stockyard, steel, and textile workers. Nor did the members examine the pro-gram to interview ex-slaves, despite their expressed concern about the FWP's treatment of African Americans. These were all programs that from Dies's point of view could have been attacked as promoting class and racial hatred. Criticism of HUAC's methods, however, does not illuminate the nature of the committee's objections to the Writers' Project. For though formulated with a cavalier treatment of the "evidence," their objections reflected the fears of their constituency and a vision of American identity, culture, and nationality that, they correctly saw, those programs did not endorse. What seemed to later historians to be conservative cultural developments were radical propaganda to many Americans in the 1930s.[10]

The committee initially focused on the New York City project, where there were, in fact, a large number of Communists and fellow travelers. In the absence of any legislation barring Communists from employment on WPA projects it would have been illegal to deny individuals work relief on the basis of their political commitments. As the symbol of American cosmopolitanism, or what Dies referred to as the invasion of America, New York was the ideal place to point to when explaining the entry of foreign ideologies into the country. The situation on the Writers' Project in New York was hardly typical of other units, but that did not interest the committee. While proving that there were Communists on the FWP was a persuasive first step from the committee's point of view, that did not necessarily prove that project publications aimed to spread propaganda that would promote class and racial hatred. To achieve this, the committee relied on the testimony of FWP workers who made such charges.

Unfortunately for historians of the FWP, the information the committee elicited on Communists on the New York City project reveals little about how that unit was run or its publications—and even less about Communist influence elsewhere in the FWP. Dies and his supporters on the committee, however, were satisfied they had unearthed enough facts to demonstrate that the FWP had been subverted by conspirators. After having proven to their own satisfaction that there were numerous Communists on the Writers' Project and after having generated numerous headlines on that point, the committee majority set out to establish what they saw as the obvious implications of the facts.

Dies seized on WPA administrator Aubrey Williams's widely reported statement that class conflict was an inevitable part of modern life. He thought Williams's statement was one more piece of evidence "that of those who are certain that they are for racial and religious tolerance, some of them openly advocate the use of class hatred to achieve some objective." Dies repeatedly linked challenges to the racial status quo with challenges to traditional labor relations and both to a Communist conspiracy. He found witnesses who shared his assumptions. Louise Lazell, an editor in the national office of the FWP, informed the committee that the guides contained a biased prolabor point of view and that this resulted from a conspiracy in the national office to insert such material. A careful reading of her testimony indicates that in her view anything referring to labor history or race relations was "criticism" and that to mention such things was to promote trouble, to be "incendiary."[11]

Dies wanted to show that FWP officials in Washington were using the agency to spread Communist propaganda. He asked Lazell if Alsberg had placed statements appealing to class hatred in the New Jersey guide. She responded, "I think Mr. Coy had done it." Dies found nothing equivocal in the words "I think" and barreled ahead: "Do you know whether he had done it upon more than one occasion?" This received the "yes" answer that Dies had wanted in the first place. By the time Dies presented his thesis as a question, Lazell was ready to endorse it: "Have you found or do you know as a fact that Mr. Coy and Mr. Alsberg, at the headquarters of the Federal Writers' Project, have shaped their material for propaganda purposes?" Propaganda, Dies and Lazell agreed, "against business and against industry as a class and against the government."[12]

As Lazell's testimony proceeded, her charges became even bolder. From the New Jersey guide, Dies moved on to the entire series:

> The Chairman: In all these Guides is it the uniform policy to array class against class?
> Mrs. Lazell: Yes.[13]

Lazell's testimony proved little more than that she was willing to approve the accusations of Dies and his allies, as in the following exchange:

> Mr. Mason: Would you say that the Federal Writers' Project was being used by a group of radicals to propagandize the States through the use of these Guides?
> Mrs. Lazell: I do; and that is just the beginning.
> Mr. Mason: And that unless we get rid of those who have the control of the policy in the Federal Writers' Project that is exactly what will be accomplished by the issuing of these Guides?
> Mrs. Lazell: Very soon.[14]

Hardly anyone else then or since thought the FWP had such influence. Historians have carefully qualified their remarks about the guides by talking about them as representing rather than creating cultural trends.

Dies was interested only in unqualified judgments that agreed with his own. He treated Ralph DeSola, a former New York City project worker who described himself as an ex-Communist, as a star witness. He welcomed DeSola's testimony about Communist activities among his fellow project workers. Nevertheless, Dies could not get DeSola to draw a connection between a Communist presence on the project and a Communist influence on FWP publications. DeSola would not support the charge that the Washington office was inserting material along the lines of class struggle, class hatred, and so on, into the guides and instructing "the State offices to expand their lines to bring that in." DeSola questioned that charge, for he remembered that "in the early days of my editorship, we received quite contrary instructions, which very much alarmed me as a loyal Communist, that we were not to class-angle anything." Dies did not value such a response, and when he could elicit no other, he got DeSola to note that he had not worked on the New York City guide in more than two and a half years.[15]

In addition to the allegations he treated as evidence, Dies cited materials from the guides as further proof. They hardly supported the charges. In some cases only a tortured textual analysis could reveal any bias. In his history of the project, former national FWP coordinating editor Jerre Mangione quoted some of the material Florence Shreve had testified was inflammatory. Mangione assumed that the absurdity of calling items such as the following inflammatory would be apparent to his readers:

"Five months of strikes in 1935 meant higher wages and the 36-hour week for members of the industrial union of the merchant shipbuilding workers of America.

"The entire structure is 8,536 feet long; it took 4½ years to build and cost $40,000,000. Thirteen workmen were killed in a series of accidents typical of those that occur on any large construction job."[16]

Both statements were either factually correct or incorrect. It was not a matter of interpretation. Where could the possible bias be? Yet Dies called this and similar material propaganda. Regardless of the fact that the evidence offered by the committee does not support the charges based on it, there was a pattern to the material on which they chose to focus. Perhaps Dies thought that the guides overemphasized positive facts about unions and negative facts about industrial working conditions, although he never clearly made that point. He seems to have regarded the connection between the examples he offered as evidence and his accusations as self-evident.

Dies focused on extracts from the Montana and New Jersey guides dealing with ethnic groups and labor. He never explained what he found objectionable in the Montana guide excerpt on ethnic groups, which mentioned that when gold was found, native whites from the Midwest and the East moved there, that Irish and German groups came to work in the first copper and silver mines, that immigrants built the railroads and then turned to farming and lumbering, and that after 1900 many Germans and Scandinavians settled the dry-land sections. Judging by the tremors the slightest mention of racial matters could set off among committee members, one suspects Dies thought his constituency would be upset by the statement, "Many of the early trappers engaged in the Montana fur trade were French-Indian; the managers of the companies were usually English or Scottish, and several of them, who married Indian women, left descendents of mixed blood."[17]

Though the committee did not overtly emphasize ethnic issues, nativist sentiment influenced the hearings. An implicit equation was made between the foreign ideology supposedly guiding the CIO and the "foreign" makeup of the organization. Likewise, patriotism and family background extending far back in American history were also equated. Evidence that one was an old-stock American was offered as proof that one was immune to un-American ideologies. One witness who accused the national staff of promoting class warfare recounted that a fellow FWP worker had called her a fascist. She told the committee that she, a descendant of Zachary Taylor, found this preposterous. She insisted she was no more a fascist than Taylor was. Here was a type of argument that even liberal FWP officials had occasion to rely on. Since Harold Kellock, the husband of national FWP tours editor Katherine Kellock, worked for the Soviet embassy, this raised charges of red influence on the Writers' Project. At the time of Katherine Kellock's appointment, FWP officials issued a press release pointing out that her ancestors had been in America since colonial times. Variations on this release were repeated whenever the issue was raised, as it was during the HUAC hearings.[18]

Dies's allegations that the New Jersey guide demonstrated FWP sympathy for the CIO were not completely without foundation. A few of the examples Dies cited from the New Jersey guide could be termed sympathetic to labor, as in the following instance: "Progressive labor continues to struggle against the power of the Court of Chancery to grant injunctions in labor disputes." The essay clearly supported legislation in labor's behalf. In this regard, the essay noted, New Jersey labor legislation was "not so progressive as the labor legislation of New York, Massachusetts, or Wisconsin." The essay concluded that New Jersey was, at last, making slow progress in the right direction. A factual statement about the American Federation of Labor's neglect of "the mass production industries which dominated New Jersey after 1900" could also be viewed as part of an argument in behalf of the CIO.[19]

The hearings linked alleged FWP sympathy for the CIO with an effort to disturb the status quo in race relations. Florence Shreve testified that in the national office of the Writers' Project "there has always been an effort to build up subtly the oppression of the Negro everywhere, in all copy." In her testimony

Shreve made no distinction between material in the state guides describing blacks and statements that advocated change in race relations. The greatest problem Sterling Brown faced was getting many states to mention blacks at all. For example, he had to explain to Florida Federal Writers that a single sentence on African Americans in Sarasota was inadequate. Brown argued that "where [the Negro] lives, what he does for a living, his homes, churches, school, social business, and professional activities deserve mention, however brief, in any representative treatment of the city's life." Brown worked hard, but with limited success, to eliminate racial stereotypes from the guides—stereotypes many white Federal Writers, especially in the South, thought of as common knowledge. But in an America where a white Anglo-Saxon Protestant Main Street was still a potent symbol of community, to acknowledge in guidebooks, as Brown put it, "that the Negro has been an integral part of American life" was bound to be viewed as radical by many.[20]

Dies, Shreve, and Lazell drew connections between a sympathetic portrayal of the CIO and a critical attitude to the status quo in race relations:

> Dies, Shreve, The Chairman: What had you been taking out? Just characterize it.
>
> Mrs. Shreve: Oh, the struggle between capital and labor; that the Negro had been downtrodden; and always—there was a word they used; I can't think of it at the moment—
>
> Mrs. Lazell: Underprivileged.
>
> Mrs. Shreve: That is it—underprivileged; the underprivileged Negro.[21]

Yet that Negroes were denied privileges accorded to whites was a legal fact. Over time, Shreve claimed, it became clear that the insertion of this material in the guide could not be accounted for by the presence of "just certain stray writers that were a little bit prejudiced."[22]

The committee was offered few examples of how the guides had actually promoted racial hatred. Dies's best evidence came instead from *American Stuff*, a volume of creative work done by Federal Writers on their free time. Dies and his allies focused on Richard Wright's short story "The Ethics of Living Jim Crow." Wright's story is a protest against both racial injustice and the idea that blacks accept the situation. His answer to the question "How do Negroes feel about the way they live?" differed from the answers whites interested in buttressing the status quo offered. African Americans only truthfully addressed the question, Wright contended, when whites were not present. For Americans like Dies, Wright was a promoter of racial hatred. Although Dies called special attention to the obscenities, the passage he entered in the record ends with

Wright's description of how southern blacks viewed their situation: "How do Negroes discuss it [race relations] when alone among themselves? I think this question can be answered in a single sentence. A friend of mine who ran an elevator once told me: 'Lawd, man, ef it wuzn't fer them polices 'n' them ol' lynch mobs, there would be nothin' but uproar down here.'"[23]

In his fiction Wright sought to make black rage known, to destroy the illusions many whites cherished, and to make it impossible to take such illusions seriously. Writing with a passionate fury, he tried to make public what he knew as the truth. To both admirers and critics, Wright's work suggested descriptive adjectives focusing on some aspect of the black anger he captured. Time and again committee members claimed there was a conspiracy to change race relations in America. Wright's story directly stated what Dies and his allies on the committee held they saw throughout the FWP publications, but with the exception of the guide to Washington, D.C., the state guides never went beyond a description of black history and life.[24]

Other representatives echoed HUAC's concern with race and radicalism. Congressman Frank Keefe's remarks on the FWP guide to Washington, D.C., provide an illuminating example of how the international crisis abroad, labor strife at home, and the fear of any change in race relations could combine in a view of the world that saw the Writers' Project as a conspiracy against American traditions. Keefe, a Republican representative from Wisconsin, thought the Washington guide showed the influence of "communist inspired agitators." He asserted that he was opposed to both "the proponents of communist and Nazi-fascism [who] are insidiously making use of the radio and the press in an attempt to transfer to America the troubles of Europe and Asia in an effort to involve us on one side or another of their numerous controversies."[25]

To meet the challenge posed by Nazism and Communism, Keefe thought, the country needed "a militant passionate revival of American patriotism." To achieve such a goal, however, loyal Americans would have to overcome the opposition of Communists who, "operating under the guise of historical research, have evidenced a common purpose to break down and destroy the patriotic impulse of the American people." The tax-supported FWP, he asserted, was one such guise. Keefe singled out the essay on blacks that appeared in the Washington guide as an example of the FWP's efforts to diminish patriotic feeling in the American people. Here, he declared, was an attempt "to portray the oppression of the Negro by the white race and thereby stimulate a feeling of class hatred."[26]

Sterling Brown, the author of the essay that so alarmed Keefe, did "portray the oppression of the Negro." His protest, however, was worded in praise of

America's democratic values, not class hatred. "In this border city, southern in so many respects," Brown maintained, "there is a denial of democracy, at times hypocritical, at times flagrant." To Keefe such statements were "insidious propaganda." He was not interested in the evidence Brown offered to support his views, for Keefe held that such assertions, whether they were right or wrong, were objectionable because they "can only result in stimulating racial intolerance." Ironically, Keefe equated criticism of racial injustice and inequality with racial intolerance.[27]

Keefe was especially upset by the claim in the D.C. guide that George Washington Parke Custis had a "colored" daughter. He found this particularly offensive because, as he explained, Custis was not only the father-in-law of Robert E. Lee but also "the stepgrandson of George Washington, the grandson of Martha Washington, and the son of George Washington by adoption, thus making him a member of the first family of our country." The FWP, according to Keefe, was attacking the founding fathers. Keefe said he spoke only in behalf of American unity and patriotism.[28]

As much as Dies and Keefe, national FWP officials voiced concern about patriotism and national unity. What emerges clearly from attacks on the FWP such as those of HUAC and Keefe is the different meanings that could be given to the same terms. In the 1930s a cultural program that challenged narrow definitions of America was inherently reformist. For Dies and a majority of the HUAC committee members mentioning the history of labor and African Americans was an unpatriotic act promoting disunity. For them America was already defined. To treat American identity and culture as fluid was to challenge the status quo. Implicitly, they held, the less said about labor conflict and African American history the better, for the best way to defend existing social arrangements was not to discuss these matters except in the language of traditional clichés. To discuss challenges to the dominant social arrangements was to give aid and comfort to those who advocated change. Such is the forceful logic behind much reactionary thinking that liberal historians often dismiss as merely crude and ignorant. From this point of view, what appears innocuous and noncontroversial to later historians constituted a deep challenge to many Americans at the time.

Americans who, like Dies, thought the FWP publications challenged their view of America were right. They were incorrect when they held that this challenge was the product of a Communist conspiracy to subvert the country. Rather, national FWP officials thought patriotism and unity were compatible with a more inclusive definition of who and what was American. In their opinion a more open definition of America could promote democratic values and accommodate different groups and interests while still achieving unity.

The official correspondence of the FWP reveals little about how national project officials felt about Dies. It is, however, possible to capture a sense of the mood in the national office through the private correspondence of a Florida FWP worker who was working closely with national officials editing the Florida guide. He sent the Florida director reports on the national office's reaction to the Dies hearings. When the news broke that members of the staff had given Dies information about "radical stuff" being planted in the New Jersey guide, there was "much seething around here." Seething or not, FWP officials could not prevent what next happened: "I neglected to tell you the important news, but you probably saw it in the paper this morning. Along about noon yesterday everybody was advised that they could not leave the building. Nobody at the time could figure out what it was about, but we soon found out." Officers of the Dies committee were "pouncing" on galley proofs of guides "purporting to be loaded with C.I.O. and Communist propaganda." He thought "they seized the revised copy that the boys have been sitting up nights to finish so they will have several versions." The next day was "dark and gloomy." The slightest office noise seemed to hold dire meaning: "I hear activity in other parts of the building and have no doubt but that it has sinister implications, i.e., Mr. Dies et al."[29]

The immediate political implications for the project were obvious: "A fine time of year to get dragged over the coals, just when Congress is coming back to town to dole out some more money." This Florida FWP worker, however, indicated no awareness of a threat to the project's very existence. Instead, he was optimistic: "The boys believe they can prove their case and discredit the gal who snitched." Furthermore, he thought, "the experience will be beneficial to the project. A lot of crackpot stuff will go in the ash can from now on, I am quite sure." Crackpot stuff, not Communist propaganda, concerned him—material from the Florida units, for example, that "branded Alabama crackers as the worst type of humanity, but admitted that Georgia crackers were high class citizens." If Dies should get hold of such copy, it "would be hot stuff for him." Washington FWP officials, he also speculated, might use such material to prove that they had been weeding out inflammatory copy sent in by the state units. So he advised the director of the Florida unit to pay special attention to the copy sent in from her unit, "to keep a weather eye on everything from now on. This place seems to be infested with spies and it's every man for himself."[30]

Whatever anger national FWP officials had toward the Dies committee they kept to themselves. Alsberg began his testimony by informing the committee that he, too, was a good anti-Communist and that as early as 1923 he had attacked the Soviet dictatorship's suppression of civil liberties. He went so far as to equate attacks on HUAC with attacks American liberals and radicals sympathetic to the Soviet Union had made against him as "a reactionary, a liberal who is slipping." He informed Dies, "I hold no brief for the people who attacked this committee. I have never attacked this committee." If his goal was to mollify his examiners, his statement, in the immediate circumstances of the hearing itself, seemed to work. Dies treated Alsberg as a friendly witness and praised him for his cooperative attitude.[31]

Alsberg attempted to repair the damage done to the FWP's reputation by earlier witnesses. While Alsberg conceded that the New York City project had been disrupted by Communists who had engaged in political activity on project time, he pointed out that this unit "is a rather small proposition in a nationwide organization." He assured the committee that he was working to restore order, and though under WPA provisions established by Congress Communists could not be barred from relief, he was seeking to keep them out of supervisory positions and from engaging in political activities during work time. When Dies moved on to the issue of promoting class hatred, Alsberg offered limited agreement. He held that the charges covered only isolated instances. Examining Alsberg on this point, Dies asked, "When this material comes into your office, do you find a great many statements that are assumptions?" It is unclear whether Alsberg was being merely clever in his answer or simply falling back into his familiar FWP editorial role: "We find statements of all kinds that are unwarranted or overstatements—claims that 'This is the biggest something or other that ever was.' . . . There is a question in Tennessee, or in Kentucky now, where the university president feels we have not been fair about some statement about the War between the States. The thing is being submitted to him. There is no question about it, that we have to watch out on that continually."[32] Dies was quick to inform Alsberg that these were not the kind of statements he had had in mind. Alsberg had, however, offered what he saw as evidence of the FWP's effort to be accurate and impartial, often to the extent of consulting outside authorities.

Regarding the New Jersey guide, Alsberg conceded that it contained objectionable material, but he blamed this on the New Jersey state staff rather than the national FWP office. From his perspective, the incident was one in which New Jersey editors, who had a "tendency . . . frankly to overstate and to sharpen statements about labor," were causing an impartial national FWP staff serious problems. Alsberg also countered charges that national FWP editors had handled the manuscript of the Montana and New Jersey guides in a way that made it possible to insert Communist propaganda at the last minute. He offered a detailed description of the handling of galley proofs and the negotiations between the FWP, the publishers, and the sponsor that even someone long involved in the book trade might have found difficult to unravel. In Alsberg's version, charges of conspiracy became merely haggling between the FWP officials, sponsors, and publishers. Because so many individuals were involved in the process, reaching final agreement on the content of a publication, Alsberg explained, was exceedingly difficult, as was determining who would pay for revisions in the galley proofs. In any case, Alsberg informed the committee that all partisan statements would be removed from the guides. Alsberg also stated that he shared Dies's view that "articles put in publications such as the guides, which are paid for by all the taxpayers, should not contain biased or partisan statements . . . or statements that take a controversial side and play up one class against another."[33]

Alsberg's concessions to Dies and his cohorts were of little benefit to the FWP. Dies and his allies attacked the administration's cultural programs, not only to hurt the New Deal politically, but also because they opposed the cultural implications of New Deal politics. In the committee report, Dies simply concluded that Alsberg accepted as true the charges brought against the FWP. In his autobiography, *The Martin Dies Story* (1963), Dies used Alsberg's testimony in the same way.[34]

In his testimony before HUAC, Alsberg had tried to convince Dies that the guides were impartial, based either on primary sources or widely accepted secondary sources, and that the list of sponsors of FWP publications—mayors, governors, chambers of commerce, and universities—constituted an impressive endorsement. Dies and his allies were not especially interested. Nevertheless, when Congress abolished the Federal Theater Project in June 1939, it allowed the FWP, soon rechristened the Writers' Program, to survive, albeit in a severely curtailed form.[35]

It made a difference that mainstream political and cultural institutions were involved in creating the guides and that the nation's major publishing houses, not noted for their radicalism, supported the FWP. Furthermore, every state in the union was included in the FWP program, and in almost every state, despite criticisms, Republicans as well as Democrats took pride in their state guides. While the Writers' Project's vision of America was unacceptable to Dies and many others, it was becoming an acceptable centrist view of America. Dies could not persuade a majority of Congress that the same people who were for racial and religious tolerance were, as he put it, also using state guidebooks to promote class hatred in order to overthrow the government. Yet, in subsequent decades similar charges would be repeated every time civil rights issues moved to the forefront of the national agenda.

In the end, Dies would not accept Alsberg's contention that the guidebooks were impartial accounts of American life and history. To a large degree Dies, not Alsberg, was right. Paradoxically, in providing a cultural component to complement the new political consensus the administration was creating, the FWP ensured that it would appear radical to those who at the time supported older conservative forms of national consensus, while appearing uncritically conservative to later historians with a radical perspective.

The New Deal both culturally and politically challenged the traditional place assigned to labor, ethnic groups, and blacks in American society. The debate over this reflects how anxious Dies and his constituency were about the relationship between class and race. They understood that in America class and race are deeply intertwined, perhaps hopelessly confused, and attempting to look at either category in a new way constituted an attack on the traditional way of regarding both.

Despite the drastic changes in their agency mandated by Congress, officials of the Writers' Program continued to try to fulfill the visions that had been developed by the Writers' Project in the years between 1935 and 1939. They also tried to convince others that those visions could be translated into programs relevant to new circumstances. That involved persuading their superiors in the administration that programs that sought to reconcile romantic nationalism and cultural pluralism, to celebrate a diverse, inclusive, and democratic national community, could result in publications contributing at first to the preparation for war and then to the war effort.

An examination of how the Writers' Program sought to create a place for itself in an administration turning from national affairs to international conflict, from reform at home to war abroad, can help illuminate how the cultural component of the New Deal's reform program adapted to the war effort. In the process, one can see how a liberal and reformist view of American culture was transformed into the basis of a new and ultimately conservative national consensus.

Chapter 10

Reform, Culture, and Patriotism

The Writers' Project Becomes the Writers' Program, 1939–1943

Congressional action in the spring and summer of 1939 drastically changed the administrative structure of the WPA arts projects. With the approach of war, the emphasis in the New Deal arts projects shifted from recovery, relief, reform, and experimentation to an attempt to institutionalize and consolidate programs that had already been enacted. Within the new guidelines established by Congress and the realities of international war, national officials of the Writers' Program sought to articulate a defensible purpose for their agency. The arguments they offered in support of their programs did not constitute a break with the FWP's original goals but a variation on them.

Many of the values that had been implicit in the approach of the FWP to the study of American culture became explicit during the Writers' Program. In response to the defense crisis, the heads of the Writers' Program continued to emphasize reconciling the realities of diversity with the need for unity. But the romantic nationalist motivation of the FWP receded as the Writers' Program slowly abandoned all efforts to fulfill the visions Alsberg and his staff had of contributing to a redefinition and flowering of American culture. The FWP had developed a cultural program compatible with New Deal reform. The Writers' Program sought to build a program on the work of the FWP that could contribute not to reform but to a united national defense effort. Here was an example of what Roosevelt had referred to as the change from Dr. New Deal to Dr. Win the War. The larger consequences were the consolidation of a liberal pluralist view of America that ironically contributed to a postwar America, which symbolically accepted diversity while ignoring the realities of class and race differences that violated democratic principles.

The congressional attack on the New Deal arts programs was two pronged. Early in 1939, under the leadership of Clifton Woodrum of Virginia, a special subcommittee of the House Appropriations Committee began hearings to determine what recommendations to make on the proposed relief bill. These hearings no more constituted a careful examination of the philosophy behind work relief and an evaluation of the performance of WPA programs than the HUAC hearings constituted a thoughtful examination of the philosophy and operations of right- and left-wing groups. Many of the same allegations made regarding the FWP in the HUAC hearings were repeated before the Woodrum committee. Both committees were more important as a reflection of a mounting conservative attack on the New Deal than for the substance of their investigations. It was not the investigations of these committees alone that led to changes in the Writers' Project. These changes were also the result of larger trends within both the Congress and the administration.[1]

With the defeat of the Supreme Court packing plan and the failure of Roosevelt's attempt to purge conservative Democrats in 1938, the alignment of congressional forces had shifted. Under pressure from a forceful conservative coalition in Congress and increasingly preoccupied with the foreign crisis abroad, the Roosevelt administration withdrew support from those reform efforts most open to attack. The WPA program, especially its arts projects, proved particularly vulnerable.[2]

In Harry Hopkins the arts projects had had a friend in high places who might not have so quickly abandoned them to their congressional critics. But illness removed Hopkins from the Washington scene between October 1937 and April 1938. After he returned, he became deeply involved in exclusively political affairs and in December was appointed secretary of commerce. His two chief assistants, Aubrey Williams and David K. Niles, regarded the art projects with more skepticism than Hopkins had. Williams considered them a "threat to the continued existence of the whole work program."[3]

The FWP owed its existence to the political and social forces that had sustained the New Deal in its successive waves of reform and experimentation; by the spring of 1939 these forces had receded. New Deal administrators responded to changing realities as they occurred and focused their energies on the consolidation and institutionalization of the reforms that had already been enacted. The age of innovation had ended. In April 1939 President Roosevelt sent Congress a reorganization plan that deprived the Works Progress Administration of its independent status, renamed it the Work Projects Administration, and placed it under the authority of the new Federal Works Agency. Previously the independence of the WPA was both symbol and evidence of the extraordinary status the relief program had enjoyed as part of the New Deal's attempt to combat the Depression. After April 1939 the WPA became just another subordinate part of the administration.[4]

In May, Col. Francis C. Harrington, who had succeeded Harry Hopkins as WPA director, told the Woodrum committee that he was willing to reduce employment on the arts projects and demand that they secure local funds to meet part of their costs, "thus eliminating their operation as Federally Sponsored projects." Harrington conveyed the impression that the administration was willing to sacrifice federal control of these programs in exchange for an appropriation that would continue the other WPA programs. At the end of June, Congress passed an Emergency Relief Act that abolished the Federal Theater Project, prohibited the existence of any project sponsored solely by the WPA (thus eliminating the national offices of the arts projects and returning their operation to the state WPA administrators), required that local sponsors be secured who would contribute 25 percent of the total cost of the program, and stated that anyone who had been employed by the WPA for eighteen months should be removed and not rehired until thirty days had passed. With the exception of Oklahoma and Missouri the state FWP programs were able to secure local sponsorship. The ease with which state FWP units secured sponsors testified to the continuing widespread support for the project within mainstream political and cultural institutions. Sponsorship by the Library of Congress maintained the existence of a national office.[5]

The Woodrum committee's discovery of a letter Alsberg had written ten years earlier to the *Nation* magazine advocating that prisoners form unions resulted in a flurry of adverse publicity. Alsberg weakly responded that the letter was written in a spirit of irony. He also pointed out that ten years had passed since he wrote the letter and it reflected nothing about his current views or how he ran the Writers' Project. Nevertheless, he had become a political liability for an administration in which the FWP was becoming a very low priority. The "termination" of Alsberg in August and his replacement by John Newsom, formerly the director of the Michigan Writers' Project, symbolized the new atmosphere that came to dominate the Writers' Project. As an administrator Alsberg may have been, in the words of one of his colleagues, "a colossus of chaos," but he had also been a creative force. Newsom, on the other hand, was more of an administrator and less of a creative editor. The immediate task before him was to see that the state guides were completed. Little work was undertaken that had not begun under Alsberg's regime. As the appointment of Colonel Harrington to succeed Hopkins "was the sign and not the cause of the triumph of organization over inspiration," Newsom's appointment was, likewise, the sign and not the cause of a similar transformation in the FWP.[6]

Congressional criticism coupled with the shift in the administration's main concerns led Writers' Program officials to lower expectations as to what they could hope to accomplish. The situation, they thought, called for realism, not dreams. An attempt to be realistic led them to try to scale down the rhetoric surrounding the agency's aspirations, for no one questioned that their most important immediate task was completing the American Guide Series. And they all knew the agency's future was uncertain. They were sensitive to the fact that WPA officials in states where the guides had not yet been completed were losing patience with projects that had produced little in their view but had received "much adverse comment." For many state WPA officials saw the Writers' Project as "a liability rather than an asset."[7]

While the Writers' Project was based on the assumption that competent personnel could be secured from the relief rolls, the truth, Newsom observed, was "this assumption, unless I am blinded by prejudice, is without foundation." In a sense, part of Alsberg's genius had been his ability to disregard such facts. Thus he had been able to conceive of, support, and administer an ambitious and innovative program. In the circumstances surrounding the Writers' Program, these facts had to be faced. The personnel situation was worse after Congress passed the 1939 relief act. Utah, Colorado, Nevada, Washington, and Alabama, Newsom concluded, lacked the competent personnel needed to complete their state guidebooks.[8]

Yet neither Newsom nor his staff could entirely abandon the goal of making significant contributions to American culture that went beyond the guidebooks in their treatment of American life. They hoped for and fought to create a future for the Writers' Program that extended beyond finishing the American Guide Series. They seemed to need such a vision to maintain their own morale. Thus, though their rhetoric may have been more subdued than that of FWP officials, they found themselves articulating plans and programs, dreams that related the Writers' Program to its origins in the Writers' Project.

Alsberg's departure signaled the disappearance of the romantic nationalism of the FWP and the emergence of the new rationale the Writers' Program offered to justify its existence in a world at war. Writers' Program officials borrowed the rhetoric of the FWP. Phrases such as "Presenting America to Americans" still proved useful. Officials of the Writers' Program, like their predecessors, were concerned with national integration, with reconciling diversity and unity. Alsberg and his staff's justification of the FWP's program took on a different meaning when repeated by officials of the Writers' Program in the new circumstances that surrounded their agency.[9]

The day after the German invasion of Poland, Newsom indicated that in the event of a national emergency the Writers' Program was ready to supply maps, population figures, and highway descriptions to interested government agencies and could easily handle press releases and prepare guide histories for the use of the military services. The FWP vision of a diverse but united nation, Newsom held, would be relevant to an America at war. The Writers' Program, he contended, could provide reports on minority groups, their geographic location, and "degree of integration." This was the FWP vision of a revitalized national culture, based on a pluralistic, inclusive, and democratic community and translated into a liberal program of social control for wartime purposes.[10]

What had already been accomplished by the FWP, national officials of the Writers' Program contended, illustrated the unique contribution their agency could make to national defense. They argued that the American Guide Series provided the basis for a new patriotism and a new sense of national unity. Their agency, they held, could "supply cultural content to patriotism" by revealing the "multitudinous life of America that rolls out behind the flag," and "by creating a sense of community growth, the American Guide Series had tended to counteract impulses arising from blind personal interests." The FWP view of America as an unfinished society in the process of becoming provided a rationale for allowing all individuals and groups in the society to participate in this growing and developing community. The Writers' Program, however, was thinking of community as a check on individualism, as a way of calling for self-sacrifice.[11]

Writers' Program officials proudly claimed that they and their FWP predecessors had "placed before the people an accumulation of cultural experience specifically American." By introducing Americans to the diversity of their country, they thought they were creating a "unified tradition" that would constitute "a powerful stimulus to integrated action." Here was the rhetoric of the FWP adapted to fit a specific national crisis. National FWP officials saw their work as contributing to a view of American identity and nationality that challenged the cultural authority of narrow definitions of who and what was American. This vision, moreover, could, as officials of the Writers' Program realized, fit in with the Roosevelt administration's desire to achieve wartime unity in a pluralistic nation without having to suppress minorities as the Wilson administration and extralegal groups had done during World War I.[12]

The Writers' Program sought to harmonize FWP themes with the mood of an administration and nation preparing for war. More than merely engaging in good public relations, the Writers' Program was meeting a widely felt need for inspiring nationalistic rhetoric and practical programs. Reviewing the Utah guide in the spring of 1941, a writer on the *Helper (Utah) Journal* declared that the book came at an opportune moment. In his view the guide helped make national identity, an abstract concept, into something concrete and thus helped Americans realize what they had to defend if they were not to lose it. The future, he pointed out, was uncertain, indeed "hazardous," and therefore "it is fitting that we think as never before upon what we have to defend, what our way of life is, and what manner of land is this in which we dwell." It was necessary, he told readers, to think of the country not only in terms of American ideals but also in terms of primordial loyalties. "What we have to defend," he argued, "is not only a national thing; it is also the incidents of our day-to-day living—the house along our street, our schools, our children . . . the matchless whole of our lives." For this reason, he concluded, the publication of the Utah guide "comes most opportunely at this moment. . . . We must know what we are fighting for, where we come from and what our identity is."[13]

From this point of view, a discussion of the Utah guide was not so much an occasion to reflect on American life as an opportunity to "reaffirm our pride in this land, our pride in ourselves and our forefathers." Pride and affirmation had been implicit in the FWP's program from the beginning, but they had been linked to the idea that American identity could be redefined in an inclusive manner that celebrated diversity while promoting national integration and a revitalized culture. The Writers' Program shifted to an emphasis on pride and affirmation at the expense of these other parts of the vision. The program did little with the theme of America as a culture still in the process of becoming, of realizing itself. That theme had reflected the FWP's ties to New Deal political and cultural programs, and most of these had become wartime casualties.[14]

The American Guide Series had been another American declaration of independence from Europe and thus part of a continuing dialogue about America's relationship to Europe. The war gave that theme a new twist. An April

1941 WPA press release that heralded the publication of the South Carolina guide stressed practical realities as well as patriotic ideals: "The guidebooks are particularly timely, because Americans can now travel only in the western hemisphere. They are introducing Americans to their own country as never before and are making people of the country appreciate their own achievements." The FWP had wanted to introduce Americans to their own country, not only to praise national achievements, but also to help them see the nation's diversity as relevant to their understanding of who and what they are, as part of their identity.[15]

Critic Lewis Gannett thought the European situation had contributed to an American literature of rediscovery that had begun not with the war but with the Depression. He saw the Federal Writers as playing a central role in that literature. The European war had intensified the trend that Gannett, uncertain about the future, thought would continue whether the United States officially declared war or not. Gannett saw the war in Europe and the events leading up to it resulting in a total reversal in American attitudes toward the Old World: "Europe is no longer our dream-land; it is a nightmare." The cultural implications of this view were reinforced by the practical realities: "The families who might have sailed for Europe are driving south on Routes 1 and 17, 41 and 51, 87, 99 and 101, and west on the great decadal routes 10, 20, 30, 40, 60 and 80— and if some at least of those numbers do not bring specific alabaster cities and fruited plains to your mind, you are not quite full-grown as a 1941 American." Gannett's rhetoric does not suggest national FWP officials' idea of travel guides that introduced American travelers to people who, while different from themselves, were fellow citizens.[16]

Meetings to draft and develop projects for the Writers' Program involving other WPA officials and interested outsiders were held frequently during 1941. Old FWP themes about the relationship between provincialism and cosmopolitanism and the need for mutual understanding and national integration were put to new uses. New Deal officials who favored religious and racial tolerance and the development of unions thought, contrary to Dies's assertions, that they were promoting national unity, not class hatred. During a period of reform such views of American culture had, as Dies recognized, liberal political implications. In a time of war they were used to promote tolerance and understanding, not to aid reform, but to ensure a united defense effort. Paradoxically, when the reform implications of the FWP's vision of America were no longer important, the Writers' Program began to express directly an American democratic ideology in a way the FWP rarely did.

The Writers' Program outlined a publications program that would have made Alsberg proud. Most of these projects had been either discussed or initiated under the FWP. The Writers' Program claimed to be dealing with "people in a changing America." It proposed books on African American folk survivals, on "people in tobacco," on "reclaiming our heritage" (a study dealing with conservation), and on American food lore, titled "America Eats," which would focus on the social and cultural rituals associated with eating and contain accounts of regional and ethnic foodways. These works were envisioned as a tribute to American creativity and pluralism. Perhaps the most ambitious undertaking was "Hands That Built America," a proposed six-volume regional study of American handicraft traditions, under the direction of Harold Rosenberg. Broadly conceived, the study was intended to "preserve a record of American craftsmen, artisans, and plain people building a nation." Individual volumes were tentatively titled "Men Working," "American Lives (biographies of non-eminent Americans)," and "Architecture for Living"; one was also planned on regional folkways. Here was a "new series" that national officials of the Writers' Program could assert in a publicity release was "the logical successor to the state guides."[17]

While valuable materials brought together in preparation for these books are kept in the Manuscripts Division of the Library of Congress and various state repositories, little of it has ever been published. These studies were wartime casualties. In a letter written two months after Pearl Harbor, the Grazing Service of the U.S. Department of the Interior backed away from its previous commitment to help the Writers' Program complete a history of western grazing. No one on the Writers' Program could have argued with the position "that events that have shaken the world, and especially those which brought the war to our shores, prompts us to weigh some of the things previously taken in stride, against trends and activities occasioned by all-out war." Newsom evidently agreed, for in February 1942 he resigned his position with the Writers' Program to join the U.S. Navy. It would not have mattered had he stayed. Further personnel reductions made it impossible to complete the grazing or other projects.[18]

"National unity," officials of the Writers' Program repeatedly declared, could be achieved "through presenting America to Americans." The very structure of their agency, they asserted, would make it a valuable addition to the national defense program. Cooperation between local units and the national office would result in an exchange of ideas and information leading to "a better understanding of the nation in all its richness and variety." In this way local and national perspectives would be integrated. As a result, they claimed, "provincialism is dissipated, while at the same time a sense of locality and a heightened regional understanding are made part of the heritage of all Americans." National cultural unity could be attained "at the same time that regional qualities are heightened and preserved." In their view, "the interrelation and interdependence of communities and the nation has always been important in American life," but this had become clearer than ever during the crisis of the 1930s. Looking ahead, they saw that "the urgencies of the decade before us make actual understanding between communities a prerequisite to national unity." Understanding would make it possible to transcend conflict. This position had also been held by FWP officials.[19]

Writers' Program officials held that the programs that had been formulated by the FWP between 1935 and 1939 were more necessary than ever during the new crisis the nation faced. Only pluralistic values could unite the nation by aiding understanding and contributing to national integration between the parts that made up the whole. Through publications produced by cooperation between local units and the national office, the Writers' Program would give local communities "familiarity with other parts of the country and the nation as a whole." The national office would enable local communities to see the "value of their peculiar treasure, frequently taken for granted," by helping them recognize that these "local phenomena are often part of large national patterns of living."[20] Every individual, every group, and every region had to be integrated into a national culture preparing for war. Writers' Program officials thought the *Jacksonville (Florida) Journal* had offered an excellent summary of the way their agency was contributing to a unified national defense effort: "In this hour— when all available manpower and industry are being mobilized for the national defense program—we should remember that an American takes pride in his community, state and nation only after he has acquired a broad knowledge of their democratic values, and has seen how he as an individual fits into the American tradition. By providing such knowledge the WPA Writers' Project is making a definite, though indirect, contribution to the national defense program."[21]

The Writers' Program continued the FWP's interest in recognizing ethnic, black, and working-class Americans as part of the national community—all groups vital to the national defense effort and all potentially a source of disunity. The war in Europe reminded everyone in the United States that ethnic identification and loyalty to countries of origin persisted among Americans, and this aroused anxiety about possible national fragmentation and disunity. The Writers' Program argued for the relevance of the FWP's liberal pluralism to the crisis at hand. In the FWP's cultural pluralism, Writers' Program officials saw a viable alternative to authoritarian suppression of any individual or group who failed to conform to narrow notions of what an American is. The Writers' Program was in line with the general approach of the Roosevelt administration. As Richard Polenberg has noted, while there was widespread fear of fifth-column activities in 1940 and 1941, "the Roosevelt administration, unlike the Wilson administration after World War I, did a good deal to reassure the public and check the hysteria." Roosevelt opposed and, when necessary, vetoed efforts to curb free speech and limit the activities of political dissidents.[22]

Thus the Writers' Program, building on the work and rhetoric of the FWP, stressed pluralism and intercultural understanding as the basis for a unified national defense effort and in this way fitted in with both administration policy and the public mood. At much higher levels of the administration than the Writers' Program, there were officials who thought that both liberal democracy and social cohesion could be obtained. "By making this a 'people's' war for freedom," one of them optimistically declared, "we can help clear up the alien problem, the negro problem, the anti-Semitic problem."[23]

Writers' Program officials thought proposed studies such as "Men at Work" could help other Americans understand labor's contribution to the nation's development. They stressed labor's loyalty to national goals. Thus, labor did not earn its place in the national community simply through citizenship or by hard work but, rather, by its patriotism. A major goal of "Men at Work" would be to "catch the spirit of American labor with its pride in craft, satisfaction in accomplishment, and desire to contribute to the national welfare."[24]

Black and social-ethnic studies should continue, Writers' Program officials held, because the materials assembled would contribute to the defense effort. While the Writers' Program in Illinois dropped many projects not deemed essential to national defense, it did continue work on its study "The Negro in Illinois." Here was a study that Writers' Program officials felt could both fulfill liberal democratic goals and aid the defense program. They planned "a study that will show the process by which the Negro has become a productive and integrated part of the culture of the industrial North, a tremendous step in the growth and development of our democracy." The bottom-line argument, however, was that this study be "continued on a limited basis because of the importance of enlisting the Negro people in the war effort." Illinois writers also planned studies of Chicago's Jews and "on adjustments of foreign born Chicagoans to life in a democracy." Their goal was to "awaken the consciousness of the populace to the advantages of living in a democracy" and to "explain the working of our government in terms the layman and especially *the new citizen* can understand" (emphasis added).[25]

A curious fact about the FWP was that it had rarely articulated an ideological patriotism. Yet countless students of American life, such as French visitor Alexis de Tocqueville and historian John Higham, have stressed the importance of ideological factors, as opposed to primordial loyalties, as the basis of American patriotism. After visiting antebellum America, de Tocqueville observed that the new nation, unlike Old World nations, was not held together by an "instinctive patriotism" that was taken for granted—a historical given that transcended in importance any ideology. Instead, Americans had a "patriotism of reflection," ideas that the majority believed all citizens had to accept if they were to be considered loyal patriots—indeed, if they were to be considered Americans at all.[26]

Working within a romantic nationalist tradition, FWP officials had been more interested in an instinctive rather than an ideological patriotism. They sought to create a sense of American nationality based on emotional bonds linked to a sense of place that Americans could take as a given, as an inheritance. Implicitly, they aligned their attempt to define American nationality with a democratic and inclusive vision of American community. The reality had been that while American nationality centered, on one level, on adherence to democratic values, immigrants and their children and the members of racial minorities, regardless of their attitude to those values, were often not seen as Americans by old-stock white Protestants. When the threat of war and then war itself became the dominant reality of national life, the Writers' Program, unlike the FWP, claimed it should help articulate a democratic ideology that would stimulate patriotic feeling. Ritualistic statements about democracy were easy to make. National FWP officials had dreamed of something more profound: a redefinition of national identity that made a democratic acceptance of one's fellow citizens a natural part of one's approach to his or her community.

The primordial instinctive loyalties the FWP and then the Writers' Program sought to develop through presenting America to Americans was linked after the invasion of Poland in the fall of 1939 to an explicit celebration of democratic values. Both forms of patriotism were combined in the idea that Americans had much to affirm, to cherish, and to be proud of. A 1941 script of an Oregon radio broadcast designed to publicize the work of the Writers' Program echoed themes found in the letters of FWP officials, prefaces to the state guides, and the comments of various critics—but added a significant new term: "We pride ourselves on having compiled a book with, if you pardon us for taking ourselves seriously—a purpose. That purpose is the understanding of America [through] intimate knowledge of the scenes and people around us. And to understand America is to love America. . . . We are selling America to

Americans."[27] Love is a value transcending ideology. To love America, FWP and Writers' Program officials held, you had to try to understand it, which in their view meant knowing, accepting, and finally embracing the nation's diversity. Understanding combined emotional feeling and intellectual knowledge. It would make possible an inclusive community. But in the summer of 1941 it was also important because, as the radio announcer in Oregon responded to the Writers' Program official, "Love, it seems to me, is an assurance of loyalty."[28]

With the publication of the final state guide, the American Booksellers' Association proclaimed the week of November 10–16, 1941, American Guide Week. They suggested it was an occasion to "Take Pride in Your Country." That slogan became the central theme of this event. WPA officials, aware that they were living in an "era when flag-waving is a popular, sometimes professional sport," feared "the adoption of such a slogan as 'Take Pride in Your Country' for another of those 'Weeks' might seem to be just a little more of the same." Of course, they were convinced it was not. Raising the possibility that it was served mainly as an opportunity to assert that American Guide Week was indeed different from those other "Weeks," that the guide series gave meaning to the slogan. They thought that "when a means to deeper understanding of the lives and deeds of the men and women who built this nation and a deeper comprehension of that which they have built is offered—then the slogan is justified."[29]

In honor of American Guide Week, President Roosevelt issued an official statement. The president tried to appeal to both an ideological and an instinctual patriotism. The guides, he declared, "ably illustrate our national way of life." He claimed they showed that an integrated nation and national identity were compatible with "the variants in local patterns of living and regional development." What in the national way of life was both compatible with and transcended variations was not specified. In this, the president did not differ from FWP and Writers' Program officials or from liberal cultural pluralists in general. He did, however, repeat their belief that the guides "will serve to deepen our understanding of ourselves as a people, and hence promote national unity." It was a faith that assumed Americans could understand and accept cultural differences as part of their national identity.[30]

As the international crisis worsened, the emphasis on democratic ideology as a source of values that transcended differences increased. The *New York Sun*, a paper hostile to Roosevelt and highly critical of the WPA, editorialized that the American Guide Series would help promote tolerance. Stephen Vincent Benét, reviewing the guides in the *New York Herald Tribune*, sounded the patriotic themes he and many others thought appropriate "to these troubled times." In the guides, he thought, Americans could study the story of national diversity. He also found evidence of American dedication to liberty and equality and pointed out that Lincoln's Gettysburg address could be found in the series. In "troubled times" Benét held Lincoln worth quoting, since Lincoln expressed sentiments Americans needed to reaffirm. "Well," Benét concluded, "we are still sticking to that—and sticking, too, to the notion on the coin—and the motto we generally only remember in times of trouble—the motto which might be the watchword of the American Guide series, E Pluribus Unum."[31]

While completion of the American Guide Series made the search of the Writers' Program for new projects more pressing, America's entry into the war was constricting the possibilities of what could be done. In September 1941, Writers' Program officials still hoped that with the guide series completed, they could turn to "individual aspects of American life and culture." At a November meeting of the Advisory Committee on Art, Music, and the Writers' Program, the participants posed urgent questions: "Can Writers' Program publications contribute to defense?" "Is the job of presenting America to Americans important under the exigencies of arming the nation?" There still seemed to be time to address once again large fundamental questions about government sponsorship of the arts that had never been resolved: "What is a 'writer'? What kind of writing can and should government employed writers do? Descriptive vs. creative writing?" The Writers' Program was as incapable as the FWP had been to address, let alone answer, these questions. In both cases the Congress and the administration determined the final answers by setting the limits within which these agencies worked.[32]

Within days after the attack on Pearl Harbor, John Newsom was arguing that the Writers' Program had a future as a government publicity bureau and, in effect, as a kind of intelligence agency. He suggested that since the Writers' Program had both national and local offices and "trained personnel residing in communities and intensely acquainted with local attitudes and problems," it could be used to explain and interpret national policies at the grassroots level. Valuable information would travel in both directions. The Writers' Program would provide "a continuous flow of information from the grassroots to Washington on all matters that must be considered if national policies are to be intelligently shaped and adjusted to fit particular local situations." Employees of the Writers' Program could "serve the war activity through collecting significant examples of local and popular forms of public information." Yet even while fighting to maintain the Writers' Program by demonstrating that it could fulfill a specific wartime need, Newsom did not abandon the idea that his agency could also make a cultural contribution. The sampling activity, Newsom insisted, also had a long-term purpose of providing "a historical and social record" for "writers and social analysts of the future." In the end, the realities of the time worked against the broad vision and against an important role for the Writers' Program, regardless of how strongly agency officials argued they could make an important contribution to the war.[33]

The attempt to tie the Writers' Program to the national defense effort was a reasonable strategy for the agency's administrators to follow. A program that could prove its relevance to the war situation had a much better chance of surviving than one that could not. With hindsight it seems that the Writers' Program had little chance of proving its value to the national defense program and to an American public preoccupied with war needs. While WPA officials maintained that "every publication that informs the public, that emphasizes American history and American heritage, or that aids public agencies in their work with the public is actually contributing to the defense of the country," some Americans denied the need not only for a Writers' Program but also for work relief programs in general. An editorial in the *Cleveland Plain Dealer* explained that while such programs had been necessary when unemployment was high and that "a certain amount of wastefulness" was acceptable to meet the needs of those "who would otherwise . . . starve," this was no longer the case "when WPA workers are rapidly being absorbed into private industry . . . [and] when defense, not relief is the major national objective."[34]

As Newsom discovered in the spring of 1941, local officials had already "felt for some time that the work the project has been doing is of doubtful value now that the National Defense program is of paramount importance." Still, Newsom "hazarded" the opinion that some cultural programs should be continued. After all, he argued, "the cultural value of the Writers' Program publications has been recognized by noted authorities in the field of letters." Nevertheless, local and state officials almost always viewed cultural projects as low priority items in the overall defense program. Rather than seeing cultural programs as part of the defense effort, they felt they had to choose between allegedly valuable cultural projects and those tangibly related to defense. They chose the latter. Publications such as guides to service academies and areas surrounding military and naval installations and bulletins advising how to "grow your own vegetables" received high priority and eventually became the only activity of most local and state units.[35]

However inevitable the demise of the Writers' Program might later look, many WPA officials had been unwilling to act as if there was no hope for a cultural program. Even as programs were being curtailed, national WPA officials persisted in having conferences. At one such conference, Margaret S. Child of the Historical Records Service complained about "unrealistic thinking." As an example, she noted, "our first conference consisted almost exclusively of a well-given discourse on choral singing in Russia, China, and Alabama—a fascinating subject to be sure but hardly one to be translated into practice by our Administration." Child was indeed more realistic than her colleagues. The defense program could not be defined broadly enough to make it a suitable vehicle for a cultural program. It was, however, the only vehicle available to the Writers' Program; that agency was not strong enough to survive independently. Instead it became a writers' unit in a larger defense program. Nevertheless, the administration's wartime cultural propaganda followed lines that the Writers' Program tried to pursue in adapting the visions of the FWP to wartime realities. That strategy was no accident, for these programs were part of an effort to create national unity without attacking national diversity and demanding cultural conformity.[36]

In retrospect it can be seen that the Writers' Program could not, after the invasion of Poland in September 1939, hope to fulfill the visions developed by Alsberg and his staff between 1935 and 1939. Newsom deserves credit for bringing the American Guide Series to completion, but while other interesting works were published during his tenure, they had grown out of projects begun before 1939. Projects like "Hands That Built America" never had a chance of being finished. The bulk of the work done at both the local and national levels was designed to meet utilitarian needs.

While the effort to tie the Writers' Program to the national defense program was not unreasonable, there probably never was a chance that such an arrangement would enable the Writers' Program to fulfill its larger goals. In March 1942 the Writers' Program became the Writers' Unit of the War Services Subdivision (formerly the Community Services Division) of the WPA. Even after this change, Merle Colby, the director of this unit, kept discussing the possibility of regional art studies and proposed conferences to discuss past programs and future activities. To a large degree Colby took a no-nonsense approach to his job, but after years of service first to the FWP and then to the Writers' Program, a part of him could not admit that the dream was dead. The dreaming went on at the same time Colby curtailed all activities not directly related to the war effort. He visited local offices of the Writers' Program to help get them in shape to provide "editorial assistance and rapidly conceived and executed writing jobs of an immediate character" and to make sure they abandoned long-range publication programs. In elaborately stilted language, he explained to state officials the change taking place. The emphasis was now on "the functional rather than the structural nature of the Writers' Project." Project workers were to regard "writing as an activity of a flexible group rather than as the product of a water tight compartment of writers." Colby stressed "service side activities rather than the product side." The long and short of this was that the Writers' Program was no longer to think of itself as an independent agency but as an adjunct of other defense-related programs. It was no longer to have its own goals but to devote itself to fulfilling the needs of others.[37]

Still, Colby kept an idea file for future undertakings that indicated he had begun with different visions for a Federal Writers' Project, though it had been some time since there had been anything in the Writers' Unit program that reflected its historical connection to Henry Alsberg and the FWP. In April 1943 Colby submitted "Final Report on Disposition of Unpublished Materials of the WPA Writers' Program" to the Library of Congress. Even in this report with its lackluster title the old visions continued to glow, for Colby thought they might still be fulfilled after the war. He hoped that "here and there in America some talented boy or girl will stumble on some of this material, take fire from it and turn it to creative use."[38]

Epilogue

Have You Discovered America?

In an effort to introduce Americans to the purposes of their program, FWP officials had asked, "Have you discovered America?"[1] The question continues to be a rhetorical device used to call up familiar themes in American culture and hopes and anxieties about that culture. When folklorist William Ferris became head of the National Endowment for the Humanities (NEH) in 1997, rhetoric similar to the FWP's about discovery and rediscovery became central to his efforts to promote a program of regional, folk, ethnic, and oral history studies. When folklorist William Ivey was later appointed head of the National Endowment for the Arts, there was some public discussion of the ascent of folklorists to control of such important cultural agencies. Hardly anyone, however, took the long perspective and remarked that folklorists were now more involved in public cultural policy than they had been since the days of the WPA. Persistent issues, inherited questions, regarding American culture are deeply embedded in the rhetoric of rediscovery.

Only one FWP theme seems to have disappeared from the rhetoric of supporters of federal programs focused on exploring the lives and cultural creativity of ordinary Americans. The assumption that such studies would both inspire American artists and reunite the artist and the community has almost vanished from the arguments still made by supporters of such programs. Thus, Merle Colby's vision of a future in which a young aspiring artist would one day rediscover FWP materials and turn them into literature is no longer the type of argument usually presented by supporters of cultural programs focused on ordinary Americans. Nor do contemporary supporters of such programs usually think they can gain support by arguing, as Benjamin Botkin and Sterling Brown did, that much of the folklore and oral history of ordinary Americans is in itself a form of literature, although they may hold this position.

Post–World War II literary criticism dismissed romantic nationalist approaches to the arts. During the war years, however, it would have seemed unlikely to most Americans interested in literature that a group of former Marxists (the Trotskyist variant) centered around the *Partisan Review* in New York City and a group of former Southern Agrarians, would find they had much in common, would form an alliance, and would dominate American literary criticism in the 1950s and early 1960s. *Partisan Review* editors rejected the literary nationalism of the 1930s as provincial and opposed to the cosmopolitanism, literary modernism, and variety of Marxism they embraced. Minus the radical politics, this view was later echoed by William Vann O'Connor, a literary critic with close ties to the New Critics, who gained prominence in the years following World War II. The New Criticism stressed a close reading of literary texts and was associated with Southern Agrarian writers, who in the 1930s had attacked industrialism as a destroyer of tradition and culture and who had advocated an agrarian program for their native South. Their view of tradition and culture was totally incompatible with the cultural pluralism of national FWP officials who thought cultural nationalism and cosmopolitanism could be compatible. In *Sense and Sensibility in Modern Poetry* (1948) O'Connor dismissed the FWP guidebooks as symbolic of the futile efforts of poets in the "Whitman-Sandburg tradition" who wrote formless and superficial poetry celebrating a vague and "synthetic myth" of America. Views such as O'Connor's contributed to a cultural climate in the postwar years that saw no purpose in studying the FWP.[2]

Nevertheless, FWP assumptions about the value of studying the lives and cultural expressions of ordinary Americans never entirely disappeared. National FWP folklore editor Benjamin Botkin tried to keep alive the Writers' Project vision in his folklore work at the Library of Congress in the 1940s, his series of regional and topical folklore anthologies beginning with *A Treasury of American Folklore* (1944), his regular column in *New York Folklore Quarterly*, and a host of activities involving what he called the utilization of folklore. Work that Botkin, Charles Seeger (a former WPA colleague, a classical composer, and one of the founders of ethnomusicology), and Alan Lomax (a former head of the Archive of American Folksong) did in the 1930s and later contributed to the folk song revival of the 1950s and 1960s. Influenced by these New Deal folklorists, scholars such as Archie Green successfully lobbied to create the annual Smithsonian folk festival, to employ folklorists in the public programs of the National Endowment for the Arts, and to expand the Library of Congress Archive of Folksong into the American Folklife Center.

Thus, the regional humanities centers William Ferris tried to establish during his time as director of the NEH embodied many of the goals the FWP had articulated earlier—goals that in a roundabout way were a legacy of the FWP and that were also a variant on an even older history of answers to inherited questions about American diversity and tradition. Both FWP officials and Ferris assumed Americans wanted and needed to rediscover their country. In both cases, the underlying assumptions were that an American society in a state of constant flux could not be defined in static terms and that the dominant culture did not provide Americans with an adequate sense of the diversity, vitality, and richness of their culture. Thus, the inherited questions FWP officials tried to answer have hardly disappeared from American life. Nevertheless, Ferris failed to create the federally sponsored nationwide infrastructure of regional humanities centers he proposed.

It is an oversimplification to end the story of the FWP by focusing on the gradual winding down of the project and its successor, the Writers' Program. FWP and Writers' Program officials never lost faith in the value of their projects and battled for ways to continue them. Botkin and his allies within the WPA programs and the scholarly world made an effort to find a permanent home in a federal agency for the FWP folklore, ethnic studies, and oral history programs. The FWP employed rhetoric about making culture accessible, the importance of a sense of place, and the link between diversity and democracy in its efforts to explain its goals and win support for its programs.

Not long after he joined the FWP, Benjamin Botkin mentioned in a letter to his wife that he had had lunch with Charles Seeger and Alan Lomax. In the same letter, he enthusiastically informed her that "I have been invited by the American Council of Learned Societies to attend a meeting of some 10 Federal Project people to discuss a plan for cooperation in research in the folk arts. This may lead to something." He was right, for these intersecting events created some of the roads that individuals interested in cultural strategy, what we think of today as cultural politics and policy, are still traveling.[3]

One of the first things Botkin did after he became national FWP folklore editor was to establish a joint WPA folklore committee. Representatives from the
Writers', Music, Theater, and Art Projects were involved as well as representatives from the WPA recreation and education divisions. The committee invited
Donald Daughtery of the American Council of Learned Societies, Harold Spivacke of the Music Division of the Library of Congress, and George Herzog
of the Columbia University Department of Anthropology to participate in its
discussions. Botkin and ethnomusicologist Charles Seeger of the Federal Music
Project cochaired the committee. Daughtery, who became a strong supporter
of the committee, initially urged it to address how WPA folklore could best be
preserved and made available. He also later encouraged committee efforts to
continue existing projects, to undertake new endeavors, and to make a permanent place in the federal government for the work the FWP had been doing and
for new ideas Botkin and Seeger developed. When it became clear by the
spring of 1939 that the FWP's days were numbered, Botkin and Seeger hoped
to use the contacts they had made through the committee to try to find a permanent home for the projects they had begun and those they still wanted to
undertake.[4]

In the summer of 1939, Botkin and Seeger knew that the reorganization of
the FWP into the Writers' Program and increasing cutbacks in WPA programs
meant that the struggle to move joint committee projects into the Library of
Congress was now more pressing than ever, and that the very future of their
projects and their ability to pursue them depended on it. They sensed that Popular Front cultural workers like themselves would be attacked as Reds. In July
Botkin wrote his brother that he had been questioned by congressional inves-
tigators, who had also confiscated some of the New York City folklore material.[5] Nevertheless, Botkin and Seeger intensified their lobbying. In August Botkin informed his wife that he had moved in with the Seeger family: "I am staying
at the Seegers' because it is less lonely, cooler, and generally agreeable, and because I can keep working on our folklore program with Charles. We practically
do nothing else—talk and eat and sleep it."[6]

Still, Botkin had to contend with conflicting realities and hopes. He had
taken a leave of absence from his position at the University of Oklahoma to
work in Washington. If there was no position for him in Washington, he would
have to return to Oklahoma soon. Yet his and Seeger's vision of what the joint
committee could accomplish if it became a permanent part of the federal establishment led him to lobby as hard as possible and to postpone the Oklahoma decision as long as possible, with the hope that his and the joint commit-

tee's future would be determined before the fall semester began.[7] Botkin's wife, however, constantly reminded him that he had to hold onto *a* job and could not afford to lose both jobs, and that that might entail returning to Oklahoma and possibly putting his dreams on hold.[8] As he struggled to establish a place for his work in the Library of Congress, Botkin provided his wife with little reassurance: "And if Charles [Seeger] has his head in the clouds . . . what of it? For seeing people and talking up my work, Charles has been more helpful than anyone."[9] Botkin not only joined Seeger in lobbying, but he also kept working on securing publication of experimental work done by the living lore units he had established in New England, New York, and Chicago.[10] In September, however, he had to return to the University of Oklahoma. Only in October did the arrangement for Botkin to work at the Library of Congress go through. He secured another leave from the University of Oklahoma to return to Washington as head of the Library of Congress unit of the Writers' Program.[11]

On one hand, when Botkin and Seeger first met, it was a time of grand new undertakings in federal cultural programs. On the other hand, it was the beginning of a time of political reaction—the emergence in the late 1930s of HUAC, which was followed in the early 1950s by Republican Senator Joseph McCarthy. It was a time of hope, promise, anxiety, and fear. Botkin and Seeger thought the New Deal could help them implement their cultural strategy and solve the problem of making a living while pursuing their goals.

Their hopes were raised and crushed as the WPA arts projects offered new opportunities and then were slowly dismantled in response to the growth of a powerful conservative coalition in the Congress and the coming of World War II. Reorienting their efforts, Botkin and Seeger, with some success, turned to the Library of Congress as a possible new base for their work. They supported programs that met what they saw as the needs of the American people for both bread and roses. Indeed, Botkin titled a paper he presented at a meeting of the Modern Language Association in 1939 "Bread and Song."[12]

In the midst of all this hope and uncertainty at home for the fate of their endeavors at promoting their cultural strategy, Botkin and Seeger faced the horror of the war they knew was coming. Indeed, for Popular Front intellectuals August 23, 1939, was a date they could not ignore. What did anti-Fascism mean after Stalin signed a pact with Hitler? The problem for them was eased after Germany attacked Russia and then when the United States and Russia became allies. They tried to give a pluralist dimension to the celebration of American nationalism and unity that the war encouraged, to help this also be a celebration and acceptance of racial and ethnic diversity.[13]

Botkin and Seeger had always seen the joint committee as just the beginning of the creation of an institutional structure for folklore studies in the government. Sharing with his wife the excitement of new ventures, Botkin wrote her "according to Daughtery and Spivacke there are big plans underway for the WPA in the Library in connection with Archibald MacLeish's cultural program."[14] The circle of individuals and institutions Botkin and Seeger were trying to involve in their cultural strategy was widening. With the support of Daughtery and Spivacke, they had already involved the American Council of Learned Societies and the Music Division of the Library of Congress. The additional support of Archibald MacLeish, librarian of Congress, had even more dramatic implications for their effort to divorce their cultural projects from relief programs. MacLeish's interest in Botkin and Seeger's program flowed logically from his cultural commitments as reflected in his *America Was Promises*, a book-length poem/photomontage about the disparity between promise and reality in Depression America, and his role as an active figure in Popular Front cultural endeavors.

Initially, Writers' Program officials discussed the possibility of the Library of Congress acting as a sponsor of Botkin's work. Botkin would be located in the library but still an employee of the Writers' Program, "loaned to the library." What he and Seeger wanted was "to get a foothold in the library" for projects that would no longer be tied to the fate of what was always regarded as a temporary relief program. They also took heart from the fact that Spivacke made it clear he wanted them. By having the work of the joint committee located in the Music Division of the Library of Congress, Spivacke thought his division would be able to establish better contacts with folklore scholars and add a folklore archive to the existing folk song archive. He wanted scholars like Botkin and Seeger working for the Library of Congress and the WPA folklore materials located in the Music Division. The relief programs interested Spivacke only to the extent that they might pay the costs of the library expanding its programs.[15]

Botkin was optimistic about the possibilities at the Library of Congress: "I have, as Spivacke put it, a wonderful opportunity. Not only Spivacke but MacLeish wants me in the Library." Botkin worked to speed the publication of some of the remaining state guides, to pursue publishing unfinished folklore books, and to create a Library of Congress folklore archive. Such influential folklorists as Stith Thompson wrote letters urging MacLeish to support such work.[16]

Botkin's superiors at the Library of Congress were impressed when he was asked to present a paper at the 1939 annual meeting of the American Historical Society. He understood that this paper, like the presentation he had given

earlier at the annual meeting of the Modern Language Association, was important for reasons of both scholarly substance and politics that clearly overlapped.
Botkin wanted to build bridges between WPA folklore studies at the Library of
Congress and literary scholars and historians. At the American Historical Association meeting he presented "Folklore as a Neglected Source of Social History" and made a case not just for what he called the prestige folklore of the
distant past but also for the folklore of the recent past and the folklore still
being created in the present.[17]

Although Botkin was helping with the state guides that had not yet been
completed, working with Morton Royse on social-ethnic studies, planning to
publish a volume of FWP occupational tall tales, and preparing with Sterling
Brown a volume of the FWP ex-slave narratives, he continued to plan for a permanent future for the joint committee. He worked enthusiastically with Spivacke on creating a classification system for the folklore archive. Once the
classification system was established, Spivacke planned to "tell Stith Thompson and other scholars that we have an archive and ask them to send in their
materials." While Botkin was eager to work on creating the archive, he was also
planning "a program for the cultural integration of folklore and folksong with
history and social science." Spivacke continued his efforts to have Seeger and
Nick Ray of the WPA Community and Recreations programs—Ray would later
become an important film director—assigned to the Music Division. He envisioned the four of them, to be joined by Alan Lomax, as taking over the work
of the joint committee. Spivacke also wanted the Music Division "to swallow
the committee," for he feared being tied up with the WPA's cycles of expansion
and retrenchment in which "newer and smaller units suffer first."[18]

As it turned out, Botkin and Seeger were not able either to implement much
of their cultural program or to establish a permanent agency to promote such
work. By July 1941, "the Project," as Botkin phrased it, "was getting put away
in storage."[19] Nevertheless, the episode was hardly without value. Botkin would
later publish a collection of FWP ex-slave narratives as *Lay My Burden Down: A
Folk History of Slavery*. Although much of the Living Lore and other FWP folklore material remained unpublished, Botkin would draw on it in *A Treasury of
American Folklore* and in his later regional and topical folklore treasuries. The
FWP and Library of Congress experiences contributed to the ideas about "applied folklore" and "utilization" that Botkin would advocate throughout his life.

Botkin could not have foreseen that during the Cold War, pretensions to
being scientific would take on a significant role in academic studies of the humanities and that a new artistic formalism would dismiss Popular Front cultural endeavors as middlebrow, without calling for any significant examination

of those endeavors. He had known during the 1930s that not all his fellow writers shared his commitments. Botkin had severely criticized the Southern Agrarians, some varieties of regionalist writing, and some forms of high modernism. He had argued that Popular Front writers focusing on neglected classes of Americans and drawing on folklore and sociology could use myth and symbol in modernist ways. What he could not have foreseen was that major trends in 1930s writing would no longer be a significant part of critical literary discourse in the postwar years.[20]

The FWP's vision and work came closest to being directly taken up again in the regional humanities centers William Ferris tried to create as head of the NEH from 1997 to the spring of 2001. Ferris's proposed centers were to be based in universities, not in urban centers as Botkin and others suggested in a 1961 "Proposal for an Applied Folklore Center."[21] Where Botkin in the late 1930s had begun moving away from regionalism as theory and practice—while still recognizing the importance of regional differences—Ferris for both theoretical and practical political reasons embraced the concept.

The FWP and Botkin struggled to help Americans see diversity, the local, and the folk as major components of the national culture. Botkin thought that "Americans as compared with other peoples are sadly deficient" when it comes to "an enjoyment of living American folklore for what it is and what it is worth." He wanted to help them see "the importance of folklore and even a healthy provincialism, as one of the ingredients, though not necessarily the most important ingredient, of a well rounded culture." He hoped that everyone— writer, artist, scholar, and ordinary citizen—who is "concerned with the materials of an American culture" would develop an interest in the nation's diverse folk and lore.[22] In his years as NEH director, William Ferris would learn how far many of the nation's humanities scholars and some of its self-appointed cultural guardians were from appreciating and examining what Botkin had wanted them and other Americans to see as an important part of American culture.

Celebrating diversity was a central theme in both the FWP and the NEH programs. Likewise, both emphasized making a diverse American culture accessible to all: "The [NEH] centers will vividly demonstrate that the humanities belong to everyone." NEH spokesperson Jim Turner declared that combined with the online encyclopedias for each state, the NEH centers "will help encourage a sense of regional belonging and understanding. . . . States have histories, pasts, local folklore. . . . These are things that can be nurtured, celebrated and made available." Echoing national FWP officials, the NEH claimed that through exploring diversity, "we rediscover our cultural roots and reaffirm our common bonds as Americans." Like national FWP officials, Ferris and his supporters within the NEH intended to introduce Americans to an America that they held was unfamiliar to them. For the NEH as for the FWP, to rediscover was to redefine and to see American identity as fluid, not static, and as emerging in the present and the future as well as being inherited from the past.[23]

The distance between Henry Alsberg's rhetoric about the significance of the American Guide Series and Ferris's about the NEH's proposed online state encyclopedias was small. Ferris maintained that the encyclopedias were an appropriate format "to rediscover America, to view her coat of many colors."[24] These encyclopedias, he claimed, would "offer a sweeping view of the landscape of knowledge within folk, popular and academic worlds." This was a slight but significant variation on the FWP guidebook approach that highlighted the vitality and creativity of ordinary Americans and refused to draw lines between high and folk expressive culture as they detailed local folkways, regional diversity, and ethnic pluralism.

The efforts of the FWP and Ferris to broaden Americans' view of their national heritage can be judged at best partial successes or partial failures, depending on one's support for such efforts and one's sense of optimism or pessimism if one does support such efforts. FWP officials knew they were seeking to broaden the vision of the national heritage. In some ways, they worked in a more supportive culture than Ferris did. Nevertheless, they recognized among some Americans an opposition to an emphasis on cultural diversity, a dismissive attitude toward folk tradition, and an inability, as Botkin put it, "to recognize or appreciate the folklore of the present."[25] Still they, like Ferris, argued for a broad view of the materials of an American culture. It is a tradition that seems never to triumph and never to disappear.

Learning about the vision and contribution of the FWP to a tradition of rediscovering America can help us assess not only the value of this New Deal agency but also why a perceived need to rediscover America is a recurrent and seemingly permanent theme in American culture. Most importantly, it can aid us in addressing the question, "Have you discovered America?" Although Ralph Waldo Emerson did not phrase the question in these words, he spoke to it and thought that trying to answer it was the task of the "American Scholar"—a role he did not limit to professors.

Notes

Abbreviations

Alsberg-Cronyn Files

Records of the Federal Writers' Project Relating to Henry G. Alsberg and George W. Cronyn, 1935–1939, Record Group 69, Central Correspondence Files of the Works Progress Administration, National Archives, Washington, D.C. Microfilm prepared by the General Services Administration, 1968, and available from Washington State University, Pullman.

BP

B. A. Botkin Papers, Personal Correspondence, University of Nebraska-Lincoln Archives, Lincoln.

DIFWPA

Works Progress Administration, Division of Information Files, Works Progress Administration records, Record Group 69, National Archives, Washington, D.C.

FWP-Couch Papers

Federal Writers' Project Papers of the Regional Director, William Terry Couch, Southern Historical Collection, University of North Carolina, Chapel Hill.

FWPLC

Federal Writers' Project file, Library of Congress Manuscripts Division, Washington, D.C.

FWPNA

Federal Writers' Project files, Works Progress Administration records, Record Group 69, Federal Writers' Project, National Archives, Washington, D.C.

HUAC

U.S. House of Representatives, Special Committee on Un-American Activities, *Investigation of Un-American Propaganda Activities in the United States*, Hearings on H.R. 282, 75th Cong., 3d sess., 1938.

Kennedy Papers
   Stetson Kennedy Papers, Southern Historical Collection, University of North Car-
   olina, Chapel Hill.
President's Papers
   Frank Porter Graham Papers, University Archives, University of North Carolina,
   Chapel Hill.
Press Papers
   University of North Carolina Press Papers, Southern Historical Collection, Univer-
   sity of North Carolina, Chapel Hill.
WPA Files
   Works Projects Administration General Files Series, Record Group 69, National
   Archives, Washington, D.C.

Introduction

1. Michael Denning, *The Cultural Front: The Laboring of American Culture in the Twentieth Century* (London: Verso, 1996).

2. Warren Susman, "History and the American Intellectual: Uses of a Usable Past,"
American Quarterly 26 (1964): 244–48, has influenced my ideas and those of many other
historians about the role of myth and ideology in American culture and in the writing
of American history.

3. Charles C. Alexander, *Here the Country Lies: Nationalism and the Arts in Twentieth-
Century America* (Bloomington: Indiana University Press, 1980), is still an important
overview of the topic it surveys and convincing in its argument that "at least in the
United States, modernist and romantic nationalist attitudes were by no means incompatible and were often complementary" (xii).

4. On this point, see Matthew Frye Jacobson, *Whiteness of a Different Color: European
Immigrants and the Alchemy of Race* (Cambridge: Harvard University Press, 1998).

5. This point is ably explored in Walter Jackson, "Melville Herskovits and the Search
for Afro-American Culture," in *Malinowski, Rivers, Benedict, and Others: Essays on Culture
and Personality*, ed. George W. Stocking Jr. (Madison: University of Wisconsin Press,
1986), 95–126.

6. Ibid., 95.

7. Harvard Sitkoff, *A New Deal for Blacks: The Emergence of Civil Rights as a National
Issue* (New York: Oxford University Press, 1978).

8. Charles I. Glicksberg, "The Federal Writers' Project," *South Atlantic Quarterly* 37
(1938): 159, 160.

9. Hans Kohn, *American Nationalism: An Interpretative Essay* (New York: Macmillan,
1957).

10. For an overview of the American intellectual community FWP national officials
were part of, see David Hollinger, "Ethnic Diversity, Cosmopolitanism, and the Emergence of the American Liberal Intelligentsia," *American Quarterly* 27 (1975): 133–51.

11. Important works pointing in this direction are Frank Kermode, *Romantic Image*
(New York: Macmillan 1957); Daniel Singal, "Towards a Definition of American Mod-

ernism," *American Quarterly* 39 (1987): 7–26; Robert L. Dorman, *Revolt of the Provinces: The Regionalist Movement in America, 1920–1945* (Chapel Hill: University of North Carolina Press, 1993); Houston Baker Jr., *Modernism and the Harlem Renaissance* (Chicago: University of Chicago Press, 1989); George Hutchinson, *The Harlem Renaissance in Black and White* (Cambridge: Belknap Press of Harvard University Press, 1995); and Wanda M. Corn, *The Great American Thing: Modern Art and National Identity, 1915–1935* (Berkeley: University of California Press, 1999).

12. Standard works on the FWP offer a good deal of information about the project while hardly discussing the vision underlying FWP studies. William F. McDonald's *Federal Relief Administration and the Arts: The Origins and Administrative History of the Arts Projects of the Works Progress Administration* (Columbus: Ohio State University Press, 1969) is based on a previously unpublished study undertaken by historians hired by the American Council of Learned Societies to write a history of the New Deal arts projects. An uneven mix of analysis and undigested government documents makes it a compendium useful primarily to the specialist. Botkin, who had served as national FWP folklore editor, was in charge of the council team's research on the FWP, and his point of view is apparent in the section on that program in McDonald's book. In *The Dream and the Deal: The Federal Writers' Project, 1935–1943* (Boston: Little, Brown, 1972), Jerre Mangione, the former national FWP coordinating editor, offers a lively account of and a loving tribute to the project, a study rich in anecdotal material but short on an analysis of the work of the FWP. Monty Penkower's *The Federal Writers' Project: A Study in Government Patronage of the Arts* (Urbana: University of Illinois Press, 1977) is the most exhaustive and fully documented examination of the organizational and administrative aspects of the FWP. Three unpublished dissertations offer additional information. See Kathleen O'Connor McKinzie's "Writers on Relief, 1935–1942" (Ph.D. diss., Indiana University, 1970); Ronald Warren Taber, "The Federal Writers' Project in the Pacific Northwest: A Case Study" (Ph.D. diss., University of Washington, 1969); and Ronnie W. Clayton, "A History of the Federal Writers' Project in Louisiana" (Ph.D. diss., Louisiana State University, 1974). Taber's and Clayton's studies are useful for the information they provide about regional matters that national studies mention only in passing. Taken together, they help clarify the organizational and administrative history of the FWP but have little to say about project work.

13. A still-important methodological essay on studying American intellectual history as a community of discourse can be found in David A. Hollinger, "Historians and the Discourse of Intellectuals," in *New Direction in American Intellectual History*, ed. John Higham and Paul K. Conkin (Baltimore: Johns Hopkins University Press, 1979), 42–63.

14. Grace Overmeyer, *Government and the Arts* (New York: Norton, 1939), 112; Lewis Mumford, "Writers' Project," *New Republic*, October 20, 1937, 306–7; Alfred Kazin, *On Native Grounds: An Interpretation of Modern American Prose Literature* (New York: Reynal and Hitchcock, 1942), 486.

15. Mumford, "Writers' Project," 307; Bernard DeVoto, "The Writers' Project," *Harper's Magazine*, January 1942, 222.

16. Kazin, *On Native Grounds*, 486; Henry Steele Commager, *The American Mind: An Interpretation of American Thought and Character since the 1880s* (New Haven: Yale University

Press, 1971), 433; Charles Comer Alexander, *Nationalism in American Thought, 1930–1945* (Chicago: Rand McNally, 1969), 45.

17. Harold Rosenberg, "Anyone Who Could Write English," *New Yorker,* January 20, 1973, 102; Mangione, *Dream and the Deal*; Penkower, *Federal Writers' Project.*

18. This point is powerfully stated in Stanley Elkins, *Slavery: A Problem in American Institutional and Intellectual Life* (Chicago: University of Chicago Press, 1976), 24–26.

19. Daniel M. Fox, "The Achievement of the Federal Writers' Project," *American Quarterly* 13 (1961): 4–5, 3, 10.

20. Paul Sporn, *Against Itself: The Federal Theater and Writers' Projects in the Midwest* (Detroit: Wayne State University Press, 1995); Christine Bold, *The WPA Guides: Mapping America* (Jackson: University Press of Mississippi, 1999). See also my "Culture on Relief: The New Deal and the Arts—A Review Essay," *Annals of Iowa* 65 (1997): 267–78.

Chapter 1

1. J. Hector St. John de Crèvecoeur, *Letters from an American Farmer* (1782; reprint, New York: Albert and Charles Boni, 1925), 54; Robert Wiebe, *The Segmented Society: An Introduction to the Meaning of America* (New York: Oxford University Press, 1973), 90, 95; Richard E. Engler Jr., *The Challenge of Diversity* (New York: Harper and Row, 1969), ix.

2. The literature on romantic nationalism, cultural pluralism, and cosmopolitanism is ample. I have relied heavily on the following secondary sources: Charles C. Alexander, *Here the Country Lies: Nationalism and the Arts in Twentieth-Century America* (Bloomington: Indiana University Press, 1980); Terry A. Cooney, "Cosmopolitan Values and the Identification of Reaction: *Partisan Review* in the 1930s," *Journal of American History* 68 (1981): 580–98; John Higham, "Ethnic Pluralism in Modern American Thought" and "Another American Dilemma," in *Send These to Me: Jews and Other Immigrants in Urban America,* by John Higham (1963; New York: Atheneum, 1975), 196–246; John Higham, *Strangers in the Land: Patterns of American Nativism* (New York: Atheneum, 1963); David Hollinger, "Ethnic Diversity, Cosmopolitanism, and the Emergence of the American Liberal Intelligentsia," *American Quarterly* 27 (1975): 133–51; R. Alan Lawson, *The Failure of Independent Liberalism, 1930–1941* (New York: G. P. Putnam's Sons, 1971); Gilman M. Ostrander, *American Civilization in the First Machine Age, 1890–1940* (New York: Harper and Row, 1970); Henry May, *The End of American Innocence: A Study of the First Years of Our Own Time, 1912–1917* (New York: Knopf, 1959); and Richard Weiss, "Ethnicity and Reform: Minorities and the Ambience of the Depression Years," *Journal of American History* 66 (1979): 566–85.

3. George L. Mosse, *The Nationalization of the Masses: Political Symbolism and Mass Movements in Germany from the Napoleonic War through the Third Reich* (New York: H. Fentig, 1975), 6. New Deal officials saw a pluralist version of cultural nationalism as an alternative to totalitarianism. This theme is clearly developed in chap. 9, "Cultural Diversity in American Life," in U.S. National Resources Committee, *The Problems of a Changing Population: Report of the Committee on Population Problems to the National Resources Committee, May 1938* (Washington, D.C.: U.S. Government Printing Office, 1938), 224–52. B. A. Botkin, national FWP folklore editor, was a contributor to this study.

4. Grace Overmeyer, *Government and the Arts* (New York: Norton, 1939), 112.

5. Henry James Jr., *Hawthorne* (London: Macmillan, 1879), 42–44; Ralph Waldo Emerson, "The American Scholar" (1837), in *The Portable Emerson*, ed. Carl Bode in collaboration with Malcolm Cowley (New York: Penguin, 1981); Van Wyck Brooks, *America's Coming of Age* (New York: B. W. Huebsch, 1915).

6. John Higham, "Hanging Together: Divergent Unities in American History," *Journal of American History* 61 (1974): 7, 10, 19, 26, 28.

7. Matthew Arnold, *Culture and Anarchy*, ed. Seymour Lipman (1865; reprint, New Haven: Yale University Press, 1994), 5; Warren I. Susman, "The Thirties," in *The Development of an American Culture*, ed. Stanley Coben and Lorman Ratner (Englewood Cliffs, N.J.: Prentice-Hall, 1970), 183; Robert Berkhofer, "Clio and the Culture Concept: Some Impressions of a Changing Relationship in American Culture," in *The Idea of Culture in the Social Sciences*, ed. Louis M. Schneider and Charles M. Bonjean (Cambridge: Cambridge University Press, 1973), 77–100. R. Hoey's remark is in his prefatory letter in FWP, *North Carolina: A Guide to the Old North State* (Chapel Hill: University of North Carolina Press, 1939). There are numerous instances of the use of the term "inventory," or a word with a similar connotation, by book reviewers and Federal Writers as a description of the guides. See, for example, "600-page Utah Guide Slated to Appear This March," February 2, 1941, clipping in box 83, WPA Files, and DIFWPA.

8. Alexander, *Here the Country Lies*, 1–71. Alexander uses the term "romantic nationalist" to cover both these groups. Although I use the term to refer only to opponents of the genteel tradition, I basically follow Alexander's argument.

9. Ibid., 7.

10. Emerson, "American Scholar," 50; Randolph S. Bourne, "Our Cultural Humility," *Atlantic Monthly*, October 1914, 503–7. See Erwin Ottomar Christiansen, *The Index of American Design* (New York: Macmillan, 1950), and Clarence Pearson Hornung, *Treasury of American Design: A Pictorial Survey of Popular Folk Arts Based upon Watercolor Renderings in the Index of American Design, at the National Gallery of Art* (New York: M. H. Abrams, 1972). Joan Shelley Rubin, *Constance Rourke and American Culture* (Chapel Hill: University of North Carolina Press, 1980), is an excellent analysis of a romantic nationalist whose approach to American studies parallels that of national FWP officials, particularly that of John Lomax and B. A. Botkin.

11. Van Wyck Brooks, "On Creating a Usable Past," *Dial*, April 11, 1918, 337–41. Van Wyck Brooks, *The Ordeal of Mark Twain* (New York: E. P. Dutton, 1920), is a famous example of Brooks's thesis that American life and culture frustrates the development of American writers. On the degree to which Brooks was a part of the genteel tradition, see James Hoopes, *Van Wyck Brooks: In Search of American Culture* (Amherst: University Press of Massachusetts, 1977); Alexander, *Here the Country Lies*, 39–40; Van Wyck Brooks, "The Wine of the Puritans" (1908), in *The Early Years: A Selection from His Works, 1908–1921*, ed. Claire Sprague (New York: Harper Torchbooks, 1968), 2–4, 8. Greenough is quoted in F. O. Matthiessen, *American Renaissance: Art and Expression in the Age of Emerson and Whitman* (New York: Oxford University Press, 1941), 145–46.

12. Hollinger, "Ethnic Diversity." Hollinger points out the limitations of focusing on psychological states, such as alienation and acceptance, at the expense of programs.

13. Malcolm Cowley, *Exiles Return: A Literary Odyssey of the 1920s* (New York: Viking Press, 1934), 11, 35.

14. Ibid., 107.

15. Richard Pells, *Radical Visions and American Dreams: Culture and Social Thought in the Depression Years* (New York: Harper and Row, 1973), 313.

16. *The American Guide and the American Guide Series: Their Task—To Introduce America to Americans*, n.d., pamphlet, box 74, FWPNA.

17. Biographical materials on Morton Royse, box 191, FWPNA, and box 210, WPA Files; John Lomax, *Adventures of a Ballad Hunter* (New York: Macmillan, 1947), 33–39; B. A. Botkin, biographical sketch in *Twentieth Century Authors, First Supplement*, ed. Stanley J. Kunitz (New York: H. W. Wilson, 1933), 101–2; Alexander, *Here the Country Lies*, 58; D. K. Wilgus, *Anglo-American Folksong Scholarship since 1898* (New Brunswick, N.J.: Rutgers University Press, 1959), 80–81; William James, *A Pluralistic Universe* (New York: Longmans, Green, 1909); Josiah Royce, *Race Questions, Provincialism, and other American Problems* (New York: Macmillan, 1908); Horace M. Kallen, *Culture and Democracy in the United States: Studies in the Group Psychology of the American Peoples* (New York: Boni and Liveright, 1924). Higham, "Ethnic Pluralism," examines the development of that concept. Barrett Wendell wrote the preface to Lomax's *Cowboy Songs and Other Frontier Ballads* (New York: Sturgis and Walton, 1910), xiii–xv.

18. Lomax, *Adventures of a Ballad Hunter*, 128–29; John Lomax and Alan Lomax, eds., *American Ballads and Folk Songs* (New York: Macmillan, 1934), xxvi, xxvii, xxx, xxxi.

19. John Lomax, "Self-Pity in Negro Folk-Songs," *Nation*, August 9, 1917, 141–45; Lomax, *Adventures of a Ballad Hunter*, 119, 124.

20. Monty Penkower, *The Federal Writers' Project: A Study in Government Patronage of the Arts* (Urbana: University of Illinois Press, 1977), 18–21; Jerre Mangione, *The Dream and the Deal: The Federal Writers' Project, 1935–1943* (Little, Brown, 1972), 53–59. Mangione's account is also the personal memoir of a national FWP official. See also "Henry G. Alsberg," biographical press release, box 74, FWPNA.

21. S. Ansky, *The Dybbuk: A Play in Four Acts*, trans. Henry G. Alsberg and Winifred Katzin (New York: Boni and Liveright, 1926); Penkower, *Federal Writers' Project*.

22. B. A. Botkin, "*Folk-Say* and *Space*: Their Genesis and Exodus," *Southwest Review* 20 (1935): 322–23. For additional biographical information, see the sketch in Kunitz, *Twentieth Century Authors*, 101–2. For an overview of Botkin's approach to folklore, see Jerrold Hirsch, "Folklore in the Making: B. A. Botkin," *Journal of American Folklore* 100 (1987): 3–38.

23. Botkin, "*Folk-Say* and *Space*," 322; B. A. Botkin, "The Folk in Literature: An Introduction to the New Regionalism," in *Folk-Say: A Regional Miscellany*, ed. B. A. Botkin (Norman: University of Oklahoma Press, 1929), 12.

24. Letters of recommendation sent to Henry Alsberg provide details about Royse's career, an outline of his intellectual biography, and evidence of the respect scholars in several fields had for his work; see esp. Spencer Miller, director, Workers' Education Bureau of America, to Alsberg, March 23, 1938, and Hilda M. Smith, specialist in workers' education, WPA, to Alsberg, March 19, 1938, box 191, FWPNA.

25. For biographical background on Brown, see the editorial foreword in Sterling A. Brown, *Negro Poetry and Drama* (Washington, D.C.: Associates in Negro Folk Education, 1937), and Sterling A. Brown, Arthur P. Davis, and Ulysses Lee, eds., *The Negro*

Caravan: Writings by American Negroes (New York: Dryden Press, 1941), 381. An undated press release, box 83, DIFWPA, provides background information on Brown and other members of the national staff.

26. On the relationship between social work, progressive reform, and the New Deal, see Allen F. Davis, *Spearheads for Reform: The Social Settlements and Progressive Movement, 1890–1914* (New York: Oxford University Press, 1967); Clarke Chambers, *Seedtime of Reform: American Social Service and Social Action, 1918–1933* (Minneapolis: University of Minnesota Press, 1963).

27. John P. Davis to Henry Alsberg, September 30, 1935, box 462, WPA Files; George Cronyn, national associate director, to Jacob Baker, "Subject: Negro Cultural Project of American Guide," November 30, 1935; Cronyn to Mary Church Terrell, December 4, 1935; Terrell to Cronyn, December 2, 1935, Alsberg-Cronyn Files. Copies of the frequent letters Alsberg sent in the early part of 1936, both inquiring about black employment on state projects and prodding state directors to hire black workers, are in the FWP-Couch Papers, and those he sent again in 1938 are in box 201, FWPNA. See also Mangione, *Dream and the Deal*, 257–59; William F. McDonald, *Federal Relief Administration and the Arts: The Origins and Administrative History of the Arts Projects of the Works Progress Administration* (Columbus: Ohio State University Press, 1972), 728–32; Penkower, *Federal Writers' Project*, 140–47.

28. Henry Alsberg to Ellen Woodward, assistant WPA administrator, April 1, July 22, 1938, FWPNA.

29. John Lomax, "Some Types of American Song," *Journal of American Folklore* 28 (1915): 1–17; John Lomax, "Supplementary Instructions No. 9 to the American Guide Manual: Folklore and Folk Customs," March 12, 1936, and "Supplementary Instructions No. 9C to the American Guide Manual: Folklore and Folk Customs—Example," August 4, 1936, box 69, FWPNA; B. A. Botkin, "The Folkness of the Folk," *English Journal* 26 (1937): 461–69; B. A. Botkin, "Manual for Folklore Studies," August 15, 1938, box 69, FWPNA.

30. B. A. Botkin, "Regionalism and Culture," in *The Writer in a Changing World*, ed. Henry Hart (New York: Equinox Press, 1937), 140–41, 154. See also Botkin, "Folk in Literature"; B. A. Botkin, "We Talk about Regionalism—North, East, South, and West," *Frontier* 13 (1933): 286–96; and B. A. Botkin, "Regionalism: Cult or Culture?," *English Journal* 25 (1936): 181–85.

31. Draft of a publicity release, "The Federal Writers' Project Does Justice to the Nationalities that Make Up America," n.d., box 83, DIFWPA; Joseph S. Roucek, Caroline F. Ware, and Morton W. Royse, "Approaches to the Study of Nationality Groups in the United States: Summary of the Discussion," in *The Cultural Approach to History*, ed. Caroline F. Ware (New York: Columbia University Press, 1940), 86–89.

32. "Portrait of the Negro as American," box 210, FWPNA. James S. Young, *Black Writers of the Thirties* (Baton Rouge: Louisiana State University Press, 1973), 3–34, 45, 134, 138–40, 147, 151–58, 165, 167, 181–88, 193, 240–41, develops the theme that young black intellectuals in this period stressed sociological analysis of black problems and saw older African American intellectuals as provincial for looking "at all problems with a racial perspective." Young treats Brown within this framework. See also Joanne

V. Gabbin, *Sterling A. Brown: Building the Black Aesthetic Tradition* (Westport, Conn.: Greenwood Press, 1985), 67–85. Brown was also a contributor to the Carnegie-Myrdal study that became the classic Gunnar Myrdal et al., *An American Dilemma: The Negro Problem and Modern Democracy* (New York: Harper and Brothers, 1944).

33. Reed Harris to Blair Bolles, December 6, 1937, as quoted in McDonald, *Federal Relief Administration and the Arts*, 694; "For Writers' Digest: Alsberg before House of Representatives," February 15, 1939, box 83, DIFWPA; M. R. Werner and Henry Alsberg, "Writers and the Government," 1936, box 83, WPA Files. See, for example, "Have You Discovered America?," n.d., box 74, FWPNA.

34. Manly Wade Wellman and Ralph Heyman to Travis Hoke, director NYCFWP, "Subject: Possible Expansion of Folklore Project," September 193[6?], box 195, FWPNA; Merle Colby, "Final Report on Disposition of Unpublished Materials of the WPA Writers' Program," April 8, 1943, box 384, WPA Files.

35. Werner and Alsberg, "Writers and the Government"; Katherine Kellock, national FWP tours editor, to Bernard DeVoto, editor *Harper's* magazine, March 1, 3, 1937, box 34, FWPNA; "For Writers' Digest: Tomorrow's Prizewinners May Be Today's Guidebook Writers," box 83, DIFWPA; "Report of the Regional Conference of the Federal Writers' Project for Region 4, held at Chicago, December 8–10, 1938," box 461, WPA Files; Franklin Folsom, executive secretary, League of American Writers, to Franklin D. Roosevelt, January 6, 1938, box 460, WPA Files; Lewis Mumford, "Talent to Order," *New Republic*, January 12, 1938, 289; Charles I. Glicksberg, "The Federal Writers' Project," *South Atlantic Quarterly* 37 (1938): 157–69.

36. Henry Alsberg to Anzia Yezierska, February 1937, box 34, FWPNA.

37. Henry G. Alsberg, "Writers and the Government: A Letter from the Director of the Federal Writers' Project," *Saturday Review of Literature*, January 4, 1936, 9; Alsberg to Harold Stein, "Subject: Creative Magazine," December 17, 1936, box 462, WPA Files. In addition to *American Stuff*, the FWP found other outlets for the off-time creative work of its members. See, for example, *American Stuff: By Workers of the Federal Writers' Project* (Darien, Conn.: n.p., 1938; special issue of *Direction*, February 1938); "Federal Writers' Number," *New Masses*, May 10, 1938, 97–127; "Federal Poets," *New Republic*, May 11, 1938, 10–12; "Federal Poets Number," *Poetry* 52 (1938): 276–83. Alsberg never succeeded in establishing a national FWP magazine of creative writing, though there were regional and state efforts, such as *Material Gathered*, published by San Francisco Federal Writers in October 1936. Mangione, *Dream and the Deal*, 241–58, and Penkower, *Federal Writers' Project*, 159–80, note the presence of creative writers on the project, some of whom later became well known.

38. "Supplement #16, Bulletin #25, WPA Sponsored Federal Project No. 1," box 331, WPA Files; Penkower, *Federal Writers' Project*, 25–26; Kathleen O'Connor McKinzie, "Writers on Relief, 1935–1942" (Ph.D. diss., Indiana University, 1970), 24–25; Edwin Bjorkman, state director, North Carolina FWP, to George Cronyn, December 12, 1935, and Henry Alsberg to Bjorkman, November 8, 1935, box 114, FWPNA.

39. Jane DeHart Mathews, "Arts and the People: The New Deal Quest for a Cultural Democracy," *Journal of American History* 62 (1975): 320.

40. Henry G. Alsberg, "Federal Writers' Project and Education," *Journal of the Na-*

tional Education Association 25 (1936): 86; "Report of the Regional Conference of the Federal Writers' Project for Region 4."

41. "Portraits of the United States: The Art Project and the Writers' Project of the Works Progress Administration" and publicity release, n.d., box 83, DIFWPA; Van Wyck Brooks to Henry Alsberg, September 18, 1938, box 461, WPA Files.

42. Milton M. Reigelman, *The Midland: A Venture in Literary Regionalism* (Iowa City: University of Iowa Press, 1975); "Federal Writers' Project Activities as Planned for the Future," talk given at the Regional Conference in Chicago, October 18, 1938, box 461, WPA Files.

43. Sinclair Lewis, *Main Street: The Story of Carol Kennicott* (New York: Harcourt, Brace and Howe, 1920), prefatory material; Mabel Ulrich, "Salvaging Culture for the WPA," *Harper's Magazine*, May 1939, 656.

44. Regional Conference in Chicago, October 18, 1938, box 461, WPA Files.

45. B. A. Botkin, "WPA and Folklore Research: Bread and Song," *Southern Folklore Quarterly* 3 (1939): 10.

46. Randolph S. Bourne, "Trans-National America," *Atlantic Monthly*, July 1916, 86–97; May, *End of American Innocence*, 282–83; Kallen, *Culture and Democracy in the United States*. On Kallen and 1930s pluralism, see Lawson, *Failure of Independent Liberalism*, 149–54.

47. Henry Alsberg to Franz Boas, November 29, 1935; Boas to Alsberg, March 10, 1936; Alsberg to Edward Kennard, March 25, 1936; Ruth Benedict to Alsberg, June 11, 1936; Alsberg to Benedict, June 18, 1936; Boas to Alsberg, June 19, 1936; Benedict to Alsberg, June 4, 1937; Alsberg to Benedict, October 1937, all in box 196, FWPNA; "Manual for a Guide to Composite America, Social-ethnic Studies," July 10, 1938, box 191, FWPNA. The term "composite America" was used repeatedly in connection with the social-ethnic studies. See the lists of planned work in the Social-ethnic Studies File, box 191, and the Negro Studies File, boxes 200, 201, FWPNA.

48. Ostrander, *American Civilization in the First Machine Age*, 318.

49. Bernard DeVoto, "The Writers' Project," *Harper's Magazine*, January 1942, 221–24; Lewis Mumford, "Writers' Project," *New Republic*, October 20, 1937, 306–7.

Chapter 2

1. Clifford Geertz, "The Impact of the Concept of Culture on the Concept of Man," in *The Interpretation of Cultures: Selected Essays*, by Clifford Geertz (New York: Basic Books, 1973), 50–51.

2. George Cronyn, associate national FWP director, as quoted in Kathleen O'Connor McKinzie, "Writers on Relief, 1935–1942" (Ph.D. diss., Indiana University, 1970), 63; editorial report, October 1936, box 461, WPA Files; Henry Alsberg to all state directors, October 17, 1935, box 50, FWPNA; "Writers' Staff Ready to Sift State History," *Indianapolis Star*, December 15, 1935, box 83, DIFWPA; Alsberg to Mabel Montgomery, state director, Alabama FWP, May 16, 1936, Alsberg-Cronyn files; Alsberg to Ellen S. Woodward, April 23, 1937, box 70, FWPNA. Alsberg used almost the same words in his memorandum to Harry Hopkins, November 6, 1936, box 70, FWPNA.

3. George Cronyn to Bruce McClure and Jacob Baker, September 18, 1935, box 461, WPA Files.

4. Ibid.; Henry Alsberg to President Franklin Roosevelt, June 18, 1937, box 462, WPA Files; U.S. Congress, House Subcommittee of the Committee on Appropriations in Charge of Deficiency Appropriations Hearings, First Deficiency Appropriations Bill of 1936, 74th Cong., 2d sess., 1936, pt. 2, 214–15. Hopkins's testimony closely follows Alsberg's memorandum to him, November 6, 1936, box 70, FWPNA.

5. "Conference on the Arts Program of the WPA, October 8, 1941," cited in McKinzie, "Writers on Relief," 267–70.

6. As quoted in Jerre Mangione, "Federal Writers' Project," *New York Times Book Review*, May 18, 1969, 2. National FWP officials kept a file devoted to their efforts to defend Katherine Kellock after Hearst editorials attacked her. It includes copies of letters to U.S. senators alleging that the appointment was a conspiracy to map and document every state for the benefit of subversive forces supported by the Soviets. Lawrence Westbrook to Aubrey Williams, February 21, 1936, box 461, WPA Files, indicates that Alsberg's superiors did not think the administration should open itself to criticism for the sake of the FWP. Thus it was "deplorable Kellock was employed in this position, not that she's not good, but there were others available, equally good." In the future, appointments should demonstrate "more care and judgment." See also Reed Harris to Oliver Griswold, "Subject: The Kellocks," February 18, 1936, box 461, FWPNA. This and other relevant materials are also in the Kellock papers.

7. McKinzie, "Writers on Relief," 32–38; Jerre Mangione, *The Dream and the Deal: The Federal Writers' Project, 1935–1943* (Boston: Little, Brown, 1972), 224–29; Monty Penkower, *The Federal Writers' Project: A Study in Government Patronage of the Arts* (Urbana: University of Illinois Press, 1977), 38–44, 162–65.

8. Henry Alsberg to Edwin Bjorkman, January 20, 1936, box 31, FWPNA; Mangione, *Dream and the Deal*, 92; Jane DeHart Mathews, *Federal Theatre, 1935–1939: Plays, Relief, and Politics* (Princeton: Princeton University Press, 1967), 102–3; William Leuchtenberg, *Franklin D. Roosevelt and the New Deal, 1932–1940* (New York: Harper and Row, 1963), 244. In memorandums and letters to Ellen Woodward, Harry Hopkins, and President Roosevelt, Alsberg and Cronyn tried to explain delays, document FWP activities, and describe what the FWP would accomplish—all in an effort to try to protect their agency from budget cuts. See Alsberg to Hopkins, November 6, 1936, box 70, FWPNA; George Cronyn to Woodward, box 461, WPA Files; Alsberg to Woodward, April 23, 1937, box 70, FWPNA; Alsberg to President Roosevelt, June 18, 1937, box 462, WPA Files.

9. George Cronyn to Ellen Woodward, December 31, 1936, box 461, FWPNA, offering explanations for slowness; Henry Alsberg to Ross Santee, state director, Arizona FWP, February 17, 1937, FWPNA.

10. See, for example, Henry Alsberg to John Doe, secretary, Rotary Club, Harrisburg, Pa., September 30, 1935, Alsberg-Cronyn files; George Cronyn to Bruce McClure and Jacob Baker, September 18, 1935, box 461, WPA Files; Henry G. Alsberg, "The American Guide," n.d., Alsberg-Cronyn files. This interest in audiences was often politically quite sensitive. See Katherine Kellock to Alsberg, "Subject: California

[handwritten margin note: Kellock & attacked Hearst]

Trailbook," March 23, 1938, box 83, DIFWPA, and Kellock to Alsberg, March 26, 1938, box 461, WPA Files, where she makes the point that "this book would please a powerful member of the House Appropriations Committee who is Nevada's lone Representative."

11. George Cronyn to Bruce McClure and Jacob Baker, September 18, 1935, box 461, WPA Files.

12. "Notes on the FWP with Special References to the American Guide, September 17, 1936," Alsberg-Cronyn files; Reed Harris to T. H. Hurt, July 13, 1937, box 461, WPA Files; Henry Alsberg, "Writers and the Government: A Letter from the Director of the Federal Writers' Project," *Saturday Review of Literature*, January 4, 1936, 9; Alsberg to John Doe, secretary, Rotary Club, Harrisburg, Pa., September 30, 1935, Alsberg-Cronyn files; FWP, American Guide Manual ([Washington, D.C.], 1935); George Cronyn to Stith Thompson, August 20, 1937, Alsberg-Cronyn files. The *San Francisco News* complained about the FWP decision to abandon plans for a history of the local labor movement. The paper wondered, "Was Washington afraid that some of the scrapped projects might stray into fields unapproved by those who see a red behind every tree?" (December 13, 1935, clipping in box 83, DIFWPA). W. T. Couch, Southeast regional FWP director, thought work on labor history in Oklahoma was suppressed by powerful political forces in the state; see interview with the author, March 12, 1972, Carrboro, N.C. On the other hand, an unsigned editorial criticism, February 26, 1937, Alsberg-Cronyn files, contains a national FWP official's complaint that the Wisconsin state essay on industry gave inadequate attention to labor disturbances.

13. Henry Alsberg to Edwin Bjorkman, state director, North Carolina FWP, January 6, 1936, box 114, FWPNA; Alsberg, "American Guide"; "Have You Discovered America?," n.d., box 70, FWPNA; FWP, American Guide Manual; Alsberg to A. F. Cleveland, vice-president in charge of traffic, Association of American Railroads, October 5, 1935, box 83, DIFWPA. In a letter to Rolls Ogden, editor of the *New York Times*, Cronyn complained about the "Topics of the Time" column of January 28, 1936; see George Cronyn to Ogden, January 28, 1936, Alsberg-Cronyn files. Words very similar to Cronyn's are used in a press release "For Writers' Digest," February 15, 1939, box 83, DIFWPA.

14. Alsberg "American Guide"; press release, Seattle, Wash., WPA, June 26, 1938, box 83, DIFWPA; "Have You Discovered America?," n.d., box 70, FWPNA; George Cronyn to Rolls Ogden, January 28, 1936, Alsberg-Cronyn files; Cronyn to W. T. Couch, Southeast regional director, September 28, 1937, FWP-Couch Papers. Articles attacking or defending the costs of the guides were printed in papers throughout the country; see, for example, "Wordboggling vs. Boondoggling," *Minneapolis Journal*, February 3, 1936, box 83, DIFWPA. The phrase "will be of value to persons in every position in our society" also appears in Alsberg's article on the FWP "New Guide to America," *New York Times*, February 9, 1939.

15. Orrick Johns, New York City FWP director, as quoted in Frederick Gruin, "Guidebook to New York," *New York Times*, July 5, 1936; Henry Alsberg, press release, November 27, 1935, box 83, DIFWPA. Similar appeals were published in newspapers throughout the country. For example, in "Each Community to Be Represented in

American Guide," *Carleton County (Minnesota) Vidette*, December 26, 1936, Mabel Ulrich, state director, Minnesota FWP, declared, "You will be performing a great civic service to your locality and your state by working on your voluntary committee." See also "American Guide Manual, Supplement 4: Volunteer Associates," December 17, 1935, box 69, FWPNA.

16. "Have You Discovered America?," box 74, FWPNA.

17. Editorial report, FWP, October 1936, box 461, WPA Files; Quincy Howe of Simon and Schuster to Jerre Mangione, December 16, 1941, box 462, WPA Files; "Prospectus: The American Guide," n.d., and "Have You Discovered America?," n.d., box 74, FWPNA.

18. Henry Alsberg to A. F. Cleveland, vice-president in charge of traffic, Association of American Railroads, October 3, 1935, Alsberg-Cronyn files. The idea that the lack of adequate American guides was a national embarrassment was one of the frequent reasons FWP officials gave to justify their existence. See, for example, "For: Writers' Digest," February 15, 1939, box 83, DIFWPA; Bernard DeVoto, "The First WPA Guide," *Saturday Review of Literature*, February 27, 1937, 8; "Prospectus: The American Guide," n.d., box 74, FWPNA.

19. "Prospectus: The American Guide," n.d., box 74, FWPNA; Alsberg, "American Guide"; Lewis Mumford, "Writers' Project," *New Republic*, October 20, 1937, 306–7.

20. "Have You Discovered America?," n.d., box 74, FWPNA. Key phrases in this document were used repeatedly by FWP officials. See, for example, Alsberg, "New Guide to America"; Mumford, "Writers' Project."

21. Alsberg, "New Guide to America"; "Have You Discovered America?," n.d., and "Prospectus: The American Guide," n.d., box 74, FWPNA; "Notes on the Federal Writers' Project with Special Reference to the American Guide," September 17, 1936, Alsberg-Cronyn files.

22. Henry Alsberg to Clevenger, October 5, 1935, box 83, DIFWPA; "Have You Discovered America?," n.d., and "Prospectus: The American Guide," n.d., box 74, FWPNA.

23. Karl Baedeker, ed., *The United States, with an Excursion into Mexico: A Handbook for Travellers* (1893; New York: Da Capo Press, 1971); Alsberg, "Writers and the Government"; see also Robert Bendimer, "When Culture Came to Main Street," *Saturday Review*, April 1, 1967, 20; Katherine Kellock to Bernard DeVoto, December 29, 1937, box 34, FWPNA. The notion that adequate guidebooks were one hallmark of a mature civilization was widely shared by those interested in the FWP. Kenneth Murdock, a student of the American Puritans, thought that FWP guides "may in time achieve the high standard maintained by the best European guidebooks." See his review of the New Hampshire guide in the *New England Quarterly* 11 (1938): 642.

24. "Have You Discovered America?," n.d., box 74, FWPNA. For example, the phrase "Seeing America First" is used as a section heading in "Prospectus: The American Guide," n.d., box 74, FWPNA. The movement to "see America first" is referred to in an unsigned letter to Fiorello La Guardia, May 16, 1936, box 11, FWPNA. FWP officials discussed the idea with individuals holding important positions in the travel industry. See Henry Alsberg to A. F. Cleveland, vice-president in charge of traffic, Asso-

ciation of American Railroads, October 5, 1935; Joseph Gaer to Alsberg and George Cronyn, January 23, 1936; "Concerning Discover America Association"; H. E. Greene to Alsberg, Harris, Cronyn, and Lockyer, "Subject: Cooperation with the 'Discover America Association, Inc.,'" January 23, 1936; Alsberg to John Doe, September 20, 1935, all in Alsberg-Cronyn files.

25. Henry Alsberg to A. F. Cleveland, October 5, 1935, Alsberg-Cronyn files; FWP, American Guide Manual; "For: Writers' Digest," February, 5, 1939, box 83, DIFWPA. National FWP officials constantly repeated that the work they were doing would aid but not compete with private business. This was a form of self-praise as well as self-defense, since they claimed no one else could undertake a task of such unprecedented magnitude and scope. See "Five Thousand Will Work on American Guide Project," *Boston Globe*, October 29, 1935, box 70, FWPNA; U.S. Congress, House Subcommittee of the Committee on Appropriations in Charge of Deficiency Appropriations Hearings, First Deficiency Appropriations Bill of 1936, 74th Cong., 2d sess., 1936, pt. 2, 214–15.

26. Response to "Critical Remarks Made by Alf Landon," box 83, DIFWPA.

27. FWP, American Guide Manual; "General Criticism of Material on Hand: New Mexico Points of Interest," box 109, and "Supplementary Instructions No. 15 to the American Guide Manual," September 15, 1936, box 70, FWPNA.

28. Paul Fussell, *Abroad: British Literary Traveling between the Wars* (New York: Oxford University Press, 1980), 212–15; Clifton Blake, "With Compliments to Vermont," *Yale Review* 27 (Autumn 1937): 214–16. Alsberg is quoted in Blair Bolles, "The Federal Writers' Project," *Saturday Review of Literature*, July 9, 1938, 19.

29. Mumford, "Writers' Project," 307.

30. Katherine Kellock, "The WPA Writers: Portraitists of the United States," *American Scholar* 9 (1940): 473.

31. "The Washington State Guide," September 10, 1941, box 83, DIFWPA; Henry Alsberg to all state directors, October 15, 1936, box 70, FWPNA; "Editorial Report," October 1936, box 461, WPA Files; FWP, American Guide Manual; Henry G. Alsberg, "Federal Writers' Project and Education," *Journal of the National Education Association* 25 (1936): 86.

32. Henry Alsberg to Cecil R. Chittenden, May 6, 1936, Alsberg-Cronyn files.

33. Press release on New York City guidebook, "For Use at Any Time before April, 1936," box 112, FWPNA. For a detailed description of how this worked in one state, see Jerrold Hirsch, "Culture on Relief: The Federal Writers' Project in North Carolina, 1935–1942" (master's thesis, University of North Carolina, 1973).

34. These field reports are in box 58, FWPNA.

35. "Notes on the FWP with special reference to the American Guide," September 17, 1936, and Reed Harris to Katherine Kellock and Members of the Tour Section, "Subject: Phrasing of Letters and Comments," February 17, 1937, Alsberg-Cronyn files.

36. Reed Harris to Oliver Griswold, "Subject: The Kellocks," February 15, 1936, box 461, FWPNA.

37. Katherine Kellock to Henry Alsberg, "Subject: Guide Manuals," January 20, February 2, 4, 1936, box 58, FWPNA.

38. Katherine Kellock to Henry Alsberg, January 20, 1936, box 58, FWPNA; Charles and Mary Beard, *The Rise of American Civilization* (New York: Macmillan, 1930), vii.

39. Henry Alsberg to Katherine Kellock, January 22, 1936, box 58, FWPNA.

40. Katherine Kellock to Henry Alsberg, October 12, 1937, box 182; Kellock to Alsberg, "Subject: Defects in Present Approach to Guidebooks," February 18, 1936, box 58; Kellock to Alsberg, "Subject: Instructions Sent to New England States on Preparation of Regional Guides," box 182, FWPNA.

41. Ruth Crawford to Henry Alsberg, July 2, 1938, FWPNA, discussing the New York City guide, states, "The foremost consideration, of course, is the convenience of the tourist, for presumably guides are written for his perusal." See, for example, "Supplementary Instructions No. 6 to the American Guide Manual," December 12, 1935, box 69, FWPNA. Alsberg's editorial criticism of state guide manuscripts reveals his view of the guide reader as a tourist. For example, he advised Ina Cassidy, state director, New Mexico FWP, on April 23, 1936, concerning material on the state's Indian population, "Unless it can be presented in a way to interest and instruct the average tourist, it would not seem to have much of a place in a guide" (box 109, FWPNA).

42. Editorial criticism, St. Petersburg, Fla., June 29, 1937, Alsberg-Cronyn files; "Supplementary Instructions No. 11D to the American Guide Manual," October 1, 1937, box 69, FWPNA; Henry Alsberg to Harrison Parkham, May 8, 1939, and unsigned criticism and editorial comment, Wisconsin Agriculture, February 24, 1938, Alsberg-Cronyn files.

43. Henry Alsberg to Maurice Howe, state director, Utah FWP, May 25, 1936, and "Supplementary Instructions No. 11B to the American Guide Manual," July 25, 1936, box 69; "Supplementary Instructions No. 15," box 70, FWPNA.

44. Unsigned, "General Criticism of Material on Hand, New Mexico Points of Interest," June 18, 1936, box 109; "Supplementary Instructions No. 15," box 70; "Supplementary Instructions No. 11C to the American Guide Manual," September 19, 1936, box 69, FWPNA. McKinzie, "Writers on Relief," 74–84, provides additional details about the manuals.

45. "Supplementary Instructions No. 11C," "Supplementary Instructions No. 11B," and "Supplementary Instructions No. 11G to the American Guide Manual," October 17, 1938, box 69; "Supplementary Instructions No. 15" and "Supplementary Instructions No. 16 to the American Guide Manual," October 21, 1936, box 70, FWPNA.

46. Henry Alsberg to Anthony Higgins, editor, Delaware FWP, June 19, 1936, and "Memorandum to the Staff, Words Frequently Misused," n.d., Alsberg-Cronyn files; "Supplementary Instructions No. 11 to the American Guide Manual," April 1, 1936, box 69, and "General Criticism on Material on Hand, New Mexico Points of Interest," June 18, 1936, box 109, FWPNA.

47. "Supplementary Instructions No. 7 to the American Guide Manual," box 69, FWPNA; Walter Pritchard Eaton, "Guides to the Beauties of New England: Writers on Relief Create a Series of American 'Baedekers,'" *New York Herald Tribune Books*, April 24, 1938, 1–2. Though national FWP officials eventually abandoned plans for a five-volume American guide divided by regions, the regionalist idea influenced the program they developed. The following works are helpful in understanding the differences

between the local color movement and the regionalism of the 1920s and 1930s: Henry D. Shapiro, *Appalachia on Our Mind: The Southern Mountains and Mountaineers in the American Consciousness, 1870–1920* (Chapel Hill: University of North Carolina Press, 1978), 6–8; R. Alan Lawson, *The Failure of Independent Liberalism, 1930–1941* (New York: G. P. Putnam's Sons, 1971), 12, 134, 135–47. Especially useful is Michael C. Steiner, "The Regional Impulse in the United States, 1923–1941" (Ph.D. diss., University of Minnesota, 1978).

48. "Have You Discovered America?," n.d., box 74, FWPNA.

49. Harry Hopkins, prefatory letter, in FWP, *Connecticut: A Guide to Its Roads, Lore, and People* (Boston: Houghton Mifflin, 1938), vii; foreword by Frank McVey, in FWP, *Kentucky: A Guide to the Bluegrass State* (New York: Harcourt, Brace, 1939), vii.

50. Prefatory letter from Massachusetts governor Charles F. Hurley and the secretary of the commonwealth, F. W. Cook, in FWP, *Massachusetts: A Guide to Its Places and People* (Boston: Houghton Mifflin, 1937); preface by Raymond Kerensky, state director, in FWP, *Iowa: A Guide to the Hawkeye State* (New York: Viking Press, 1938), vii.

51. Foreword by Ralph M. Tirey, president, Indiana State Teacher's College, in Writers' Program, *Indiana: A Guide to the Hoosier State* (New York: Oxford University Press, 1941) vi; introduction by Roy F. Nichol, in Writers' Program, *Pennsylvania: A Guide to the Keystone State* (New York: Oxford University Press, 1940), v.

52. "Supplementary Instructions No. 15," box 70, FWPNA; Thomas Hartshorne, *The Distorted Image: Changing Conceptions of the American Character since Turner* (Cleveland: Case Western University, 1968), 101–13, refers to the FWP guides as part of the evidence that "the concept of national character found little or no place in the wholesale and rather desperate attempt during the 1930s to discover what was going on in the country and what the people of the United States were thinking and doing."

53. FWP, *Illinois: A Descriptive and Historical Guide* (Chicago: A. C. McClung, 1939), 3; Irving L. Dillard, "People and Character," in Writers' Program, *Missouri: A Guide to the "Show Me" State* (New York: Duell, Sloan and Pearce, 1941), 3; Writers' Program, *Indiana: A Guide to the Hoosier State* (New York: Oxford University Press, 1941), 3; Writers' Program, *Arizona: A State Guide* (New York: Hastings House, 1940), 4; FWP, *Tennessee: A Guide to the State* (New York: Viking Press, 1939), 3; FWP, *Mississippi: A Guide to the Magnolia State* (Viking Press, 1938), 3; FWP, *Montana: A State Guide Book* (New York: Viking Press, 1939), 3–8.

54. Writers' Program, *Alabama: A Guide to the Deep South* (New York: Hastings House, 1941), 3.

Chapter 3

1. Monty Penkower, *The Federal Writers' Project: A Study in Government Patronage of the Arts* (Urbana: University of Illinois Press, 1977); Richard Pells, *Radical Visions and American Dreams: Culture and Social Thought in the Depression Years* (New York: Harper and Row, 1973), 316; FWP, *Tennessee: A Guide to the State* (New York: Viking Press, 1939), 86.

2. Ronald Warren Taber, "The Federal Writers' Project in the Pacific Northwest: A Case Study" (Ph.d. diss., University of Washington, 1969), 171; Karal Ann Marling, "A

Note on New Deal Iconography: Futurology and the Historical Myth," *Prospects* 4 (1979): 435–37, also notes the virtual absence of the present, of the Great Depression, from New Deal mural art.

3. Warren Susman, "History and the American Intellectual: Uses of a Usable Past," *American Quarterly* 26 (1964): 244–48.

4. "Supplementary Instructions No. 11C to the American Guide Manual," September 19, 1936, box 69, and "Supplementary Instructions No. 16A to the American Guide Manual," May 26, 1937, box 70, FWPNA.

5. See, for example, Francis V. O'Connor, ed., *Art for the Millions: Essays from the 1930s by Artists and Administrators of the WPA Federal Art Project* (Greenwich, Conn.: New York Graphic Society, 1973).

6. FWP, *Montana: A State Guide Book* (New York: Viking Press, 1939), 96.

7. FWP, *Tennessee: A Guide to the State* (New York: Viking Press, 1939), 120.

8. Unsigned, "Editorial Report on State Copy: New Mexico History," December 29, 1936, box 109; "Supplementary Instructions No. 15 to the American Guide Manual," September 15, 1936, and "Supplementary Instructions No. 16 to the American Guide Manual," October 21, 1936, box 70; Frank Manuel to Henry Alsberg, July 1, 1978, box 182, FWPNA.

9. FWP, *Minnesota: A State Guide* (New York, Viking Press, 1938), 57; Writers' Program, *The Ohio Guide* (New York: Oxford University Press, 1940), 21; Writers' Program, *Indiana: A Guide to the Hoosier State* (New York: Oxford University Press, 1941), 13.

10. Writers' Program, *Arizona: A State Guide* (New York: Hastings House, 1940), 49.

11. Writers' Program, *Ohio*, 29.

12. FWP, *Illinois: A Descriptive and Historical Guide* (Chicago: A. C. McClung, 1939), 37.

13. Writers' Program, *Alabama: A Guide to the Deep South* (New York: Hastings House, 1941), 56–60; Writers' Program, *Louisiana: A Guide to the State* (New York: Hastings House, 1941), 52.

14. Writers' Program, *Ohio*, 37.

15. See, for example, Writers' Program, *Ohio*, 133, and FWP, *Delaware: A Guide to the First State* (New York: Viking Press, 1938), 143–44. Project correspondence documents the effort of the national office to promote this point of view. See, for example, unsigned criticism of the Oklahoma art essay, June 9, 1937, box 189, and "Suggestions Pertaining to the Guidebook Art Essays," n.d., box 188, FWPNA. See also Jane De-Hart Mathews, "Arts and the People: The New Deal Quest for a Cultural Democracy," *Journal of American History* 62 (1975): 316–39.

16. FWP, *Tennessee*, 154; Writers' Program, *Washington: A Guide to the Evergreen State* (Portland, Ore.: Binfords and Mort, 1941), 120; FWP, *Illinois*, 128.

17. "Story of Art Told in the American Guide Series," June 6, 1939, box 83, DIFWPA.

18. FWP, *Illinois*, 109; unsigned, "Illinois Art, Line by Line Report," n.d., box 187, FWPNA.

19. Fred Lowenstein, "Utah Art," n.d., box 190; unsigned, "Philadelphia, Painting and Sculpture Unsatisfactory," March 5, 1937, box 189; Lowenstein comments on controversy over Indiana art essay, n.d., box 187, FWPNA.

20. FWP, *Iowa: A Guide to the Hawkeye State* (New York: Viking Press, 1938), 140, 146–49. See also Matthew J. Baigell, *The American Scene: American Painting of the 1930s* (New York: Praeger, 1974), and James M. Dennis, *Grant Wood: A Study in American Art and Culture*, rev. ed. (Columbia: University of Missouri Press, 1986), for an analysis of the regionalism of these painters, which differs from the regionalism of national FWP officials. Baigell argues, "Regionalist painting came to stand for an art of rural and country views, apolitical in content, often nostalgic in spirit, and generally unmindful of the effects of the Depression" (*American Scene*, 55). Baigell's assessment of the regionalist painters seems accurate. The problem is the general tendency to equate all manifestations of 1930s regionalism with an endorsement of rural life and a rejection of the city. The regionalist painters and the southern Agrarians capture only one aspect of 1930s regionalism. Lewis Mumford, University of North Carolina sociologists led by Howard Odum, and national FWP officials developed an equally significant aspect of regionalism. They saw regionalism as compatible with diversity, as a way of promoting national integration and of integrating metropolitan areas with their hinterland. See Writers' Program, *New Mexico: A Guide to the Colorful State* (New York: Hastings House, 1940), 169; unsigned, "Suggestions for the Organization of the Essay on Art [Missouri]," n.d., box 188, FWPNA.

21. For biographical material on Seidenberg, see the Roderick Seidenberg file, Press Papers. In various autobiographical works Mumford mentions Seidenberg as part of his circle. See Lewis Mumford, *Sketches from Life: The Autobiography of Lewis Mumford, the Early Years* (New York: Dial Press, 1982), 174, and *My Works and Days: A Personal Chronicle* (New York: Harcourt Brace Jovanovich, 1979), 162, 518.

22. Roderick Seidenberg, "I Refuse to Serve," *American Mercury*, January 1932, 91–99. See also the brief biography of Seidenberg in the notes on the *American Mercury* authors, ibid., 128.

23. Seidenberg, "I Refuse to Serve," 98–99.

24. Roderick Seidenberg, "The Much Promised Land," *Freeman*, March 1922, 621; Seidenberg file, Press Papers.

25. Roderick Seidenberg, *Posthistoric Man: An Inquiry* (Chapel Hill: University of North Carolina Press, 1950) and *Anatomy of the Future* (Chapel Hill: University of North Carolina Press, 1961).

26. Roderick Seidenberg to Darel McConkey, "Subject: Excerpts from Lewis Mumford's criticism of the New York State Essay, relative to Buffalo," August 30, 1938, box 188, FWPNA; Lewis Mumford, "Writers' Project," *New Republic*, October 20, 1937, 307.

27. Lewis Mumford, *Sticks and Stones: A Study of American Architecture and Civilization* (New York: Boni and Liveright, 1924) and *The Brown Decades* (New York: Harcourt, Brace, 1931). See also the discussion in Charles C. Alexander, *Here the Country Lies: Nationalism and the Arts in Twentieth-Century America* (Bloomington: Indiana University Press, 1980), 123–24; Writers' Program, *Louisiana*, 148; FWP, *Minnesota*, 140–41.

28. "Supplementary Instructions No. 3 to the American Guide Manual," December 16, 1935, box 69; unsigned, "Vermont Architecture Essay," March 1, 1937, box 190; Roderick Seidenberg, "Ohio, Cleveland Architecture," December 14, 1936, box 189,

FWPNA; Louis Sullivan, "The Tall Office Building Artistically Considered," in *Kindergarten Chats and Other Writings*, by Louis Sullivan (New York: Wittenborn, Schutz, 1947), 202–13.

29. "Supplementary Instructions No. 3," box 69; Roderick Seidenberg to Joseph Gaer, September 28, 1938, box 188, and to James G. Dunton, state director, Ohio FWP, July 7, 1937, box 189, FWPNA; Writers' Program, *New Mexico*, 148.

30. FWP, *Connecticut: A Guide to Its Roads, Lore, and People* (Boston: Houghton Mifflin, 1938), 80; FWP, *Maine: A Guide to "Down East"* (Boston: Houghton Mifflin, 1937), 86.

31. F. A. Gutheim, "Architecture in Washington," May 1, 1937, box 190, FWPNA.

32. Unsigned, "Vermont Architectural Essay," January 13, 1937, box 190, FWPNA.

33. Unsigned, "Wisconsin Essay on Architecture," February 18, 1937, box 190, FWPNA; editor's introduction to *Carolina Dwelling, toward Preservation of Place: In Search of the North Carolina Vernacular Landscape*, ed. Doug Swaim (Raleigh: School of Design, 1978), 6:18.

34. Writers' Program, *Oklahoma: A Guide to the Sooner State* (Norman: University of Oklahoma Press, 1940), 94; "Supplementary Instructions No. 3," box 69, and Roderick Seidenberg to Professor Rexford Newcomb, University of Illinois, April 8, 1936, box 187, FWPNA.

35. Louis H. Sullivan, *The Autobiography of an Idea* (New York: Press of the American Institute of Architects, 1924); Sullivan, *Kindergarten Chats*, 43, 177. Peter Link Abernethy Jr., "Whitman and Architecture: A Study of His Influence on Sullivan and Wright" (master's thesis, University of North Carolina, 1965), is suggestive. The emphasis on developing art out of indigenous cultural materials pervades all the guides but is perhaps most explicitly stated in FWP, *Iowa*, 146, and Writers' Program, *Missouri: A Guide to the "Show Me" State* (New York: Duell, Sloan and Pearce, 1941), 176, with their chronicles of the triumph of native subject matter over "the isms of European art."

36. Memorandum, F. A. Gutheim to Roderick Seidenberg, "Subject: Wisconsin Architecture Essay," December 19, 1936, box 190; F. A. Gutheim, "Architecture in Wisconsin," March 18, 1937, box 190, FWPNA.

37. Roderick Seidenberg to Horace R. Chadbourne, state director, Missouri FWP, February 6, 1937, box 188; Seidenberg to Professor Rexford Newcomb, University of Illinois, April 8, 1936, box 187; Lowenstein, untitled criticism of Texas art essay, August 11, 1937, box 190, FWPNA.

38. Henry G. Alsberg, "Wisconsin Essay on Art," June 21, 1938; John Lyons to Alsberg, September 13, 1938; and Alsberg to Lyons, September 22, 1938, box 188; unsigned criticism, "West Virginia: Literature and the Arts," June 25, 1939, and F. A. Gutheim to Roderick Seidenberg, "Subject: Architectural Essay on Kentucky," December 24, 1936, box 190, FWPNA. See also Gutheim to Seidenberg, "Subject: Georgia Architecture Essay," December 18, 1936, box 187, FWPNA.

39. Stella Hanau to Roderick Seidenberg, March 5, 1939, box 187, FWPNA; Writers' Program, *Georgia: A Guide to Its Towns and Countryside* (Athens: University of Georgia Press, 1940), 188; FWP, *Illinois*, 108.

40. Writers' Program, *Arkansas: A Guide to the State* (New York: Hastings House, 1941), 154; unsigned, "Suggestions for the Organization of Essay on Art" [Missouri], n.d., box 188, FWPNA.

41. See, for example, Matthew Arnold, "The Literary Influences of Academies," in *Matthew Arnold's Essays in Criticism*, ed. Sister Thomas Marion Hoctor (Chicago: University of Chicago Press, 1968), 42; John Henry Raleigh, *Matthew Arnold and American Culture* (Berkeley: University of California Press, 1957), 150–53. Raleigh documents and analyzes the enormous impact of Arnold on American cultural and literary critics of all types.

42. Arnold, "Literary Influences of Academies," 42; Lowenstein, "Utah Art," n.d., and unsigned criticism, "West Virginia: Literature and the Arts," June 25, 1939, box 190, FWPNA; Roderick Seidenberg to John T. Frederick, October 18, 1937; Seidenberg to George A. Rollins, acting state director, Illinois FWP, February 19, 1937, FWPNA.

Chapter 4

1. Bernard DeVoto, "New England via the WPA," *Saturday Review of Literature*, May 14, 1938, 4, 14.

2. FWP, *Vermont: A Guide to the Green Mountain State* (Boston: Houghton Mifflin, 1937), viii; Writers' Program, *Wisconsin: A Guide to the Badger State* (New York: Duell, Sloan and Pearce, 1941), vii, viii.

3. FWP, *Nebraska: A Guide to the Cornhusker State* (New York: Viking Press, 1939), v.

4. D. W. Meining, "Symbolic Landscapes: Some Idealizations of Ordinary Landscapes," in *The Interpretation of Ordinary Landscapes: Geographical Essays*, ed. D. W. Meining (New York: Oxford University Press, 1979), 178.

5. FWP, *Illinois: A Descriptive and Historical Guide* (Chicago: A. C. McClung, 1939), 203; FWP, *Iowa: A Guide to the Hawkeye State* (New York: Viking Press, 1938), 189.

6. Writers' Program, *Arizona: A State Guide* (New York: Hastings House, 1940), 187, 188, 194.

7. Mary Hornaday, "'New Light on America' Folklore and Detail about the Past and Present of the United States Are to Be Made Available in the American Guide, a Volume Being Prepared as a WPA Project," *Christian Science Monitor*, November 11, 1936; clipping also in box 460, WPA Files.

8. Frederick Gutheim, "America in Guide Books," *Saturday Review of Literature*, June 14, 1941, 5.

9. Charles Merz, *The Great American Bandwagon: A Study of Exaggerations* (New York: Literary Guide of America, 1929), 19.

10. "History, Romance, Literature along U.S. No. 1," draft, n.d., box 83, DIFWPA; "Maine to Florida," *New York Times Book Review*, March 20, 1938, 4.

11. Matthew Arnold, *Civilization in the United States: First and Last Impressions of America* (Boston: DeWolf, Fiske, 1900), 170–81. John Henry Raleigh, *Matthew Arnold and American Culture* (Berkeley: University of California Press, 1957), 12–13, 47–87, is informative and perceptive. See also George Cronyn to all editors—state guide, "Subject: Checking State MS," January 14, 1937.

12. "Supplementary Instructions No. 11C to the American Guide Manual," September 19, 1936, box 69, FWPNA; Katherine Kellock, "The WPA Writers: Portraitists of the United States," *American Scholar* 9 (1940): 474; Gutheim, "America in Guide Books," 3.

13. "Supplementary Instructions No. 11E to the American Guide Manual," October

17, 1938, box 69, FWPNA. See also Katherine Kellock to Henry Alsberg, "Subject: California Trailbook," March 23, 1938, box 83, DIFWPA.

14. Critique of Baedeker guide to the United States, n.d., box 83, DIFWPA; FWP, *Tennessee: A Guide to the State* (New York: Viking Press, 1939), 134.

15. "Picture Books: A Circular Presenting the Techniques for Compiling State Picture Books," May 31, 1940, box 70, FWPNA; untitled press release critiquing 1909 Baedeker guide to the United States, n.d., box 83, DIFWPA.

16. Writers' Program, *Arizona*, 199, 193.

17. Ibid., 193.

18. Nancy K. Hill, *A Reformer's Art: Dickens' Picturesque and Grotesque Imagery* (Athens: Ohio University Press, 1981), 12–19.

19. As quoted in John Forster, *The Life of Charles Dickens* (London: Cecil Palmer, 1928), 370.

20. Writers' Program, *Arizona*, 281.

21. FWP, *Connecticut: A Guide to Its Roads, Lore, and People* (Boston: Houghton Mifflin, 1938), 538; Writers' Program, *Arizona*, 281.

22. Writers' Program, *Alabama: A Guide to the Deep South* (New York: Hastings House, 1941), 267, 378.

23. FWP, *Connecticut*, 529.

24. Writers' Program, *Wisconsin*, 396–97.

25. Ibid., 331–34.

26. My use of the terms "identity," "possession," and "orientation" has been strongly influenced by Eric Rosenberg, "Toward a Theory of Place Meaning," in *Carolina Dwelling, toward Preservation of Place: In Search of the North Carolina Vernacular Landscape*, ed. Doug Swaim (Raleigh: School of Design, 1978), 6:20–27, and Meining's introduction to *Interpretation of Ordinary Landscapes*, 1–7. See Henry G. Alsberg, as quoted in Jerre Mangione, *The Dream and the Deal: The Federal Writers' Project, 1935–1943* (Boston: Little, Brown, 1972), 241; "Supplementary Instructions No. 11E," box 69, FWPNA; W. T. Couch to Edwin Bjorkman, June 5, 1936, August 3, 1938, FWP-Couch Papers.

27. Henry Alsberg to J. Frank Davis, state director, Texas FWP, n.d., Alsberg-Cronyn files.

28. Barbara Novak, *American Painting of the Nineteenth Century: Realism, Idealism, and the American Experience* (New York: Praeger, 1969), 23.

29. The following works have been helpful in my thinking about how the guides treat the landscape and seek to create monuments: Meining, *Interpretation of Ordinary Landscapes*; Charles Rosen and Henri Zerner, "Enemies of Realism," *New York Review of Books*, March 4, 1983, 31–32; Hill, *Reformer's Art*, 12–29; Neil Harris, *The Artist in American Society: The Formative Years, 1790–1860* (New York: George Braziller, 1966), 193.

30. FWP, *Tennessee*, 434, 459; FWP, *North Carolina: A Guide to the Old North State* (Chapel Hill: University of North Carolina Press, 1939), 170; FWP, *Maine: A Guide to "Down East"* (Boston: Houghton Mifflin, 1937), 131; FWP, *Tennessee*, 274; Writers' Program, *Arizona*, 196–99; Writers' Program, *Indiana: A Guide to the Hoosier State* (New York: Oxford University Press, 1941), 166–69.

31. FWP, *Tennessee*, 436, 439–40.

32. Ibid., 436, 458, 459, 462.

33. FWP, *North Carolina*, 538.

34. FWP, *Tennessee*, 507.

35. FWP, *North Carolina*, 495.

36. Ibid., 275–90.

37. Ibid., 276, 278.

38. Ibid., 529.

39. Katherine Kellock to Bernard DeVoto, February 24, 1938, December 29, 1937, box 34, FWPNA.

40. Daniel M. Fox, "The Achievement of the Federal Writers' Project," *American Quarterly* 13 (1961): 4–5.

41. Ibid., 5.

42. Ralph Waldo Emerson, "The American Scholar," in *Nature*, ed. Robert E. Spiller and Alfred R. Ferguson (Cambridge: Belknap Press of Harvard University Press, 1971), 67.

43. Ibid., 5. Whitman uses the words "Here is not merely a nation but a teeming Nation of nations" in "By Blue Ontario's Shore," in *Leaves of Grass: Comprehensive Reader's Edition*, ed. Harold W. Blodgett and Sculley Bradley (New York: New York University Press, 1965), 343. Illinois Federal Writer Nelson Algren used Whitman's line "Land tolerating all, accepting all" as an evocative head note for an unpublished FWP manuscript titled "Soloman and Morris: Two Patriots of the Revolution." The B'nai B'rith, a Jewish fraternal organization, may have sponsored this work. Whitman's line can be found in *Leaves of Grass*, 460. A photostat of the Algren manuscript is in Kenneth G. McCollum, comp., *Nelson Algren: A Checklist* (Detroit: Gale Research, 1973), 86–107. See also F. O. Matthiessen, *American Renaissance: Art and Expression in the Age of Emerson and Whitman* (New York: Oxford University Press, 1941), 138.

44. Emerson, "American Scholar," 67; Ralph Waldo Emerson, "The Poet," in *Essays: Second Series* (Philadelphia: David McKay, 1980), 44, 43. In *American Renaissance*, Matthiessen stressed the desire of writers of the American Renaissance to attain "an organic union between labor and culture" (xiv–xv). The appeal of these writers, especially Walt Whitman, to writers during the Great Depression merits separate study. Such a study should compare and contrast the meaning Whitman had for writers in the pre–World War I years, the 1920s, and the 1930s. Parts of the story can be gleaned from Henry May, *The End of American Innocence: A Study of the First Years of Our Own Time, 1912–1917* (New York: Knopf, 1959); Christine Stansell, *American Moderns: Bohemian New York and the Creation of a New Century* (New York: Henry Holt, 2000); James E. Miller, *The American Quest for a Supreme Fiction: Whitman's Legacy in the Personal Epic* (Chicago: University of Chicago Press, 1979); Frederick J. Hoffman, *The Twenties: American Writing in the Postwar Decade* (New York: Free Press, 1962); and William Vann O'Connor, *Sense and Sensibility in Modern Poetry* (Chicago: University of Chicago Press, 1948). Matthiessen's own classic study reflects an aspect of the 1930s interest in Whitman. See also Newton Arvin, *Whitman* (New York: Macmillan, 1938).

45. My view of Whitman and the problem of creating an American epic has been influenced by Roy Harvey Pearce, *The Continuity of American Poetry* (Princeton: Prince-

ton University Press, 1961), 59–69, 69–83, 210–20, and Miller, *American Quest for a Supreme Fiction*, ix, 31–43.

46. Susan Sontag, *On Photography* (New York: Farrar, Strauss and Giroux, 1977), 27; William Stott, *Documentary Expression in Thirties America* (New York: Oxford University Press, 1973), 49. This discussion draws heavily on Stott's *Documentary Expression in Thirties America.* Stott, however, is not as explicitly analytical as he might have been about the role of documentary expression in creating a shared sense of community that transcends class, ethnic, and regional divisions—a sense of sharing in a common culture —although the idea is implicit in such remarks as "One who considers a certain work a human document identifies with the self it reveals; otherwise, he would not call it human" (8) and "This is what documentary must do if it is to work social change: talk to us, and convince us that we, our deepest interests are engaged" (28). Stott correctly emphasizes both the reformist and the conservative aspects of the documentary tradition but inadequately examines how it contributes to consensus.

47. Conroy as quoted in Stott, *Documentary Expression,* 120.

48. Bernard DeVoto, "The Writers' Project," *Harper's Magazine,* January 1942, 181; Lewis Mumford, "Writers' Project," *New Republic,* October 20, 1937, 306–7.

49. Allport as quoted in Stanley Coben, "A Study in Nativism: The American Red Scare of 1919–20," *Political Science Quarterly* 79 (1964): 52–75.

50. Sontag, *On Photography,* 76.

51. Dean MacCannell, *The Tourist: A New Theory of the Leisure Class* (New York: Shocken Books), 13, 45.

52. Ibid., 56, 83.

53. Henry Alsberg to Lewis Mumford, October 4, 1938, box 195, FWPNA.

54. In thinking about travel books as literature, I have benefited greatly from Paul Fussell, *Abroad: British Literary Traveling between the Wars* (New York: Oxford University Press, 1980), which has broader implications than the subtitle indicates and constitutes a stimulating discussion of the travel genre in general, esp. pp. 37–50, 57, 62–64, 168, 202–15. In addition to Fussell, I have found the following works helpful in thinking about the cultural and social meaning of travel: Victor Turner and Edith Turner, *Image and Pilgrimage in Christian Culture: Anthropological Perspectives* (New York: Columbia University Press, 1978), 7–8, 15, 39; MacCannell, *Tourist,* 46, 125, 150; Valene E. Smith, ed., *Hosts and Guests: The Anthropology of Tourism* (Philadelphia: University of Pennsylvania Press, 1977); and Michael S. Schudson, "On Tourism and Modern Culture," *American Journal of Sociology* 84 (1979): 1240–58, a review treating these works.

55. Rosen and Zerner, "Enemies of Realism." Stimulating approaches to reading the vernacular landscape can be found in Wilbur Zelinsky, *The Cultural Geography of the United States,* rev. ed. (Englewood Cliffs, N.J.: Prentice Hall, 1992); Amos Rapoport, *House Form and Culture* (Englewood Cliffs, N.J.: Prentice Hall, 1969); and Meining, *Interpretation of Ordinary Landscapes.*

56. F. O. Matthiessen, *From the Heart of Europe* (New York: Oxford University Press, 1978), 74.

Chapter 5

1. Sterling Brown, "The Approach of the Creative Artist," *Journal of American Folklore* 59 (1946): 506; B. A. Botkin, "Folklore as a Neglected Source of Social History," in *The Cultural Approach to History*, ed. Caroline Ware (New York: Columbia University Press, 1940), 312.

2. Caroline C. Ware, introduction to Ware, *Cultural Approach to History*, 5.

3. August Meier and Elliot Rudwick, *Black History and the Historical Profession, 1915–1980* (Urbana: University of Illinois Press), xi, 1, 73–122; Peter Novick, *That Noble Dream: The "Objectivity Question" and the American Historical Profession* (Cambridge: Cambridge University Press, 1988), 172–74; J. L. Lowes, letter of recommendation, B. A. Botkin student file, Harvard University Archives, Cambridge, Mass.

4. Novick, *That Noble Dream*, 339–40.

5. Robert Sklar, ed., *The Plastic Age, 1917–1930* (New York: George Braziller, 1970), 14.

6. The phrase "tribal twenties" is borrowed from John Higham, *Strangers in the Land: Patterns of American Nativism* (New York: Atheneum, 1963), 264–99. See also John Higham, "Ethnic Pluralism in Modern American Thought," in *Send These to Me: Jews and Other Immigrants in Urban America*, by John Higham (New York: Atheneum, 1975), 198–218.

7. Alain Locke, ed., *The New Negro: An Interpretation* (New York: Albert and Charles Boni, 1925; reprint, New York: Atheneum, 1968), xvi; Robert Hayden, preface to Locke, *New Negro* (1968), xiii. Nathan Huggins, *Harlem Renaissance* (New York: Oxford University Press, 1971), emphasizes how much the ideas of Harlem Renaissance figures paralleled those of American writers such as Van Wyck Brooks, who focused on the alleged weaknesses, strengths, and potential of American culture measured against the achievements of European literature. Thus in Huggins's view the Harlem Renaissance was as typically American as Emerson's and Brooks's declarations of cultural independence.

8. Horace Kallen, *Culture and Democracy in the United States: Studies in the Group Psychology of the American Peoples* (New York: Boni and Liveright, 1924), 61; Horace Kallen, "Democracy vs. the Melting Pot," *Nation*, February 18–25, 1915, 220. Important overviews are provided in Higham, "Ethnic Pluralism," 196–230; R. Alan Lawson, *The Failure of Independent Liberalism, 1930–1941* (New York: G. P. Putnam's Sons, 1971), 134, 149; Richard Weiss, "Ethnicity and Reform: Minorities and the Ambience of the Depression Years," *Journal of American History* 66 (1979): 566–85.

9. Locke, *New Negro* (1968), 15.

10. See, for example, B. A. Botkin, "The Folk in Literature: An Introduction to the New Regionalism," in *Folk-Say: A Regional Miscellany*, ed. B. A. Botkin (Norman: University of Oklahoma Press, 1929); B. A. Botkin, "Serenity and Light," in symposium "Regional Culture in the Southwest," *Southwest Review* 15 (1929): 492–93; B. A. Botkin, "We Talk about Regionalism—North, East, South, and West," *Frontier* 13 (1933): 286–96; B. A. Botkin, "Regionalism and Culture," in *The Writer in a Changing World*, ed. Henry Hart (New York: Equinox Press, 1937), 140–57; B. A. Botkin review of *Color* by Countee Cullen, *Daily Oklahoman*, April 11, 1926.

11. B. A. Botkin, "Self-Portraiture and Social Criticism in Negro Folk Song," *Opportunity*, February 1927, 42.

12. George Brown Tindall, "Southern Negroes since Reconstruction: Dissolving the Static Image," in *Writing Southern History: Essays in Historiography in Honor of Fletcher M. Green*, ed. Arthur S. Link and Rembert W. Patrick (Baton Rouge: Louisiana State University Press, 1967), 337–61; B. A. Botkin review of Sterling Brown, *The Negro in American Fiction* and *Negro Poetry and Drama*, *Opportunity*, June 1939, 184.

13. See the introduction by Sterling Stuckey to *The Collected Poems of Sterling A. Brown*, selected by Michael S. Harper (New York: Harper and Row, 1980), 12. *Southern Roads*, Brown's first volume of poems, was originally published in 1932. See Joanne V. Gabbin, *Sterling A. Brown: Building the Black Aesthetic Tradition* (Westport, Conn.: Greenwood Press, 1985), 170.

14. Henry Louis Gates Jr., *Figures in Black: Words, Signs, and the "Racial" Self* (New York: Oxford University Press, 1987), 227.

15. Arthur Huff Fauset, "Introduction: Homage to Sterling A. Brown," in *Sterling A. Brown: A UMUM Tribute*, 2nd ed., ed. Black History Museum Committee (Philadelphia: Black History Museum UMUM Publishers, 1976), 4; Sterling Brown, "A Century of Negro Portraiture in American Literature," *Massachusetts Review* 7 (1966): 12.

16. "Biographical Sketch of Sterling Brown," in Black History Museum Committee, *Sterling A. Brown*, 5.

17. Nathaniel A. Sweets, "Prof. Brown at Lincoln University," in Black History Museum Committee, *Sterling A. Brown*, 47.

18. James Weldon Johnson, "Preface to the First Edition," in *The Book of American Negro Poetry*, ed. James Weldon Johnson (1922; reprint, New York: Harcourt, Brace and World, 1958), 41–42. The 1958 reprint edition includes the preface to the original edition of 1922 and to the revised edition of 1931.

19. Ibid., 9; Gates, *Figures in Black*, 180; James Weldon Johnson, "Preface to the Second Edition," in Johnson, *Book of American Negro Poetry*, 4, 5.

20. Johnson, "Preface to the First Edition," 41; Johnson, "Preface to the Second Edition," xiii–xv.

21. Alain Locke, "Sterling A. Brown: The New Negro Folk-Poet," in *Negro: An Anthology*, ed. Nancy Cunard (London: Wishart, 1934), 115.

22. Ibid.

23. Botkin review of *The Negro in American Fiction* and *Negro Poetry and Drama*, 184.

24. Paul Radin, *Primitive Man as Philosopher* (New York: D. Appleton, 1927), viii; Paul Radin, *Method and Theory of Ethnology* (1931; reprint, New York: Basic Books, 1966), esp. 120–22. Botkin specifically refers to Radin's views in "The Folk and the Individual: Their Creative Reciprocity," *English Journal* 27 (1938): 128.

25. Sterling A. Brown, Arthur P. Davis, and Ulysses Lee, eds., *The Negro Caravan: Writings by American Negroes* (New York: Dryden Press, 1941), 825–26.

26. Sterling A. Brown, *The Negro in American Fiction* (Washington, D.C.: Associates in Negro Folk Education, 1937), 2, 1; Sterling A. Brown, "Negro Character as Seen by White Authors," *Journal of Negro Education* 2 (1933): 179–201; Sterling A. Brown, "Imitation of Life: Once a Pancake," *Opportunity*, March 1935, 87.

27. See Roi Ottley and William J. Weatherby, eds., *The Negro in New York: An Informal*

Social History (New York: New York Public Library, 1967), and materials in Ann Banks, ed., *First Person America* (New York: Knopf, 1980; reprint, New York: Norton, 1991), for examples of the diversity of African American studies undertaken by the Writers' Project. Among the major studies Brown planned were a history, "The Portrait of the Negro as American"; a study of slavery, "Go Down, Moses"; and a work titled "The Underground Railway." See boxes 200 and 201, FWPNA.

28. Lawrence Reddick, "A New Interpretation for Negro History," *Journal of Negro History* 22 (1937): 27; Botkin, "Folklore as a Neglected Source of Social History," 309; V. F. Calverton, "The Negro," in *America Now: An Inquiry into Civilization in the United States*, ed. Harold E. Stearns (New York: Charles Scribner's Sons, 1938), 493.

29. Unsigned "General Criticism: Wisconsin, the Negro Race," April 13, 1937; unsigned, "Ohio State Guide: Racial Elements: American Negroes," n.d.; unsigned, "Louisiana State Guide: Ethnology, Negroes," n.d., all in FWPLC, arranged by state in folders labeled "American Guide: Racial Elements."

30. Unsigned, "General Criticism: Wisconsin," and Sterling Brown, "Alabama: Birmingham," May 28, 1937, FWPLC; Writers' Program, *Alabama: A Guide to the Deep South* (New York: Hastings House, 1941), 133.

31. Sterling Brown, editorial criticism, "Florida: St. Augustine," July 31, 1937, and Sterling Brown, "Florida: Sarasota," September 29, 1937, Alsberg-Cronyn files.

32. Unsigned editorial criticism, "Alabama: Florence," September 25, 1937, and Myrtle Miles to George Cronyn, October 4, 1937, FWPLC.

33. GBK, editorial criticism, "North Carolina: Folkways and Folklore," November 19, 1938, FWPLC.

34. Edwin Bjorkman to W. T. Couch, November 15, 1937, FWP-Couch Papers; Myrtle Miles to Henry Alsberg, August 10, 1937, box 201, FWPNA.

35. Edwin Bjorkman to W. T. Couch, November 15, 1937, FWP-Couch Papers; Bjorkman to Couch, December 13, 1937, box 201, FWPNA.

36. As quoted in "Take It Easy Ike!," *The State*, October 21, 1939, mimeographed copy in FWP-Couch Papers.

37. FWP, *North Carolina: A Guide to the Old North State* (Chapel Hill: University of North Carolina Press, 1939), 4; "Take It Easy Ike!," FWP-Couch Papers.

38. Draft essay on the Negro in Beaufort, South Carolina; Mabel Montgomery to Henry Alsberg, May 4, 1937; Sterling A. Brown to Alsberg, May 14, August 11, 1937, box 201, FWPNA.

39. Mabel Montgomery to Henry Alsberg, May 4, 1937; Sterling A. Brown to Alsberg, May 14, August 11, 1937, box 201, FWPNA.

40. Edwin Bjorkman to W. T. Couch, November 15, 1937, FWP-Couch Papers.

41. See draft "Stories of Negro Survival Types in Coastal Georgia," box 201, FWPNA; George W. Stocking, *Race, Culture, and Evolution: Essays in the History of Anthropology* (New York: Free Press, 1968), 64–90, 195–233.

42. Proposal for a book to be titled "The Portrait of the Negro in America," n.d., box 210, FWPNA; W. T. Couch to Eudora Richardson, Virginia state FWP director, October 24, 1939, FWP-Couch Papers; W. T. Couch, interview with the author, March 12, 1972, Carrboro, N.C.

43. FWP, *Mississippi: A Guide to the Magnolia State* (New York: Viking Press, 1938), 8.

44. Writers' Program, *Virginia: A Guide to the Old Dominion* (New York: Oxford University Press), 86.

45. Ibid.

46. There are undated outlines and descriptions of "Go Down, Moses" and "Portrait of the Negro as American," boxes 200 and 201, FWPNA.

47. Writers' Program, *The Negro in Virginia* (New York: Hastings House, 1940); "For Immediate Release, August 15, 1939, 'The Negro in Virginia' Most Revealing Book of Its Kind According to Federal Writers' Project Editor," DIFWPA.

48. Writers' Program, *Negro in Virginia*, 3.

49. The quotation comes from an undated essay by Sadie McKee. New members of the Writers' Unit of the Library of Congress were required to learn about the FWP, its purpose, program, and products. Their first assignment was to write an essay about the project. Their essays reflect their attempts to understand the visions behind the FWP programs, especially those of Morton Royse, Sterling Brown, and B. A. Botkin, who were all working on the Writers' Unit. These materials are in box 210, FWPNA.

50. Writers' Program, *Survey of Negroes in Little Rock and North Little Rock* (Little Rock: Urban League of Greater Little Rock, 1941).

51. Arna Bontemps and Jack Conroy, *They Seek a City* (New York: Doubleday, Doran, 1945).

52. Oscar Handlin, *The Uprooted: The Epic Story of the Great Migrations That Made the American People* (New York: Grossett and Dunlap, 1951), 3; John F. Kennedy, *A Nation of Immigrants* (New York: Harper and Row, 1964); Higham, *Strangers in the Land*, 21; Marcus L. Hansen, *The Problems of the Third Generation Immigrant* (Rock Island, Ill.: Augustana Historical Society, 1938), 5.

53. Higham, *Strangers in the Land*, 236–63, 151.

54. For example, see W. H. Auden, "America Is NOT a Melting Pot," *New York Times*, March 18, 1972; *Forum*, November 1909, 434–35; Philip Gleason, "The Melting Pot: Symbol of Fusion or Confusion?," *American Quarterly* 16 (1964): 20–46; Higham, "Ethnic Pluralism," 196–230.

55. Higham, "Ethnic Pluralism," 196–230.

56. "American Guide Manual Supplement Number 15," n.d., box 69, FWPNA.

57. FWP, *Minnesota: A State Guide* (New York: Viking Press, 1938), 118; FWP, *Maine: A Guide to "Down East"* (Boston: Houghton Mifflin, 1937), 170; FWP, *New Jersey: A Guide to Its Present and Past* (New York: Viking Press, 1939), 124, 318; Writers' Program, *Pennsylvania: A Guide to the Keystone State* (New York: Oxford University Press, 1940), 66.

58. FWP, *New Jersey*, 125.

59. FWP, *New Hampshire: A Guide to the Granite State* (Boston: Houghton Mifflin, 1938), 3.

60. FWP, *Massachusetts: A Guide to Its Places and People* (Boston: Houghton Mifflin, 1937), 51.

61. FWP, *New York: A Guide to the Empire State* (New York: Oxford University Press, 1940), 110; Writers' Program, *Pennsylvania*, 4.

62. FWP, *Iowa: A Guide to the Hawkeye State* (New York: Viking Press, 1938), 78.

63. FWP, *Minnesota*, 77–80.

64. FWP, *The Armenians in Massachusetts* (Boston: Armenian Historical Society, 1937), 9.

65. FWP, *The Italians of New York* (New York: Random House, 1938), 225.

66. FWP, *The Bohemian Flats* (Minneapolis: University of Minnesota Press, 1941), 2.

67. FWP, *The Italians of Omaha* (Omaha: Independent Printing Co., 1941), 33, 38, 49.

68. FWP, *Armenians*, 144–45.

69. FWP, *Italians of Omaha*, 7; FWP, *Italians of New York*, 35.

70. Henry Alsberg to All State Directors, n.d., description of studies for a composite America, box 191, FWPNA.

71. "Socio-ethnic Studies Manual," September 1938, box 191, FWPNA.

72. Proposed study of Greek Americans, n.d., box 191, FWPNA.

73. Henry Alsberg to Morton Royse, December 29, 1939; memorandum, Royse to Alsberg, March 21, 1939; Royse to Cleavenger, state FWP director, Colorado, November 21, 1938; "Socio-ethnic Studies Manual," box 191, FWPNA. See also the general accounts in William F. McDonald, *Federal Relief Administration and the Arts: The Origins and Administrative History of the Arts Projects of the Works Progress Administration* (Columbus: Ohio State University Press, 1969), 43; Jerre Mangione, *The Dream and the Deal: The Federal Writers' Project, 1935–1943* (Boston: Little, Brown, 1972).

74. Joseph S. Roucek, Caroline F. Ware, and Morton W. Royse, "Approaches to the Study of Nationality Groups in the United States: Summary of the Discussion," in Ware, *Cultural Approach to History*, 86–89.

75. Federal Writers' Project, *The Albanian Struggle in the Old World and New* (Boston: The Writer, Inc., 1939); Morton Royse to Henry Alsberg, November 21, 1938, box 191, FWPNA.

76. B. A. Botkin, "WPA and Folklore Research: Bread and Song," *Southern Folklore Quarterly* 3 (1939): 14.

Chapter 6

1. Allan Nevins, *The Gateway to History* (Boston: D.C. Heath, 1938), iv.

2. Roy Rosensweig and Barbara Melosh, "Government and the Arts: Voices from the New Deal Era," *Journal of American History* 76 (1989): 596–608.

3. Jacquelyn Dowd Hall, James Leloudis, Robert Korstad, Mary Murphy, Lu Ann Jones, and Christopher B. Daly, *Like a Family: The Making of a Southern Cotton Mill World* (Chapel Hill: University of North Carolina Press, 1987).

4. See, for example, Clifford Lord, ed., *Ideas in Conflict: A Colloquium on Certain Problems in Historical Society Work in the United States and Canada* (Harrisburg, Pa.: Association for State and Local History, 1958); Martha Jane Zachert, "The Second Oral History Colloquium," *Journal of Library History* 3 (1968): 173–78; Elizabeth I. Dixon, "Arrowhead in Retrospect," *Journal of Library History* 2 (1967): 126–28; Gould Coleman, ed., *The Third National Colloquium on Oral History Held at the Center for Continuing Education, University of Nebraska, Lincoln, November 22–25, 1968* (New York: Oral History Association, 1969); Gould Coleman, ed., *The Fourth National Colloquium on Oral History, Held at Airlie House, Warrenton, Virginia, November 7–10, 1969* (New York: Oral History Association, 1970).

5. "Is Oral History Really Worth While?," in Lord, *Ideas in Conflict*, 34–36.

6. Richard Dorson, "Oral Tradition and Written History: The Case for the United States," in *American Folklore and the Historian*, by Richard Dorson (Chicago: University of Chicago Press, 1971), 129–44; Richard Dorson, "Oral Literature, Oral History, and the Folklorist," in *Folklore and Fakelore: Essays toward a Discipline of Folk Studies*, by Richard Dorson (Cambridge: Harvard University Press, 1976), 127–44; remarks by Roger Welsch at the panel Philip Crowl chaired, "Interdisciplinary Views on Oral History," in Coleman, *Third National Colloquium*, 19–24.

7. John Bodnar, "Power and Memory in Oral History: Workers and Managers at Studebaker," *Journal of American History* 75 (1989): 1201–21; Barbara Allen, "Story in Oral History: Clues to Consciousness," *Journal of American History* 79 (1992): 606–11. The special issue of *Journal of American History* on memory was later published in book form as David Thelen, ed., *Memory and American History* (Bloomington: Indiana University Press, 1990).

8. Important examples of this trend are the essays in Michael Frisch, ed., *A Shared Authority: Essays on the Craft and Meaning of Oral and Public History* (Albany: State University of New York Press, 1990), xvi; Sherna Berger Gluck and Daphne Patai, eds., *Women's Words: The Feminist Practice of Oral History* (New York: Routledge, 1991); Ronald Grele, ed., *Envelopes of Sound: The Art of Oral History* (New York: Praeger, 1990); Alessandro Portelli, *The Death of Luigi Trastulli and Other Stories: Form and Meaning in Oral History* (Albany: State University Press of New York Press, 1991), viii.

9. Joel Lieber, "The Tape Recorder as Historian," *Saturday Review of Literature*, June 11, 1966, 98, noted, "One of Columbia's rules of thumb is that, except for a few fragments, tapes are erased and reused—'much to the horror of psychologists with their interests in speech slips and inflections.'" Lieber is quoting Louis Starr, Nevins's successor as director of the Columbia University oral history program. Starr could not imagine developments that would make historians as interested as psychologists and other social scientists in the actual language of the interviewers.

10. Allan Nevins, "Oral History: How and Why It Was Born," *Wilson Library Bulletin* 40 (1966): 600–601.

11. John Higham, *History: The Development of Historical Studies in the United States* (Engelwood Cliffs, N.J.: Prentice Hall, 1965), 80–84, 121, 206.

12. Nevins, *Gateway to History*, iii–iv.

13. Ibid., iii, 3.

14. Ibid., iii, 342–54, iv.

15. Charles Morrisey, "Oral History as a Classroom Tool," *Social Education* 32 (1968): 546.

16. David Steven Cohen, ed., *America, the Dream of My Life: Selections from the Federal Writers' Project's New Jersey Ethnic Survey* (New Brunswick, N.J.: Rutgers University Press, 1990), 1; C. Stewart Doty, ed., *The First Franco-Americans: New England Life Histories from the Federal Writers' Project, 1938–1939* (Orono: University of Maine at Orono Press, 1985), 2; C. Stewart Doty, "Going to the States: Testimony from the Franco-American Life History Narratives in the Federal Writers' Project, 1938–1939," *Contemporary French Civilization* 7 (1983): 275–92.

17. Ann Banks, ed., *First Person America* (New York: Norton, 1991), xx.

18. Tom E. Terrill and Jerrold Hirsch, eds., *Such as Us: Southern Voices of the Thirties* (Chapel Hill: University of North Carolina Press, 1978), xiii; Banks, *First Person America*, i–ii; David Thelen, as quoted in Banks, *First Person America*, ii.

19. Nancy J. Martin-Perdue and Charles L. Perdue Jr., eds., *Talk about Trouble: A New Deal Portrait of Virginians in the Great Depression* (Chapel Hill: University of North Carolina Press, 1996), 22.

20. I. A. Newby, *Plain Folk in the New South: Social Change and Cultural Persistence, 1880–1915* (Baton Rouge: Louisiana State University Press, 1989), 9.

21. Ibid., 3.

22. Jacquelyn Jones, "'Tore Up and a-Movin': Perspectives on the Work of Black and Poor White Women in the Rural South," in *Women and Farming: Changing Roles, Changing Structures*, ed. Wava G. Haney and Jane B. Knowles (Boulder: Westview Press, 1988), 15–34; Jack Temple Kirby, *Rural Worlds Lost: The American South, 1920–1960* (Baton Rouge: Louisiana State University Press, 1987).

23. Charles T. Davis and Henry Louis Gates Jr., introduction to *The Slave's Narrative*, ed. Henry Louis Gates Jr. and Charles T. Davis (New York: Oxford University Press, 1985), xi, xii.

24. For an introduction to the debate about the FWP ex-slave narratives as a historical source, see Jerrold Hirsch, "Reading and Counting," review essay on Paul D. Escott, *Slavery Remembered: A Record of Twentieth-Century Slave Narratives*, in *Reviews in American History* 6 (1980): 312–17; John W. Blassingame, "Using the Testimony of Ex-Slaves: Approaches and Problems," *Journal of Southern History* 41 (1975): 473–92.

25. For these type of statistics, see Paul D. Escott, *Slavery Remembered: A Record of Twentieth-Century Slave Narratives* (Chapel Hill: University of North Carolina Press, 1979). On the idea of oral history as a conversational narrative, see Ronald Grele's two articles, "Movement without Aim: Methodological and Theoretical Problems in Oral History," in Grele, *Envelopes of Sound*, 126–54, and "A Surmisable Variety: Interdisciplinary and Oral Testimony," *American Quarterly* 27 (1975): 175–95. Examining another FWP oral history project, Jerrold Hirsch and Tom Terrill suggest a way of approaching this kind of material. See "Conceptualization and Implementation: Some Thoughts on Reading the Federal Writers' Project Southern Life Histories," *Southern Studies: An Interdisciplinary Journal of the South* 18 (1979): 351–62; Blassingame, "Using the Testimony of Ex-Slaves," 487; Escott, *Slavery Remembered*, 316.

26. Jerrold Hirsch, foreword to the new edition of *Lay My Burden Down: A Folk History of Slavery*, ed. B. A. Botkin (1945; reprint, Athens: University of Georgia Press, 1989), xiii.

27. From different perspectives, Ronald Grele, "Movement without Aim" and "Surmisable Variety," and Michael Frisch, "Oral History and Hard Times: A Review Essay," *Red Buffalo*, nos. 2 and 3 (n.d.), 217–31, discuss similar interpretive issues. Frisch's essay is reprinted in Frisch, *Shared Authority*, 5–13.

28. Mrs. Ida Cooley (formerly Ida Moore) to Jerrold Hirsch, n.d.; Terrill and Hirsch, *Such as Us*, 243.

29. Terrill and Hirsch, *Such as Us*, 284.

30. For a sociological perspective on what goes on during an interview, see chap. 5, "What Kind of Truth Do You Get?" and chap. 6, "Toward a Transactional Theory of Interviewing," in *Elite and Specialized Interviewing*, by Lewis Anthony Dexter (Evanston, Ill.: Northwestern University Press, 1970), 119–62. On the poor white genre, see Shields McIllwaine, *The Southern Poor White: From Lubberland to Tobacco Road* (Norman: University of Oklahoma Press, 1939); Sylvia Jenkins Cook, *From Tobacco Road to Route 66: The Southern Poor White in Fiction* (Chapel Hill: University of North Carolina Press, 1976); FWP, *These Are Our Lives* (Chapel Hill: University of North Carolina Press, 1939).

31. John Dollard, *Caste and Class in a Southern Town* (New Haven: Yale University Press, 1937), 33–42; Hortense Powdermaker, *After Freedom: A Cultural Study in the Deep South* (1939; reprint, New York: Viking Press, 1968), xv; Leonard Doob, "Poor Whites: A Frustrated Class," in Dollard, *Caste and Class*, 445–84; Nathan Asch, *The Road: In Search of America* (New York: Norton, 1937), 7; Margaret Jarman Hagood, *Mothers of the South: Portraiture of the White Tenant Farm Woman* (Chapel Hill: University of North Carolina Press, 1939), 63–64; Doty, *First Franco-Americans*; Banks, *First Person America*; Cohen, *America*.

32. Blassingame, "Using the Testimony of Ex-Slaves."

33. Herbert T. Hoover, "Oral History in the United States," in *The Past before Us: Contemporary Historical Writing in the United States*, ed., Michael Kammen (Ithaca: Cornell University Press, 1980), 396.

34. Dennis Tedlock, "Learning to Listen: Oral History as Poetry," in Grele, *Envelopes of Sound*, 106–26.

35. Francis Berry, *Poetry and the Physical Voice* (London: Routledge and K. Paul, 1962), 7.

36. Terrill and Hirsch, *Such as Us*, 34, 190.

37. Edwin Bjorkman to W. T. Couch, October 26, 1938, FWP-Couch Papers.

38. Barnette Yarborough to Eri Douglass, July 19, 1937; John Lomax to Myrtle Miles, June 22, 1937; Lomax to William Cunningham, June 8, 1937, box 192, FWPNA.

39. Brown's "Notes by an editor on dialect usage in accounts by interviews with ex-slaves," June 20, 1937, is in "Slave Narratives: A Folk History of Slavery in the United States from Interviews with Former Slaves," Library of Congress Microfilm, xxvii–xxix.

40. Henry Bennett to Mrs. Wharton, February 21, 1941, box 191, FWPNA; John Lomax, *Adventures of a Ballad Hunter* (New York: Macmillan, 1947), 190; Virginia P. Brown and Laurella Owens, *Toting the Lead Row: Ruby Pickens Tartt, Alabama Folklorist* (Alabama: University of Alabama Press, 1981); Bennett to Mrs. Wharton, evaluations, February 25, 1941, box 191, FWPNA.

41. C. H. Wetmore to Mrs. Wharton, February 20, 1940; Botkin, *Lay My Burden Down*, xi; B. A. Botkin, "Criteria for Slave Narratives," December 16, 1940, box 191, FWPNA.

42. The argument that transitions became more age-graded and uniform in the twentieth century is clearly presented in John Modell, Frank Furstenberg, and Theodore Hershberg, "Social Change and Transition to Adulthood in Historical Perspective," *Journal of Family History* 1 (1976): 7–32. It is an important theme in Tamara

Hareven, ed., *Transitions: The Family and the Life Course in Historical Perspective* (New York: Academic Press, 1978); John Demos and Spence Boocock, eds., *Turning Points: Historical and Sociological Essays on the Family* (Chicago: University of Chicago Press, 1978); and George B. Tindall, "Beyond the Mainstream: The Ethnic Southerners," *Journal of Southern History* 50 (1974): 15.

43. Lutz K. Berkner, "The Stem Family and the Developmental Cycle of the Peasant Household," *American Historical Review* 77 (1972): 398–418, and "The Use and Misuses of Census Data for the Historical Analysis of Family Structure," *Journal of Interdisciplinary History* 5 (1975): 721–38.

44. Banks, *First Person America*, iv–v.

Chapter 7

1. FWP, *These Are Our Lives* (Chapel Hill: University of North Carolina Press, 1939), x–xi.

2. On Dies and Woodrum, see Chapters 9 and 10.

3. For an overview of the topic, see Shields McIllwaine, *The Southern Poor White: From Lubberland to Tobacco Road* (Norman: University of Oklahoma Press, 1939), and Sylvia Jenkins Cook, *From Tobacco Road to Route 66: The Southern Poor White in Fiction* (Chapel Hill: University of North Carolina Press, 1976).

4. Clare de Graffenried, "The Georgia Cracker in the Cotton Mills," *Century*, February 1891, 483–98; Lois McDonald, *Southern Mill Hills: A Study of Social and Economic Forces in Certain Textile Mill Villages* (New York: A. L. Hillman, 1928), 144; Frank Tannenbaum, *Darker Phases of the South* (New York: G. P. Putnam's Sons, 1924), 117. For a recent review of writings on southern poor whites that demonstrates the persistence of these images, see I. A. Newby, *Plain Folk in the New South: Social Change and Cultural Persistence, 1880–1915* (Baton Rouge: Louisiana State University Press, 1989), 1–19.

5. Henry Alsberg to Edwin Bjorkman, May 25, 1936, Editorial Correspondence, FWPNA; W. T. Couch to Bjorkman, May 26, 1935, FWP-Couch Papers. For a fuller history of the FWP in North Carolina, see Jerrold Hirsch, "Culture on Relief: The Federal Writers' Project in North Carolina, 1935–1942" (master's thesis, University of North Carolina, 1973).

6. W. T. Couch to Mrs. Leonard K. Elmhirst, October 17, 1935, President's Papers.

7. See also Frank Porter Graham to George Foster Peabody, May 30, 1935; Graham to Charles Dabney, November 5, 1935; Graham to E. C. Lindeman, November 7, 1935; Couch to Graham, November 5, 1935; Graham to Edwin R. Embree, November 16, 1935, President's Papers.

8. Dixon Wecter, *The Age of the Great Depression, 1929–1941* (New York: Macmillan, 1948), 159–60. Older images of the South, however, persisted. Stark Young's *So Red the Rose* (1934) and Margaret Mitchell's *Gone With the Wind* (1936) portrayed, with enormous success, a moonlight-and-magnolias South.

9. C. Hugh Holman, *The Roots of Southern Writing: Essays on the Literature of the American South* (Athens: University of Georgia Press, 1972), 103. Holman has called for a reexamination of the work of writers such as Erskine Caldwell and T. S. Stribling. He ar-

gues that they, too, are part of the Southern Renaissance. Although Caldwell wrote with deep feeling for the plight of southern poor whites and blacks, his unique mixture of comedy, naturalism, and outrage often confused his readers. As Carl Van Doren once wisely remarked, "Mr. Caldwell has interested different readers for different reasons" (Carl Van Doren, "Made in America: Erskine Caldwell," *Nation*, October 18, 1933, 443). For example, the explicit sexual humor in *God's Little Acre* (1934) led to an attempt to suppress the book. This, no doubt, gained Caldwell many readers whose interest in the book was limited. The most extreme example of the Agrarian attitude toward Caldwell's writings is John Donald Wade's remark that Caldwell's work "deals in short with just the sort of people sophisticated New Yorkers and would be New Yorkers—the major part of the book buying population of America—can at once most envy and marvel over and deplore" (Wade, "Sweet Are the Uses of Degeneracy," *Southern Review* 1 [1936]: 456). See also Donald Davidson, "Erskine Caldwell's Picture Book," *Southern Review* 3 (1938): 15–23. The *Southern Review* was an Agrarian organ.

10. W. T. Couch, "Landlord and Tenant," *Virginia Quarterly Review* 14 (1938): 311.

11. W. T. Couch to Henry Alsberg, May 14, 1937, Editorial Correspondence, FWPNA.

12. May E. Campbell to Henry Alsberg, May 14, 1937; W. T. Couch to Edwin Bjorkman, March 11, 1937; Bjorkman to Couch, March 30, 1938, FWP-Couch Papers.

13. Henry Alsberg to W. T. Couch, July 9, 1937, FWP-Couch Papers; William F. McDonald, *Federal Relief Administration and the Arts: The Origins and Administrative History of the Arts Projects of the Works Progress Administration* (Columbus: Ohio State University Press, 1969), 667; William Cunningham, assistant to the national FWP director, to Couch, May 24, 1938, FWP-Couch Papers.

14. W. T. Couch to Henry Alsberg, April 22, 1938, FWP-Couch Papers.

15. Rupert B. Vance, *Human Factors in Cotton Culture* (Chapel Hill: University of North Carolina Press, 1929), 260; W. T. Couch to Henry Alsberg, April 22, 1938, FWP-Couch Papers.

16. [Couch?] to [?], "Memorandum Concerning Proposed Plans for Work of the Federal Writers' Project in the South," July 11, 1938, FWP-Couch Papers (internal evidence points to Couch as the author); FWP, *These Are Our Lives*, ix–x.

17. For a discussion of the FWP ex-slave narratives, see Chapters 5 and 6 of this study.

18. These outlines are reprinted in Tom E. Terrill and Jerrold Hirsch, eds., *Such as Us: Southern Voices of the Thirties* (Chapel Hill: University of North Carolina Press, 1978), 283–88.

19. Ida Cooley (formerly Ida Moore) to the author, n.d.

20. W. T. Couch, "Recommendation to the Rosenwald Foundation," January 11, 1940, Press Papers.

21. W. T. Couch to Henry Alsberg, June 2, July 7, 1938, FWP-Couch Papers.

22. Ibid., July 7, 1938.

23. Ibid.; Henry Alsberg to W. T. Couch, July 8, 1938, FWP-Couch Papers; telephone interview with Paul Green, April 4, 1972, Chapel Hill, N.C.; Green to Alsberg, July 11, 1938, FWPNA; Couch to Alsberg, August 5, 1938, and Alsberg to Couch, September 8, 1938, FWP-Couch Papers.

24. George W. Coan Jr., North Carolina WPA administrator, to W. T. Couch, August 24, 1938, FWP-Couch Papers. Shortly thereafter Virginia was removed from Couch's region.

25. W. T. Couch to May E. Campbell, December 5, 1938, box 35, FWPNA; Couch to Andrews, August 30, 1938, FWP-Couch Papers; Couch, interview with the author, March 12, 1972, Carrboro, N.C.; Couch to Bernice Kelly Harris, October 13, 1938, FWP-Couch Papers.

26. Rupert Vance to W. T. Couch, January 28, 1939; Paul Green to Couch, February 3, 1939, FWP-Couch Papers.

27. Bernice Kelly Harris submitted a life history of a minister, which Couch found inadequate. It made him wonder "whether it is possible to get cultivated people to talk—I mean really talk and tell about themselves and their feelings about people and things." See W. T. Couch to Harris, January 30, 1939; memorandum from Couch to state directors, FWP, subject: "Answers to Frequent Queries on Life Histories," n.d.; Couch to Henry Alsberg, January 25, 1939, FWP-Couch Papers.

28. William McDaniel to W. T. Couch, May 6, 1939; Dean Newman to McDaniel, subject: revision of "Lived Too Long," January 25, 1939, FWP-Couch Papers.

29. FWP, *These Are Our Lives*, xii; William McDaniel to W. T. Couch, February 6, 1939; Edwin Bjorkman to Couch, January 13, 1939, FWP-Couch Papers; Couch to Mrs. Howard Mumford Jones, June 21, 1939, Press Papers.

30. FWP, *These Are Our Lives*, 313; W. T. Couch to Henry Alsberg, March 26, 1939, FWP-Couch Papers.

31. Muriel Wolff to W. T. Couch, September 15, 1938; Couch to Wolff, September 19, 1938, FWP-Couch Papers.

32. FWP, *These Are Our Lives*, x–xi, xiii–xiv.

33. W. T. Couch to Douglas Southall Freeman, March 25, 1939, FWP-Couch Papers.

34. FWP, *These Are Our Lives*, x–xi, xiii–xiv.

35. Undated biographical sketches of most of the contributors to *These Are Our Lives* can be found in the FWP-Couch Papers. Additional background on Harrison, Dunnagan, and Massengill can be obtained from the Records of the Alumni Association, Alumni House, University of North Carolina, Chapel Hill.

36. Bernice Kelly Harris, *Southern Savory* (Chapel Hill: University of North Carolina Press, 1964), 181–205; Bernice Kelly Harris, interview with author, March 11, 1973, Seaboard, N.C.; Harris to W. T. Couch, January 11, 1939, FWP-Couch Papers; Willis S. Harrison to the author, June 24, 1973; Ida Cooley (formerly Ida Moore) to the author, n.d.; James Aswell to Mary Barrett, head of the essays division, national office FWP, June 5, 1939, FWP-Couch Papers.

37. William McDaniel to W. T. Couch, January 20, 1939, FWP-Couch Papers.

38. FWP, *These Are Our Lives*, 21.

39. Ibid., 375–76.

40. Mary-Carter Roberts, "Book Points Out What Every One Knows and Does It without Skill or Beauty," *Washington Star*, May 21, 1939, clipping in FWP-Couch Papers; "Voice of the People," *Time*, May 1, 1939, 33; William Shands Meachum, "35 Southerners Tell Their Life Stories," *New York Times*, May 21, 1939, clipping in Press Papers; Charles Beard to W. T. Couch, April 14, 1939, FWP-Couch Papers.

41. Robert Register, "Book Delves into History of People," *Greensboro Daily News*, May 21, 1939, clipping in Press Papers.

42. Virginius Dabney, "Realities on Tobacco Road," *Saturday Review of Literature*, May 7, 1939, 5.

43. This is undoubtedly what made it possible for both southern newspapers and organs of the Communist press to praise the book. See Richard H. Rovere, "FWP's Americana: A Guide to New York and the Lives of Thirty-five Southerners," *New Masses*, June 27, 1939, and Harold Preece, "A Southern Epoch: 'These Are Our Lives' Tells the Story of People Who Toil," *Daily Worker*, June 6, 1939, clippings in Press Papers.

44. Donald Davidson to W. T. Couch, May 7, 1939, Press Papers.

45. Erskine Caldwell to W. T. Couch, n.d., Press Papers.

46. W. T. Couch to William McDaniel, February 20, 1939; Couch to Henry Alsberg, February 28, 1939; Couch to Muriel Wolff, December 15, 1938; Couch to Alsberg, March 25, 1939, FWP-Couch Papers.

47. W. T. Couch to Josiah Bailey, April 27, 1939; Couch to Frank Porter Graham, May 4, 1939; Couch to Henry Alsberg, May 18, 1939, FWP-Couch Papers.

48. Henry Alsberg to W. T. Couch, June 20, 1939, FWP-Couch Papers. On June 24 Couch sent letters to the following committee members: Carter Glass (D., Va.); Alsa Adams (D., Colo.); John Bankhead (D., Ala.); James Byrnes (D., S.C.); and Richard Russell (D., Ga.), FWP-Couch Papers.

49. W. T. Couch to Mrs. Franklin D. Roosevelt, April 26, 1939; "Answers to Queries on Federal Writers' Project," Couch to Harold W. Landlin of the American Council of Learned Societies, June 7, 1943, Press Papers. The nation's leading publishers campaigned openly and addressed a public letter to Congress in support of the Writers' Project. See "Publishers Praise Federal Writers' Project," *Publishers' Weekly*, May 20, 1939, 1817, and "Publishers' Letter on Federal Writers' Project," *Publishers' Weekly*, May 27, 1939, 1919.

50. Henry Alsberg to W. T. Couch, August 8, 1939; Couch to Alsberg, August 10, 1939, FWP-Couch Papers.

51. Clarke A. Chambers, *Paul U. Kellogg and the Survey: Voices for Social Welfare and Social Justice* (Minneapolis: University of Minnesota Press, 1971); Paul U. Kellogg to W. T. Couch, July 25, 1939; Ellsworth Faris to Couch, July 29, 1939, Press Papers.

52. W. T. Couch to Ellsworth Faris, August 3, 1939, Press Papers.

53. Hadley Cantril to W. T. Couch, October 23, 1939, Press Papers; Howard Odum to Couch, September 16, 1939; Couch to May E. Campbell, September 18, 1939; Couch to Archibald MacLeish, November 3, 1939, FWP-Couch Papers; Couch to Allen Tate, December 7, 1939, Press Papers.

54. W. T. Couch to George Reynolds, Julius Rosenwald Fund, December 6, 1939, Press Papers; Couch to David H. Stevens, Rockefeller Foundation, President's Papers. These negotiations with the Rosenwald, Rockefeller, and other foundations did not prove as fruitful as Couch had hoped. However, several grants were obtained from the Rosenwald Fund for individual writers to work on life histories. Only one of these manuscripts was ever published. Jay Saunders Redding's *No Day of Triumph* (New York: Harper and Brothers, 1942) attempted to portray the life of the black masses.

55. W. T. Couch to C. E. Triggs, director, community service projects, November 27, 1939, Press Papers.

56. Harvey Swados, in *The American Writer and the Great Depression*, ed. Harvey Swados (Indianapolis: Bobbs-Merrill, 1996), 47.

Chapter 8

1. B. A. Botkin, "Folklore as a Neglected Source of Social History," in *The Cultural Approach to History*, ed. Caroline Ware (New York: Columbia University Press, 1940), 308. Lawrence Levine, *Black Culture and Black Consciousness: Afro-American Folk Thought from Slavery to Freedom* (New York: Oxford University Press, 1977), and Charles Joyner, *Down by the Riverside: A South Carolina Slave Community* (Urbana: University of Illinois Press, 1984), draw heavily on FWP materials and offer excellent examples of what a marriage between folklore and history can accomplish.

2. Monty Penkower, *The Federal Writers' Project: A Study in Government Patronage of the Arts* (Urbana: University of Illinois Press, 1977), 66–67. The FWP's Negro Studies File contains repeated queries from Sterling Brown about black employment on the state FWP projects; see boxes 200, 201, FWPNA. The FWP-Couch Papers contain letters written in the fall of 1938 from W. T. Couch to each of the state directors in the Southeast asking about black employment on the FWP in their states. From these sources it is possible to estimate black employment on the FWP in the South.

3. Frank Friedel, *F. D. R. and the South* (Baton Rouge: Louisiana State University Press, 1965), and George B. Tindall, *The Emergence of the New South, 1913–1945* (Baton Rouge: Louisiana State University Press, 1967) (vol. 10 of *History of the South*, ed. Merton Coulter and Wendell H. Stephenson), 607–49, are still good starting points for understanding the forces limiting New Deal reform in the South.

4. For interpretations that stress the emergence of modern southern thought from Victorianism and the relationship of the idea of the South to modern fragmented society and the heritage of romanticism, see Daniel Joseph Singal, *The War Within: From Victorian to Modernist Thought in the South* (Chapel Hill: University of North Carolina Press, 1982), esp., xi–33, 198–260, 111–52, and Michael O'Brien, *The Idea of the American South* (Baltimore: Johns Hopkins University Press, 1979), 2–59, 220–23.

5. Henry Alsberg to Lewis Mumford, October 4, 1938; Alsberg to Ellen Woodward, April 1, July 22, 1938, box 195, FWPNA.

6. For an overview of New Deal folklore programs, see Jerrold Hirsch, "Cultural Pluralism and Applied Folklore: The New Deal Precedent," in *The Conservation of Culture: Folklorists and the Public Sector*, ed. Burt Feintuch (Lexington: University Press of Kentucky, 1988), 47–67; John Lomax, *Adventures of a Ballad Hunter* (New York: Macmillan, 1947), 128–29; John Lomax and Alan Lomax, eds., *American Ballads and Folk Songs* (New York: Macmillan, 1934), xxvi, xxvvii, xxx, xxxi.

7. See, for example, John Lomax, "Self-Pity in Negro Folk-Songs," *Nation*, August 9, 1917, 141–45; John Lomax, "'Sinful Songs' of the Southern Negro," *Musical Quarterly* 20 (1934): 177, 179; Lomax, *Adventures of a Ballad Hunter*, 128–29. See also Jerrold

Hirsch, "Modernity, Nostalgia, and Southern Folklore Studies: The Case of John Lomax," *Journal of American Folklore* 105 (1992): 183–207.

8. For an overview of Botkin's career and ideas, see Jerrold Hirsch, "Folklore in the Making: B. A. Botkin," *Journal of American Folklore* 100 (1987): 3–38; 13. See, for example, B. A. Botkin, "Folk and Folklore," in *Culture in the South*, ed. W. T. Couch (Chapel Hill: University of North Carolina Press, 1934), 578–93.

9. B. A. Botkin to Henry Alsberg, March 24, 1938, FWPNA. See also, for example, B. A. Botkin, "Regionalism and Culture," in *The Writer in a Changing World*, ed. Henry Hart (New York: Equinox Press, 1937), 140–57, and B. A. Botkin, "The Folk and the Individual: Their Creative Reciprocity," *English Journal* 27 (1938): 121–35.

10. B. A. Botkin, "The Folkness of the Folk," *English Journal* 26 (1937): 465, 467–68; B. A. Botkin, "The Folk in Literature: An Introduction to the New Regionalism," in *Folk-Say: A Regional Miscellany*, ed. B. A. Botkin (Norman: University of Oklahoma Press, 1929), 12; Botkin, "Folklore as a Neglected Source of Social History"; Botkin, "Folk in Literature," 9–10; Botkin, "Folk and the Individual"; B. A. Botkin, "We Called It 'Living Lore,'" *New York Folklore Quarterly* 14 (1958): 97–198.

11. Botkin, "Regionalism and Culture," 141, 156–57; B. A. Botkin, "We Talk about Regionalism—North, South, East, and West," *Frontier* 13 (1933): 286, 291–93; B. A. Botkin, ed., *A Treasury of Southern Folklore: Stories, Ballads, Traditions, and Folkways of the South* (New York: Crown, 1949), xxi–xxii, 479, 646, 729.

12. Botkin, "Folkness of the Folk," 465–69. Perhaps the most moving expression of the Regionalist's desire to reconcile southern and American identities is found in Howard Odum's *An American Epoch: Southern Portraiture in the National Picture* (New York: H. Holt, 1930).

13. Botkin, "We Talk about Regionalism," 291–92; B. A. Botkin, "*Folk-Say* and *Space*: Their Genesis and Exodus," *Southwest Review* 20 (1935): 330–31; B. A. Botkin, "Regionalism: Cult or Culture?," *English Journal* 25 (1936): 182; Allen Tate, "Regionalism and Sectionalism," *New Republic*, December 23, 1931, 159; Botkin, "Regionalism and Culture," 141.

14. Botkin, "Regionalism and Culture," 141; Botkin, "Folk and the Individual," 126.

15. Botkin, "We Called It 'Living Lore,'" 197; B. A. Botkin, "'Living Lore' on the New York City Writers' Project," *New York Folklore Quarterly* 2 (1946): 252–63.

16. [Couch?] to [?], "Memorandum Concerning Proposed Plans for Work of the Federal Writers' Project in the South," July 11, 1938, FWP-Couch Papers. On this point I have been influenced by Wernor Sollors, "Modernization as Adultery: Richard Wright, Zora Neale Hurston, and American Culture of the 1930s and 1940s," *Hebrew University Studies in Literature and the Arts* 18 (1990): 109–55.

17. W. T. Couch to Mrs. Leonard K. Elmhirst, October 17, 1935, President's Papers. See also the discussion of Couch in Singal, *War Within*, 265–301.

18. W. T. Couch, speech delivered at South Georgia Teachers' College, Collegeboro, Ga., March 12, 1937, FWP-Couch Papers; W. T. Couch, "Landlord and Tenant," *Virginia Quarterly Review* 14 (1938): 309–12; W. T. Couch, "The Agrarian Romance," *South Atlantic Quarterly Review* 32 (1937): 429.

19. See W. T. Couch, preface to FWP, *These Are Our Lives* (Chapel Hill: University of North Carolina Press, 1939), ix–xx.

20. Allen Tate, "Knowledge and Reporting in the South," *Free America* 3 (1939): 18–20.

21. Couch made clear the problems he thought the outlook of ordinary white southern field-workers created in getting black life histories in memorandum from William T. Couch to all state directors, FWP, subject: "Answers to Frequent Queries on Life Histories," n.d., FWP-Couch Papers.

22. Chalmers S. Murray to Mabel Montgomery, July 8, 1937, box 192, FWPNA. Anyone dipping into both the FWP former slave interviews and Page's work will be struck immediately by the frequent similarities. Graduate papers in David Donald and Syd Nathans's Harvard seminar helped call my attention to this fact. The dominance of the white South's view of slavery in popular culture, literature, and history had profound cultural and political consequences. In Francis Pendelton Gaines, *The Southern Plantation Tradition: A Study in the Development of the Accuracy of a Tradition* (New York: Columbia University Press, 1924), and Paul Buck, *The Road to Reunion, 1865–1900* (Boston: Little, Brown, 1937), scholars close to the plantation tradition, and unembarrassed by and sympathetic to the assumptions underlying it, have offered insights into the tradition's pervasiveness that less sympathetic students of the subject need to understand.

23. *The American Guide and the American Guide Series: Their Task — To Introduce America to Americans*, n.d., pamphlet, box 74, FWPNA.

24. Gaines's *Southern Plantation Tradition* can be treated as both a secondary source indirectly supporting my analysis and a primary source providing evidence for my interpretation. Among more recent works, see Paul Gaston, *The New South Creed: A Study in Southern Mythmaking* (New York: Oxford University Press, 1970), and Charles Reagan Wilson, *Baptized in Blood: The Religion of the Lost Cause* (Athens: University of Georgia Press, 1980), 177–202.

25. Gaston, *New South Creed*, 167–86; Writers' Program, *Alabama: A Guide to the Deep South* (New York: Hastings House, 1941), 184; FWP, *Mississippi: A Guide to the Magnolia State* (New York: Viking Press, 1938), 8; Writers' Program, *Georgia: A Guide to Its Towns and Countryside* (Athens: University of Georgia Press, 1940), 8; Writers' Program, *Louisiana: A Guide to the State* (New York: Hastings House, 1941, 292.

26. Writers' Program, *Texas: A Guide to the Lone Star State* (New York: Hastings House, 1940), 570, 631.

27. Ray Stannard Baker, *Following the Color Line: An Account of Negro Citizenship in the American Democracy* (New York: Doubleday, Page, 1908), 44.

28. FWP, *Mississippi*, 223; Writers' Program, *Alabama*, 184.

29. See draft, "Stories of Negro Survival Types in Coastal Georgia," n.d., box 201, FWPNA.

30. FWP, *Mississippi*, 76–86; Gaines, *Southern Plantation Tradition*, 63.

31. Gaines, *Southern Plantation Tradition*, 3.

32. Ibid., 4.

33. B. A. Botkin, "WPA and Folklore Research: Bread and Song," *Southern Folklore Quarterly* 3 (1939): 14. For a fuller analysis of this point and a reconsideration of the historical, literary, and moral value of *Lay My Burden Down*, see Jerrold Hirsch, foreword to the new edition of *Lay My Burden Down: A Folk History of Slavery*, ed. B. A. Botkin (1945; reprint, Athens: University of Georgia Press, 1989), ix–xxx; Botkin, *Treasury of Southern Folklore*, xxi.

Chapter 9

1. HUAC, pt. 4, 3135. See Alsberg's testimony before the Dies committee, esp. HUAC, pt. 4, 2887, 2889, 2903–8; Henry Alsberg to Ellen Woodward, assistant WPA director, April 1, August 26, 1938, and Alsberg to Lewis Mumford, September 25, 1938, box 195, FWPNA.

2. Alfred Kazin, *On Native Grounds: An Interpretation of Modern American Prose Literature* (New York: Reynal and Hitchcock, 1942), 486; Henry Steele Commager, *The American Mind: An Interpretation of American Thought and Character since the 1880s* (New Haven: Yale University Press, 1971), 433; Charles Comer Alexander, *Nationalism in American Thought, 1930–1945* (Chicago: Rand McNally, 1969), 45; Richard Pells, *Radical Visions and American Dreams: Culture and Social Thought in the Depression Years* (New York: Harper and Row, 1973), 315.

3. Jerre Mangione, *The Dream and the Deal: The Federal Writer's Project, 1935–1943* (Boston: Little, Brown, 1972), 289–326; Monty Penkower, *The Federal Writers' Project: A Study in Government Patronage of the Arts* (Urbana: University of Illinois Press, 1977), 195–210. For Dies's treatment of the Federal Theater Project, see Jane DeHart Mathews, *The Federal Theatre, 1935–1939: Plays, Politics, and Relief* (Princeton: Princeton University Press, 1967), 198–235. For a broad overview of Dies and the committee, see Albert Alexander, "The President and the Investigator: Roosevelt and Dies," *Antioch Review* 15 (1955): 106–16; Walter Goodman, *The Committee: The Extraordinary Career of the House Committee on Un-American Activities* (New York: Farrar, Strauss and Giroux, 1968); John R. Poe Jr., "Martin Dies: The Development of a Southern Anti-Communist" (master's thesis, University of North Carolina, 1973); August Raymond Ogden, *The Dies Committee: A Study of the Special House Committee for the Investigation of Un-American Activities, 1938–1944* (Washington, D.C.: Catholic University Press, 1945).

4. Poe, "Martin Dies," stresses Dies's relationship to the Populist and Progressive tradition; see esp. 54–57, 77–83. Surprisingly, the thesis that the "radical right" is an outgrowth of Populism has not been argued in a sustained fashion regarding Dies, when he might better fit the theory than Joseph McCarthy does. In the case of Dies, too, the relationship between reaction, reform, and mainstream politics is more complex than consensus historians acknowledged; see Martin Dies, *The Trojan Horse in America* (New York: Dodd, Mead, 1940), and David Brion Davis, ed., *The Fear of Conspiracy: Images of Un-American Subversion from the Revolution to the Present* (Ithaca: Cornell University Press, 1971), 1, 205–9, 263–70. On the persistence of earlier cultural conflicts in the 1930s, see Leo P. Ribuffo, *The Old Christian Right: The Protestant Far Right from the Great Depression to the Cold War* (Philadelphia: Temple University Press, 1983), and Richard Polenberg, *One Nation Divisible: Class, Race, and Ethnicity in the United States since 1938* (Viking Press: New York, 1980; Pelican Books ed., 1981), 15–45.

5. Martin Dies, "Immigration Crisis," *Saturday Evening Post*, April 20, 1935, 27; Louis Adamic, "Aliens and Alien-Baiters," *Harper's Magazine*, November 1936, 561–74.

6. Dies, "Immigration Crisis," 27, 105; W. J. Cash, *The Mind of the South* (New York: Knopf, 1941), 305.

7. *New York Times*, August 18, 1935.

8. Ibid.; Poe, "Martin Dies," 72–74, 54–56, 61–63, 66; Martin D. Irish, "Proletarian South," *Journal of Politics* 2 (1940): 247.

9. Poe, "Martin Dies," 22–44; Thomas as quoted in ibid., 34. On the conservative revolt in Congress, see James T. Patterson, "Conservative Coalition Forms in Congress," *Journal of American History* 52 (1966): 746–65, and James T. Patterson, *Congressional Conservatism, 1933–1939* (Lexington: University Press of Kentucky, 1967).

10. Goodman, *Committee*, 24–58; Mathews, *Federal Theatre*, 198–235; Mangione, *Dream and the Deal*, 289–326; Penkower, *Federal Writers' Project*, 195–210.

11. HUAC, pt. 4, 3109–10, 3113–14, 3112.

12. Ibid., 3113, 3114.

13. Ibid., 3119.

14. Ibid., 3120.

15. Ibid., 2406, 2407.

16. Mangione, *Dream and the Deal*, 305.

17. HUAC, pt. 4, 2645–49, 2653.

18. Ibid., 3117, 2898.

19. FWP, *New Jersey: A Guide to Its Present and Past* (New York: Viking Press, 1939), 86–87, 84.

20. HUAC, pt. 4, 3122; Sterling Brown, "Florida: Sarasota," September 29, 1937, Alsberg-Cronyn Files; Sterling A. Brown, Arthur P. Davis, and Ulysses Lee, eds., *The Negro Caravan: Writings by American Negroes* (New York: Dryden, 1941), 825. For a cultural analysis of the history of Main Street as a symbol, see D. W. Meining, "Symbolic Landscapes: Some Idealizations of Ordinary Landscapes," in *The Interpretation of Ordinary Landscapes: Geographical Essays*, ed. D. W. Meining (New York: Oxford University Press, 1979), 178.

21. HUAC, pt. 4, 3123.

22. Ibid.

23. Richard Wright, "The Ethics of Living Jim Crow," in FWP, *American Stuff: An Anthology of Prose and Verse by Members of the Federal Writers' Project* (New York: Viking Press, 1937), 39–52; HUAC, pt. 2, 1010–11.

24. HUAC, pt. 4, 2645–49, 2653.

25. *Congressional Record*, 84, 1939, pt. 4, 3930, 3931.

26. Ibid., 3931.

27. Ibid.; FWP, *Washington: City and Capital* (Washington, D.C.: U.S. Government Printing Office, 1937), 90.

28. *Congressional Record*, 84, 1939, pt. 4, 3114–15.

29. Maxwell Hunter to Carita Corse, November 28, December 3, 4, 1938, Kennedy Papers.

30. Ibid., December 4, 1938.

31. HUAC, pt. 4, 2887, 2889, 2908.

32. Ibid., 2903, 2904.

33. Ibid., 2904–7.

34. Penkower, *Federal Writers' Project*, 209–11; Martin Dies, *The Martin Dies Story* (New York: Bookmailer, 1963). In the committee report Dies simply concluded that Alsberg

accepted as true the charges brought against the FWP. See U.S. House of Representatives, *Report of the Special Committee on Un-American Activities—Pursuant to H. Res. 282*, 75th Cong., 4th sess., 1939, 31.

35. Penkower, *Federal Writers' Project*, 209–11; Mangione, *Dream and the Deal*, 330; Kathleen O'Connor McKinzie, "Writers on Relief, 1935–1942" (Ph.D. diss., Indiana University, 1970), 241, 243–44.

Chapter 10

1. Jerre Mangione, *The Dream and the Deal: The Federal Writers' Project, 1935–1943* (Boston: Little, Brown, 1972), 289–326; Monty Penkower, *The Federal Writers' Project: A Study in Government Patronage of the Arts* (Urbana: University of Illinois Press, 1977), 204–12; Walter Goodman, *The Committee: The Extraordinary Career of the House Committee on Un-American Activities* (New York: Farrar, Strauss and Giroux, 1968), 3–88; James Patterson, *Congressional Conservatism, 1933–1939* (Lexington: University Press of Kentucky, 1967), 288–324. See also James MacGregor Burns, *Roosevelt: The Lion and the Fox* (New York: Harcourt Brace and World, 1956), 291–380.

2. Mangione, *Dream and the Deal*, 329.

3. Kathleen O'Connor McKinzie, "Writers on Relief, 1935–1942" (Ph.D. diss., Indiana University, 1970), 203.

4. William F. McDonald, *Federal Relief Administration and the Arts: The Origins and Administrative History of the Arts Projects of the Works Progress Administration* (Columbus: Ohio State University Press, 1969), 305–11.

5. Harrington's statement before the committee is quoted in McDonald, *Federal Relief Administration and the Arts*, 310; Mangione, *Dream and the Deal*, 330; Penkower, *Federal Writers' Project*, 209–10; McKinzie, "Writers on Relief," 241, 243–44.

6. Penkower, *Federal Writers' Project*, 211; Jerre Mangione, "Federal Writers' Project," *New York Times Book Review*, May 18, 1969, 2; Mangione, *Dream and the Deal*, 331–33; McDonald, *Federal Relief Administration and the Arts*, 307.

7. J. D. Newsom to C. M. Triggs, "Subject: Completion of the American Guide Series," December 21, 1939, box 463, WPA Files.

8. Ibid.

9. Untitled press release, August 28, 1941, box 83, DIFWPA.

10. J. D. Newsom to Florence Kerr, September 9, 1939, box 463, WPA Files.

11. Memorandum, Greene to Brummett, December 12, 1941, as quoted in McDonald, *Federal Relief Administration and the Arts*, 689, 692.

12. Ibid.

13. Walter M. Kiplinger to Virginia Price, weekly defense bulletin, defense effort editorial from the April 3, 1941, *Helper (Utah) Journal*, April 24, 1941, box 463, WPA Files.

14. Ibid.

15. South Carolina press release, April 30, 1941, box 83, DIFWPA.

16. Lewis Gannett, "Reading about America," *Publishers' Weekly*, May 3, 1941, 1818–19.

17. "Program and Publications for the Fiscal Year 1942," n.d., box 83, DIFWPA; Walter M. Kiplinger, director, public activities program, to H. P. Drought, Texas State

Works Project administrator, "Subject: Hands That Built America," August 11, 1941, box 384, WPA Files; untitled press release, August 28, 1941, marked "no release," box 83, DIFWPA; "Meeting of State and Regional Representatives for a discussion on Objectives, Methods, and Techniques of the WPA Writers' Program, during the Coming Year," Washington, D.C., May 26, 27, 28, 1941, "Public Activities Program of the Community Service Division, Work Projects Administration," Federal Works Agency, box 463, WPA Files. There is an undated description of the proposed study "Hands That Built America," box 384, WPA Files. In the fall of 1941 newspapers such as the *South Bend [Indiana] Tribune*, October 27, 1941, attacked the "America Eats" project as a "foolish boondoggle"; see clippings in box 83, DIFWPA. The subject now has academic status as a research topic, the accompanying bibliographies are useful, and there has been interest in the "America Eats" manuscript. See Charles Camp, "Foodways in Everyday Life," *American Quarterly* 34 (1982): 278–90, and Charles Camp, "America Eats: Toward a Social Definition of American Foodways" (Ph.D. diss., University of Pennsylvania, 1978).

18. R. E. Rutledge, director, Grazing Service, U.S. Department of the Interior, Salt Lake City, Utah, to J. D. Newsom, February 5, 1942, box 384, WPA Files. A description of the proposal "History of Grazing," circular, June 6, 1940, is in box 70, FWPNA, offering suggestions on a technique for compiling data, writing, and editing material for a history of grazing. See also Penkower, *Federal Writers' Project*, 231; Mangione, *Dream and the Deal*, 348.

19. J. D. Newsom to Walter M. Kiplinger, "Subject: Information on New Program for National Advisory Committee," September 9, 1941, box 461, WPA Files; press release, August 28, 1941; "Writers' Program publicity activities," n.d., box 83, DIFWPA; "Meeting of State and Regional Representatives," box 463, WPA Files; "WPA Writers' Map Interesting Program for Coming Months," August 30, 1941, box 83, DIFWPA.

20. J. D. Newsom to Walter M. Kiplinger, "Subject: Information on New Program for National Advisory Committee," September 9, 1941, box 461, WPA Files; press release, August 28, 1941; "Writers' Program publicity activities," n.d., box 83, DIFWPA; "Meeting of State and Regional Representatives," box 463, WPA Files; "WPA Writers' Map Interesting Program for Coming Months," August 30, 1941, box 83, DIFWPA.

21. As quoted in the report "Meeting of the State and Regional Representatives" box 463, WPA Files.

22. Richard Polenberg, *One National Divisible: Class, Race, and Ethnicity in the United States since 1938* (New York: Viking Press, 1980), 45, 53. The treatment of Japanese Americans, however, was a major exception and a gross violation of civil liberties.

23. As quoted in ibid., 47.

24. "National Defense Activities of the Illinois Writers' Project," May 16, 1941, box 464, WPA Files.

25. Ibid.

26. John Higham, "Hanging Together: Divergent Unities in American History," *Journal of American History* 61 (1974): 5–28; Alexis de Tocqueville, *Democracy in America*, 2 vols., ed. Phillips Bradley, trans. Henry Reese and Francis Bowen (New York: Vintage Books, 1945), 1:241–44; Arthur Mann, *The One and the Many: Reflections on American Identity* (Chicago: University of Chicago Press, 1979), 46–47.

27. Radio script, June 13, 1941, Records Relating to the WPA Writers' Project in

Oregon, 1935–1942, Records Group 69, Central Correspondence Files of the WPA, National Archives, Washington, D.C. Microfilm prepared by the General Services Administration and available from Washington State University, Pullman.

28. Ibid.

29. "WPA Announces American Guide Week, November 10 to 14," release October 12, 1941, box 83, WPA Files; "American Guide Week Planned for November 10th–16th," *Publishers' Weekly*, October 11, 1941, 1463–64; from Howard Staub, state headquarters, WPA, New Haven, Conn., release, November 9, 1941, box 83, DIFWPA.

30. Roosevelt as quoted in "American Guide Planned for November 10th–16th," 1463–64.

31. *New York Sun*, December 31, 1941; Stephen Vincent Benét, "Patchwork Quilt of These United States: At Last We Have Guidebooks to All Our Commonwealths," *New York Herald Tribune*, December 28, 1941.

32. "Agenda: Meeting of the Advisory Committee on Art, Music, and the Writers' Program," November 1–4, 1941, box 464, WPA Files.

33. J. D. Newsom to Walter M. Kiplinger, December 12, 1941, box 461, WPA Files.

34. "WPA In Ohio Information Release," June 4, 194[?], box 83, DIFWPA; *Cleveland Plain Dealer*, May 22, 1941, clipping in box 464, WPA Files.

35. J. D. Newsom, field report, Michigan, March 20, 1941, box 464, WPA Files; press release (describing the bulletin), "Grow Your Own Vegetables," December 1, 1941, box 83, DIFWPA.

36. Margaret S. Child to Florence Kerr, February 27, 1942, box 384, WPA Files.

37. Merle Colby, field report, Illinois, January 20–27, 1942, box 464, WPA Files; Colby, field report, Massachusetts, September 26–29, 1942, box 384, WPA Files; Penkower, *Federal Writers' Project*, 234–37.

38. Merle Colby, "Final Report on Disposition of Unpublished Materials of the WPA Writers' Program," April 8, 1943, box 384, WPA Files.

Epilogue

1. "Have You Discovered America," n.d., box 70, FWPNA.

2. Terry A. Cooney, "Cosmopolitan Values and the Identification of Reaction: *Partisan Review* in the 1930s," *Journal of American History* 68 (1981): 580–98; Lawrence Schwartz, *Creating Faulkner's Reputation: The Politics of Modern Literary Criticism* (Knoxville: University of Tennessee Press, 1988), esp. chap. 3, "The Origins of a New Literary Consensus: The New Critics and the New York Intellectuals," 72–98; William Vann O'Connor, *Sense and Sensibility in Modern Poetry* (Chicago: University of Chicago Press, 1948), 27, 19, 30, 179, 206.

3. Ben Botkin to Gertrude Botkin, May 29, 1938, BP.

4. William F. McDonald, *Federal Relief Administration and the Arts: The Origins and Administrative History of the Arts Projects of the Works Progress Administration* (Columbus: Ohio State University Press, 1969), 719; Elizabeth Dwyer-Schick, "The Development of Folklore and Folklife Research in the Federal Writers' Project, 1935–1943," *Keystone* 20 (1975): 18–20. See also Elizabeth Dwyer-Schick, "Review Essay: Folklore and Govern-

ment Support," *Journal of American Folklore* 89 (1976): 476–87; "Minutes: First Meeting Joint Committee on Folk Arts, W.P.A.," December 7, 1938, box 195, FWPNA; Herbert Halpert to B. A. Botkin, October 4, 1938, 1939; "Draft: Coordinating Committee on Living Folklore, Folkmusic and Folk Art, Federal Project Number One, Works Progress Administration," November 23, 1938, box 195, FWPNA. The "Draft" outlines the aims, functions, and program of the committee and lists members and consultants.

5. Ben Botkin to Harry Botkin, July 5, 1939, BP.

6. Ben Botkin to Gertrude Botkin, August 5, 1939, BP.

7. Ibid., August 29, 30, 1939.

8. Gertrude Botkin to Ben Botkin, August 30, 31, September 2, 4, 6, 7, 9, 1939, BP.

9. Ben Botkin to Gertrude Botkin, August 10, 1939, BP.

10. Ibid., August 31, 1939.

11. Ibid., August 27, 1939.

12. B. A. Botkin, "WPA and Folklore Research: Bread and Song," *Southern Folklore Quarterly* 3 (1939): 6–14.

13. Gertrude Botkin to Ben Botkin, August 23, 24, September 2, 1939; Ben to Gertrude, September 3, 4, 1939, BP.

14. Ben Botkin to Gertrude Botkin, January 2, 1939, BP.

15. Ibid., August 21, 14, September 27, August 15, 1939.

16. Ibid., August 15, 1939.

17. Ibid., December 26, 1939; B. A. Botkin, "Folklore as a Neglected Source of Social History," in *The Cultural Approach to History*, ed. Caroline Ware (New York: Columbia University Press, 1940), 309–15.

18. Ben Botkin to Gertrude Botkin, November 11, 1939, BP.

19. Ben Botkin to Harry and Rhoda Botkin, November 24, 1941, BP.

20. B. A. Botkin, "We Talk about Regionalism—North, South, East, and West," *Frontier* 13 (1933): 291–93; B. A. Botkin, "Regionalism: Cult or Culture," *English Journal* 25 (1933): 182–83; B. A. Botkin, "Regionalism and Culture," in *The Writer in a Changing World*, ed. Henry Hart (New York: Equinox Press, 1937), 147–53; B. A. Botkin, "Unliterary Literature," *Trend* 2 (1935): 234–35; B. A. Botkin, "The Folk and the Individual: Their Creative Reciprocity," *English Journal* 27 (1938): 121–35.

21. B. A. Botkin, "Proposal for an Applied Folklore Center," *New York Folklore Quarterly* 17 (1961): 151–54.

22. B. A. Botkin, ed., *A Treasury of American Folklore: Stories, Ballads, and Traditions of the People* (New York: Crown, 1944), xxii, xxvi.

23. Susan Wenner, "Reviving Regional Roots," *Family Tree Magazine*, August 21, 2001, ⟨http://www.Familytreemagazine.com/magazine_aug01.a⟩; "NEH Launches Initiative to Rediscover America through Regional Studies: Multiyear program will establish 10 centers for the study of regional characteristics," December 2, 1999, ⟨http://www.neh.gov/news/archive/19991202b.html⟩.

24. William Ferris, "On Encyclopedias," ⟨http://www.uiowa.edu/~humiowa/wf-172001.htm⟩.

25. Botkin, *Treasury of American Folklore*, xxii.

Index